PRECIOUS COMMODITY

HISTORY OF THE URBAN ENVIRONMENT

Martin V. Melosi and Joel A. Tarr, Editors

Precious Commodity

PROVIDING WATER FOR AMERICA'S CITIES

MARTIN V. MELOSI

University of Pittsburgh Press

For Nonno and Nonnie

Published by the University of Pittsburgh Press, Pittsburgh, Pa., 15260
Copyright © 2011, University of Pittsburgh Press
All rights reserved
Manufactured in the United States of America
Printed on acid-free paper
10 9 8 7 6 5 4 3 2 1

Library of Congress Cataloging-in-Publication Data

Melosi, Martin V., 1947–
The sanitary city : environmental services in urban america from colonial
times to the present / Martin V. Melosi. — Abridged ed.
p. cm. — (History of the urban environment)
Includes bibliographical references and index.
ISBN-13: 978-0-8229-5983-0 (pbk. : alk. paper)
ISBN-10: 0-8229-5983-6 (pbk. : alk. paper)
1. Municipal water supply—United States—History. 2. Sanitary
engineering—United States—History. 3. Refuse and refuse disposal—
United States—History. 4. Municipal services—United States—History.
I. Title.
TD223.M45 2008 2011
363.6'10973—dc22   2007046149

Contents

Acknowledgments

Working on this book brought back many wonderful memories (some not so good!) about all of the different projects that contributed to its completion. I was somewhat surprised by how many times I examined water from a variety of perspectives; never really thinking of myself as a water historian. I talked with Joel Tarr about my original conception for the book, and these conversations helped me to cast and recast the project until it reached this final iteration. I also benefited from the reviewer reports, especially one that suggested I focus on public versus private responsibility for the management and delivery of water. This was just the idea I needed to pull together what seemed to be disparate studies. Other reviewers pushed me to clarify, explain, and otherwise hone my own conclusions. I took the criticisms seriously and did my best to learn from them.

I especially want to thank Cynthia Miller and the staff at University of Pittsburgh Press. We have worked together on many projects—my own and others—and I find the relationship eminently professional and perpetually cordial. I hope to do more with the press as new ideas crop up.

I also can't forget the essential role of my wife, Carolyn. She may not believe that she is central to my research and writing process. But without her love, patience, and care, I wouldn't be able to find the time nor the inclination to produce books—an experience that I always regard as challenging and satisfying.

Finally, this book is dedicated my dad's parents—Victor and Jennie Melosi—who are now long departed. It was sad to have lost them (as well as my own folks) in a very short time span some years ago, yet my memories of Nonno and Nonnie remain vivid to this day. What joy of life I embrace comes in great measure from them. It is almost a cliché to view immigrants to the United States like them as among the most hopeful of Americans. Yet they constantly demonstrated a delight with the little pleasures of daily life, and maintained an abiding devotion to their family. Thank you.

Introduction

WATER—TRULY A PRECIOUS COMMODITY

A common and oft-repeated statement is that "water is the next oil." Nothing could be farther from the truth. The comparisons, of course, are understandable. Oil has become scarcer and more expensive. We have reached peak oil and the world faces a downward spiral—fast or slowly depending upon who you believe—to the bottom of that energy barrel. Fresh water, too, is a finite resource with demand on the rise, and inevitably, higher prices to follow. Concerns abound regarding water as a fixed supply, often with limited access, and perpetually undervalued in terms of cost. One set of statistics claims that demand for water in the United States in the past thirty years has tripled, while the population has doubled. Global consumption of water appears to be doubling every twenty years—twice the rate of population growth.[1] As historian John McNeill quaintly noted, "[t]he clearest thing about the history of water is that people use a lot more now than they used to."[2] Enterprising business leaders look on these challenges as opportunities to turn the problems of peak water into profits. Some engineers and scientists look upon the reality of limited water supplies as an occasion to change hydro-management techniques to "grow water," that is, to modify existing engineered water systems to function more naturally and to allow for water reuse through recycling processes.[3]

To treat the problem of water supply as if its resolution can be found through some technical black box ignores the fundamental issue of who controls water and why. This is not to demean the search for efficient ways to provide sufficient water, to cease taking into account better methods of allocating the resource, or to ignore methods to sustain the available supplies. Rather, it is to state emphatically that the control of water supplies—whoever has it—strongly influences promotion of efficient technologies, determines allocation, and, to some degree at least, has something to say about the ultimate sustainability of water systems.

Precious Commodity takes a look at public and private responsibility for water from a historical perspective and from a variety of vantage points. It concludes, not surprisingly, that the institutional setting within which decisions over water are made has a profound impact on allocation and use. Concerns about a "fresh water crisis" now or in the past give too much attention to gross statistics on population growth and levels of consumption and not enough to who manages water supply and why that matters.

The following eight chapters focus mainly on urban American topics, but also make some attempt to move beyond those borders. All of them focus on questions of public and private responsibility in some fashion. Among the issues raised are the following:

- The effort to "harness" American rivers brought into play questions concerning property rights and public management opportunities. Water as a contested resource was played out through these issues.

- A major justification for the first public water supply and wastewater systems in American cities rested on a rather misinformed notion of disease transmission that nevertheless set a pattern for municipal control for generations.

- While the development of modern American waterworks in the nineteenth century was a success story at the time, the inflexible systems left little room for serious modifications in the future.

- The building of big dams by the federal government was the most graphic symbol of water as a public resource. Their construction, use, and possible dismantling have been and continue to be the subject of public regulation and public policy, as well as environmental concern.

- San Jose's long lasting private water system was an anomaly but demonstrates how circumstance and contingency can challenge orthodoxy. In the end, the private system survived in part because of its association with the Santa Clara Valley Conservation District—a public entity.

- Public and private uses of water obviously are not limited to water supply. A water artery—in this case Buffalo Bayou running through Houston—linked the past and present political, social, and economic history of the community, serving both public and private interests.

- While Houston followed the public service model in developing its modern water supply system, that system was crucial to private development and was sometimes shaped by the needs of the private sector—especially, in this case, the oil refining and petrochemical industries.

- The emerging global movement by multinational companies to privatize water supply systems raises important questions about water as a public good or an economic commodity. It also raises questions about the loss of local control to absentee owners and managers far removed from the area of service delivery.

These are issues I have raised during the course of my career with respect to water history in an attempt to understand institutional influences in the delivery and allocation of a vital resource. As I stated previously, I had never really considered myself a water historian. I feel different about that today, not only because I have written more extensively on the topic than I realized but because I have also been involved in the International Water History Association as, among other things, a board member for its journal, *Water History.*

As is my wont, I am constantly trying to connect pressing current environmental issues with their past histories. If this is doing "history in the moment," I must plead guilty. Yet I firmly believe that history has much to tell us about our current state of affairs, can raise pertinent questions of long-standing importance, and can sometimes help us to move beyond present discourse that is more of the heart than the head.

I came to the study of water primarily through my longtime interest in the urban environment. My first foray into that area was through the study of solid waste—garbage—as a way of understanding the public health and environmental views of people living in cities in nineteenth- and twentieth-century America. The study of garbage—although this is not the proper descriptive term for all solid waste—brought me to a mundane subject that had impact on everyone. By looking at what people threw away and why, I came to understand what they kept and thus what they valued.

Water entered the picture for me in two ways. First, in completing a book on America's energy history, *Coping with Abundance,* I needed to learn about waterpower, dams, and so forth in developing my larger picture of energy production.[4] Turning to what became *The Sanitary City* several years later, I wanted to expand my study of city services to treat water supply, wastewater, and solid waste conceptually as "sanitary services" to understand their collective impact on confronting public health and environmental issues affecting cities over a relatively long period of time and over a large geographic area.[5]

Common to both books, concerning water at least, was the lingering question of who was responsible for controlling the resource and what were the implications of that control. I suppose my early experiences as a political and diplomatic historian had me framing many issues in a political context, thus I remained extremely curious about the wielding of power as it influenced public health and environmental decisions. An interest in private control was not so well developed in my work, but studying water supply and other water uses began my thinking more deeply about questions such as privatization.

Spurring those intellectual curiosities were the current debates over potential scarcities, a supposed fresh water crisis, and the challenge to publicly managed water systems by water corporatists. Further sustaining my interest in water, but not represented in this collection, were queries about the intersection of energy development and the need for water with respect to biofuels, for example, and cooling water for atomic power plants that negatively impacted rivers as thermal pollution. My current research on atomic energy takes up some of these water questions, but as yet I don't have sufficient work completed to showcase such studies here. The questions that this new research raises fit the pattern of my previous work on water, however.

The issues stated above—with respect to the eight chapters in this book—bind together pragmatic concerns over the control of water with an appreciation of the inherent limits of this precious commodity. Social scientists and others have been debating how to understand water as a resource for years. Is it a renewable or a nonrenewable resource? Traditionally water has been regarded as renewable, at least in the sense that hydrologic cycles circulate it with very little lost in the process. Running water (flowing rivers) is often regarded as a fugitive resource like wildlife, especially in efforts to define property rights for obvious reasons. Only groundwater is likely to be viewed as nonrenewable, especially if aquifers cannot be sufficiently recharged. Groundwater also has been regarded as a common pool resource that may be owned by a surface property owner under which the groundwater collects. Therefore, the physical qualities of water as a resource play a major role in determining its use, and by whom, and its potential ownership. Natural resource policies, however, may be determined by property rights theory, theories based on scarcity, various other economic-based theories, and to a broader extent, ecological approaches built more upon scientific analysis than economics.[6]

Another central issue necessary to understanding control of water rests upon the idea of water as a commodity. The controversy over privatization in recent years revolves, in part at least, around a concern among critics that water is becoming commodified, thus undermining the public's access and right to it. Probably it is more accurate to say that water has long been a commodity—a resource—to be bought and sold, and what we actually might be observing today is essentially a recommodification of water.

Underlying the debate over this issue is a question of control. As engineer and city planning professor Peter Rogers astutely observed: "Most people in everyday use do not regard water as an end in itself. It is a commodity, consumed directly or used as an input to other processes. The problem is that most people understand water this way at an individual level but treat water differently when they gather collectively to make decisions about the future use of water."[7] Who is and who should be responsible for providing, allocating, and managing water? These are questions central to any discussion of any resource—but few resources are so central to life itself as water.

In this case, the typical schism rests upon water as a public utility (or public good) versus water as a private commodity (or exclusive economic good). Such a paradigm is much too simple, a little too murky, and much too dichotomous. Water is a commodity whether it is managed and/or allocated by government or by a private business—or anything in between. But how that commodity is treated and for whose benefit is likely a more important question.

Water as a medium also serves myriad purposes—human sustenance, agricultural irrigation, sanitation, fire protection, military defense, power generation, transportation, and more—and thus contested uses must be understood and explained to obtain a proper context in which to evaluate wants and needs. Underlying water's uses are cultural traditions, various hierarchies, and social perceptions and conditions—all influencing control and allocation.[8]

A difficult question is whether we must accept fresh water as part of the commons or subject it to ownership. Historically water has been treated as a public resource to be used or managed by a variety of entities; in other cases the view of water as property is at the heart of control. As one study noted, "[t]he struggle to control water is a struggle without end."[9]

This volume is meant to address the question of control of water primarily in the United States with a principal focus on urban water use. Two chapters discuss riverine issues beyond the city in order to deal with broader questions of water management, water law, and a variety of water uses over time. But even these chapters should inform the discussion of urban water, since a great amount of water used in cities comes from rivers. One chapter takes on a more global perspective by raising questions related to public and private water management and control beyond existing political borders. In this case, the chapter attempts to raise questions about water as a borderless resource as well as a resource contested within and without national boundaries—and a resource recommodified in a new global setting.

The chapters in *Precious Commodity*, with the exception of the last one, represent some of my previously published articles, chapters, or excerpts from longer studies. I have attempted to limit duplication, to give primary attention to the role of local, state, and national management of water resources, to approach questions of privatizing water supplies in the past and present, and also to confront issues related to water pollution and questions of health. As a group, I am hopeful that the chapters will shed light on efforts to control and manage a vital resource that often defies such control and management.

A section of "Further Reading" has been included in the back matter to offer historical accounts on key water issues written since approximately 2000. Water history is becoming a field unto itself, and in 2001 the International Water History Association (IWHA) was established. At this time there are more than five hundred members from over seventy countries represented in the IWHA. Historians of water also are to be found in many other professional historical societies and associations, and many more writers on the subject fill the electronic pages of Amazon.com and other purveyors of books and articles. Beyond the printed page, water history is the subject of documentaries—like the recently aired *Liquid Assets* produced by Penn State Public Broadcasting and Ken Burns's *The National Parks: America's Best Idea*—as well as innumerable news shows and a variety of public forums on key water issues.

Precious Commodity looks at the apparent tension between public and private responsibility for and control of water. It explores how those seeming polarities function in a riverine context (with respect to dams), for urban water supply and wastewater systems (in regards to arteries of transportation and economic activity), and through the efforts of water corporatists (hybrid approaches and public or private partnerships also have evolved under certain conditions).

In the largest sense, reliance on water goes much deeper into history than dependence on oil. Truth be told, "water is the next water"—if such a phrase makes any sense at all.

PRECIOUS COMMODITY

CHAPTER ONE

"Improving" Rivers in America

FROM THE REVOLUTION TO THE PROGRESSIVE ERA

RIVERS AS RESOURCE

This chapter was extracted from a book I coauthored with David Billington and D. C. Jackson, *The History of Large Federal Dams: Planning, Design, and Construction,* which was underwritten by the Bureau of Reclamation, U.S. Army Corps of Engineers, and the National Park Service (NPS). Although dealing with "federal involvement in dam construction" in general, the book gave greater focus to the West, where many of the largest federal dams were built. For reasons that had to do more with funding than scholarly appraisal, the Tennessee Valley Authority (TVA) dams were not included in the study, although it should be noted that the Bureau of Reclamation and the U.S. Army Corps of Engineers built the vast majority of major federal dams in the United States. Beyond the discussion of several important dam projects, the book provided substantial detail on the federal role in dam building and the importance of the U.S. Army Corps of Engineers and the Bureau of Reclamation in that venture. My role was largely to contextualize the book in two of the nine chapters, while my colleagues did almost all of the "heavy lifting" and detailed work on dams in the remaining seven chapters.

The History of Large Federal Dams could only begin with a discussion of rivers. Most obviously, to understand dams is to understand what rivers do, how they have been perceived, the role they play in resource management, and the legal structure that emerged to regulate their use. The chapter reproduced here functioned as chapter 1—an introduction, offering a prelude to a much more detailed analysis of specific questions relating to the building and maintenance of large federal dams. Because of the book's focus, the important role of groundwater—especially in urban development—was not addressed.

As historians Christof Mauch and Thomas Zeller stated, "Sources of both abundance and destruction, life and death, rivers have always had a powerful hold over humankind. They run through every human landscape, whether mythical or actual."[1] In every place on earth, rivers have played a major role in providing transport; water for drinking, agriculture, commerce, and industry; water for power; sources of food; carriers of waste; and places of recreation. For urban development, rivers along with groundwater have been most essential. Rivers historically have transcended their practical value to take central roles in religion and human culture in general, as icons and symbols and as metaphors.[2]

For the purposes of *Precious Commodity,* this chapter is meant to set context, to make the point that the human imprint on America's riverine history—public and private—has been central from the earliest days of the republic. In essence, the intrinsic value of rivers—their ability to remain "forever wild"—was superseded quickly and aggressively by a human demand for control of a vital resource, maybe the most vital resource. Questions over private access to water and its use—be it riparian rights or prior appropriation—were mitigated by the courts, by state action, and by federal laws. At the heart of the question of water rights is property rights, and while the two are intertwined, the history of water has been a story as much about use as ownership.

This chapter particularly highlights the contesting consumers vying for fresh water—including cities—and the historical forces that played a role in allocating the resource in the nineteenth and twentieth centuries. Because they were so dramatic, contests in the "arid" West received a great amount of coverage. But debates over flood control, transportation, and industrial and urban uses of water in the "moist" East—beginning at the Mississippi River—are no less important and receive critical attention as well. In such an expansive country as the United States, as Peter Rogers noted, "public goals concerning water policy have continually shifted because the nature of the problems has changed as the country has grown, both in size and in affluence."[3]

As the contested role of rivers as resource intensified in the nineteenth and into the twentieth century, problems and policies not only changed but became more complex. This first chapter sets the stage for debates over public and private responsibility for water that will be explored in a number of ways in the chapters to follow. "Harnessing" rivers on a national scale meant commodifying water and controlling its use, practices that persisted as fresh water flowed in and out of cities (as most of chapters 2 through 7 especially will testify). Since riverine flows rarely if ever stop at urban boundaries, questions of public and private responsibility for the control of water do not end there either.

THE AMERICAN WATERSHED SYSTEM

The great rivers and their tributaries in the United States are the primary source of the water bounty and are major symbols of American regionalism, ultimately binding together disparate areas into a powerful whole.

The American watershed system is an awesome force. The Mississippi Basin alone drains more than 40 percent of the country's land from the Appalachian Mountains in the East to the Rockies in the West. To the North, the St. Lawrence River drains the Great Lakes. In the Southwest, the Colorado River traverses seven states and Mexico on its route to the Gulf of California, and the Rio Grande forms part of the nation's southern boundary. Along the Pacific Coast, the Columbia River gathers water from the Rocky Mountains and the Cascades, and the Sacramento and San Joaquin Rivers collect water from the Sierra Nevada, linking inland valleys to the Pacific Ocean. The geological and human history of the United States is linked inextricably to its rivers.[4]

American rivers were symbols of a burgeoning nation in the eighteenth and nineteenth centuries. They inspired romantic renderings at the hands of artists, and in some cases—as with painters of the Hudson River School in the 1820s—they were depicted as detailed landscape features with physical and even human qualities.[5] But at times they were regarded as untapped or underutilized resources, raw material waiting to be harnessed, managed, and exploited for human benefit. In the neoclassical tradition of the eighteenth and early nineteenth centuries, "The 'proper' channel for a river is not necessarily the one it has carved for itself: By means of canals and locks it can be guided by men along a straight and level line, thereby improving upon natural design." Rivers, therefore, were most attractive "when they yielded to humanity's needs, whether as mechanisms of transportation or as sites for nascent towns."[6] For aesthetic and for practical reasons, wild rivers served little purpose, historian Theodore Steinberg noted: "As the [nineteenth] century progressed, a consensus emerged on the need to exploit and manipulate water for economic gain. A stunning cultural transformation was taking place, a shift in people's very perception of nature. By the latter part of the nineteenth century, it was commonly assumed, even expected, that water should be tapped, controlled, and dominated in the name of progress—a view clearly reflected in the law."[7] Steamboats, canals, and dams became the technologies of choice to accomplish those goals.

THE RISE OF AN INDUSTRIALIZING NATION

The impulse to "improve" waterways was stimulated by the profound changes transforming the young nation. Beginning as early as 1820, the Industrial Revolution ushered in a period of unprecedented economic development for the United States. Manufacturing began to challenge agriculture as the nation's leading economic enterprise. While agriculture was responsible for the largest single share of production income before the Civil War, the growth and importance of manufacturing, especially in the East and along the Great Lakes, rose rapidly during the decades that followed the war. In 1859, there were 140,000 industrial establishments in the United States—many of them hand or neighborhood industries. Forty years later, there were 207,000 industrial plants, excluding hand and neighborhood industries.[8]

The economic transformation of the nation paralleled the rise of cities. The first federal census in 1790 showed that city dwellers represented less than 4 percent of the nation's population. Urban growth stagnated until 1820, but by the end of the decade the urban population had almost doubled.[9] While only seven out of every one hundred Americans lived in cities or towns at that time, the urban population grew by 552 percent (from 1.1 million to 6.2 million) between 1830 and 1860, which was the fastest rate of urbanization the nation had ever experienced.[10]

Industrialization also inspired the mechanization of agriculture and stimulated demand for a variety of products that helped to build a national market economy. Irrigation ultimately became a tool for expanding the agricultural market in the West to supply a variety of goods for growing urban centers at home and abroad. As early as the 1770s, an emerging capitalist economic system was evident in the Northeast, the Mid-Atlantic region, the South, and the back country. A booming transatlantic market for grain and other agricultural products, a rising number of American capitalist entrepreneurs, surplus labor available to work for wages, and state and national governments encouraging and promoting economic growth underlay the emergence of a market revolution along the American rural frontiers.[11]

The promise of economic growth had long attracted the interest of government. In the manufacturing belt of the East Coast and the Great Lakes, the states and the federal government had been active agents in stimulating commerce and industrialization. Competition between the states beyond the Appalachians for access to ports on the Atlantic had been intense. Rivalries between the states for a variety of public works projects focused on economic opportunities to be won and lost.

THE ORIGINS OF FEDERAL WATER RESOURCE POLICY

With respect to water resource issues, rivalries between the states suggest a partial answer for an increased role by the federal government. However, no comprehensive water resource policy ever emerged in the nineteenth or twentieth centuries. Federal navigation policy, flood-control policy, and irrigation policy were conceived and administered separately over the years, and water issues even today remain a combination of local, state, and national interest.[12] Supporters of national initiatives for water and navigation projects chronically vied with advocates of states' rights, who opposed outright subsidies for waterway construction. Steering a middle course, an emerging "water bureaucracy"—including the U.S. Army Corps of Engineers, the Bureau of Reclamation, and the TVA—often urged government planning without directly challenging state control of water projects.[13]

There is merit in Richard N. L. Andrews's observation that federal responsibility for water resource management "evolved almost unintentionally from the convergence of nineteenth-century public-land and internal-improvements policies."[14] Disposal of public lands set several precedents about how the federal government would deal with the nation's resources. At one time or another, more than 78 percent of the nation's 2.3 billion acres was owned by the federal government. There was no uniform method of land distribution during early colonial days. Since much of the frontier remained within the boundaries of the states after the American Revolution, state legislatures often developed the first land schemes to deal with estates confiscated from Loyalists. Land speculation on federal lands initially focused on the Ohio River region, an area wedged between the new nation and the vast frontier. After the Louisiana Purchase, a new land law that lowered the minimum purchase to a quarter section (160 acres) made western migration attractive to easterners and European immigrants. Between 1850 and 1900, the number of farms in American territory increased from 1.4 million to 5.7 million. Indian land rights, however, were often ignored or manipulated in providing settlers with land. In essence, much of the productive land in the West had already been claimed before the famous Homestead Act of 1862, and after its initial disposal, former public land increasingly became a speculative commodity.[15]

The disposal of public lands was not merely an end in itself from the first land ordinances in the eighteenth through the nineteenth century, the federal government intended to generate revenue and to stimulate economic development by a rapid transfer of public lands to private individuals. This was not accomplished without fierce debate, characterized most graphically by Thomas Jefferson's image of a nation of self-sufficient yeomen farmers and Alexander Hamilton's promotion of manufacturing, inland navigation, and the development of new economic markets.

In dealing with the states, the federal government could offer public lands in exchange for their support on development projects or other policies. Public lands also were used to provide capital for private businesses, such as the railroads. The first land laws in the 1780s and 1790s (including the Northwest Ordinance of 1787), however, were primarily directed toward using land to raise revenue, to retire the public debt, and to create a market in western lands.[16]

While land subsidies for public works projects were not provided for in federal law, many land grants were made to subsidize road building, river improvements, and railroad construction. For public lands to have value, they needed to be accessible to facilitate settlement and the transportation of raw materials and crops to the East and to Europe. The federal government funded "internal improvements" through general revenues, the sale of public lands, and land grants.[17] But as John Lauritz Larson perceptively observed, "the campaign for internal improvements, so universally appealing in the abstract, proved incredibly controversial at all levels of government as soon as workmen struck their spades into the earth."[18]

Prior to 1789, private investors provided internal improvements. At the Constitutional Convention of 1787, Benjamin Franklin was the primary advocate for federal sponsorship for internal improvements, but he could not carry the day. The Constitution ultimately reserved that responsibility for the states. However, with poor economic conditions in many states, Congress began appropriating funds for specific improvements beginning in 1802. In 1808, Secretary of Treasury Albert Gallatin submitted his report recommending federal aid for a system of roads and canals that would link the Atlantic seaports with the nation's interior.[19]

Artificial canals became the foremost technology in the early nineteenth century to connect the riverine system to the sea. The virtue of such canals was to "free" rivers from their natural courses and to direct them into channels that would serve the economic ends of the nation.[20] East Coast rivers were only navigable up to the fall line, a barrier at the foothills of the Appalachians. In the late eighteenth century, several short canals and the twenty-seven-mile Middlesex Canal in Massachusetts had been constructed, but by 1816 only about a hundred miles of canals existed in the United States. These human-made waterways proved to be demanding engineering feats and financial liabilities, and it became difficult to find investors for new projects.

The construction of the Erie Canal, linking Albany and Buffalo by means of an artificial waterway 364 miles in length, set off a canal boom in the United States that ultimately attracted federal dollars to future projects. The New York legislature authorized the construction of the Erie Canal in 1817 without a promise of federal support, and the canal was completed in 1825. By 1840, various states had invested approximately $125 million in 3,200 miles of canals. Between 1815 and 1860, the total public and private expenditures for canal construction was about $195 million. While the federal government had refused to help New York State build its canal, and states were the primary financial contributors in the early canal era, the federal government ultimately provided financial support through land grants and subscribed more than $3 million in canal company stock. Expensive enlargement programs, the Panic of 1837, and competition from railroads brought the canal boom to an end by the 1840s.[21]

WATER LAW AND THE USE OF RIVERS

MILLS AND DAMS IN THE EARLY INDUSTRIAL ERA

Complicating the creation of a national water resource program was the fact that fresh water, unlike land, was common as opposed to private property. Navigable waterways, for example, could not be treated like the public lands, that is, could not be disposed of to generate revenue or to promote economic development. They were open to common use and thus required special treatment. Water usage also was subject to unique practices imbedded in the law.[22]

Water, among other things, was an important source of energy before and during the early stages of the Industrial Revolution and was thus the focus of voluminous litigation over water rights. The bulk of litigation arose from disputes over the use of streams for waterpower.[23] Mills and dams raised for the first time legal questions over the relationship between property law and private development, when "antidevelopmental doctrines of the common law first clashed with the spirit of economic improvement."[24] Evolving water rights law had a greater impact on the effort to adapt private law doctrines to the promotion of economic growth than any other branch of law.

The water mill inevitably came into conflict with other stream uses. Aside from the waterwheel, the dam was the most essential element of a mill. Preindustrial dams were low, crude structures designed to increase water fall by raising the stream level. The dam created a storage reservoir, or millpond, that not only obstructed navigation and log floats but also the seasonal movement of fish.[25]

Water mills challenged prevailing water rights law and practices such as riparian rights, commonly recognized in the eastern United States in the eighteenth and nineteenth centuries. This English common-law doctrine granted ownership of a water privilege with the land bordering the two banks of the stream. The landowner did not own the stream, but only the rights of water usage. Even usage was subject to rights and claims of other users, including navigation interests, owners of riparian farmlands above and below a specific water privilege, lumber and other commercial interests, upstream communities, and mill owners themselves.[26]

Before the nineteenth century, common-law doctrines were generally based on the natural flow of water, and jurists rarely looked with favor on the use of water to irrigate or to run machinery. Possessing a narrow view of the productive capacity of water, they generally placed strict limits on its appropriation.[27] With the onset of the Industrial Revolution, the increasing number of conflicting claims and shades of interpretation of privilege challenged the water rights of riparian owners.[28]

Since navigation rights had priority on streams sufficiently large to carry regular traffic, the parts of the law referring to that activity were the least controversial. As power needs increased, government officials began to favor mill owners—especially in New England—over other riparians. This also was true for capitalists who wanted to divert water from natural sources to build canals.[29]

The most typical water rights controversy pitted downstream riparian landowners against upstream owners whose dams obstructed the natural flow of water for mills or irrigation. Other cases pitted upstream mill owners against downstream mill owners or landowners flooded by the dam. Some courts virtually refused to recognize any right to interfere with the flow of water to a mill.[30]

"Reasonable use," or a balancing test, was the most important challenge to the common-law doctrine of riparian water rights. Although the concept did not find general acceptance until around 1825, some early decisions set the stage. By the Civil War, most courts accepted a balancing test in which reasonable use of a stream depended on the extent of detriment to riparian landowners downstream.[31]

In determining reasonable use, it was common to take into account what constituted a proportionate share of the water. In *Cary v. Daniels* (1844), however, Massachusetts Chief Justice Lemuel Shaw tended to weaken the standard of proportionality by giving priority to the proprietor who first erected his dam, thus placing greater emphasis on maximizing economic development at the expense of equal distribution of the water privilege.[32] Not until the nineteenth century was a theory of priority used offensively to maintain a right to obstruct the flow.[33] What brought on the change was the building of large dams, which widened the possibilities for injury by causing potential damage to mill owners both upstream and downstream from the dam.

The two doctrines—reasonable use and prior appropriation—were becoming less and less interchangeable, at least as they operated within the context of economic development in the emerging industrial age. Thus a tension between the two, which had moved beyond the natural rights doctrine characteristic of preindustrial societies, found its way into the courts. By midcentury, almost all courts rejected prior appropriation because it so obviously interfered with competition. Riparian rights, modified by reasonable use, prevailed in the East in dealing with economic development. In addition, the advent of the steam engine and the railroad made concessions to mill dams and canals temporary.[34]

WATER LAW IN THE WEST

While waterpower development and canal building framed much of the water law in the East, in the West mining activity and agriculture helped shape the law.[35] The traditional interpretation stresses that water rights in the nineteenth-century West, as opposed to the East, have been closely associated with the prior appropriation doctrine.[36] When Anglo-American settlers arrived in the West, neither land nor water rights issues had been clearly resolved. Until the Civil War, the federal government controlled the public domain. Legislation enacted by Congress in the 1860s and 1870s, however, recognized the rights of settlers to utilize water on the public lands for a variety of purposes. Thus, the prior appropriation doctrine in the West owes a great deal to local circumstance.[37] Donald Pisani, however, has persuasively argued that "water law evolved slowly in both California and the West, constructed piece by piece, like a quilt, rather than from whole cloth." The courts and legislatures, he added, "rarely looked beyond immediate economic needs" in determining water rights.[38]

THE WESTERN SETTING

In humid eastern America water is an essential resource. But control over water resources does not define the central character of that society. In contrast, water is dramatically scarce in the arid West and that "precious liquid" occupies a pivotal position in regional development and in the larger political economy. Much of the West's historical character arises from a pervasive lack of rainfall.[39] It has become clear that water resources development is a key factor in regional growth.[40] Moreover, in the history of western water use, the work of the federal government—in particular the U.S. Reclamation Service after 1902 and the U.S. Army Corps of Engineers after 1933—has had enormous influence in transforming the environment and fostering economic development.[41]

Precipitation in the West is not evenly distributed over the landscape, and while billions of gallons of water might be dumped on the desert in the period of a few days or weeks, such storms can be spaced years apart. With much surface water originating either as seasonal snowmelt or infrequent torrential rainstorms, the ability to support widespread agriculture—as well as mining, municipal growth, and hydroelectric power development—has by necessity become dependent upon artificial means of controlling water.

Leaving aside groundwater that can be lifted to the surface by either wind-mills or electric pumps, irrigated agriculture depends upon water diverted from rivers, transported in canals, and then distributed over fields to sustain crops. The engineering techniques and the political instruments devised to foster irrigation in the West later comprised the basis for water resources de-velopment throughout the nation.

THE CALIFORNIA DOCTRINE, 1851–1886

During the California gold rush, the right to a claim went to the first person working it. Not surprisingly, this "first in time, first in right" principle (or prior appropriation doctrine) could also apply to water—a commodity es-sential to mining. A miner did not acquire property in the running water itself, but only its use if he continued to work the claim. But this prior appro-priation doctrine coexisted with riparian rights in the 1840s and early 1850s, since many miners did not want streams diverted from their natural courses. The California State Legislature, eager to promote mining, supported prior appropriation for the gold country in 1851, the state court accepted it in 1855, followed by its congressional endorsement for public lands generally in 1866.[42] The federal action endorsed prior appropriation not only for min-ing but also for agricultural, manufacturing, and other uses, and it further acknowledged the states' power to regulate water rights. The prior appro-priation doctrine promoted economic development but gave no preference to communities over individuals. Eventually every western state endorsed some form of the doctrine, and nine states adopted it as their sole water law.[43]

In practice, prior appropriation worked well enough when water was abundant, but when water was scarce it created confusion. An appropriator could sue to defend his rights, and the courts reviewed the records to deter-mine a prior claim. But the amount of water available was not always known. A title established in one case protected an appropriator from one claimant only. Although the states gradually evolved more orderly approaches, the system remained confused.[44]

Although California set a precedent in the application of prior appropria-tion, riparianism also gained legal recognition early in the state's history. In 1850, the first legislature adopted as its basic system English common law, subsequently modified by state courts in response to statutory and case law, and "for nearly three decades the state dealt with the problem of two contra-dictory legal systems by reaffirming the legitimacy of both and seeking to soften their differences." However, when irrigation appeared necessary for some forms of agriculture, the courts demonstrated flexibility, "taking a cue from eastern states, which had begun modifying their riparian law tradition in favor of some appropriation practices."[45]

Drought in the 1860s and 1870s, and especially increased irrigation, threatened to challenge the uneasy status quo. The development of refrigerated railroad cars, for example, meant that high-profit fruit and vegetable crops produced through irrigation could be shipped to distant markets.[46]

While the California courts ruled in favor of some irrigation under riparianism by the 1870s, accommodation had not been made for an irrigation boom. During the 1880s, the area of irrigated land in the arid West increased four- or fivefold. The clash of the water doctrines reached an acme in 1886. In *Lux v. Haggin,* the California Supreme Court affirmed a dual system of water rights, the so-called California Doctrine.[47] The court held that riparianism was law in California, applicable in all private lands and public lands that became privately owned. An appropriator could have a superior claim if he used the water before a riparian user had acquired the property. Timing was crucial.[48] As unpopular as the decision was within the public at large—since large landholders would be affected much less than small farmers—the California Doctrine eventually was adopted along the Pacific Coast (Washington and Oregon) and in the Great Plains (Nebraska, Oklahoma, Texas, Kansas, North Dakota, and South Dakota).[49]

In the 1880s, Colorado invalidated riparian rights to surface water and began enforcing appropriative rights under state authority. Prior appropriation became the sole water right and came to dominate much of the Rocky Mountain region. Five other states (Utah, Wyoming, Arizona, New Mexico, and Idaho) soon accepted the Colorado Doctrine, with Montana and Alaska following in the early twentieth century.[50]

A third approach developed in Wyoming, emphasizing a different type of enforcement. The state constitution gave the state title to all water. Officials could reject water claims and overturn existing appropriations not believed to be in "the public interest." In essence, the so-called Wyoming Doctrine gave greater protection to appropriators than under the Colorado system. Besides Wyoming, Nebraska, Oklahoma, North Dakota, and South Dakota claimed full control over their water.[51]

Despite the flurry of activity that led to the three major water doctrines, water rights—let alone water policy—were not completely rationalized, nor were conflicts ended among economic interest groups. Battles over irrigation, farming and livestock raising, mining, and the demands of urban growth kept the water issue at center stage.

Inevitably, the federal government would be active in the controversies, which was welcomed by some and not welcomed by others. The commitment in the early twentieth century to the construction of federal dams in every major watershed occurred in the wake of the long-contested uses of water. That water law favored the states only complicated the ability of federal dams to provide stored water to a variety of consumers. However, under the property clause (Article 4, Section 3) of the U.S. Constitution, the federal government had legal authority to accept, manage, and dispose of public domain lands, and this provided the basis for subsequent laws and regulations pertaining to public lands and other resources. With regard to water resource policy, the federal government presumably holds "reserve rights" to enormous amounts of annual water flows in the West, since it was the earliest formal owner of the public lands. However, the federal government has never fully asserted these rights and the U.S. Supreme Court has never formally recognized them.[52]

Prior appropriation exacted heavy social and environmental costs in the West. Water was an economic commodity, although private gain resulting from the use of water did not translate into revenue for the states. Instead, several large corporations and monopolies benefitted, and many farmers adopted wasteful irrigation practices. Prior appropriation led to a rapid economic development that "exacerbated the boom-and-bust mentality endemic to the mining industry, encouraging speculation and maximum production." Moreover, it failed to preserve water quality as did riparian rights, and it allowed vast environmental destruction.[53]

Environmental policy was in the developmental stages in the late nineteenth century.[54] The emergence of resource conservationism, as opposed to nature preservation, grew out of concern about the depletion of natural resources, which could stall further economic development.[55] Resource exploitation was central to the actions of a rapidly industrializing society; laissez-faire capitalism was more regaled than condemned for stoking the fires of economic growth.[56] Particularly in the West, where the forests, rivers, and mineral wealth were directly linked to economic opportunity, conservationism was largely dismissed in the nineteenth century.[57] But even practical concerns, such as the marshaling of such a scarce resource as water, generated intense conflict. A more widely held interest was how to tap yet-to-be exploited water sources.

THE U.S. ARMY CORPS OF ENGINEERS IN THE NINETEENTH CENTURY

The U.S. Army Corps of Engineers and the Bureau of Reclamation have been the most important government bodies responsible for water resource management in the United States. Their stories are central to riverine history.

THE CORPS AND THE FRENCH ENGINEERING TRADITION

In a March 16, 1802, congressional act, the U.S. Army Corps of Engineers was separated from the Corps of Artillerists and Engineers and stationed at West

Point, New York. This act not only marked the reestablishment of a separate U.S. Army Corps of Engineers (first created in 1779), but also founded the U.S. Military Academy. The Military Academy remained under the charge of the corps until 1866.[58]

The American engineering profession in the nineteenth century was being shaped by two European traditions. One emphasized the civilian "builder mechanic" model of the British; the other, the military, formally trained engineer in the French (or Continental European) style.[59] Of the two European engineering traditions, the French was the older—linked to the rise of a powerful monarchy in the sixteenth and seventeenth centuries. French engineering successes included a high point in canal engineering with the 149-mile-long Languedoc Canal opened in 1681.[60]

The U.S. Army Corps of Engineers became the chief American standard-bearer for French engineering. The key to the corps' preference for French engineering rested not only in its connection to the military, but to the role of the military within the state.

The influence of French engineering in the United States actually began during the American Revolution. The reputation of the French engineers, plus their country's sympathies for the rebelling colonies, resulted in a period of seven years when French military engineers organized and trained the American army's engineering corps.[61] It is not surprising that when the U.S. Army Corps of Engineers was reestablished in 1802, it embraced the French engineering tradition and sought to implant it at West Point.[62]

The influence of the French at West Point did not simply shape the engineering style and dictate the engineering methods, but it also imbued the corps with an interest in scientific design, natural philosophy, applied mathematics, and a commitment to large, state-supported projects.[63] But even those engineers who entered the corps did not focus exclusively on military projects. They helped map the West, constructed coastal fortifications and lighthouses, built jetties and piers for harbors, and mapped navigation channels.[64]

COMMERCE, NAVIGATION, AND THE "STEAMBOAT CASE"

The U.S. Army Corps of Engineers' water projects in the early nineteenth century focused primarily on navigation. With the economic climate of the nation improving after the War of 1812, the steamboat came of age. In the West, the steamboat was vital to commerce and travel. Only 17 steamboats operated on western rivers in 1817, but there were no less than 727 by 1855.[65]

While states' rights advocates typically objected to direct federal subsidies for waterway construction, they were less likely to block indirect types of federal aid, such as scientific surveys.[66] In 1820, Congress appropriated

$5,000 for a navigation survey of the Ohio and Mississippi Rivers from Lou-
isville to New Orleans. In the next few years, the corps also made surveys of
harbors, coastal areas, and lead mines on the upper Mississippi. It also built
jetties and breakwaters along the Massachusetts coast and at Presque Isle in
Lake Erie. Army engineers had demonstrated their ability to deal with a variety of civilian projects. Nevertheless, direct federal aid to waterways fared
little better than other forms of internal improvements in the early nineteenth century.[67]

The Supreme Court ruling of 1824 in the case of *Gibbons v. Ogden* (the
"Steamboat Case") changed that and also initiated the corps' regular participation in civil works and led to its role in maintaining the nation's inland waterways.[68] The case, producing the Supreme Court's first interpretation of the
commerce power of the federal government, originated in 1807, when Robert R. Livingston and Robert Fulton acquired a steamboat monopoly from
the New York legislature. Subsequently, they also petitioned other states and
territorial legislatures for similar monopolies in the hope of developing a national network of steamboat lines. Only Orleans Territory accepted their pe-
tition and awarded them a monopoly on the lower Mississippi.

Competitors, aware of the potential of steamboat navigation, challenged
Livingston and Fulton, arguing that the commerce power of the federal
government was exclusive and superseded state laws. Legal challenges followed, and in response the monopoly attempted to undercut its rivals by
selling them franchises or buying their boats. Former New Jersey governor
Aaron Ogden had tried to defy the monopoly but ultimately purchased a li-
cense from its assignees in 1815.[69] He entered business that year with Thomas
Gibbons from Georgia, but the partnership collapsed three years later when
Gibbons ran an unlicensed steamboat on Ogden's route. The former partners
ended up in the New York Court of Errors, which granted a permanent injunction against Gibbons in 1820.

Gibbons appealed to the U.S. Supreme Court, arguing as he did in New
York that the monopoly conflicted with federal law. After several delays, the
Court began discussing the meaning of the commerce clause in 1824, which
by that time had become an issue of wider interest. Congress was debating a
bill to provide a federal survey of road and canal routes. Southerners, in particular, were growing increasingly sensitive to what the resolution of these
issues would mean to them as sectional disputes, especially over slavery,
were heating up.

Chief Justice John Marshall could not ignore the political ramifications
of *Gibbons,* and thus in the unanimous decision he avoided stating flatly that
the federal government had exclusive power over commerce. Marshall ar-
ticulated a broad construction of the commerce clause, but he also tried to

accommodate state regulation of local problems and state demands for the principle of free trade. The New York monopoly was struck down, however, based on the argument that national law took precedence over state law in cases of conflict.[70]

While *Gibbons* did not settle the issue of the extent of federal power over commerce, it did provide an expansive interpretation of commerce. Marshall stated that "commerce, undoubtedly, is traffic, but it is something more, it is intercourse. It describes the commercial intercourse between nations, and parts of nations, in all its branches."[71] This included river navigation, giving impetus to further federal river and harbor improvements, and thus providing an opportunity for the corps to play a central role in planning and construction along commercial routes.[72] Although the corps began to assume responsibility for flood control in the 1880s, river and harbor work comprised a large part of its mission in the nineteenth century.[73]

FRENCH TRADITION VERSUS FRONTIER TECHNIQUES

Shortly after the Supreme Court rendered its judgment in *Gibbons,* President Monroe signed the General Survey Act on April 30, 1824, which gave him the authority to employ engineers and corps officers to survey "routes of such roads and canals as he may deem of national importance in a commercial or military point of view, or necessary for the transportation of the public mail." In gaining this role in civil works, including the planning and politics of internal improvements, the corps essentially became "the engineering department of the federal government."[74] One month later, Monroe signed an additional bill for improving navigation over sandbars in the Ohio River and for removing snags from the Ohio and Mississippi. The $75,000 appropriation was the first that Congress had issued for work in inland navigable waters.[75]

In 1826, Congress passed the Rivers and Harbors Act authorizing surveys and construction for more than twenty water projects on the Atlantic and Gulf coasts and on the Great Lakes. Combining both planning and construction, it is regarded as the first law of its kind, and it eventually became the model of enabling legislation for the corps' navigation improvement program and later for flood control. The act significantly expanded the work of the corps in waterways engineering.[76]

The expanding federal program on rivers and harbors was shrouded in controversy between 1824 and the beginning of the Civil War. The corps could not escape the controversy in these volatile years. It was caught between the forces contesting the internal improvements issue, especially as the primary agent for executing federal rivers and harbors projects. It also continued to be locked in a contest over the application of "the polytechnic orientation that promoted theory and standardization at the expense of frontier technique."[77]

Between 1824 and 1831, the corps attempted to develop a comprehensive, national system of internal improvements through its Board of Engineers for Internal Improvements. It consisted of the French Army Engineer Brigadier General Simon Bernard (who served under Napoleon), Colonel Joseph G. Totten of the U.S. Army Corps of Engineers, and civil engineer John L. Sullivan.[78] The plan called for three main projects: canals between the Chesapeake and the Ohio and between the Ohio and Lake Erie and improvements to navigation on the Ohio and Mississippi Rivers; a series of canals connecting the bays to the north of Washington, D.C.; and a road from Washington to New Orleans. By 1827, thirty-five examinations and surveys were conducted, but nothing more. By 1830, local political considerations became more influential than the overall plan in defining priorities, and it soon became the practice of Congress to adopt laws with this in mind.[79]

NAVIGATION AND THE BEGINNING OF RIVER DAMS, 1824–1865

For navigation improvements on the Ohio and Mississippi Rivers in the early nineteenth century, the U.S. Army Corps of Engineers focused on snag removal and channel deepening. Thousands of snags—possibly more than 50,000—threatened transportation daily, accounted for the majority of steamboat losses before 1826, and, along with other isolated obstructions, were responsible for three-fifths of all steamboat accidents until 1849.

Under the Rivers and Harbors Act of 1827, Congress made the first in a series of annual appropriations (through 1838) for the removal of obstructions, reflecting a clearer understanding—after one failed contract—that snag removal had to be ongoing. A year earlier, Henry M. Shreve had been appointed superintendent of Western River Improvements and was given responsibility for snag removal. He built the first steam-powered snag boat, the *Heliopolis,* launched in 1829. Shreve's operation was so successful that no boats were lost on the Ohio River due to snags in 1832, and the drop in insurance rates on steamboat cargoes between 1827 and 1835 reflected the vast improvements in clearing the channels.[80]

The other major improvement in river navigation in the 1820s was to deepen channels across sand and gravel bars.[81] Major Stephen H. Long conducted an early experiment with wing dams (or spur dikes) on the Ohio River near Henderson Island, Kentucky, about one hundred miles below Louisville.[82] The structure (two rows of 1,400 piles filled with brush) extended from the bank at a forty-five degree angle partway into the river. It narrowed the width of the channel, thus increasing the velocity of the current and deepening the channel itself while also slowing water flow close to the riverbanks. The wing dam was the primary method of deepening channels on the Ohio and several of its tributaries until the late nineteenth century. Long's project at Henderson Island, and a similar use of a wing dam carried out under the direction of Shreve at the Grand Chain near the mouth of the Ohio, led to a congressional appropriation in 1831 for additional dikes on the Ohio River. Some bars were dealt with effectively, but no system of wing dams was in place before the Civil War.[83]

Snag and boulder removal in some relatively minor tributaries of the Ohio River were inadequate to make them viable for steamboat navigation, thus a slack water system of locks and dams arose in the 1830s. Dams were placed across a stream at intervals insuring a minimum depth of water year-round. Each dam had a lock through which vessels passed. By the mid-1840s, such systems were in operation on the lower Kentucky River and also on the Green and Barren, the Licking, the Muskingum, and the Monongahela Rivers.

Once in place, these early slack water systems faced financial and technical problems. Inadequate capital for repairs and maintenance delayed completion and limited their operation. Poor engineering and construction, as well as flooding and icy conditions, limited service. Revenues did not meet expectations, such as the Kentucky River project, suspended in 1842 after the building of five dams. A Muskingum project, completed in 1842, showed profit for a decade but then faced financial problems. The most successful project was one on the lower Monongahela River, which benefitted from coal shipments to Pittsburgh. Even state-supported, open-channel projects had financial problems. On the Kanawha River, smaller boats took advantage of the improvements, but large coal barge tows could not.[84]

Until 1852, relatively little river work was carried out by the U.S. Army Corps of Engineers or the Corps of Topographical Engineers.[85] Even with the Rivers and Harbors Act of 1852, which provided funds for dike repair and construction on the Ohio and for building new snag boats, navigation improvement was sporadic at best for several years.[86] The Democrats won the 1852 election, kept power until 1860, and consistently opposed internal improvements, so that Congress did not pass another general rivers and harbors bill until after the Civil War.[87]

POSTWAR NAVIGATION AND THE OHIO RIVER, 1866–1885

The years after the war witnessed a shift from specific open-channel improvements—especially the elimination of obstructions or bypassing them with canals—to elaborate plans for slack water systems and storing flood-

waters in large reservoirs on the headwaters.[88] Pressure for federal involvement intensified especially because states' rights interests had been quelled.
And the Republican Party, strongly committed to federal public works, was
in control. Despite the rising competition from the railroads, the government focused on the Mississippi River because of its commercial importance.

In June 1866, Congress appropriated approximately $3.7 million for
about 50 projects and almost 40 examinations and surveys across the country. In the 1870s alone, total appropriations reached almost $54 million.
Between the end of the Civil War and 1882, U.S. presidents signed sixteen
river and harbor bills and federal appropriations for river and harbor projects
totaled over $91 million. In 1882, Congress provided $18.7 million for 371
projects and 135 surveys.[89]

As a result of the Rivers and Harbors Act of 1866, William Milnor Roberts was appointed to oversee improvements and to conduct surveys of the
Ohio. In his 1869 report, he provided a "radical" plan for a slack water, lock,
and dam canalization. Colonel William E. Merrill, who replaced Roberts
in 1870, supported the proposal because of its relatively successful use on a
number of tributaries.[90]

Ironically, those coal shippers, who were dominating Ohio river commerce and who stood to benefit from a deepened channel and year-round
navigation, argued that the dams would obstruct the channels, require
breaking tows to pass through the locks, and demand heavy tolls. In addition, the flatboat and rafting trade objected because the proposal would sac-
rifice the natural navigation of the river for ten months of the year to gain
two additional months of navigation for larger vessels. Others warned of
possible increased flood heights, stagnant slack water pools, and silting of
river channels.

In the wake of such criticisms, Merrill began exploring alternatives. He
sent his deputy to examine movable dams in Europe where 124 movable
dams had been completed. Such dams could be raised to increase depths
during shallow periods and then lowered when the water was higher.[91] As
a result, in 1874 Merrill recommended that a series of movable dams be utilized in the canalization of the Ohio River with the first experimental movable dam and lock to be built at Davis Island near Pittsburgh. While critics
complained loudly, he received support from the Ohio River Commission, a
variety of shipping interests, and the Grange—a farmer group that hoped to
undercut railroad costs. With the additional support of the Senate Committee on Transportation Routes, Congress appropriated funds for the project in
1875. Work began in 1878 and eventually was completed in 1885.[92]

Completion of the Davis Island Dam opened a new era in the improvement and navigation of the western rivers. It also marked the modern era of lock design in the United States. While only a 174-mile section between Pittsburgh and Marietta was completed by 1896, a series of about fifty dams extended slack water navigation along the Ohio by 1929.[93]

THE UPPER MISSISSIPPI AND THE HEADWATER DAMS, 1866–1899

In 1866, after many attempts to channelize the upper Mississippi, Congress appropriated $400,000 for a four-foot-deep channel between Minneapolis and St. Louis. In 1878, before the channel project was completed, Congress authorized the corps to seek a depth of four-and-a-half feet through the use of a wing and closing dam.[94] As a result of the deepening project, the banks gradually moved inward thus constricting the river and also changing the landscape.[95] The Mississippi River Commission, established in 1879, had set a goal of a minimum year-round channel depth of six to four-and-a-half feet from St. Louis to St. Paul, the results of which would fundamentally change the physical character of the river. Methods proposed included low-water dams to concentrate the flow of water in the main channel, spur dikes or wing dams to narrow the channel in places where the river was too wide, protection of the river banks from erosion, and occasional dredging. In addition, the Congress authorized reservoirs on the headwaters of the upper river to store surplus water during the wet season.[96]

In fact, as early as 1870, Brevet Major General G. K. Warren recommended construction of forty-one reservoirs on the St. Croix, Chippewa, Wisconsin, and Mississippi Rivers. In 1878, Representative William D. Washburn of Minnesota raised the issue of the reservoirs again, in part to benefit his own flour mills at St. Anthony and also to counter the growing railroad challenge. In 1880, in spite of opposition from St. Paul, Congress made its first of several appropriations for these headwaters dams, thus beginning a project that would be one of the earliest large-scale systems of reservoirs constructed in the United States.[97]

Congress initially authorized five headwater dams. They all were located upriver from St. Paul on the main stem and tributaries of the upper Mississippi near the river's source at Lake Itasca. The corps built all of them at lake outlets in remote areas with no existing roads and few settlements. The isolation of the sites led to initial construction with timber. At the turn of the century, the dams were reconstructed with concrete.[98]

Initially, civic leaders and businessmen in St. Paul had opposed the reservoirs for fear that they would give Minneapolis an unfair economic advantage, and lumbermen in northern Minnesota worried that the dams would constrain their logging activities. Predictably, the railroads also had op-

posed the project. While it was anticipated that improved steamboat navigation would be the primary beneficiary of the project, commercial interests
in Minneapolis and St. Paul benefitted the most, particularly lumber, flour
milling, and waterpower.[99]

In addition to political and economic rivalries, the construction of the
headwater dams also highlighted social and environmental problems that
would plague dam projects in the twentieth century. For example, the land
to be inundated by the construction of the Lake Winnibigoshish and Leech
Lake Dams belonged to approximately 1,300 Chippewa Indians. Constructing the dams required taking a substantial amount of timber from the area.
Also, opening the dams damaged or destroyed the Chippewas' wild rice
fields, some of their fisheries, and tamarack and cedar tree stands.[100]

The improved ability to transport lumber by water, aided by the construction of the headwater reservoirs and dams, increased water pollution
along the upper Mississippi. Sawmill refuse, already a serious problem in the
Minneapolis area by the late 1870s, obstructed river navigation. The corps
and many river interest groups favored a refuse act to prohibit such dumping.
Lumber interests, however, fought such action, in part at least because they
were not the only culprits. Minneapolis dumped approximately five hundred tons of refuse into the Mississippi each day.[101]

Changes in federal law were meant to address in some fashion pollution
problems like those faced on the upper Mississippi. With the Rivers and
Harbors Act of 1899, especially section 13 (the Refuse Act), loopholes were
closed and the law made illegal the casting of "any refuse matter of any kind
or description" into navigable waters without permission of the secretary of
war. In time, the act of 1899 would be regarded as a seminal piece of legislation in the recognition of water pollution as a major problem. It did not, however, seriously reduce pollution along the upper Mississippi or other rivers.[102]

As settlement increased along the nation's great rivers and their tributaries, a wide array of environmental issues complicated the use of the waters,
including how to best manage sewage and industrial pollutants and urban
and agricultural runoff. Also, the impact of river improvements themselves
in the form of dredging, canalizing, and dam and reservoir construction
would raise serious concerns about silting, land inundation, flooding, and
threats to fisheries.

The U.S. Army Corps of Engineers would find themselves in the midst
of these controversies. The corps' status as the lead federal bureau in water
resources development was challenged at the turn of the century by the creation of a new federal bureau focused on the arid West.[103]

WATER IN THE WEST—ORIGINS OF
THE RECLAMATION SERVICE

THE WEST BEFORE THE NINETEENTH CENTURY

Cultivation of irrigated crops in the West predates the arrival of both Spanish and Anglo-American settlement. For instance, the Hohokam and their predecessors used canal irrigation on the Santa Cruz River in the Tucson area as early as 1,200 BC, and canal irrigation was well established in the Phoenix area by about 500 AD. Some of these canals were quite large even by modern standards. In addition, the Pueblo Indians of the Rio Grande Valley were using canal irrigation at the time of Spanish contact in 1540. By the time Europeans first explored the Southwest in the sixteenth century, Hohokam culture had vanished, a victim of unknown environmental or cultural forces. But their canals survived largely intact; in the 1860s they were cleaned out and re-excavated by Anglo-American settlers who transformed them into irrigation canals that still lie at the heart of Phoenix's hydraulic infrastructure. But prehistoric Indian irrigation did not sustain the bulk of native food production in the West; many tribes made no attempt to use riverflow for agriculture, and they had little or no impact on the riparian environment.[104]

In the seventeenth century, the Spanish took control over what later became the southwestern United States, bringing with them an understanding of agricultural techniques suitable for an arid environment. That knowledge supplemented Pueblo irrigation skills. Their settlements in the Southwest involved some development of irrigation, most notably at San Antonio, in the pueblos settlements of the upper Rio Grande, and at the Franciscan missions of California. On the whole, however, Spanish irrigation initiatives were limited in scope and did not involve the construction of large storage dams.[105] Not until large numbers of pioneers from the eastern United States began moving westward in the mid-nineteenth century did interest in large-scale development of western water resources become manifest.

WATER AND MORMON MIGRATION

The first Anglo-Americans to embrace the possibilities of irrigation technology were Mormon refugees who emigrated to Utah's Salt Lake Valley in the late 1840s. To survive in the wilderness, they quickly began diverting creeks that flowed from the Wasatch Mountains, using the water for crops. This was first accomplished at City Creek in Salt Lake City and quickly spread along mountains of the Wasatch Front that form the eastern edge of the Great Basin.

Mormon settlements centered around the small streams were able to erect numerous irrigation systems that did not depend on large dams or lengthy canals. Extending less than five miles on average, Mormon canals typically supported small communities comprised of farms less than thirty acres in size.[106] Early irrigation systems in Utah comprised a relatively rudimentary technological achievement, but they proved successful in supplying food, and the communal settlements helped to inspire western agrarian development. The Mormons' success in building irrigation-based communities set a precedent for later pioneers seeking to colonize the West.

Most early non-Mormon irrigation development did not depend upon a strong social mission tying settlers together. For example, Anglo-American agricultural settlement in Arizona's Salt River Valley dates to the late 1860s and represents a much more prosaic endeavor. In 1867 "Jack" Swilling, a former Confederate Army officer formed the Swilling Irrigation Canal Company and quickly cleared out an ancient Hohokam canal. Swilling's canal extended a mile-and-a-half across the desert and then curved back toward the Salt River; farmland "under the ditch" could now be cultivated using water from the river, and resulting crops could be sold to the army outpost at Fort McDowell. By 1870, the townsite that became Phoenix had been laid out, and the Anglo-American settlement of central Arizona began to grow slowly as it met the needs of the local army encampment.[107]

CALIFORNIA WATER DEVELOPMENT

In central California agriculture became a major economic activity as early as the 1850s when crops were cultivated for sale in the gold mining camps of the Sierra Nevada. In addition, the fertile lands of the Sacramento River Valley were developed as large farms to export wheat through the busy port of San Francisco. These wheat fields depended upon nutrients and moisture that had accumulated in the soils over hundreds of years, and, initially, they did not require irrigation. As the soils were depleted, the attractiveness of nonirrigated agriculture began to fade while commercial interest in irrigation development increased, especially in the drier lands of the San Joaquin River Valley that lay to the southeast of San Francisco.

By 1886, there were twenty-one irrigation colonies in the Fresno region, covering 45,000 acres and supporting 7,500 residents. Real estate speculators and large landholding syndicates promoted these colonies, which drew water from the Kings River or (less frequently) from the San Joaquin River.[108]

Irrigation development in the San Joaquin Valley also centered around large tracts of land in the low-lying areas adjoining the river in the region north of Fresno and south of Stockton. By the late 1860s, much of this rich riparian land was under the control of a consortium of influential San Francisco businessmen headed by William Ralston of the Bank of California.

Ralston and his partners soon formed the San Joaquin and Kings River Canal and Irrigation Company. In the early 1870s, the company planned a valley-wide irrigation system capable of watering hundreds of thousands of acres of land.[109] Although the company was willing to invest its own money in those parts of the system that would divert water on to the low-lying lands that it directly controlled, they were hesitant to underwrite any broader scheme without government assistance.

Rebuffed by the state legislature, Ralston approached the federal government with hopes of obtaining a large land grant and associated canal rights-of-way that would make the project economical. This plan also failed. However, in early 1873, Congress authorized $6,000 for a Board of Irrigation Commissioners to study the water resources of central California. Their report did nothing to further Ralston's efforts to obtain federal help, but it was a precursor of large, federally sponsored projects that were implemented in California in the 1930s. Furthermore, the report enhanced the nation's political consciousness that western agriculture represented a potentially major segment of the burgeoning national economy.

THE EXPLOITS OF JOHN WESLEY POWELL

By the mid-1880s, most of the small streams in the West had been diverted for irrigation and other uses. It was becoming evident to some that larger dams on the major rivers would be needed to expand water supplies. In 1888, a Senate resolution called for the Department of the Interior to identify possible reservoir sites and to protect them for future development. Later that year, Congress passed another resolution designating the U.S. Geological Survey as the body to examine the arid region, determine the capacity of streams and where irrigation could be practiced, and arrive at the cost of construction and the capacity of possible reservoirs.[110] It was the publication of John Wesley Powell's *Report on the Lands of the Arid Regions of the United States* in 1879 that had opened the eyes of Americans to the significance of irrigation development.[111] Appointed director of the Geological Survey in 1881, Powell quickly became a major spokesman for development of the West's water resources. With Powell as a primary proselytizer, the notion that "reclaimed" land in the West might serve a larger national purpose began to assume momentum.[112]

Socially concerned citizens intent on countering the seemingly baneful effects of industrial development in eastern cities saw irrigation as a way for population growth in rural settlements. Recalling Madison's idea of a continental nation and Jefferson's agrarianism, advocates of this irrigation crusade considered western reclamation an ideal means for small family farms to foster the American ideal that life rooted to the soil was better than life despoiled by the "evil" city. Powell became prominently associated with this idealistic crusade.

In 1888, Congress authorized Powell to head the Irrigation Survey to explore the potential for developing western water resources. Among the many young engineers who participated in this work were Frederick Haynes Newell and Arthur Powell Davis, both of whom would later serve, respectively, as chief engineer and director of the U.S. Reclamation Service.[113] The legislation creating the Irrigation Survey offered no indication that the bureau was conceived as a direct antecedent for federal sponsorship or financing of irrigation projects. However, the legislation did give Powell and his staff the power to "withdraw" public land from entry to prevent private ownership claims from impeding economical construction of a storage reservoir.[114] In essence, the withdrawal authority was to preclude speculators from using information gathered by survey personnel to purchase, at cheap prices, choice public lands that might later be sold for large profits.

Speculative exploitation by large landowners ran counter to the ideal of western irrigation for small-scale, independent farmers. But with no stated mechanism for using the Irrigation Survey's data, the idea that reservoir sites could be closed indefinitely to private development aroused alarm among many westerners who already owned land in the arid region. This consternation found political expression in the person of Senator William Stewart of Nevada who, in his capacity as chairman of the Senate Select Committee on Irrigation and the Reclamation of Arid Lands, prompted Congress to cut off funding for the Irrigation Survey in the summer of 1890.[115] Furthermore, Congress enacted a law in 1891 allowing individuals and private irrigation companies to file claims to reservoir sites on public lands, providing that construction work begin within five years.[116]

THE SENTIMENTAL AND PRACTICAL DURING THE 1890S

Powell had come to realize that most of the best irrigable land had already fallen into private hands by the 1890s. He created an uproar by announcing this fact at the National Irrigation Congress of 1893 in Los Angeles.[117] The following year, Powell resigned from the Department of the Interior, becoming a victim of the "triumph of sentimentalism" among those who championed the social primacy of the small family farm.[118]

Opening the West to a new generation of yeoman farmers was popular even among American citizens at large, many of whom had only the vaguest concept of western reclamation. In the early twentieth century, sentiment for promoting family farms in the arid West found political expression in a national reclamation program; but while this federal program would espouse the ideals of the irrigation crusade, it would also provide benefits to large tracts of land that had long since been removed from the public domain.

Political efforts to promote reclamation also continued. Francis G. Newlands, Nevada's member of the House of Representatives, Senator Francis E. Warren of Wyoming, and Senator Joseph M. Carey of Wyoming, persisted in seeking support for western agriculture during the 1890s.[119] While it remained politically unfeasible to advocate a federally controlled reclamation program, Congress did pass the Carey Act in 1894, which authorized the federal government to cede up to a million acres of public land to states on their assurance that the acreage would be developed through viable irrigation projects. Eventually, these projects proved important in some northern states such as Idaho, but the Carey Act proved too cumbersome overall, failing to open the public domain to widespread irrigation.[120]

Western reclamation in the 1890s has no simple narrative trajectory leading inevitably to the establishment of the U.S. Reclamation Service in 1902. Rather, a variety of private interests as well as state and local politicians promoted initiatives to increase agriculture and land values. Among the most prominent of these advocates of western irrigation was George Maxwell, a California lawyer who, in 1897, organized the National Irrigation Association to call for federal legislation benefitting western agriculture. But also important in the adoption of the Reclamation Act of 1902 were several broader factors, including: the depression of the 1890s that crippled construction of private irrigation projects in the West and drove down the value of irrigable land; the rapid disposal of public land to grazing interests and land speculators after 1889; and the desire of leading railroads to boost their traffic in the West and to sell farmland.[121]

THE CHITTENDEN SURVEY OF 1897

In another strategy to attract federal support for western irrigation, Senator Warren adopted the model of "river and harbor improvement" so successfully used by eastern states in garnering government assistance. In 1896, he called for a survey of reservoir sites in Wyoming and Colorado to help reduce floods in the Missouri and Mississippi River Basin. Warren justified federal support because the Missouri was an interstate river, and because Wyoming, Colorado, New Mexico, Arizona, Utah, and Nevada previously had received no benefits from river and harbor improvements authorized by Congress.[122]

Warren won approval in May 1896 for the survey. At his request, the U.S. Army Corps of Engineers appointed Captain Hiram Chittenden to direct it. He traveled throughout the West inspecting irrigation systems, and he examined reservoir sites at the headwaters of the Platte and Laramie Rivers in Wyoming and Colorado. While he held little enthusiasm for flood control from reservoirs placed in the lower Missouri and Mississippi River Basin, Chittenden nonetheless recommended the construction of dams at five reservoir sites that were well suited to support irrigation development. Avowing that such reservoir construction could "properly be carried out only through public agencies," he also advised that all water stored behind government-built reservoirs be "absolutely free to the people forever, just as the canals, harbors, and other public works are free for general use without toll or levy of any kind."[123]

Chittenden's report of December 1897 attracted the interest of western irrigation advocates, but the attention of the nation as a whole was rapidly becoming absorbed by the impending war with Spain. Senator Warren could not entreat Congress to consider an expansion of Chittenden's work until early 1899. In addition, his attempts to utilize a rivers and harbors appropriation for dam and reservoir construction were thwarted by eastern congressmen who argued that the Constitution gave a clear mandate for government control over interstate rivers, but the water stored behind upstream reservoirs was not to be owned or controlled by the federal government. Despite intense lobbying and political maneuvering on Warren's part, the federal "rivers and harbors" appropriation of 1899 authorized no expenditure for western storage dams, and the issue of federal support for reclamation remained unresolved.[124]

While Congress vacillated in the 1890s, privately financed projects continued to open land for settlement. Some proved viable, others failed.[125] In California, the most prominent state initiative for locally controlled irrigation districts experienced only limited success.[126]

NEWELL, ROOSEVELT, AND THE MOVE TO RECLAMATION

Although nineteenth-century irrigation settlements in the West proved the feasibility of building diversion dams and distribution canals, the financial risks associated with building large, remote storage reservoirs and lengthy feeder canals through rough terrain discouraged private financiers.[127] By the turn of the century, the possibility of "capturing the floods" for widespread irrigation remained much more a vision than a reality. Because huge quantities of floodwater were lost to the ocean or dissipated in desert lakes, political support for federal intervention began to grow stronger and found its leading advocate in Frederick H. Newell.[128]

As the U.S. Geological Survey's chief hydrographer in 1894, Newell's mandate was to measure flows in America's rivers. Initially he could not advocate a large-scale federal reclamation program. However, in the late 1890s, this changed with the foundering of the Carey and Wright acts. By 1900,

Newell was interacting with key western businessmen and politicians to promote a federal role in irrigation among the capital's political leadership.[129]

Newell had attended the contentious Irrigation Congress of 1893 that reacted vehemently to Powell's report on the paucity of prime irrigable land in the public domain. In fact, Newell even gave a speech to the Irrigation Congress echoing Powell's remarks.[130] He projected a romantic image of yeoman farmers populating arid public lands in 1902 with his book, *Irrigation in the United States:* "The national government, the owner of these arid lands, is the only power competent to carry this mighty enterprise to a successful conclusion."[131]

In 1901, Congressman Newlands—working closely with Newell—submitted a joint proposal with Senator Henry Hansbrough of North Dakota to fund federal irrigation projects from proceeds derived from public land sales.[132] In addition, Newlands received assistance from George Maxwell, who, through his leadership of the National Irrigation Association, continued to lobby on behalf of a national reclamation program. While political support for federal irrigation appeared to be rising within Congress, President William McKinley showed little interest.

Everything changed when Theodore Roosevelt became president following McKinley's assassination in September 1901. Roosevelt was an irrepressible outdoorsman and an ardent conservationist who would not be afraid to wield the power of the federal government in directly influencing and promoting the nation's economic life. Roosevelt believed that government should play a major role in conserving, and efficiently using, the nation's natural resources. Conservation of water in the West soon became a high priority for Roosevelt. In his first formal message to Congress in December 1901, Roosevelt explicitly endorsed federal support for irrigation. Roosevelt proclaimed that "it is as right for the national government to make the streams and rivers of the arid region useful by engineering works for water storage as to make useful the rivers and harbors of the humid region by engineering works of a different kind."[133]

With the new president's vigorous support, Newlands's bill sailed through Congress and Roosevelt signed it into law on June 17, 1902. The National Reclamation Act (Newlands Act) advocated a national perspective and a scientific approach to natural resource management.[134] As originally enacted, the act directed the secretary of the interior to select irrigation projects without any further review or authorization by Congress. Construction would be undertaken directly by the Department of the Interior, acting through the newly formed U.S. Reclamation Service.[135] Upon completion of each project, the farmers benefitting from increased water supply were to repay all construction costs to the federal government. Theoretically, the repaid money would then be available to fund other federal reclamation projects.

Unlike the Carey Act, state governments would play no role in the program's implementation. The National Reclamation Act contained provisions for "reserving" public lands served by irrigation projects to insure that speculators would not take advantage of planned improvements, and it stipulated that farms benefitting from the irrigation be 160 acres or smaller. The act also allowed land already in private ownership to receive water from the federal projects without prejudice. But it also reflected the enduring legacy of the "irrigation crusade" by specifying that no farmer operating an irrigated tract larger than 160 acres could benefit from water supplied by a Reclamation Service project.

In the summer of 1902, responsibility for administrating the fledgling Reclamation Service fell to Newell, who became the Reclamation Service's first chief engineer. After years of lobbying and proselytizing, Newell now faced the challenge of actually implementing large-scale dam and water supply projects. Although he possessed no real experience in the construction of major engineering works, Newell could not afford the luxury of slowly learning the skills required to plan, design, construct, and operate reclamation projects. The political circumstances that fostered the establishment of the Reclamation Service also encouraged—and in fact almost demanded—that the new federal bureau prove its service to the nation by building large storage dams in the West as quickly as possible. The federal government was widely perceived as a savior possessing the technical skills and financial resources necessary to "make the desert bloom" and to open a new era of regional growth.[136]

The stage was set for the great confrontation between the professional and military U.S. Army Corps of Engineers and the amateur and civilian Reclamation Service. But the amateurs, with strong presidential backing, would quickly become professional just as the corps, with continuing congressional support, became increasingly civilian.

PROGRESSIVISM AND WATER RESOURCES

PROGRESSIVISM, CONSERVATION, AND EFFICIENCY

In the nineteenth century, fresh water was a commodity and rivers needed to be channeled or otherwise modified to "improve" them. These notions were not abandoned in the early twentieth century, but they were certainly modified by the efficiency concepts imbedded in progressivism, by early stirrings about the multiple uses of rivers, and by growing interest in hydropower. By the late 1920s, the stage was set for the arrival of the Big Dam Era in the 1930s.

Conservation became an important national issue in the Progressive Era. Proponents were increasingly dismayed by the wanton waste and destruction of natural resources in the name of economic progress. Some, like John Muir, viewed preservation of public lands and pristine waterways as the only way to stave off the worst impulses of the industrial age. But many other conservationists favored the management of natural resources and their efficient use. In his conservation message to Congress in 1907, President Theodore Roosevelt stated:

> As a nation we not only enjoy a wonderful measure of present prosperity but if this prosperity is used aright it is an earnest of future success such as no other nation will have. The reward of foresight for this nation is great and easily foretold. But there must be the look ahead, there must be a realization of the fact that to waste, to destroy, our natural resources, to skin and exhaust the land instead of using it so as to increase its usefulness, will result in undermining in the days of our children the very prosperity which we ought by right to hand down to them amplified and developed.[137]

Proponents did not want to undermine development per se, but they questioned short-term private gain at the expense of long-term public benefit. Progressive Era government regulation challenged the notion of unfettered private exploitation of resources by asserting a utilitarian ethic based on "the greatest good for the greatest number." But more than some generalized communal ideal was a commitment to efficient use of those natural resources. Problems could be solved, they believed, if well-trained experts armed with the techniques of applied science and located within the government were the spearheads of change. These experts came from a variety of fields, including hydrology, forestry, agrostology, geology, anthropology, and civil engineering.[138]

MULTIPURPOSE STIRRINGS

During the early years of Theodore Roosevelt's presidency, problems associated with forestry received central attention. But the evolution of American conservation policy depended upon more than the application of scientific forestry practices.[139] To conservationists, issues concerning timber and grass were directly linked to water. Roosevelt often stated that water conservation had to be associated with forest reserves, which preserved watersheds in timbered regions. For his part, Chief Forester Gifford Pinchot supported a concept of management of forest reserves that integrated the protection of watershed and grazing rights with timber management.[140] It was western water development in particular that shaped the burgeoning conservation movement in the early twentieth century. The promotion of a federal irrigation program, debate over water rights, the problem of speculation, and concern over siltation "gave rise to extensive ideas about water conservation." Historian Samuel Hays also argued that these issues "became crystallized into an overall approach and by 1908 emerged as a concept of multiple-purpose river development," although that conclusion may exaggerate the actual commitment to multipurpose development by more than a decade.[141] The promotion of hydroelectric power—both in the East and the West—also was crucial to the rise of the multipurpose movement, but not until the end of World War I.[142]

Beginning in the late nineteenth century, hydraulics data and new theories of natural resource development and control helped bring into question water as a single-purpose resource. Interest in irrigation, floodwaters, new sources of urban water supply, hydroelectric power, and navigation stimulated promotion of broader economic development plans for whole river basins. Such plans included the protection of watersheds, headwater reservoirs, and coordination of the various water uses.[143] The U.S. Geological Survey is credited with advocating the idea of water as a resource with many uses. The Reclamation Service, which was constructing reservoirs for irrigation purposes, saw the possibility of combining irrigation storage with hydroelectric power production. However, the Reclamation Act made no provisions for hydropower, and Congress did not authorize the bureau to take up its general development and sale until 1906.[144]

Conservation leaders within the Roosevelt administration faced an array of problems raised by various water uses and proposed water uses, but they also began to envision the possibilities of basin-wide river development. An emerging viewpoint was to avoid opportunities lost. Pinchot echoed these sentiments: "To develop a river for navigation alone, or power alone, or irrigation alone, is often like using a sheep for mutton, or a steer for beef, and throwing away the leather and the wool."[145]

The multipurpose approach ultimately reinforced the notion that the federal government needed to take the lead on river development because of the complexity of the issues and because of the many jurisdictions involved. (This was not always popular with state governments or the U.S. Army Corps of Engineers, however.) From a practical perspective, the multipurpose approach was not only meant to deal with whole river basins but with such matters as the size, type, design, and purpose of dams.[146]

Attention to inland waterways navigation proved an opportunity for federal officials to implement the multipurpose viewpoint. Waterways associations and related groups, particularly in the Mississippi Basin, called for federal aid to increase navigable depths along the rivers but appeared to have little concern for a broader approach. However, a common interest in a deep channel navigable by oceangoing vessels—from the Gulf of Mexico to Chicago—seemed to offer a chance to promote such a plan.[147] Combining the development of hydroelectric power with the navigation goals, the argument went, could provide revenue to pay for the desired river improvements.[148]

Standing in the path of the deep channel was the U.S. Army Corps of Engineers, which blocked efforts at acquiring construction funds for the basinwide plan. Some believed that the corps was stubbornly clinging to the single-use philosophy of the past, but the corps had good reason to regard the multiple-use idea as impractical at the time. Hydroelectric power had yet to compete on the open market with other forms of energy. River transportation was facing stiff competition from railroads. And the idea of building dams large and inexpensive enough to be practical had not been tested.[149]

Alternately, Representative Newlands concluded that congressional statutes imposed clear limits on corps functions, and that the corps itself narrowly interpreted the functions assigned to it by Congress. Of course, the corps may have simply been protecting its long-standing leadership role in determining waterways policy, fending off all other contenders. However, several members of Congress also were impediments to multipurpose development. They opposed efforts by the administration to coordinate the activities of agencies concerned with water resource policy because they did not want to have their influence eroded.[150]

W. J. McGee, a geologist and anthropologist, an associate of John Wesley Powell, and a former member of the Geological Survey, was the primary architect and promoter of the new waterways movement connected to the Roosevelt administration. To circumvent the traditionalists in the corps and the Rivers and Harbors Committee, McGee urged the president to appoint a commission to examine possibilities for integrated river basin development.[151] In 1907, Roosevelt appointed the Inland Waterways Commission (IWC), stating that the time had come to merge "local projects and uses of inland waters in a comprehensive plan designed for the benefit of the entire country."[152] This clearly placed Roosevelt behind multipurpose river development. Beginning in April, the IWC devoted much of its time to problems of navigation, but it also appointed a subcommittee to examine the water power issue.[153] In February 1908, the commission issued its report recommending that future plans "shall take account of the purification of the waters, the development of power, the control of floods, the reclamation of lands by irrigation and drainage, and all other uses of the waters or benefits to be derived from their control."[154]

Resistance from the U.S Army Corps of Engineers to the multipurpose approach arose at several junctures. The corps opposed the recommendation of the Geological Survey's chief hydrographer, Marshall O. Leighton, to regulate streamflow with reservoirs. Brigadier General William H. Bixby believed that the hydrographer's data was too limited to make such claims and that the economic feasibility of the idea was questionable. While Bixby's position did not demonstrate overt hostility to the multipurpose approach, it did reflect extreme caution in abandoning basic corps principles and historic practices.[155]

The IWC also recommended that a National Waterways Commission be established to coordinate the work of the corps, the Reclamation Service, the Department of Agriculture's Forest Service and Bureau of Soils, and other federal agencies.[156] But the corps objected to bureaucratic changes proposed in the report that would undermine its authority and stressed the primacy of navigation in federal river development. This viewpoint carried significant weight in Congress.[157] When Newlands presented a bill to carry out the recommendations of the IWC—particularly to centralize all water resource issues under a single agency—it received a frosty reception in the Senate, and the bill eventually died.[158]

Ultimately, a joint congressional commission was created by the Rivers and Harbors Act of 1909. While not the vehicle for multipurpose river development that advocates hoped for, it called for several navigation improvements, regulation of wharves and terminals, prevention of deforestation near mountain streams, and legislation promoting water power development. It also recommended a federal reservoir system for flood control based on multipurpose benefits. At this stage, the corps remained unconvinced that the multipurpose approach had broad applicability; although by World War I, Congress expanded its program to include flood control along with navigation.[159]

A spirited controversy over the damming of Hetch Hetchy Valley in Yosemite National Park further intensified the debate over water use, and in so doing, also drove a wedge among conservationist groups. In San Francisco, disagreements surrounding the franchise held by the Spring Valley Water Company led to a provision in 1900 for a municipal water system. Reform Mayor James D. Phelan applied to the secretary of the interior for dam construction permits along the Tuolumne River running through the Hetch Hetchy Valley in the northern part of Yosemite National Park. The secretary denied Phelan's request, but the new secretary of the interior, James R. Garfield, accepted the application in 1907 because he was not very interested in guarding resources for aesthetic purposes and because he felt that the 1906 earthquake and fire in San Francisco demonstrated a real need for plentiful water.[160]

San Francisco officials were ecstatic, but opposition mounted. Spring Valley Water Company voiced its objections, as did farmers in Modesto and Turlock, who claimed the water of the Tuolumne. However, the opposition of preservationist John Muir and a throng of wilderness advocates turned the dispute into a national debate.[161] The effort to invade the Hetch Hetchy Valley infuriated Muir. "Dam Hetch Hetchy!" he declared, "As well dam for water-tanks the people's cathedrals and churches, for no holier temple has ever been consecrated by the heart of man."[162]

Muir failed to attract support from President Roosevelt, who was torn between his relationship with Muir, concern about the reaction of Californians, and his sympathy for resource conservationism. Muir then began a public campaign to win support for protecting the Hetch Hetchy Valley. Approval of the Hetch Hetchy project was successfully blocked in Congress in 1909, but a bill was passed in 1913 to transfer the proposed site to San Francisco. In 1923, the O'Shaughnessy Dam on the Tuolumne River was completed.[163]

The Hetch Hetchy controversy not only shattered Muir's vision of the protection of the Sierra Nevada but also divided the conservation movement. In the hearing before Congress over the Raker Bill to approve the project, Muir and his allies squared off against Pinchot and supporters of resource conservation. It was a bitter squabble. Pinchot and Muir had been friends and allies in several conservation battles. With Hetch Hetchy, Muir clearly divorced himself from the utilitarian approach that Pinchot had come to represent.[164]

Hetch Hetchy also was about hydroelectric power and to some degree multiple use. San Francisco had turned to the valley for water but also identified three hydroelectric sites for future development. To defenders of the Hetch Hetchy, hydroelectric power was "the Trojan Horse of the whole fight" since dam advocates had been cool toward seriously considering alternative sites that could provide water but little prospect of hydropower. An amendment to the 1913 act required the city to distribute hydropower from the valley directly to consumers.

This action put the private utility, Pacific Gas and Electric (PG&E), on the same side with Muir, but for different reasons. The city's efforts, however, to contract with PG&E as an agent for Hetch Hetchy power met with resistance from supporters of private power. The debate was settled in 1945 when San Francisco leased a transmission line from PG&E to deliver its power to the city. Public power was defeated at this site, but not the desire for multiple use.[165]

From a national perspective, hydropower was a key component in the evolution of multipurpose river development and hence in the later construction of large federal dams. With respect to the latter, the recurrent use of storage reservoirs to increase capacity is linked to the use of hydropower.[166] The generation of power is one of the prime benefits of running or falling water, making it an essential resource to be conserved through wise use. It also was considered by proponents of multiple use as a means to underwrite the cost of dam building and river development in general.

Prior to the advancement of hydroelectric power in the late nineteenth century, almost 66 percent of the waterpower in use in the United States was concentrated in the North Atlantic States (primarily New York and New England). The amount of water horsepower in use by eastern manufacturers far outstripped similar use in the rest of the country. By 1920, however, demand for the distribution of waterpower potential shifted to the Rocky Mountain and Pacific Coast States thanks largely to electricity. By 1890, hydroelectric power had been successfully applied in Europe and was making inroads in the United States.[167]

While a plant in Appleton, Wisconsin, was the first to utilize falling water to generate electricity in the early 1880s, the harnessing of Niagara Falls in the mid-1890s brought major national attention to hydroelectric power.[168] Since the mid-nineteenth century, there had been strong interest in utilizing the water of Niagara Falls for power production. The falls were an excellent choice because of their steady flow and their proximity to large populations. Until the advent of alternating current (AC) and efficient dynamos, the project was impractical. However, as the technology changed and the market for electricity increased, the development of the falls became more practical. In 1895, the first of three 5,000 horsepower AC generators was installed. The completion of the plant marked the beginning of large-scale hydroelectric generation in the United States. With less fanfare, hydroelectric power generation began in the West—as early as 1889 in Oregon, followed by similar ventures in California, Washington, and Montana.[169]

Governmental regulation related to hydroelectricity evolved with the technology. Private hydroelectric dams on waterways in the East and Midwest increasingly interfered with navigation. Urged on by the U.S. Army Corps of Engineers, Congress attempted to regulate dam construction through the Rivers and Harbors Acts of 1890 and 1899, requiring that dam sites and plans for dams on navigable rivers be approved by the corps and the secretary of war before construction. Regardless, between 1894 and 1906 Congress issued thirty permits for private dams, mostly along the Mississippi River.[170]

Prior to the twentieth century, waterpower sites in the public domain were claimed by private companies without any effort by the federal government to reserve those sites or regulate their use. Part of the reason was ambiguity over federal jurisdiction, and part was the lag in identifying waterpower as a central feature of water conservation and wise use. The first step toward waterpower conservation occurred in 1901, with passage of the Right-of-Way Act. Although primarily intended as a way of facilitating reclamation and irrigation programs adjacent to public lands, it was broadened to cover many utility functions. The secretary of the interior could grant rights-of-way over public lands for dams, reservoirs, waterpower plants, and transmission lines.

Private companies continued to fight for more favorable legislation, but they accepted the permit system. By 1916, power facilities in the national forests represented 42 percent of the total developed power in the western states. President William Howard Taft's appointment of Richard Ballinger as secretary of the interior in 1909 weakened the new regulatory scheme. Ballinger refused to apply the Forest Service permit system to waterpower sites in the public domain. In 1911, Walter L. Fisher succeeded Ballinger and decided to follow Garfield's policy. He had to contend with the General Land Office, which regarded the permit system as illegal, and thus he gave the Geological Survey the responsibility for administering it. The revised permits included a fifty-year limited grant and imposed a waterpower fee ("conservation charge").[171]

These efforts did not resolve the problem of waterpower development on navigable streams. An important issue was the relationship between the multipurpose development of waterways and the question of financing such development. In the 1903 veto of private construction of a dam and power stations on the Tennessee River at Muscle Shoals, Alabama, Roosevelt protected the site for later government development, but he also helped to establish the principle of national ownership of resources previously considered only of local value. In this particular case, Roosevelt recommended using revenue from power production to finance navigation improvements.

The General Dam Act of 1906 standardized regulations concerning private power development, requiring dam owners to maintain and operate navigation facilities—without compensation—when necessary at hydroelectric sites. The act helped to clarify the role of the federal government in safeguarding river navigability and, in a general way, also strengthened federal regulatory authority in the area of water that already had been established with respect to forest land. A 1910 amendment to the 1906 act more closely linked hydropower to plans for waterway improvements by requiring the U.S. Army Corps of Engineers to take hydropower development into account when evaluating dam construction permits. The emphasis of the amendment was on hydropower as a financing mechanism for navigation and flood-control projects.[172]

The 1906 act and the 1910 amendment, however, engendered strong disagreements of interpretation of water development. Traditionally, the U.S. Army Corps of Engineers viewed power dams as obstructions to expanding navigation, and they were only slowly moving toward a broader viewpoint. The Taft administration, like the corps, looked at dams essentially as obstructions to navigation and was no more supportive of a multipurpose approach, approving hydropower franchises that required neither a limited permit nor compensation. Prior to World War I, hydroelectric power development continued to remain a private venture.[173]

In general, the Woodrow Wilson administration showed little interest in conservation issues. For example, Democrats usually had not favored expanding government power to withdraw public lands from use, which limited equal access to resources. However, the issue of private development of hydroelectric power on navigable rivers in the public domain remained a lively issue in the Wilson presidency.[174]

The desire to "improve" rivers through human technology had not disappeared in the United States by the end of World War I. Indeed, the demand on water resources had become greater. Large dams, rather than artificial canals and steamboats, would become the primary tools to harness rivers. And during the course of the next several decades, dam building greatly accelerated the changes humans imposed on riverine water.

CHAPTER TWO

How Bad Theory Can Lead to Good Technology

WATER SUPPLY AND SEWERAGE
IN THE AGE OF MIASMAS

ORIGINS OF PUBLIC WATER AND WASTEWATER SYSTEMS

This chapter grew out of research for my book *The Sanitary City*. It was first presented as a paper in 1998 at a small conference, "Inventing for the Environment," convened by the Lemelson Center for the Study of Invention and Innovation at the Smithsonian's National Museum of American History in Washington, D.C. The intent of the conference was to focus on historical issues that demonstrated "the complex relationship among invention, innovation, and the environment."[1] The ideal or belief grounding all symposia and other activities sponsored by the center has been "the conviction that historians and innovators have much to learn from each other." In the case of "Inventing for the Environment," that strategy "seemed particularly appropriate in the case of environment-related inventions, where so much of current practice is based on assessments of past conditions and patterns of change."[2]

The case of developing the first public water and wastewater systems in the United States fit nicely within the boundaries of the conference charge. That a misinformed notion about disease transmission (the miasmatic theory) led to a relatively sensible approach for dealing with the threat of epidemics (environmental sanitation) in the face of limited or no scientific evidence was a stroke of good luck. Unfortunately, the response did not result in a total solution to the problem of disease transmission, and ultimately it proved dangerously flawed. Whatever the limitations of putting the miasmatic theory into practice, the resulting sanitary infrastructure formed the basis of water and wastewater systems to this day. Such systems as originally constructed, however, proved to be little more than transportation networks for bringing water into homes and businesses and whisking wastes away from them—and essentially relocating those wastes to a more distant sink. It would take the new theory of bacteriology to underscore the need for filtration and treatment as a replacement for—or at least a complement to—environmental sanitation. Even then, "pollution" would only connote *biological* pollution for many years. Engineers and others were not so quick to regard industrial wastes, for example, as threatening to health for years to come.

I share with Ernest S. Griffith the opinion that public utilities, particularly water, "made possible the modern city."[3] In trying to understand how and why sanitary services developed in the United States in the nineteenth century, several themes became obvious: there was a connection between the kind of technology put on or in the ground to provide access to clean water and waste disposal and the prevailing attitudes toward health and the environment in general; viewed from a system's perspective, water supply and wastewater technologies reflected those prevailing attitudes; and access to pure water and waste disposal—because of their impacts on health—were viewed by civic leaders as community services requiring public management and control.

The essential irony growing out of these circumstances, as stated above, was that until the 1880s or 1890s, people got it wrong about what caused disease. Miasmas, vapors, smells, and decaying matter did not cause disease as the prevailing "filth theory of disease" purported; bacteria caused disease. Yet despite this crucial misunderstanding, contemporaries drew an association between what constituted a health threat and the need to move waste away from human contact and to avoid water that looked or smelled bad. The act itself—environmental sanitation—had a positive impact on health, but for an entirely erroneous reason. Nevertheless, the interconnection between miasmas and the need for sanitary services beginning in the United States in the late nineteenth century was an important element in promoting these services within the bounds of public responsibility. In some places, France for instance, such a correlation did not result in an overwhelming commitment to public sanitary services as was the case in the United States. For many generations much of the water used in Paris, for example, was and is provided by private companies. A possible explanation for why most American cities turned to public water supplies and public sanitation systems through at least the late twentieth century had much to do with the growing demand for local control of city affairs—more "home rule"—that justified claiming jurisdiction over as many community services as possible. A complementary reason was the increasing ability of cities to generate their own revenue streams. Timing also was decisive for a public option. For example, many business owners at the time became less confident that privately owned systems could ensure adequate fire protection. Conversely, when revenue began to dry up and when competing administrative entities—cities, counties, special districts—vied for the management and funding of public services, local control seemed less important with outsourcing and privatization as possible solutions.

Historian Charles Jacobson has made a very useful observation that different services and utilities took place in "very different historical settings" and thus developed very different management and control trajectories. Comparing waterworks, electric utilities, and cable television, he stated that in the late nineteenth century "waterworks represented a critical element in a distinctively growth-oriented American style of city-building, elements of which have survived to the present day."[4] The historical context helps to explain the public ownership pattern for waterworks, since in all three of the services he studied nongovernmental ownership initially prevailed. In the case of water, he added, the change in the pattern of ownership occurred primarily because—at least in major cities—municipal governments ultimately could and wanted to invest heavily in waterworks, while private franchises often assumed that the return on investment would not be sufficient. Also, he argued, "Private firms may face risks of exploitation and even outright expropriation once large investments are tied up in fixed facilities." Heavy investment in waterworks, therefore, often appeared not to be worth the financial risk.[5]

Jacobson himself conceded that the history of public policy toward waterworks and other services could not be explained solely in terms of economics.[6] My argument rests more upon the notion that the move toward public responsibility for sanitary services in the United States in the nineteenth century emerged in a period where bad science did indeed lead to good technology—a basic technology that remained unchallenged for years.

HOW BAD SCIENCE CAN LEAD TO GOOD TECHNOLOGY

In his *Service Delivery in the City*, political scientist Bryan D. Jones claimed that "delivering services is the primary function of municipal government. It occupies the vast bulk of the time and effort of most city employees, is the source of most contacts that citizens have with local government, occasionally becomes the subject of heated controversy, and is often surrounded by myth and misinformation. Yet, service delivery remains the 'hidden function' of local government."[7] Service delivery is a "hidden function" largely because it often blends so invisibly into the urban landscape; it is part of what we expect a city to be. While economic forces are essential to the formation of cities in the United States, urban growth depends heavily on service systems that shape the infrastructure and define the quality of life.

In the mid- to late nineteenth century, when sanitary services became essentially municipal responsibilities, the decision to choose between available technologies was informed by the prevailing environmental theory of the day. Before the twentieth century, when the initial technologies of sanitation were implemented, the miasmatic (or filth) theory of disease strongly influenced choice. From the 1880s through the end of World War II, choices were informed by bacteriological theory. Sometime after the war, new theories of ecology broadened the perspective of sanitary services beyond the health outlook. These health and environmental theories were sufficiently widespread to constitute environmental paradigms.

The Age of Miasmas began in the seventeenth century, when American cities faced poor sanitary conditions and suffered the crippling effects of epidemic diseases with only a vague understanding of their cause. By the nineteenth century, a few larger cities had developed community-wide water supply systems with rudimentary distribution networks, but cities continued to regard waste disposal as an individual responsibility. The powerful worldwide influence of the English "sanitary idea" in the middle of the nineteenth century, however, linked filth with disease and provided a clearer rationale and newer strategies for improving sanitary services in England and beyond. In his *Report on the Sanitary Condition of the Labouring Population of Great Britain* (1842), the English lawyer and sanitarian Sir Edwin Chadwick took a bold stance on the need for an arterial system of pressurized water that would combine house drainage, main drainage, paving, and street cleaning into a single sanitary process. Although this remarkable hydraulic system was never implemented, nineteenth-century English sanitarians and engineers became the leaders in setting standards for water and wastewater systems throughout Europe and North America.

English theories of sanitation helped to provide the environmental context for augmenting new technical systems in the United States and elsewhere. The development of North American water and wastewater systems in the mid- to late nineteenth century depended heavily on the expertise of English civil engineers and English public health leaders, on the implementation or adaption of English sanitation technology, and on the absorption of English environmental values.

Rapid population growth and the proliferation of cities produced great potential breeding grounds for disease and increased the need for improved health and sanitation measures. Though no American city grew as rapidly as London, English sanitary reform attracted a receptive audience in the United States. The sanitary idea was persuasive because it became easier to compare urban problems after 1830 than it had been in a previous era of limited urban growth.

Charles E. Rosenberg, in his classic study *The Cholera Years*, acknowledged the transformation in American thinking about disease that occurred in the nineteenth century. Focusing on New York's cholera epidemics of 1832, 1849, and 1866, he made the following observations: "Cholera in 1866 was a social problem; in 1832, it had still been, to many Americans, a primarily moral dilemma. Disease had become a consequence of man's interaction with his environment; it was no longer an incident in a drama of moral choice and spiritual salvation."[8] The change in mind-set was gradual and not entirely conscious, but the days of viewing disease as God's wrath were passing.

Throughout much of the nineteenth century, however, it remained simplest to blame the poor, the infirm, or members of nonwhite races for the scourge of epidemic disease. Rosenberg further noted that "when in the spring of 1832 Americans awaited cholera, they reassured themselves that this new pestilence attacked only the filthy, the hungry, the ignorant."[9] Newly arriving immigrants raised the greatest fears, especially when they were crammed into grimy and dilapidated housing. Ironically, cholera—"the poor man's plague"—made victims of the very people accused of breeding the disease. In New York, blacks and Irish immigrants were the most frequent casualties. Persons born in Ireland accounted for more than 40 percent of the deaths in New York. In Philadelphia, the case rate was nearly twice as great among blacks as among whites.[10]

In southern cities, cholera also was considered a class disease and most especially a race disease. As Howard N. Rabinowitz noted, "although poor whites could be found near industrial and other unpleasant sites, the alleys and rear dwellings of the cities were almost entirely the province of the blacks." These were areas where cholera lurked, and poor housing often meant high mortality rates. In Richmond, Nashville, Atlanta, and other southern cities, cholera appeared first in black neighborhoods.[11] Local governments in Charleston, for example, emphasized social cohesion as a major objective. Thus, poor health conditions threatened all citizens, and public and private funds were intermingled in an attempt to develop an effective health care system. Some historians have even argued that health and disease control facilities were generally more advanced in southern cities. Disease was "a constant companion" there, since freezing temperatures that killed bacteria and viruses arrived so late in the autumn. Nevertheless, fighting epidemics often was not successful, especially since an understanding of contagion was so primitive.[12]

Yellow fever, unlike cholera, spared blacks more than whites. People of West African descent suffered least. In the great yellow fever epidemic of 1878, only 183 of 4,046 victims in New Orleans were black, even though one-third of the city's population was black. In Memphis, where at least 14,000 of the 20,000 people remaining in the city through the epidemic were black, only 946 of the more than 5,000 yellow fever deaths in the city occurred in the "colored population."[13]

Anticontagionism was eventually discredited, but its widespread adoption in the nineteenth century was a victory for empiricism and rationalism over sermonizing and moral outrage. Environmental sanitation appealed to simple logic and to the senses, offering a way for people to participate directly in cleaning the cities and, ostensibly, to eradicate disease. That it misrepresented the root cause of disease was a serious (sometimes fatal) flaw, but its call for the removal and disposal of waste materials was a worthy objective.

In the wake of England's sanitary idea and Chadwick's report, the miasmatic theory of disease "emerged into practical vitality" during the 1850s. Based on empirical observation of the relation between filth and disease, the theory at first was somewhat crude, inferring that organic decomposition per se caused disease, that is, that no specific relationship existed between a particular kind of decomposing substance and a particular infirmity. Eventually filth was recognized as the medium for transmitting disease instead of the primary source of contagion. This perspective provided a bridge to the eventual acceptance of the germ, or bacteriological, theory.[14]

Although the germ theory—bacteria rather than putrefaction or foul smells caused disease—was not firmly established until after 1880, in one form or another the idea of contagion had been circulating since the sixteenth century or earlier. It was, however, incorrect in detail until Louis Pasteur and Robert Koch clearly linked a specific organism with a specific disease. In 1871, an advocate of the germ theory was severely criticized in *Scientific American* for postulating that yellow fever was caused by a living organism. Only a few years later, during the epidemics of 1878 and 1879, the belief that a germ caused yellow fever was more widely accepted.[15]

Controversy over contagionism in the middle of the nineteenth century, especially the competition among theories dealing with the generation of living particles, made it easier for anticontagionism to find a cordial reception.[16] The first two of four major cholera pandemics in the nineteenth century won converts to the anticontagionist cause. Erwin H. Ackerknecht perceptively argued that anticontagionists were "motivated by the new critical scientific spirit of the time," while contagionists supported old theories that seemed never to have been carefully examined.[17]

The emphasis on environment over personal habits of hygiene in Chadwick's report set the tone for the strategies to be employed in combating disease and improving sanitation for much of the remaining century. Perhaps the earliest graphic example of Chadwick's influence in the United States was *The Sanitary Condition of the Laboring Population of New York*, an 1845 study published by New York City inspector John H. Griscom. *The Sanitary*

Condition began as an addendum to Dr. Griscom's first report as city inspector. That 1842 document, *A Brief View of the Sanitary Condition of the City*, included a commentary with particular emphasis on the state of the poor. New York's aldermen were so displeased with Griscom's characterization of the city's sanitary condition and with his call for preventive action that they chose not to reappoint him. Undaunted, Griscom expanded the commentary into a small book with a title reminiscent of Chadwick's own report.[18]

The Sanitary Condition—the first in-depth study of health problems in New York—covered many topics. It called for the expansion of the public water supply, the construction of an underground sewer system, and the development of a program of street cleaning and refuse removal. The study was infused with the environmental view of disease and was based on what the historian John Duffy called "the general acceptance of the symbiotic relationship between physical and moral health." Griscom, like Chadwick, decried the unnecessary physical evils that were responsible for widespread sickness and premature deaths among the poorer classes and that subsequently inspired moral decay. Prevention of disease was his greatest hope for reversing these ominous trends.[19]

Despite the dramatic disclosures, and the reformist momentum provided by Chadwick and other European sanitarians, little immediately came of Griscom's efforts. New York was infamous as an extraordinarily unhealthy city with problems so complex and political webs so entangled that one report could not change entrenched practices or reverse long-standing policies of neglect.[20]

The earliest technologies of sanitation nevertheless began to spread to several American cities in an era of rapid urban growth after 1830, and especially in the wake of the English sanitary idea in the 1840s. Primary attention was given to water supply and, to a lesser extent, sewerage. Before 1800, most cities and towns had depended on a combination of water carriers, wells, and cisterns to meet their needs. Even during the first several decades of the nineteenth century, several larger cities and many smaller towns continued to rely on local sources of supply. Unless they hired water peddlers, each citizen used no more than five gallons per day.

Community-wide water supply systems developed slowly in American cities. In 1801, Philadelphia had become the first to complete a waterworks and municipal distribution system, sophisticated even by European standards. The necessary health, economic, and technical factors converged to produce what became a model for future systems. Yet the Philadelphia waterworks also was something of an anomaly, since it did not spark an immediate nationwide trend. Concern for the health of the citizenry prompted the campaign for a waterworks in Philadelphia. Despite imprecision in determining disease causation in the late eighteenth century, the correlation between pure water and good health was nevertheless an early driving force in dealing with epidemics. Scott's *Geographical Dictionary* described the water in the densest areas of the city as having become "so corrupt by the multitude of sinks and other receptacles of impurity, as to be almost unfit to be drank."[21]

Unsettled by ravaging yellow fever attacks in 1793 and 1798, political and business leaders formed a committee of the common council to deal with epidemics. The consensus view was that polluted water from wells and cisterns caused the fever and that the city's private wells should be replaced by a community-wide system. Not only would the waterworks eradicate the disease; it also could be used to clean the streets, to provide fresh water for drinking and bathing, and to enhance the beauty of the city by supplying water to public fountains.[22] Attention to finding a new source of water had arisen before the common council's action. In 1789, after a yellow fever epidemic struck Philadelphia, Benjamin Franklin suggested that it was necessary to go beyond the city limits to find a pure water supply. In fact, in 1792 he had added a codicil to his will, leaving money to the city to finance a central water system using Wissahickon Creek as a supply. Until the inception of water filtration and treatment, and methods derived from the study of bacteriology, seeking new supplies (as opposed to purifying the old ones) was the only alternative to tainted sources.[23]

After examining various options, the committee accepted the proposal of Benjamin Henry Latrobe.The English-born engineer was also a practicing architect, who later worked on the U.S. Capitol from 1802–1817. He recommended a system to pump water from the Schuylkill River and to distribute it through mains made of bored logs. He proposed that the water would be moved by a steam engine along the river up to a tunnel running under the streets and then by gravity to a pump house at Centre Square in the city. Another steam engine at Centre Square would pump the water to reservoir tanks at the top of the building, and then gravity would distribute water through the rest of the system. Latrobe began the task in 1799 and completed it in 1801. In 1811 the city's Watering Committee replaced Centre Square with a larger plant in a different location. The engineer Frederick Graff, Latrobe's former assistant, called for a pumping station along the Schuylkill at the foot of Fairmount rise (beyond the city limits), with construction of a reservoir on top of the hill in the city. The new facility was completed in 1815. Steam pumps again were employed, but the waterworks converted to more reliable water power in the 1820s. The Fairmount Waterworks served Philadelphia until 1911.[24]

Though not without its flaws, Philadelphia's waterworks was considered by many to be the most advanced engineering project of its time. Especially after its construction, Philadelphia had a system with a much greater capacity than existing demand (until the 1870s at least), unlike comparable cities such as New York, Boston, and Baltimore.[25] To promote its use, citizens were initially offered free water for several years. Despite the fear of epidemics, many citizens had not been completely convinced to give up "their cold well water for the tepid Schuylkill water." But 2,850 dwellings were receiving water from the new system by 1814.[26]

The construction of a major waterworks in Philadelphia was widely publicized, but a national trend of adoption was not evident until late in the century. Inexperience in dealing with such a major project, in part at least, helps to explain why urban population growth exceeded construction for so many years. Despite the limitations of the new water systems, the few American cities that turned to community-wide approaches set patterns for the modern sanitary services of the near future. Protosystems offering rudimentary distribution networks, pumping facilities, and new sources of supply were precursors to more elaborate centralized citywide systems adopted by many cities and towns by the late nineteenth century. As in England, the application of these new technologies ran ahead of an effective understanding of the causes of disease and pollution; nevertheless, they attempted to enhance the healthfulness of the city and provide better protection against fire.

Early in the nineteenth century, a few water supply protosystems began to appear in major American cities.[27] However, the number of waterworks multiplied at an increasingly accelerated rate from 1830 to 1880. At first, they almost doubled in twenty years. In the 1870s alone, they more than doubled. By 1880, some water supplies were evolving into modern citywide systems. Not only did they deliver greater quantities of water over a larger area; they also included rudimentary safeguards to ensure purity. A growing preoccupation with water quality (a direct result of the sanitary movement) was bringing attention to filtration techniques and new methods of water treatment. City leaders and sanitarians were demanding more from their water supply service than convenience at the tap.

By the 1870s, the trend toward more public water supplies was evident. The crucialness of adequate supplies of water to meet the needs of citizens, commercial establishments, and industry—and the emerging mandate of cities to protect the public health—meant that authorities in the largest urban areas at least wanted centralized systems under their direct control. Boosterism was an additional motivation, since an effective water system was a powerful promotional tool for city leaders seeking to enhance a city's economic base. Though many water companies had been very profitable, capital investment in the more modern systems (with reservoirs, pumps, and elaborate distribution networks) was steep, and operating costs were on the rise. Private service, therefore, was gradually phasing out in several communities. In addition, public control of the water supply enhanced the authority of city government relative to that of the legislature or that of rival cities, thus private owners often were under pressure to sell out, particularly through less lucrative franchises.

The desire of city leaders to convert private systems into public ones, or to build new public systems, rested on more than the will to do so. The central issue was the ability of cities to incur debt to fund major projects and to sustain the high costs of operating the new technologies of sanitation. As the nineteenth century unfolded, city finances underwent changes in scope and complexity that ultimately made the development of public sanitary systems achievable.[28] In most cases, a combination of local circumstances and the experience of other cities influenced the shift from private to public.[29]

Boston suffered under many years of water supply politics before it developed a system in the 1840s. In 1796, Governor Samuel Adams approved a General Court Act creating the Aqueduct Corporation, which constructed a line from Jamaica Pond in Roxbury to the city. The system was extended in 1803 with the addition of new mains and fire plugs. There was no further attempt to improve the system until 1825. Between 1825 (a year in which the city suffered a great fire) and 1846 (a period in which several epidemics rocked the city), civic leaders were embroiled in debate over the water supply.

Those in favor of a municipal supply were persistent, and the issue remained alive in the 1840s. A water referendum in December 1844 resulted in a major victory for proponents of a municipal system. Long Pond (later renamed Lake Cochituate) was selected as the city's source of supply, to be purchased at city expense. But who should hold general powers over the water supply system was not resolved. The city did not gain the legal authority to establish a municipal supply until 1846.[30] In that year the General Court passed Boston's Water Act, which provided for the development of Long Pond under the direction of a Water Board. The city was authorized to finance construction with up to $3 million in municipal bonds. (The entire Cochituate system cost almost $4 million.)

In October 1848, the Cochituate Aqueduct opened, ushering in an era of municipal control of water supply in Boston. The switch from private to public management was not the only reason for the significant improvement. As historian Fern L. Nesson argued, the completion of the Cochituate system also changed the focus of water supply debates. It placed control and monitoring of the water system in the hands of experts, under whose influence Boston was favored by avoiding future water shortages and escaping the devastation of epidemic disease. "What had been a popular, political issue," Nesson stated, "became a technical issue initiated by an administrative request to the General Court for permission to add to the water supply system."[31] The success of the Boston system, therefore, elevated the stature of technical experts and also reinforced the faith in environmental sanitation.

Outside of a core of emerging major cities in the industrial East and a few others sprinkled throughout the country, the transition from private companies to municipal service more typically occurred in the late 1860s and after. For example, Buffalo did not establish its municipal system (by acquiring a privately held plant) until 1868. The Jubilee Spring Water Company had distributed spring water through log pipes as early as 1826, followed by the Buffalo Water Company (1849), which tapped the Niagara River. The latter's facilities provided the nucleus for the public system.[32]

The first waterworks in Chicago was not established until 1840, under the auspices of the Chicago City Hydraulic Company. Lake Michigan was used as the primary source of water, and the company built the city's first pumping station and reservoir. The distribution lines only reached a small portion of the southern and western divisions, while four-fifths of the city continued to obtain its water from the polluted Chicago River or from water carriers. In the wake of a cholera epidemic in 1852, city officials exercised their option and assumed control of the system. Since the epidemic was believed to have originated with the wells, the Lake Michigan supply gained greater significance in the years after 1852.[33]

Milwaukee's first recognized waterworks was built in 1840 for the United States Hotel, while most citizens received their water from local springs and wells. In response to citizen pressure, the common council passed an ordinance in 1857 to authorize the issuance of bonds to finance the Milwaukee Hydraulic Company. It also gave the company some property for a water tower. The project was never completed, and a second attempt by Hubbard and Converse of Boston (1859) was sidetracked by the Civil War. In March of 1861, the state legislature passed a bill preventing the issuance of new city bonds. Serious progress on a waterworks did not commence until 1868.[34]

The St. Louis Water Works was built in the 1830s. As early as 1821, however, general concern about fire hazards led to demands for a better water supply. In 1823 the mayor began promoting the idea for a citywide system, and finally in 1829 the city council offered a $500 prize for the best plan. A committee also made inquiries in other cities, especially Philadelphia and New Orleans.[35] Within a short time, St. Louis officials signed a contract with Wilson and Company. The work began in 1830, but, as historian Richard Wade noted, "no water moved through the pipes until the next decade."[36]

In the South, municipal water systems were rare in this period. In Reconstruction Era Atlanta, plans moved ahead for a new waterworks, but its primary thrust was to serve business and industrial needs and fire protection, not to supply potable supplies. Without a creditable municipal water supply, the more affluent turned to purchasing spring water or other pure sources or depended on their own wells. In black neighborhoods, however, drainage was poor, sewer outfalls often dumped wastes there, and wells were badly polluted. Likewise in Memphis, little attention was given to residential water service.[37]

As changes in the administration of waterworks were slowly evolving after the middle of the nineteenth century, far less subtle changes were taking place in water supply technology. New sources of supply became necessary when old sources could no longer meet growing demand or became severely polluted, bringing up questions of quantity and quality. The only viable alternatives were abandoning older sources, then digging new wells; pumping water from nearby lakes, rivers, and streams; seeking more distant sources; and filtration (but not until the 1870s). Good location was a significant advantage for cities forced to change or augment their water supplies. Filtration (and treatment), however, eventually helped to defy the limits of location, especially as the miasmatic theory was challenged by those who found dangers in polluted water beyond smells and discoloration.

In some cases, cities took only modest precautions to ensure a good supply of water. St. Louis, for example, used the same system of pumping muddy river water into a single 330,000 gallon reservoir until 1871. The reservoir also served as a sedimentation basin. Pumping, with two rotary pumps originally bought for use on fire engines, occurred only during daylight hours, while the reservoir was used to supply demand at night.[38]

For Chicago, location offered new sources in close proximity to population centers. When the town was founded in 1833, the water of the Chicago River—a relatively sluggish stream with two branches that divided the city—was considered pure, with some variation in quality from season to season. Water also was drawn from shallow wells, since the site of the town was only a few feet above the level of Lake Michigan. In the 1850s, especially as the Chicago River became more of an open sewer, the public water supply was pumped from an inlet basin on Lake Michigan near Chicago Avenue (a distance of 3,000 feet from the mouth of the Chicago River). Lake Michigan offered a magnificent alternative as a water source, extending over 22,400 square miles and with a watershed of 69,000 square miles.

As the city grew (more than 100,000 people in 1860), and as the lake water close to shore became increasingly polluted, the intake pipe was moved further out and deeper into the lake. In 1863, the common council approved a plan of the Board of Public Works to construct a two-mile tunnel burrowed under the lake bottom connected to a new intake. This first lake tunnel was completed in 1866 at an estimated cost of $600,000. The project proved to be a much more difficult and complex engineering task than anyone imagined. Duel and Gowan, the Harrisburg, Pennsylvania, engineering firm that won the contract, was faced with several problems in tunneling below the lake bed. Most difficult was connecting the shore and lake points on a straight line. Despite the arduousness of the task, this first lake tunnel only supplied the needs of the city until 1871. After the Chicago fire of that year, a new tunnel and pumping station were built for the west side of the city.[39]

Most major cities that were growing as rapidly as Chicago did not have the advantage of such a convenient water source to meet the increasing demand. More consideration had to be given to distant sources. But these cities would need to confront two of the same problems Chicago faced in developing effective citywide service: skyrocketing capital costs and the sheer scale and complexity of the engineering task required to develop a new supply and distribution system.

The Old Croton Aqueduct (1842) is regarded as a sublime engineering feat and as a symbol of the conquest of nature in service to the urban population explosion. The Croton Aqueduct project is also an important example of changes in the scale and complexity of modern water supply systems. Several attempts to solve New York's water problem failed in the early part of the nineteenth century. The Manhattan Company's willingness to build an aqueduct from the Bronx River to Manhattan Island never materialized. Efforts to revive the plan in the 1820s likewise fizzled. In 1835, the fortunes of the city changed. Citizens, frustrated by the poor state of well water and frightened by the most recent serious outbreak of cholera, were ready to support a new plan. In a rare moment of political harmony, the voters, the state legislature, and the New York common council agreed to construct an aqueduct from the Croton River in Westchester County, running forty-one miles to New York.

The Croton project won out over the Bronx project because the source was much larger—estimated at 40 million gallons per day—and could be delivered to the city, without pumps. Even with the savings in the construction and maintenance of such machinery, the aqueduct cost approximately $9 million to $10 million.[40] The task of building the aqueduct was first entrusted to Major David Bates Douglass. Douglass, however, lacked experience with large public works, especially one that required building a variety of structures: a dam, an enclosed masonry conduit, bridges and embankments, and a huge reservoir. A good surveyor, he had consulted on railroad and canal projects and taught civil engineering at West Point and New York University, but he had never carried out such a large project. In addition, he

had a major personality clash with the chairman of the water commissioners, Stephen Allen. Douglass was fired in October 1836, but at least he had
routed most of the aqueduct before his departure.

The commissioners replaced Douglass with John B. Jervis. A self-trained
engineer with vast work experience, Jervis served as a supervising engineer
on a portion of the Erie Canal (1823) and as chief engineer of the Delaware
and Hudson Canal (1827). In both cases, he had worked his way up through
the ranks of the projects. Based on his canal experience, he was in demand
for many other similar ventures.[41] In regard to the task facing Jervis on the
Croton project, the historian Larry Lankton noted: "This was no ordinary
engineering work, no mundane railroad or canal. It was literally to become
a lifeline to Manhattan, sustaining hundreds of thousands of lives. It had to
be exceptionally dependable and durable. It had to work and it had to last."[42]

Jervis confronted the task of building what was to be the largest modern aqueduct in the world with great aplomb. Innovative design techniques
had to be employed to make sure that the aqueduct could remain operational
across a variety of terrains and could withstand the intense winter cold. To
maintain a uniform grade, the aqueduct ran through tunnels dug into hills
and was carried by bridges constructed over ravines and streams. When the
Croton Aqueduct was opened on July 4, 1842, it safely carried 75 million gallons per day, 15 million more than Jervis originally calculated. At the time,
it seemed that the project would meet the demands of the city for years into
the future. But by 1860 the Croton Aqueduct was delivering its maximum,
and it was pushed to provide as much as 105 million gallons per day before a
new line was built.[43]

New York's need to supplement water supplied by the Croton Aqueduct
became apparent in the 1870s. During droughts and in cold winter months,
more water was consumed than was received, requiring the drawing of extra
water from other sources in the city. Refilling the reservoirs took a great deal
of time because of the limited capacity of the aqueduct, while millions of gallons of water ran over the Croton Dam simply unavailable for use.[44]

Despite its great overall success, the Croton system had not been built
without technical difficulties, input from several special interests, contract
irregularities, and discrimination in service delivery. The insurance industry, for example, wielded substantial influence in seeing that the aqueduct
was completed quickly in order to reduce fire damage claims. The industrial
community likewise was anxious for a pure and abundant supply of water.
Construction work, however, was sometimes haphazard, as when water
mains were run through sewer lines. And despite the fact that the aggregate water production increased dramatically with the aqueduct, availabil-

ity of supplies tended to favor the middle class over the poor. Affluent lower wards, for example, received more pipes than poorer upper wards.[45]

Major projects in a few other cities followed the construction of the Croton Aqueduct. Boston completed its aqueduct (half the length of the Croton) in 1848. Another major engineering feat, much of the Cochituate Aqueduct ran through deep trenches covered with dirt. It terminated at Brookline in a twenty-acre reservoir, where the water was then moved along large mains to two distributing reservoirs. The cost of the project was approximately $4 million.[46] The Washington Aqueduct, built to supply the nation's capital with water from the Great Falls of the Potomac (fourteen miles from the city), began construction in 1857 and was completed in December 1863.[47]

Distant sources of supply received great attention from major cities because they offered large and dependable quantities of water, but also because they provided alternatives to polluted or infected sources in the local area. Smaller communities, without a sufficient tax base or other financial resources, were hard pressed to seek distant sources. For many communities the lack of viable options for dealing with polluted water supplies was the weakest link in the early systems. The transformation of protosystems into modern waterworks required methods for ensuring—or at least improving—water quality. The gradual introduction of filtration and new techniques for water distribution held some promise for accomplishing that goal.

The search for pure water was made difficult because determining what constituted a tainted supply was little understood in the Age of Miasmas. Taste and smell substituted for scientific testing in most assessments of water quality. Some physicians warned patients not to drink hard water or water with vegetable and animal matter in it, fearing that it would harm the kidneys or produce stomach and intestinal maladies. In 1873, the president of the New York Board of Health, a chemistry professor at Columbia University, advocated the consumption of lake or river water stating that "although rivers are the great natural sewers, and receive the drainage of towns and cities, the natural process of purification, in most cases, destroys the offensive bodies derived from sewage, and renders them harmless."[48]

It was the British physician John Snow's research on cholera in the 1850s that established a clear link between epidemic disease and polluted water that was not based simply on the test of the senses. Snow's work on waterborne transmission of disease inspired Dr. William Budd's studies of typhoid fever. Like Snow, Budd determined that typhoid was spread through water supplies contaminated with human feces.[49] Of the possible waterborne diseases that threatened American cities, typhoid fever was the worst. "The disease means little to us today since it is no longer a threat to modern cities," stated historian Michael P. McCarthy, "but it frightened the urbanizing world of the late nineteenth century."[50]

The typhoid bacillus could be contracted by direct contact with a "carrier" or through contaminated food such as milk, raw fruits and vegetables fertilized with night soil, and shellfish found in polluted waters. Most often it was spread when excreta from a victim entered the water supply directly or as untreated sewage. Detecting the disease posed something of a problem because the incubation period was approximately fourteen days. Typhoid fever produced vomiting and diarrhea leading to dehydration and was accompanied by high fevers. Children, in particular, were most susceptible to the disease.[51] Not only was the disease a threat to human life, but it could severely damage the reputation of a city trying to attract new citizens and new business enterprise.[52] It was a scourge to be avoided if at all possible.

By the turn of the century, various approaches to ensuring a pure water supply and limiting waterborne disease emerged from the bacteriological and chemical laboratories supported by agencies such as the Massachusetts Board of Health. But the first means of water purification readily available to cities in the late nineteenth century—one that fit within the context of the filth theory—was filtration through sand or gravel to improve the clarity, odor, and color of the water.

As early as the ninth century, Venetians filtered water from cisterns through beds of sand. The first filtering system for a public water supply was likely established in Paisley, Scotland, in 1804.The Chelsea Water Works in London (1827) employed a "slow sand" (or English) filter, which was the archetype for later models and eventually found its way to the United States. Berlin's water was filtered in 1856, and by 1865 several European cities followed its example.[53]

In 1835, a noted American engineer, Samuel Storrow, was the first to recommend the use of filtration in the United States. "If the supply be originally taken from a river," Storrow wrote in his book on waterworks, "it will be liable at some seasons of the year to be very much loaded with impurities, and it is important to have, in connection with the reservoirs, filtering beds, by means of which it may be cleansed of them, before it is introduced into the distributing pipes."[54]

Albert Stein, the designer of Richmond's waterworks, was the first to attempt to filter a public water supply in the United States in 1832. Pumping water from the James River, Stein prepared a sand filter in the reservoir, but he could not get it to operate effectively. During the next forty years, several major cities, including Boston, Cincinnati, and Philadelphia, considered installing sand filters, but they were too expensive at the time.[55]

A major step forward, but not recognized immediately as such, was

James P. Kirkwood's *Report on the Filtration of River Waters, for the Supply of Cities, as Practiced in Europe, Made to the Board of Water Commissioners of the City of St. Louis* (1869). In 1865, Kirkwood (an engineer) recommended that Cincinnati and St. Louis employ filters in their water systems. At the time, Kirkwood was engaged by a joint committee of the city council and the waterworks trustees of Cincinnati to report on a new water source. He suggested that one or more of the committee visit Europe to examine the filters in person, but nothing came of it.

Kirkwood was then hired by the city of St. Louis to survey locations for supply works along the Mississippi River. Upon recommendation of a plan that included filtration, the water commissioners instructed him to travel to Europe "and there inform himself in regard to the best process in use for clarifying river waters used for the supply of cities, whether by deposition alone, or deposition and filtration combined." While he was gone, however, opposition to Kirkwood's plan had led to a clean sweep of the commission and replacement with members unwilling to underwrite the cost of a filtration system. The city would not even publish his report as a city document, and did not filter its water until fifty years later.[56]

Kirkwood's report ultimately became a bible of sorts for those cities interested in copying the European experiments. For several years after its completion, however, little additional firsthand knowledge was gathered about the various European systems.[57] By the early 1870s, a few cities began to recognize the value of filtering water. Poughkeepsie, New York, built the first American slow sand filter in 1870–1872; it was based on the designs in Kirkwood's report. This decision was particularly noteworthy because the filter was to be used on Hudson River water, a notoriously polluted supply.[58]

By 1880, there were only three slow sand filters in the United States and none in Canada. But experimentation continued even if adoptions were sluggish. The Europeans, to the contrary, forged ahead with several slow sand filters, and in Buenos Aires in the 1880s experiments were conducted on the suitability of various filtering materials. Information about the experiments in filtration, as well as other crucial information about water supplies, was disseminated more effectively because of the organization of the American Water Works Association (1881) and the New England Water Works Association (1882), both of which published their proceedings. Other engineering societies and public health organizations added to the rich body of data, making its way even to the smallest town in the 1880s and after.

Several Americans were pioneers in disseminating information about the quality of water and the value of filtration in this period. Professor William Ripley Nichols of the Massachusetts Institute of Technology, a leading authority on water quality, had argued that sand was the only practical medium for large filtration operations, but that evidence was poor on whether sand filtration would purify polluted water efficiently. Colonel John T. Fanning, a well-respected hydraulic engineer, published a major treatise on waterworks in 1877, in which he discussed the water purification methods used in Europe.[59]

Along with experiments in filtration, a variety of pumping techniques and changes in pipe technology helped to transform older protosystems into modern, centralized waterworks. Aside from gravity systems, steam pumps were increasingly employed directly at the source (especially in the 1870s) as a way of moving water to reservoirs, tanks, and standpipes.[60] Wooden pipe was adequate in low-pressure gravity systems, but could not withstand the action of high-pressure pumping engines. Wooden mains were sometimes modified by strapping iron bands around the staves. By 1850, iron pipe was coming into wider use in the United States, especially in high-pressure systems. The transition from wood to iron, however, was not uniform throughout the country. Some water utilities continued to use wooden pipe until the 1930s. In the West, especially, wood was used for large aqueducts, irrigation, hydroelectric plants, and hydraulic mining.[61]

For all the improvements begun by private companies through municipal franchises, accessibility to water supply was still largely linked to class. Affluent neighborhoods and the central business district received the lion's share of water, while the working-class districts often relied on polluted wells and other potentially unhealthy local sources. As Sam Bass Warner Jr. astutely observed about a later period, "the mode of construction of water supply and sewerage systems divides the responsibility between municipal capital on the one side and the individual installations of middle-class homeowners and home builders for the middle-class market on the other."[62] This observation applies to the pre-1880 period of private water companies as well, insofar as those outside of the middle and upper classes were unable to tap into the water supply, which at that point was available only to a limited market.[63]

The basic form and function of modern waterworks were established by 1880. Major cities began to devise financial plans based on enhanced revenue generation and long-term debt to plan construction and maintenance of new systems or to secure old systems from private companies. Sources of supply were no longer limited to local wells, ponds, and streams. Distribution extended over wider areas, owing (in part, at least) to the use of iron pipe and a variety of pumping techniques. And a concern for water quality led to research on and, in some cases, implementation of filters. All these changes occurred in the Age of Miasmas, which placed a pure and plentiful water supply squarely at the heart of environmental sanitation.

By the late nineteenth century, waterworks were generally regarded as a public enterprise, justified as such because of the need to protect the public health and to supply water on a citywide basis. As with wastewater systems and solid waste collection and disposal in later years, modern citywide water supply systems were conceived in an Age of Miasmas. The structure of those systems and their functions were linked inextricably to the goals of environmental sanitation, that is, to utilize the prevailing sensory tests of purity to deliver a product that would not only be free of disease but also would be utilized to mitigate against disease. Plentiful supplies of water, for example, could help to flush away stench-ridden wastes.

Despite the fact that massive increases in piped-in water proved to be a major reason for wastewater systems, water supply and sewerage were addressed separately in the nineteenth century. However, the justification for wastewater systems also was graphically linked to the precepts of environmental sanitation. The leap of logic from liquid wastes to solid wastes was made possible by the adherence to environmental sanitation, to a point of view that almost etched in stone the primary directive that wastes had to be removed from the presence of humans as quickly as possible to preserve the public health. In essence, sanitary services in this period were little more than elaborate transportation networks (or water and waste redirection systems).

The underground sewer was a logical embodiment of the goals of environmental sanitation, as were the sanitary landfill and the incinerator. These technologies were meant to distance humans from their wastes and discards—materials that presumably had imbedded in them the threat of disease.

Whole systems were designed, therefore, to meet the ends of environmental sanitation. Water supply systems began with a protected source—or one that could be purified through filtration or treatment. The new distribution system of pipes and pumps removed from the individual responsibility for filling containers at a public well or local watercourse and made the waterworks—private and public—responsible for bringing water directly to each consumer. Implicit in this system was a guarantee that the supply met the prevailing standards of purity. With respect to wastewater systems, citizen responsibility also was at a minimum. Combined or separate sewer pipes whisked effluent from homes and businesses and placed responsibility for disposal in the hands of the city. The objectives of environmental sanitation had been met because human contact with the waste—at least at the source—was dramatically reduced. In the case of refuse, on-site pickup served the same purpose as water or sewer pipes.

Within the context of nineteenth-century environmental sanitation, sanitary services were at their best in the areas of collection and delivery of water and collection of effluent and solid wastes. Insofar as pure water was delivered efficiently and initial human contact with wastes was minimized, these services fulfilled their major objective. A change in environmental paradigm—from miasmas to bacteria—did not disrupt these methods of collection, nor influence major changes in "front-of-the-pipe" components in these technologies of sanitation. The new age of bacteriology, however, did help to identify and ultimately confront "end-of-the-pipe" problems, namely pollution. The major weakness of environmental sanitation as a concept was its limited attention to disposal of effluent and refuse after they had been directed away from homes and businesses.

With the onset of the Bacteriological Revolution, water pollution, in particular, received greater and more pointed attention. Scientists, physicians, and engineers now had a much better idea of what they were looking for in the fight against communicable disease and a clearer idea of how to combat biological pollutants. Older methods, such as dilution of wastes in running water, had value under proper circumstances, but the primary focus centered on treatment. The goals of environmental sanitation were no longer regarded as sufficiently broad to deal with the several confounding problems of waste disposal or to ensure the purity of a water supply. Without attempting to change the basic structure of the technologies of sanitation, experts introduced new methods of water testing and focused increasing attention on refining treatment technologies. Never in question, however, was the basic precept of designing permanent, citywide sanitary systems; the basic designs originating in the Age of Miasmas were not substantively changed in the twentieth century. How extraordinary it was, however, that such significant technical systems as water and wastewater infrastructure depended so heavily on what proved to be flawed science.

CHAPTER THREE

Pure and Plentiful

THE DEVELOPMENT OF MODERN WATERWORKS
IN THE UNITED STATES, 1880–2000

MODERN AMERICAN WATERWORKS

This chapter was a distillation of draft sections from *The Sanitary City* on water-works prepared for a special issue of *Water Policy*, the official journal of the World Water Council. Edited by Martin Reuss, formerly of the U.S. Army Corps of Engineers' Office of History, the topic of the special issue was "Historical Perspectives on Global Water Challenges" and in large measure grew out of a conference entitled, "Water in History: Global Perspectives" held in Aberystwyth, Wales, in 1999. The event was a crucial step toward the initiation of the International Water History Association.

The shift in momentum toward public municipal waterworks began in the mid-nineteenth century, as was made clear in chapter 2. After 1880 or so, new theories of disease generation—bacteriology—transformed waterworks from transportation mechanisms into systems with a much greater capacity to deliver water of high quality through an array of filtration and treatment technologies. Underground sewer systems became more widespread through the country as well, carrying away unwanted liquid wastes to destinations far removed from human senses and deposited mostly in rivers, lakes, and oceans. This action, therefore, did not mitigate against pollution but merely relocated it. Despite often tapping sources of water beyond their borders and deferring pollution elsewhere, contemporary public officials and municipal engineers viewed these achievements as among the most important of the time. They had helped to create sanitary systems that, they believed, were permanent and well worth the substantial investment—but were not necessarily self-sustaining.

Those who were responsible for modern water supply and wastewater systems at the turn of the twentieth century and a few decades beyond had a right to be proud of these accomplishments in many respects. While no one could guarantee an absolutely safe and plentiful supply of water at all times nor dispose of wastes without potential consequences in other locations and jurisdictions, American cities could boast of a legitimate success story. Several decades later in the wake of an acknowledged "infrastructure crisis" with deteriorating water pipes, overworked treatment facilities, and a burgeoning population, the assertion of a permanent solution to municipal sanitary needs seemed a little naive—or at least a little too optimistic and unrealistic.

In more recent years, choices facing city leaders about their decaying or overstressed sanitary systems are seriously constrained. Ripping out existing systems and replacing them with something entirely new is exceedingly impractical. Investing substantial resources in repairs and extensions vies with other city priorities on a regular basis, especially in economic hard times. Walking away from managing water and wastewater systems—thus leaving the responsibility to some private company—is essentially thinking what had been the unthinkable. Privatization of waterworks in the United States was almost always "off the table" several years ago. How could the city turn over one of its few revenue generators such as water service to the private sector? Such improbable thoughts have crept back into the public debate as the burden of maintaining and expanding sanitary services rises and as city coffers—and those of other governmental entities—shrink. While the federal government underwrote—or contributed to—several such local projects since the 1930s, its withdrawal from funding them beginning in the 1980s only exacerbates the problem.

Water supply and wastewater systems clearly have been subject to what economists and others have called "path dependence." Although definitions vary, simply put path dependence exists "when the present state of a system is constrained by its history."[1] This suggests that decisions made early along the path—or early in the decision-making process—are very difficult to abandon or reverse in the present. It becomes almost impossible to break away from sanitary systems so long in use and to replace them with something entirely new. Going from a rigidly constructed centralized system, for example, to a more flexible, modular, decentralized system is almost impossible. You can expand on what you have or repair it, but you are unlikely to tear it out and start again.

For all of the positive good that modern sanitary services have provided over the years, sustaining their value to a community has been one of the most daunting tasks of municipal authorities. Continually extending the city's reach beyond its borders for new sources of water supply creates tensions with those in the hinterland, diverts valuable resources from one land use to another, intensifies institutional rivalries, and pits the public interest of urbanites against other public interests and holders of private property. Disposal of wastes also may threaten those within or beyond the city's boundaries. In addition, the tremendous increase in nonpoint pollution from runoff, flooding, and other sources is most often beyond the ability of fixed treatment plants to capture.

The following chapter discusses in some length the story of the United States' path since 1880 to about 2000. Disease outbreaks attributable to problems at public water treatment systems have steadily declined. But in 2002, thirty years after the passage of the Clean Water Act—"a critical law for ensuring the health of our nation's citizens"—about 1,000 community drinking water systems still violated the Environmental Protection Agency's Surface Water Treatment Rule.[2] In 2000, 16,202 wastewater treatment facilities and 21,264 sewer systems were operating in the United States and served approximately 208 million people. Nevertheless, Combined Sewer Overflows (CSOs)—containing raw sewage with pathogens, solids, debris, and toxic pollutants—create serious health problems and have resulted in beach closures, shellfish bed closures, and water supply contamination.[3] The path has been bumpy and the success of the once-hailed water and wastewater systems continually needs to be examined and reexamined. Among the difficulties facing cities and the nation is that such infrastructure needs chronically compete with other problems for attention and funding. But as the promotional material for *Liquid Assets: The Story of Our Water Infrastructure*, a documentary first released on PBS in October 2008, noted: "These systems—some in the ground for more than one hundred years—provide a critical public health function and are essential for economic development and growth. Largely out of sight and out of mind, these aging systems have not been maintained, and some estimates suggest this is the single largest public works endeavor in our nation's history."[4]

PURE AND PLENTIFUL

Water supply, like other sanitary services (wastewater and solid waste systems), has been and remains indispensable for the functioning and growth of cities; it is part of the urban circulatory system. Sanitary services are not organic entities but specialized technical systems—technologies of sanitation—that help to shape the apparatus of modern cities. In addition, the study of urban water supply is an important vehicle for revealing environmental thought as it relates to urban life and city development in general. Technical changes in sources of supply, distribution networks, filtration, and treatment are central to the discussion, as are the environmental implications of the evolving systems.

Modern citywide water supply systems, as demonstrated in chapter 2, were conceived in an Age of Miasmas (prior to 1880), that is, at a time when prevailing public health ideas blamed disease transmission on decaying matter, foul smells, and "bad air." Sanitarians, engineers, and city officials, among others, linked the structure of those systems and their functions to the goals of environmental sanitation, utilizing sensory tests of purity to deliver a product that would be free from known diseases and would remove wastes from direct human contact. With the advent of the Bacteriological Revolution (roughly 1850–1945), when the cause of disease transmission developed a sound scientific basis, and then into the era of the new ecology (after 1945), when a more holistic view of the environment emerged, a greater awareness of environmental inputs and outputs prevailed. However, traditional emphasis on permanent, centralized systems, going back at least to the turn of the twentieth century, exposed limitations in their functions. Modern waterworks were successful in coping with many biological and chemical pollutants, but by the late twentieth century they faced severe challenges from nonpoint pollution sources and groundwater contamination.

1880–1920

By the late nineteenth century, faith in environmental sanitation as the primary weapon against disease lost followers. Bacteriology placed more emphasis on finding cures for disease as opposed to prevention, which had been the mainstay of sanitary reform since the 1840s. Nonetheless, the commitment to develop elaborate urban infrastructure for water services was not deterred by the changing notions of health and disease. By 1920, many American cities could boast about plentiful sources of pure water and water systems that were taking greater account of how to confront waterborne epidemics.

In the era of bacteriology water supply systems increasingly relied upon centralized organizational structures and capital-intensive technical innovations. They continued to fulfill the traditional objectives of providing water but with greater attention to biological pollution risks. The prevailing goal in the late nineteenth and early twentieth centuries was to transform the evolving systems into more comprehensive public, citywide systems that afforded permanent solutions to the delivery of water. In this way, specific project design took precedence over long-term urban planning.

It would appear that the new public health and the rise of bacteriology would have blunted enthusiasm for investing so heavily in various technologies of sanitation. Yet few people denied the inherent value of pure and plentiful water. In 1870, the total number of waterworks stood at 244; by 1924, cities had constructed approximately 9,850 waterworks.

A variety of systems were in use. Some were expanded versions of the

older protosystems[5] with larger and increasingly distant surface water supplies, more and bigger reservoirs and settling tanks, and extended distribution networks. Some waterworks employed more efficient pumps, with
several using electrical power. The most advanced systems devoted greater
attention to water purity through the introduction of filters and water treatment. Technical improvements often led to greater water availability and use
but did not ensure against all epidemic diseases or pollution.

Many city leaders concluded that control of the sanitary quality of its water service would be difficult if the supply remained in private hands. The
push for municipal ownership had as much to do with the desire to influence
the growth of cities as to settle disputes with private companies over specific
deficiencies.[6] Major cities tended to support public systems earlier and more
uniformly than any other class of cities. In 1890, more than 70 percent of cities with populations exceeding 30,000 had public systems. In 1897, 41 of the
50 largest cities (or 82 percent) had public systems.[7]

Metering water usage became a powerful management tool in administering the water supply in public systems. Ostensibly employed as a way to
set rates, the use of water meters was equally important as a means to check
waste and to anticipate future expansions of the system. By 1920, metering
had made notable strides. While only about 30 percent of the cities metered
at the pump, more than 600 of 1000 cities surveyed metered at the tap; 279
cities metered all taps.[8]

New sources of supply became necessary when old sources could no
longer meet demand or became severely polluted. On the Pacific coast, Los
Angeles is the best example of relentless penetration into the hinterland in
search of water. Los Angeles was a community poised to become a major city
at the turn of the century. With a population of approximately 200,000 and
most every physical blessing imaginable, it lacked one important component—water. A drought from 1892 to 1904 forcefully drove home that point.
The story of the quest for water in Los Angeles for the next several years is
one of the most dramatic episodes of the period.[9]

The extension of the distribution network also made the modern water
systems more complex. Technological innovations produced three types
of supply systems: those that supplied water by gravity (New York and San
Francisco); those that supplied water entirely by direct pumping (Chicago,
Detroit, and Des Moines); and those that supplied water by pumping from
elevated storage tanks (St. Louis, Cleveland, and Kansas City, Kansas). The
method influenced the amount and kind of piping used in the system, and
the street plan and topography determined the layout. Thus uniformity in
the networks were not possible, and cities had to carefully match their distribution network to their sources of supply.[10]

Bacteriological laboratories, filtration plants, and treatment facilities also added new dimension to the modern water systems. Enthusiasm for bacteriology sometimes unduly discredited the work of chemists in evaluating water supply. Until the mid-twentieth century, engineers and medical and public health experts paid greater attention to biological forms of pollution linked to epidemic diseases than to industrial and other chemical pollutants. While some individuals placed too much faith in filtration as the panacea for waterborne epidemics, the investment nevertheless proved worthwhile in improving the quality of water in almost every community that employed it. Yet unqualified acceptance of filtration was not immediate. The cost could be prohibitive, and there was widespread debate over the most suitable forms of filtration to employ.[11]

The noted engineer M. N. Baker identified five eras of water treatment in America. The first ended in 1870, roughly coinciding with James P. Kirkwood's *Report on the Filtration of River Waters*. During this time, some waterworks employed sedimentation to clarify muddy water, others used "natural" filtration—or infiltration basins and galleries. In some cases, several small, rather primitive filters strained some of the largest materials. A second era, from 1870 to 1890, saw the introduction of slow sand and rapid sand—or mechanical—filters. Implementation was erratic, and the principles of bacteriology were not well enough entrenched to inform the most effective use of the filters. The rapid sand filter was an American invention. Aside from the enhanced speed of filtering, the chief distinction between the English and the American filters was the cleaning process. The former was cleaned manually, while the latter used mechanical devices—water jets, reverse-flow wash, or revolving sand agitators or stirrers.[12]

The third era, from 1891 to 1900, is noted for the beginnings of scientifically designed slow sand filters and better designed mechanical filters. The Lawrence Experiment Station in Massachusetts led the way to improved filtration. It became the leader in water-purification research in the nation.[13] Possibly the most important discovery in these years was that an improved slow sand filter could remove typhoid germs from river water, proving what only had been surmised in other cases. This third era, however, remained a time of uncertainty in the application of the new filtration technologies, especially in the South and West where muddy or hard river water posed different problems than those of the East, Midwest, and even Europe.[14]

The years 1901–1910 marked the fourth era in which the rivalry between slow sand and mechanical filters intensified. Water treatment, as opposed to filtration, made important strides in the first decade of the twentieth century. Several cities added chlorine to their water, and the federal government experimented with copper sulfate for algae control. Sanitarians had been able to convince city leaders that typhoid and related diseases were preventable through a combination of filtration and treatment, and their eradication was a measure of water purity. Facilities such as East Jersey Water Company's Little Falls plant conducted tests on coagulants. Other sites experimented with a variety of measures to protect water supplies.[15]

The idea of disinfecting water was discovered well before the twentieth century. Even before chlorination of water became popular, sewage had been chlorinated in England, France, and the United States. In 1896, sanitary engineers introduced bleaching powder in Austria. The next year, waterworks personnel applied chlorine gas to a test filter at Adrian, Michigan. In 1909, chemists produced liquid chlorine, which offered a much easier method of dispersal. By 1918, engineers were installing chlorination equipment as far west as California. A dramatic decline in typhoid fever rates followed the use of chlorine in many locations. Despite the optimistic reports, there remained some concern among citizens about "doping the water" with chemicals. While this fear arose before the turn of the century, it never completely died out.[16]

Baker regarded the years from 1910 to the 1930s as an era when filter plants and the use of chlorination became widespread. His forecast was somewhat optimistic, since statistics suggest that filtration and disinfection spread less rapidly than he believed. Nevertheless, a movement toward purified water supplies was underway after 1910.[17] Because most engineers, public health experts, and other sanitarians in this era linked purity with waterborne diseases, concern over water pollution per se focused primarily on bacteria in the water, rather than on the impact of industrial pollutants or other toxic materials. Not until after World War I did health experts view industrial wastes as a major problem affecting water purity and complicating the process of sewage treatment.[18]

1920—1945

From the end of World War I to the end of World War II, neither the quality nor character of sanitary services underwent substantial change. The challenge for municipal officials, engineers, planners, and sanitarians was to adapt those services to urban growth increasingly characterized by metropolitization and suburbanization, on the one hand, and demand for such services in numerous small towns and rural communities, on the other hand. Decision making in this period was complicated by two major disruptions to American life: the Great Depression and World War II. From a fiscal perspective, the economic calamity beginning in the late 1920s changed the very nature of city and federal relations and resulted in transforming what had been essentially local service delivery into systems increasingly influ-

enced by regional and national concerns and interests. Water supply was
linked into regional systems or mired in an array of jurisdictional disputes.
By World War I, water pollution issues and the capturing of distant sources
of pure water supplies by major cities already had demonstrated that the
largest systems had impacts well beyond city limits.

Despite the up-and-down cycles of the economy from the 1920s to the
1940s, national trends in the construction and expansion of waterworks
continued to indicate steady growth. Many of the new systems were rudimentary ones in numerous small communities. In 1940, there were approximately 14,500 waterworks in the United States.[19] Although the rate
of growth was strongest from the 1890s through the early 1920s, increases
in the 1930s were significant due to the infusion of federal funds during the
New Deal.[20]

The relative stability of the waterworks business in the interwar years
occurred with some significant changes in the management of the water
supply systems. The need for greater cooperation between political entities
in the acquisition and delivery of water was becoming obvious, especially in
response to metropolitan and suburban growth patterns in major cities. In
some parts of the country, special water districts sprouted up in the 1920s,
especially for the development of water resources and the delivery of adequate service.[21]

Without question, the greatest change in the development, extension,
management, and financing of water supply systems in the interwar years
came with the new role of the federal government. During the New Deal,
the Public Works Administration (PWA) financed between 2,400 and
2,600 water projects with a price tag of approximately $312 million. This
sum amounted to half of the total expenditures for waterworks for all levels
of government. The Federal Emergency Relief Administration (FERA), the
Civil Works Administration (CWA), and the Works Progress Administration (WPA) spent another $112 million for work relief on municipal water
projects. Smaller communities felt the greatest impact of these funds. For the
first time they were able to finance public systems, treatment facilities, and
distribution networks. In fact, almost three-fourths of the projects financed
went to communities with less than one thousand people.[22] While federal
support stimulated development of new waterworks and provided resources
for improving others, wartime priorities ultimately shifted federal funds
away from local sanitary services.[23]

With respect to water purity, the interwar years witnessed a better understanding about what constituted water pollution and a greater sensitivity
to consumer demands for water that was not only clean but soft, odorless,
and tasteless. By the 1920s the process of purifying and treating water was

significantly refined. There was more complete preliminary clarification of water prior to filtration, better mechanical filtration, better controlled use of chlorination, new procedures for reducing odors and tastes, attention to corrosive elements in water, broader use of aeration, and progress in softening water.[24] This is not to suggest that all water problems had been worked out. Debate continued on when to filter water versus when to chlorinate it and when sewage treatment was preferable to filtration.[25] Since World War I, hundreds of cities had built water filters. In 1926 there were 635 filter plants in the United States serving approximately 24 million people, of these plants, the lion's share (588) were of the rapid sand type. While the depression slowed development temporarily, in 1939 there were filtration facilities at 2,188 plants (but only 97 slow sand filters). In 1938, 37 million Americans used filtered and chlorinated water, 26 million used partially purified water, and 17 million used untreated water.[26]

Despite the efforts of waterworks to offer a more palatable product to consumers, the techniques of filtration and disinfection did not undergo substantial change in the interwar years. Water pollution at the source, however, emerged as a national issue. Some experts believed that public concern over water pollution was a driving force for change. While there was no accurate way to measure the level of the public's interest in water pollution, a diverse array of groups from conservationists to coastal oystermen, fishermen, and shrimpers spoke out publicly against environmental threats to the nation's waterways.[27] There is also little doubt that public health officials, engineers, scientists, and other experts took the issue seriously and began to recognize the problem of water pollution in broader terms than before.

By international standards, the United States was faring better by the 1930s, in terms of waterborne disease, than it had in the past. Of sixteen countries surveyed in 1912, the United States was ranked twelfth in the lowest typhoid rate; in 1932, eleventh out of twenty—one place higher than France, and substantially better than Spain, Portugal, Italy, Czechoslovakia, Greece, Japan, Chile, and South Africa.[28]

While bacterial measures of water purity maintained a strong influence, health experts began to take industrial pollutants more seriously as a better understanding of their composition became known and as new studies pointed to the immense quantities entering the nation's watercourses. Among the problems identified were the hindrance in the proper operation of water treatment facilities, the consumption of oxygen that reduced the dilution power of running water, the problem of fish kills, and the increase in taste and odor problems in drinking water. A 1923 report indicated that industrial wastes had affected no less than 248 water supplies throughout the United States and Canada.[29]

The states, more than the municipalities or the federal government, were the centers of action for new legislation to control stream pollution. In the early and mid-twentieth century, this issue remained the major focus of concern over the disposal of municipal and industrial wastes. The states generally opposed any extension of federal regulatory authority in the area of water pollution control, preferring to confine federal involvement to investigation and research and possibly to acting as a coordinating body.[30] The first state legislation to control stream pollution was written in 1878 in Massachusetts. It gave the Massachusetts State Board of Health the power to control river pollution caused by industrial wastes. All but four states established such divisions by 1927.[31] But in 1931, only nineteen states gave health departments sole jurisdiction over laws enforcing stream pollution.[32] However, as early as World War I, states were establishing boards and commissions designed to regulate water pollution. These new bodies often were given expanded power over industrial as well as municipal pollution. The results of checking water pollution were often disappointing, however.[33]

Before national legislation was enacted, interstate compacts were the primary institutional means, other than the courts, to deal with water pollution issues between the states. The agreements could be formal treaties ratified by the appropriate state legislatures and approved by Congress, or they could be informal cooperative agreements entered into by the states themselves. States passed legislation for river compacts in 1921; legislators drafted the first interstate river compacts for the Colorado and La Plata Rivers the following year.[34]

Harold W. Streeter, senior sanitary engineer of the U.S. Public Health Service in Cincinnati, referred to advances in water purification and sewage treatment as a "general broadening viewpoint" on stream pollution and control. Streeter credited "the growth of public interest in stream pollution as a nation-wide problem" as the stimulus for this change.[35] More likely, the deepening experience of research scientists, engineers, public health experts, and sanitarians in confronting water pollution problems was responsible for the budding environmental insight. The broadening viewpoint was an indicator that the old debate over environmental sanitation versus individual health, which framed the transition from the filth theory to the germ theory of disease, was beginning to be put aside, and a more sophisticated environmental outlook was emerging.

Uncertainty prevailed as to whether effective efforts were underway to eliminate stream pollution. Expert and public concern over stream pollution and sewage disposal helped to accelerate state regulatory responses to water pollution in the interwar years, but federal action lagged considerably. Nevertheless, what had been essentially a local issue—the development and maintenance of a water supply system—now was inextricably linked to state and even national concerns and policies.

1945—1970

Relentless growth on the periphery and deterioration of the central city characterized post–World War II urban conditions and affected the maintenance and development of technologies of sanitation. Urban sprawl placed increasingly stiff demands on the providers of water supply. Concern over decaying infrastructure, most especially at the urban cores, raised important questions about the permanence of the sanitary systems devised and implemented in the nineteenth and early twentieth centuries. However, an array of mounting social ills—characterized in the aggregate as an "urban crisis"—increasingly shifted attention away from infrastructure problems.

Sanitary services not only were situated within a new social and political context after 1945 but within a changing environmental context as well. The emergence of the new ecology and the modern environmental movement produced a paradigm in which people viewed sanitary services with different eyes. The last of a series of *Fortune* articles on infrastructure (December 1958) stated flatly that water supply and sewerage "remain a signal failure in public works."[36] This assessment was harsh, but many older water supply and sewerage systems were in decline by the mid-1940s. The Committee on Public Information for the American Water Works Association reported in 1960 that of the approximately 18,000 functioning water facilities in the United States one in five had a deficient supply, two in five had inadequate transmission capacity, one in three had defective pumping, and two in five had weaknesses in their treating capacity.[37]

Decisions about improving water supply systems had to be made within a framework of rapid urban growth and increasing water usage, especially with the availability of new appliances—automatic dishwashers, washing machines, and air conditioners—in many middle-class homes. Further concentration of industry in metropolitan and unincorporated areas also increased the need for more water, as did demands for service in unincorporated residential communities.[38]

New waterworks continued to come online, especially in the expanding metropolitan periphery and in smaller cities and towns no longer able to depend on private wells and more rudimentary water systems. In 1945 there were approximately 15,400 waterworks in the United States supplying about 12 billion gallons per day to 94 million people. By 1965, there were more than 20,000 waterworks supplying 20 billion gallons per day to approximately 160 million people.[39] By the mid-1960s, 83.4 percent of water supply facilities (cities with a population of 25,000 or more) were publicly owned.[40] Between 1956 and 1965, $10 billion was spent for new construction and additions in the United States. The annual value of the water placed waterworks within the nation's top ten largest industries.[41]

Postwar water supply problems were exacerbated by several causes: uneven distribution of facilities for storing water and pumping and transporting water from available supplies to areas of greatest demand; chronic shortages of water in the Southwest and West; and increased pollution of traditional sources of potable water. Some cities had long depended on distant supplies of surface water. San Francisco's primary reservoirs were as much as 150 miles from the city; Los Angeles and San Diego drew water from as far away as 550 miles. In some cases, supplies were tapped beyond state boundaries leading to intense battles for control. However, these problems were more exaggerated in the arid West than in the East or South.[42]

Distribution problems resulted from the location of water facilities in central cities, which often serviced the larger metropolitan area and outlying suburban communities. It was frequently in the interest of the central city to extend waterlines to the suburbs to maintain a healthy economic climate in the metropolitan area. For suburbs, growth was impossible without adequate services. In some cases there was reluctance on the part of central cities to extend distribution lines outward if there was no guarantee of future annexation. In several cases, real estate developers or alternative public entities constructed pipelines beyond the existing city limits to make outlying suburbs attractive to future annexation. In the 1960s the central plant in Chicago supplied water on a contract basis to approximately sixty suburban communities. The number of special districts and other administrative arrangements were increasing in number in response to the need for water.[43]

From the vantage point of the total water system, the cost of distribution represented as much as two-thirds of a utility's investment.[44] Difficulties of extending new distribution lines were exacerbated by undersized pipes, over-extension of mains, and problems in design. The internal corrosion of distribution lines, which had received little attention through the late 1960s, reduced carrying capacity, produced discolored water, and caused bad tastes and odors.[45]

Filtration, a major breakthrough in the late nineteenth century, faced serious scrutiny in the postwar years.[46] While there had been little improvement in filter design for fifty years, new pretreatment equipment—that aided the performance of rapid sand filters—became available in the 1960s. Filtration in general remained expensive, and the cost seemed to be out of proportion to its contribution in the treatment process.[47] Even the widely adopted practice of chlorination attracted doubters. In 1966, chlorination was used by 99 percent of all municipalities that chemically disinfected their supplies. Concern, however, arose over the ability of chlorination to keep up with increasing water demand. Also, tests showed that chlorine was not effective against all microorganisms, at least in the concentrations used in existing waterworks systems.[48]

A new water additive, fluoride, was used for the purpose of reducing the incidence of tooth decay, a chronic disease especially in children. Communal fluoridation began in Grand Rapids, Michigan; Newburgh, New York; Evanston, Illinois; and Brantford, Ontario, in 1945.[49] Proponents of fluoridation believed that it could reduce cavities by 60 percent. Many scientific and public health organizations, including the U.S. Public Health Service and the American Dental Association, endorsed the use of fluoride in water supplies as a safe, effective, and inexpensive practice.[50] After 1951, when the benefits of fluoridation were first announced, public acceptance was on the rise. Simultaneously, organized opposition to the use of fluoride in drinking water also intensified. Some of the opposition was similar to that raised against chlorination, that is, skepticism about any compound added to a natural water supply. Some criticisms were more bizarre and reflected the paranoia rampant in the 1950s due to the Cold War and the fear of communism.[51] Critics of the practice filed local lawsuits and supported national legislation to ban fluoridation. In the long run, support of key public health and scientific groups and the positive results from usage led to increasingly greater application of fluoride to public water supplies.[52]

While problems of distribution and treatment were serious after 1945, public attention was directed toward dramatic claims of water shortages and drought in the West and Southwest. But more significant from a national perspective was intensifying concern over water quality. In the postwar years, attention to water pollution broadened considerably from the focus on biological contaminants to a wide variety of chemical contaminants. One important reason for the change was the substantial decline in a number of waterborne diseases and confidence in available methods and technologies in combating those that remained.[53] Aside from the known health hazards, there were unknown or little-known dangers, especially from thousands of new organic chemicals coming on the market after World War II in such products as detergents and pesticides, through a variety of industrial processes, and from nuclear technology.[54] Criticism of general water quality led some to portray water pollution as a national disgrace and to decry the United States as an "Effluent Society."

Some studies tried to downplay the extent and scale of the national water pollution problem. The Drinking Water Standards, however, gave increasing attention to toxic chemicals and soluble minerals that made their way into the water supply. Following their revisions in 1946, the American

Water Works Association voluntarily adopted the standards for all public water supplies.[55] Concern remained that the standards had not gone far
enough in dealing with a range of toxic or potentially toxic substances found
in water. The encouraging news was that scientists were using several new
analytical techniques as early as the 1940s to detect and monitor some trace
elements and toxins, such as DDT. By 1970, however, the ability to evaluate hazards from microchemical and microphysical substances was far from
comprehensive.[56]

Those who viewed water pollution as a growing national problem be-
moaned the inadequate number of good treatment facilities. By the end of
World War II, construction of new sewage and industrial waste treatment
plants had literally ceased. A 1961 estimate concluded that adequate fresh
water needs for the immediate future would require municipalities to spend
$4.6 billion, and another $575 to $600 million per year was needed just to
retire the backlog of industrial waste treatment facilities.[57]

Local authorities and their health departments were ill-prepared to identify sufficient resources to satisfy the treatment requirements, let alone to
effectively curb further pollution. By the 1950s, more than twenty states did
not have truly comprehensive water pollution control apparatus, although
efforts continued to establish interstate compacts to deal with transborder
issues of water pollution. Even in the states with direct-type legislation, requirements might be set low in the face of pressure from industry or other
interests.[58] In 1948, the Eightieth Congress passed and President Truman
signed the first major federal water pollution control legislation. The Water
Pollution Control Act empowered the federal government to participate in
the abatement of interstate water pollution. However, it limited federal enforcement to interstate problems with the consent of the participating states
and thus constrained the federal role in controlling water pollution. The
1948 act also was unwieldy and difficult to enforce.[59]

The Federal Water Pollution Control Act Amendments of 1961 continued the cooperative approach between the federal government and the states
in several provisions. Federal jurisdiction, however, expanded beyond interstate waters to include navigable waters or essentially all major waterways
in the United States. The 1961 amendments also made it possible for states
to benefit more substantially from federal grants. Like New Deal water and
sewer programs, the water pollution acts were a greater boon to smaller cities and towns, rather than a complete answer to the water pollution problem
of many watersheds.[60]

Possibly the most important, and certainly the most controversial, water
pollution bill in the period was the Water Quality Act of 1965. The federal
government became more deeply involved in water quality management and

in establishing water quality standards. Debate over federal versus state authority raged again as did the battle over what constituted excessive pollution levels and clean water. Advocates hoped that the new law would change the strategy underlying the country's water pollution programs from "one of containment to one of prevention."[61] Yet, the gap between aspirations for cleaner water and more carefully monitored sewage discharge, on the one hand, and actual federal support, on the other hand, remained wide by 1970.

As in the case of water supply systems, the postwar economic boom and the dynamic expansion of metropolitan America obscured the chronic deterioration of the infrastructure and the inability of cities to keep pace with sanitary needs. Water supply systems were failing to live up to expectations and foretold a soon-to-be unsettling fear of a new era of crisis.

1970—2000

In the wake of the "infrastructure crisis," water supply avoided the most dire predictions about decay and deterioration in several major studies. A report in 1987 stated that a national water supply "infrastructure gap" of the magnitude that "would require a substantial federal subsidy" did not exist. Urban water supply systems as a whole, it concluded, "do not constitute a national problem."[62] This assessment was based on comparisons with other components of the nation's infrastructure. Water needs appeared modest when compared with highway repair and replacement estimated in the mid-1980s to reach a twenty-year "needs level" of approximately $2 trillion. Needs studies set price tags of $125 billion for water supply repairs, expansions, and improvements.[63] The relatively small, but hardly insignificant, number masked problems that had been building for years. Some experts, looking beyond the statistics, charged that many drinking water systems were outdated, faced massive leaks, were poorly maintained, and relied on pipes a hundred or more years old.[64] Broadening federal regulatory authority over water pollution and the tightening of water quality standards were first steps in recognizing the severity and complex nature of water pollution in the 1970s.

In the aggregate, availability of supplies to meet water demand appeared stable in the period. But aggregated data sometimes masked major droughts and chronic water shortages in urban centers located in arid regions of the country. In many respects, local circumstances and local conditions continued to strongly influence the operation and performance of the water supply systems.

Water issues tended to be defined in technical terms by experts operating in allegedly apolitical agencies that faced little public review. Aside from substantial administrative discretion, public works bodies were, as one study

noted, "repositories of expertise" about their service area and often were active in mobilizing outside client groups (vendors, suppliers, and equipment
manufacturers) in support of their work. While privatization made in-roads
into several service areas in recent years, water supply remained largely a
public venture.[65] Regionalization of the water industry attracted considerable attention, especially the Metropolitan Water District in California and
the Metropolitan Sanitary District of Greater Chicago. However, "local pa-
rochialism" in water supply systems was not overcome despite the urging of
some national studies.[66]

Financing of water supply also demonstrated the persistent local nature
of sanitary service delivery after 1970. Statistics from the early 1980s indicate
that state and local governments were primarily responsible for 83 percent
of the expenditures for municipal water supplies. Federal funds for water
projects were on the decline in the 1970s, and capital spending by all governments for water resources had fallen by 60 percent from the late 1960s to the
late 1980s.[67]

In an era of heightened concern over a range of environmental risks
threatening the nation's water supplies, outbreaks of waterborne diseases
continued to decline. Diseases such as cholera and typhoid fever had been
virtually eliminated. Disinfection continued to be regarded as one of the
most important, if not the most important, steps in water treatment to assure that a supply was hygienic. Chloramines were regarded as having a limited impact on viral agents in the water, however, and thus attention turned
to alternative disinfectants such as other halogens, bromine, and iodine.
Most significantly, chlorine disinfection produced some undesirable by-
products, including trihalomethane (THM). In attempts to control THM,
researchers took a new look at ozone because of its high germicidal effectiveness, its ability to combat odor, taste, and color problems, and its benign
decomposition.[68]

By the mid-1970s, despite its impressive record, chlorination came under severe criticism as a cancer risk. A report issued in 1974 alleged a causal
relationship between the use of Mississippi River water (which contained
large quantities of chlorinated sewage effluent) and the incidence of cancer.
While some authorities later questioned the validity of the study, it led to an
increased awareness of chemical contaminants in water supplies and the impact of chlorination on them. The Environmental Protection Agency (EPA)
set the first THM limits in 1979.[69] Fluoridation did not suffer the same deep
scrutiny as disinfection, but debate over its use persisted. In 1990, waterworks staff added fluoride to the water supplies of 57 percent of the American people.[70]

As in the case of waterborne disease, there appeared to be measurable improvement in surface water quality in several locations throughout the country in the 1970s and 1980s.[71] Serious pollution problems remained in other surface waters areas but were not confined to any one region. With over 300,000 factories in the United States using water, a variety of toxic materials found their way into surface supplies. Some of the discharges were routine, others accidental.[72]

While surface water continued to be a major source of supply for municipal and industrial uses, for irrigation, and for generating electricity, groundwater use was on the rise, especially for community water systems in smaller and medium-sized cities. Groundwater was the source for 80.4 percent of all community water systems. In non-community water systems, 96 percent were served by groundwater sources. Groundwater use is significant because it met a specialized need in many communities as a primary source of drinking water. By the end of the 1980s, more than 50 percent of the U.S. population depended on groundwater as the main source of drinking water. Groundwater was available nearly everywhere in the United States, but its quantity and quality varied by region. The maximum average well yields were located along the West Coast, Nevada, and Idaho. The smallest yields were generally found in the western mountain ranges. In the East and South, groundwater was used primarily for domestic and industrial purposes; in the West, for irrigation.[73]

While depletion of groundwater was a chronic concern for many years, the question of quality had rarely been an issue. Beginning in the 1970s, that hallowed belief came into question, but it took time to determine the general quality of the nation's groundwater. Sources of contamination included waste disposal practices, irrigation return flows, spills, abandoned oil and gas wells, and leaks from buried tanks and pipelines. From 1978 to 1981, contamination forced hundreds of wells to close.[74]

The 1970s also witnessed an increased awareness of nonpoint pollution as a major cause for concern. By 1990 it was estimated that more than 50 percent of America's total water quality problems were attributed to agricultural, industrial, and residential nonpoint sources. Runoff into water courses contained asbestos, heavy metals, oil and grease, salts, manures, pesticides and herbicides, construction site pollutants, bacterial and viral contaminants, hydrocarbons, and topsoil.[75]

The federal role in water supply issues grew significantly after 1970 as more comprehensive federal regulations imposed stiffer water quality and effluent standards. In 1971 the EPA was given responsibility for water quality, and it set standards for twenty-two contaminants. Because of the limits on the success of previous legislation and because of the desire to broaden the water quality program, the Federal Water Pollution Control Act of 1972—

later renamed the Clean Water Act—passed Congress with overwhelming support and became a critical turning point in national water quality legislation.[76] The act was meant to reduce the quantity of pollutants discharged into surface waters by setting two goals: first, to attain water quality in navigable waters suitable for fisheries and for swimming (the so-called fishable-swimmable goal) by 1983 and to mandate that all publicly owned wastewater treatment facilities provide secondary treatment by 1988 (originally 1983); and second, to achieve a zero pollutants discharge goal by 1995. These goals were meant to change the basic strategy of federal water quality management by replacing in-stream water quality standards (ambient water quality standards) with limits on the discharge of pollutants from industrial point source discharges and municipal wastewater treatment plants (technology-based standards). The 1977 amendments to the Clean Water Act continued the emphasis on technology-based standards by increasing federal funding from 75 percent to 85 percent for projects employing "innovative" technologies.[77]

Despite its role in the improvement of water quality, the Clean Water legislation of the 1970s did not meet with its original timetable, did not operate with the authorized funds, and did not achieve its antipollution targets.[78] In several respects, the new legislation was guided by powerful historic forces in dealing with effluent, that is, a dependence on highly centralized, capital-intensive water supply filtration and wastewater treatment facilities designed to capture point sources of pollutants entering watercourses or returning to consumers via those watercourses. These mechanisms, in and of themselves, were not capable of addressing water pollution in all its manifestations, especially problems such as groundwater contamination and stormwater runoff.

In the 1980s, Congress and some federal agencies made efforts to bolster groundwater protection authority. Nonpoint pollution, however, proved to be the most perplexing pollution issue to confront in the late twentieth century largely because its causes were so diverse, existing treatment systems were ill-suited to deal with it, and prevailing regulations had long ignored it. Not until the passage of the 1987 amendments to the Clean Water Act was there statutory language attempting to resolve what had become a heated battle over nonpoint sources and stormwater runoff.[79]

The legislative history of water pollution abatement after 1970 demonstrates the difficulty in addressing a wide array of pollution problems. Establishing quality standards also proved perplexing and much too large an issue to be ignored. Whatever its value as a general critique of the state of public works in the United States, the "infrastructure crisis" was not sufficiently broad to effectively characterize the state of water supply systems in recent

years. Granted, technologies of sanitation often reflected myriad problems
of an aging and deteriorating infrastructure. But equally important is the fact
that these services, which began as protosystems in the nineteenth century
and evolved into sophisticated centralized systems in the twentieth, were
not designed to anticipate problems such as groundwater contamination
and nonpoint pollution. Particularly in the case of the latter, the conceptual
framework within which those systems were designed and built focused on
problems of epidemic disease and—eventually—an array of point source
pollutants, but they did not allow for—and arguably could not anticipate—
the kinds of environmental problems posed by runoff and nonpoint sources.
If there was an infrastructure crisis for water supply, it was of a different type
than other public works. In addition, the demands on the water supply had
increased dramatically since the nineteenth century. With improvement
over time, and a rise in expectations, it is not surprising that water supply
systems left a mixed legacy.

By the twentieth century, many American cities established permanent,
centralized citywide water supply systems. This was a major accomplish-
ment. Water was readily available for home and business use, for combating
fires, and for tasks too numerous to mention. Cities were spared the most serious consequences of many waterborne diseases. However, while sanitarians, engineers, and city officials could take justifiable pride in making their
cities more sanitary, modern water supply systems failed to address some
new and different environmental problems.

By the late nineteenth century, waterworks were generally regarded as
public enterprises, justified as such because of the need to protect the public
health and to supply water on a citywide basis. With the onset of the Bacteriological Revolution after 1880, water pollution, in particular, received
attention along with municipal control of the precious resource. Scientists,
physicians, and engineers now had a much better idea of what they were
looking for in the fight against communicable disease than they did in a prior
era dominated by the miasmic—or filth—theory of disease. Thus they had a
much clearer idea on how to combat biological pollutants. Without changing
the basic structure of the technologies of sanitation developed in the mid-
nineteenth century, experts introduced new methods of water testing and
focused attention on refining treatment technologies. Never in question,
however, was the basic precept of designing permanent, citywide sanitary
systems; the basic designs originating in the nineteenth century were not
changed in the twentieth.

While bacteriology contributed effectively to eradicating biological pollution, it offered less in addressing other environmental problems, particu-

larly industrial wastes and the new toxic chemicals entering water supplies. The new ecology after World War II brought into focus a more sophisticated notion of the extent of water pollution, especially through better measurement techniques. The basic structure of the water supply system did not change, but a better understanding of its capabilities did.

The new ecology offered a greater awareness of environmental inputs and outputs, which could help maximize the value of sanitary services. Water supply systems also delivered valuable service through continual refinements. However, the traditional emphasis on permanent, centralized systems ultimately exposed limitations in their functions. Since all technologies of sanitation were capital intensive, they required continual maintenance and repair. The publicly acknowledged infrastructure crisis in the 1970s and 1980s demonstrated a lack of commitment to adequately maintaining existing systems. Other priorities in city budgets strongly influenced their fate, as did a variety of fiscal constraints. Water supply systems, like other infrastructure issues, were caught between the choice of investing in existing technologies or expansion to meet new demand. Also, choices concerning the development of new water supply systems in recent years were constrained by initial choices made in the nineteenth century.

The decision to invest in a distant water supply, pumping stations, filtration, and treatment facilities gave a certain degree of comfort to city leaders in the past who believed they were creating monuments to good sanitation and effective service delivery. The emphasis on project design as opposed to long-range planning often meant that future generations could not choose to abandon these systems and begin again, but they must maintain or expand them—even if the systems are inadequate—or face extraordinary costs. It was not so much that flawed technologies were chosen initially, but that systems were designed to be permanent, to resist change in order to justify their worth to the contemporary community. In essence, the systems lacked flexibility, that is, they were not capable of substantial alteration due to changes in fiscal conditions or changes in urban growth patterns. More recent demands for "modular flexibility" in the design of infrastructure (a decentralized versus a centralized system, for example) is a response to the realization that past practices in the construction and use of technical systems have severely limited choice for contemporary decision makers.[80]

With respect to problems of pollution, it is clear that the modern water supply systems have limited value in dealing with certain kinds of pollutants not present or not considered significant in the initial design of the systems. Of particular note is nonpoint source pollution. Designers of the systems and decision makers in the nineteenth and early twentieth centuries cannot be faulted for failing to anticipate these problems, after all these decisions took place during the "century of technological enthusiasm," as coined by historian Thomas P. Hughes, when the centralizing tendencies of government were strong.[81]

The commitment to permanent, centralized technical systems to resolve sanitary problems in fact left little room for adapting those systems to meet new and serious challenges. In other words, they built in permanence but not resilience. Historical circumstances strongly influence the recent choices available for sanitary services whether decision makers like it or not. Water supply systems, originating in the nineteenth century and continuing to the present, have an impressive, but not altogether flawless, record of achievement. As part of the circulatory system of the city, they contributed mightily to the environmental well-being of millions of Americans, but they also expose limitations that require attention today.

CHAPTER FOUR

The Environmental Impact
of the Big Dam Era

THE IMPACT OF DAM BUILDING

This piece was the concluding chapter in *The History of Large Federal Dams: Planning, Design, and Construction*, and as such, it deals especially with the story and environmental impacts of big dam development. This chapter also had a western orientation largely because of the book's strong emphasis on the Big Dam Era, lasting from 1935 to 1965, which gave us, among others, Hoover, Grand Coulee, and Glen Canyon Dams located west of the Mississippi River. The dynamic impact of dam building and the contradictory perceptions of dams themselves, however, raise several universal issues beyond the geographic focus represented here.

The most dynamic means of harnessing a river is dam building. Although there are countless small private dams throughout all of the watersheds in the United States, the biggest and most impressive are those constructed with public money. The Big Dam Era of the early twentieth century was the most memorable dam-building period of all, but such mammoth construction was by no means restricted to one brief moment in history. In more recent years, the majesty of the great dams, and many less grand structures, faced severe criticism as impediments to the free flow of rivers, destroyers of fish populations, potential disaster risks, and more.

The swing from human-made wonder to environmental threat should come as no surprise. Dams always have been contested technology. Among their strong advocates, for example, dams offered flood control, irrigation, urban water supply, electric power, and recreational opportunities. Despite the rationalization for multipurpose use—and thus the ability to serve numerous consumers—the uses of dams, dam water, dam-built lakes and reservoirs served different people in different ways and often led to government regulations setting priorities or outright battles (legal and otherwise) between users. The battle for water rights and water use pitted city leaders against farmers, city against city, and cities against small towns. Even if the contesting parties could resolve their differences, dam building created other losers too. Flooding land for reservoirs wrested property from Native Americans, small farmers, and others, changing arable landscapes into artificial waterscapes. Intensive construction of dams and reservoirs sometimes threatened land considered too sublime to be disrupted or flooded. Anadromous fish such as salmon perished or were vastly diminished. Water flow was altered or altogether stopped along great stretches of formerly free-flowing rivers.

Dams, in fact and in theory, represent a rather simple technical idea with very complex implications. It is precisely because big dams, especially, were public ventures that this chapter was included here. Particularly in the New Deal years and beyond, dams were graphic examples of the spread of federal water activity into a variety of new arenas. That period also saw the maturing of national resources planning of which dams also were a central objective.[1] Possibly the most telling example of the federal role in river management was the Pick-Sloan Compromise in 1944 to deal with conflicting interests over flood control in the Missouri River Valley. Some cities along the river sided with the U.S. Army Corps of Engineers and others with the Bureau of Reclamation. Congress intervened and produced a compromise that allowed the corps to manage dams, navigation, and flood control in downstream areas, and gave the Bureau of Reclamation management of upstream reservoirs for irrigation, municipal use, and power production. This led to a massive dam- and levee-building program in the Missouri River Valley and beyond.[2]

Big dams are indeed the most graphic symbol of a program that proclaims water as a public resource. Not only are the largest and most significant dams public ventures, but their construction, use, and possible dismantling have been and continue to be the subject of public regulation, public policy, and public concern.

THE ENVIRONMENTAL IMPACT OF THE BIG DAM ERA

In a 1941 book, *American Bridges and Dams*, Paul Zueker wrote: "Of all works of engineering, the perfect bridge most nearly approaches the realm of art—the dam, the realm of nature." Dams compared with "God's immovable mountains." Zucker went on to suggest that, "no other achievement of peaceful civilization during the last two decades on this war-torn earth has contributed more to the welfare of future generations than the building of dams in this country." The dam's legacy consisted of storing water, averting and controlling floods, irrigation, conservation of soil, improving navigation, and generating electrical energy. "It is natural," he concluded, "that a vast country of mighty rivers, like the United States, should excel in the construction of dams."[3]

About forty years after Zucker's book appeared, an international movement against current dam-building practices emerged, comprised of numerous environmental, human rights, and social activist groups from a variety of local, regional, national, and international anti-dam campaigns. Criticisms abounded: dams flooded valleys, displaced farmers, and blocked fish migrations. Dams reduced water quality. Dams changed forever natural riverine flows. Dams were shortsighted structures that drew funds away from other potentially sounder technologies. For some, the conclusion was obvious—destroy or decommission the dams and free the rivers.[4]

The story of dam building and its environmental impacts is not as neatly explained as the opposing views imply. However, it is safe to say that the perception of large dams, their economic and societal value, and their environmental implications have undergone considerable change in recent years. Dams have been used to manage river flow since ancient times, but not until the heyday of the Big Dam Era in the United States was the promise of controlling rivers fully realized. The change in perception of the role of dams over the last half-century or more—from economic boon to unwelcome obstruction—is at once palpable but with complex undertones and no absolute consensus.

Harnessing rivers into service to humankind was the major objective of the Big Dam Era. Construction in this period ran the gamut from the twenty-six dams of the Tennessee Valley Authority (TVA) in the East to the pre–World War II giants, the Hoover (1936) and Grand Coulee (1941; plant and pumps ready for operation in 1951) Dams, and Glen Canyon Dam (1964) in the West.[5] In this sense, the Big Dam Era elaborated on the legacy of Progressive Era water policy, bent on maximizing the efficient use of a vital natural rcsource. Sometimes the aim was to reduce flooding and to improve navigation. In other cases, flowing water was manipulated to provide abundant sources for irrigation and urban use or to produce electricity. Multipurpose projects attempted to accomplish all of these goals. To the builders of Shasta Dam (1944), for example, controlling "the temperamental waters of the Sacramento area" meant an opportunity to build an agricultural and industrial empire in the Central Valley of California.[6] As historian Mark Harvey observed, "dams, the traditional dictum went, harnessed 'wild' and 'untamed' rivers and transformed them into calm, docile waterways."[7]

Dams also were great symbols of American achievement. In the 1950s, the American Society of Civil Engineers listed Hoover Dam and Grand Coulee Dam as two of the seven civil engineering wonders of the United States; in 1964, it crowned Glen Canyon Dam as the outstanding engineering triumph of the year.[8] The mighty structures were viewed at once as symbols of the coming of age of the modern West, as the product of American engineering know-how, and as sublime renderings that improved rivers and complemented nature's aesthetic. Power production, in particular, gave dams a great reach well beyond the site of their construction, transforming hinterland into cities. Several conservationists also envisioned dams as "the cornerstone of social policy extending well beyond cheap hydroelectricity." Regional development programs, they believed, would have economic and social benefits, especially for the underprivileged.[9]

Dam builders and a variety of other interests also had pragmatic reasons for extolling the virtues of big dams. Especially in the years of the Great Depression, massive federal construction projects, like dams, meant jobs and long-lasting financial security for farmers tending irrigated lands and for cities in search of stable and plentiful water supplies. The likely maximum number of workers employed at any one time at Hoover Dam was 5,200 workers; more than 7,000 for Grand Coulee; and 10,500 for Fort Peck Dam. Several commentators argued that the electricity generated by big dams showed its worth particularly in World War II and in the Cold War.[10] One set of estimates stated that water development projects in the United States resulted in 26,000 miles of channeled waterways, 58 million acres of irrigated land, 30 million kilowatts of hydroelectricity, and flood control through 400 large dams.[11]

Despite the enthusiasm over dam building from the 1920s to the early 1960s, some people—namely the rural poor, small farmers, Native Americans, Latino communities, and even some farm families of means—failed to enjoy fully the benefits of the new construction. Displacement of people prior to inundation or construction often affected those with little political or economic leverage. Since World War II in particular, several Indian reservations were affected by the construction of federal dams on major rivers. Nine thousand acres of Seneca land were taken along the Allegheny River for the building of the Kinzua Dam (1965). Fort Mohave, Chemehuevi Valley, Colorado River, Yuma, and Gila Bend reservations in Arizona and California lost land to dam projects in the Colorado River Basin. In 1960, 190 Indian families on the Standing Rock Sioux Reservation lost land to proposed flooding for the Oahe Dam (1962) in the Missouri River Basin. Bonneville Dam (1937) displaced the Indian dip-net fishery at the Cascades; the Dalles Dam (1957), also on the Columbia, eliminated the prized fishing site of Celilo Falls. And the list goes on.[12] While not directly affected in the way some Native Americans were, some easterners, nevertheless, resented federal dollars flowing to the West to underwrite the big dam projects, at least until dam building in the East began to accelerate after 1945. In the Midwest, where few deep canyons made giant dams possible or where dams threatened marshlands necessary to sustain bird hunting, the Big Dam Era was not always welcomed. Even in the West, a variety of terrains and economic interests influenced support for these massive public works projects. Some small farmers in the West, for example, who may have looked to the dams and reservoirs as a source of plentiful water, ultimately lost out to corporate farms and big irrigators, and others saw the water directed toward urban development instead of rural preservation.[13]

Early indicators also appeared that raised questions about the physical implications of the big dams before the emergence of the modern environmental movement in the 1960s. As one historian noted, dam building "was conceived within American conservation tradition—the tradition of utilitarianism which stressed efficient control of nature in the public interest."[14] However, some conservation-minded people held reservations about big dam projects. Karl E. Mundt, congressman from South Dakota, noted in 1943 that "dams which are properly designed and wisely built can expand recreational and conservation assets just as certainly as improper and unwise dams can destroy them."[15] Other conservationists questioned dam building for power production and irrigation as a "national mania" or even a "national menace." Field naturalist William Finley argued that "some of these projects destroy existent wealth or endanger some other resource."[16]

The tone and the focus of environmental concern over dam building evolved dramatically in the 1960s. What had been viewed as projects of great economic hope and possibility were now being critiqued more closely in terms of erosion of downstream channels, changes in fish population and riparian vegetation, water evaporation loss, displacement of native peoples, dwindling scenic wonders, and urban sprawl. Even the utilitarian value of dams came into question as dam infrastructure began aging, raising growing concern about performance and safety. Within environmental circles, especially, emphasis shifted from the value of dams to the value of scenic and wild rivers. The realization that the United States was the second most dammed country in the world, and that most major rivers in the lower forty-eight states were regulated by some combination of dams, locks, or diversions, made the preservation of undammed rivers more important.[17]

The account of the environmental implications of big dam building in the United States during the twentieth century is at once a story of the contested use of natural resources and changing perceptions, values, and symbols of human-made structures.

THE ECONOMIC AND SOCIAL IMPACTS OF DAMS

In the 1920s and 1930s, the economic potential of big dams appeared so great that it was difficult to look beyond the expectation of material progress. Hoover Dam was an archetype for such speculation. Constructed between 1931 and 1935 on the Lower Colorado River, the massive arch-gravity dam was not only meant to protect downstream communities from flooding but to stimulate economic growth through the production of hydropower for southern Arizona, Nevada, and Southern California, and to provide bountiful supplies of irrigation water for the Imperial Valley. The cost of construction would be recouped by the generation of electrical power to be produced by sixteen main turbines with a rated capacity of 1,735,000 horsepower. Los Angeles and surrounding communities also would reap the benefits of the dam through the construction of the Colorado River Aqueduct. Water, indeed, was a crucial factor in the rapid growth of the city, which was transformed from a community of 500,000 in 1920 to a major urban center of 2 million in 1952. During the war, electricity generated at Hoover Dam (at the time, still called Boulder Dam) provided power for steel and aluminum mills and for Douglas, Lockheed, and North American aircraft plants that accounted for one-fifth of the nation's aircraft production. In the postwar years, Hoover Dam power helped stimulate the growth of tourism, especially centered in the burgeoning gambling mecca of Las Vegas.[18] As one writer noted in 1936, water was "the miraculous developer . . . of the Southwest."[19]

Water and hydroelectricity were intimately woven with urban growth in general in the twentieth century. In the Big Dam Era, rural life became less attractive as agribusiness came to marginalize small farmers, more power encouraged industrial growth, and metropolitan areas looked ever outward for new sources of water and energy. Between 1920 and 1940, the urban population of the United States increased from 54.2 million to 74.4 million.[20] While metropolitan growth was less uniform in the West than in the old manufacturing belt, for instance, metropolitan population growth as a proportion of the region's population exceeded other U.S. regions by 1960 (64 percent compared to 62.5 percent).[21] Between 1930 and 1970, striking expansion took place in several western and southern cities, in particular. San Diego increased from 94 to 307 square miles; San Jose from 8 to 117; Phoenix from 10 to 247; and Jacksonville from 26 to 827.[22]

In volume, consumption of water by irrigation and industrial purposes greatly exceeded municipal uses. In the West, nondomestic uses of water—particularly irrigation—outstripped all others.[23] But it was the consumption of electrical power where cities—along with industry—dominated the market from the power production of big dams. As historian Carl Abbott stated, "easily transmitted over long distances, hydroelectric power facilitated the industrial growth of cities from Spokane to Los Angeles to Austin."[24]

In the Pacific Northwest, it was believed that Grand Coulee Dam could transform the regional economy. This New Deal project was meant to spearhead a "planned promised land" along the Columbia River. Completed in 1941, Grand Coulee was the centerpiece of an enterprise that resulted in the largest single reclamation project undertaken in the United States. The project was believed to have an intended irrigated area of more than 2.5 million acres and was, for some time, the world's largest hydroelectric power generator. The dam would generate more than 6.18 million kilowatts of electricity, dwarfing even the awe-inspiring production of Hoover Dam and eventually irrigating more than 556,000 acres of land (far less than originally contemplated). It returned more than $4 billion directly through the generation of power and became well known for providing electricity for aircraft manufacturing, the production of magnesium and aluminum, and powering the Hanford atomic installation near Richland, Washington, central to the building of the first atomic bomb toward the end of World War II.[25] Some contemporaries and a later generation of historians and others questioned this unbounded enthusiasm for the economic benefits of dam building and were convinced that too little thought went into long-range regional planning. But euphoria over economic gain wavered very little among those prepared to reap the benefits of increased power production, better navigation, municipal water supply, and irrigated farmlands.[26]

ENVIRONMENTAL THREATS: FLOODING AND SILTING

Environmental implications of dam building were always part of the equation, but the vantage point in the Big Dam Era strayed little from the desire to control nature and manage its resources. Indeed, dam building focused on environmental issues linked directly to resource development or a selective form of preservation. Flood control, for example, rested upon the assumption that rivers needed to be predictable and not threaten the built environment.[27] In constructing Hoover Dam, calculations revealed that previous river discharge had varied from a few thousand to more than 300,000 cubic feet per second, depending on the amount of runoff or the occurrence of floods. In the Lower Colorado River Delta area, protective levees had been constructed along a 150-mile stretch, but half of the headworks and levees had been destroyed by the river. In 1905, the river had breached the levees inundating the Imperial Valley and discharging millions of gallons of water and creating the Salton Sea over a period of 18 months. Reclamation construction engineer Walker R. Young stated in 1937 that "without regulation, the river had little value to the lower basin area."[28] The official history of Hoover Dam noted that Lake Mead "swallows the floods."[29] Few had to be convinced of the benefit.

In the mid-1930s, the orientation of many engineers, and the policy of government agencies responsible for flood-control measures, remained focused on structural solutions to water problems, meaning the building of dams, levees, and floodwalls to curb flooding. Indeed, states, levee boards, cities and counties, railroads, and other groups also built levees and other water control works, making uniform flood-control policy—beyond the building of structures at least—especially difficult. The Boulder Canyon Project Act of 1928 was among the first large multipurpose water projects to include substantial flood control measures. The Flood Control Act of 1936 established flood control for navigable waters and their tributaries as an essentially federal activity.[30] Despite the increased federal authority over flood control and the urgings of some experts, acceptance of floodplain management beyond a simple structural approach was slow in developing.[31] Debates over cost-benefit guidelines only complicated the picture, and, into the 1960s, reliance on structures to prevent flooding dominated policy decisions. Yet, some critics argued, "despite the billions invested in flood control dams, levees, and other works, flood losses had been steadily mounting."[32]

Like flood damage, silting was recognized as an environmental danger to be reckoned with. On the Hoover Dam project, it was estimated that the Colorado River carried annually from 88,000 to 137,000 acre-feet of silt to the delta. Concern centered on obstructing the diversion works and the effects that silt-laden water had upon irrigation, especially the building up of the ground elevation with material of "questionable value." Trapping the silt in the reservoir appeared to be a workable solution, since it was believed that at the rate of buildup it would take many years. E. W. Lane, a consulting engineer with the Bureau of Reclamation and former head of its Hydraulic Lab, and J. R. Ritter, chief of the Hydrology Division, Branch of Project Planning in Denver, noted that, "a number of different people have studied the rate at which Lake Mead will be filled with sediment. They are unanimous on the point that it will have a long, long life."[33]

Unfortunately, an understanding of the broader implications of silting was not well appreciated in the Big Dam Era. Building dams, indeed, trapped silt in reservoirs, reducing the tons of deposits. However, silt contained nutrients essential to the survival of fisheries downstream and in coastal waters. Reducing silt, therefore, had lasting ecological consequences. In a similar sense, focus on the "silt menace" was not matched with an understanding of the potential problems caused by salinity. Reservoirs and other water development structures led to an increase in the salinity of many rivers, especially by the 1950s, due, in part, to highly saline runoff from irrigated land and also to reduced river flows. Increased upstream water diversion also led to seawater intrusion into estuaries and river deltas.[34] Silt "control," like flood "control," was, therefore, a kind of early environmental or nonecological approach to the physical impact of dam building—a commitment to harnessing natural events through human technologies.

DAM FAILURES AND DAM SAFETY

In the Big Dam Era, dam safety was essentially regarded as an engineering issue linked to proper design and construction. Faith in the safety of well-designed dams was not misplaced, especially for major dams. Nonetheless, the potential for disaster or even a near failure rested on several possible factors: the unpredictability of flooding, uncertainties in the geologic setting, seepage through foundations and embankments, defects in design and construction, and liquefaction under earthquake conditions.[35]

Embankment dams (a massive water barrier composed of soil, sand, clay, or rock), especially in comparison with masonry and concrete structures, were a particular concern in the early twentieth century. Into the 1920s, some engineers believed that restrictions on height should be placed on embankment dams in case of overtopping. Deficiencies of hydraulic fills also became an area of concern. Sheffield Dam, near Santa Barbara, a twenty-five-foot-high earthfill structure, failed as a result of an earthquake in June 1925. The dam was seven miles from the epicenter of a 6.3 Richter magnitude quake. The embankment and the foundation were comprised primarily of loose silty sand, and seepage had saturated the foundation and the lower part of the fill, resulting in liquefaction of the foundation during the earthquake. Such events led to increasing interest in using instruments to study the performance of dams. The Engineering Foundation, for example, sponsored experiments on Stevenson Creek Dam (a thin-arch, sixty-foot-high structure) in California. It had been constructed in 1926 especially for testing.[36]

The failure of St. Francis Dam (1926), completed by the Los Angeles Department of Water and Power to the northwest of the city, on March 12, 1928, set off intense efforts to improve dam safety in California, especially with respect to new dam construction. Regarded as one of the worst civil engineering disasters in the twentieth century, the failure of St. Francis Dam resulted in over 400 people dead or missing and $15 million in property damage. The collapse occurred just before midnight. Billions of gallons of water rampaged down the San Francisquito Valley, carrying concrete blocks as large as 10,000 tons downstream for a mile or more. The massive surge destroyed a concrete powerhouse, roared through Saugus, and crashed through a work camp at Kemp and several other communities, before spilling into the Pacific Ocean fifty miles from the damsite.[37] Although not on par with the destruction caused by the Johnstown Flood in Pennsylvania, which resulted in 2,200 deaths, the failure of St. Francis Dam was significant because it was a concrete structure, 205 feet in height, rather than an earthen structure. There had been some workers and ranchers who had said the dam was unsafe, but the chief engineer of the Los Angeles waterworks, William Mulholland of the infamous Owens Valley-Los Angeles water controversy of the 1910s and beyond, had inspected the dam on the very day of the disaster and had not been concerned about some cracks in the concrete and some slight leakage. Mulholland's assessment and his close association with the design and building of the dam shattered his reputation and ended his career. The more than a dozen investigations after the disaster, however, were inconclusive and often conflicting. Most of them agreed, nonetheless, that the design had not been sufficiently reviewed by independent experts and that the foundation of the dam was weak.[38] Beyond the public outcry about the disaster, the dam-building industry was jarred by the failure of a prominent arch-gravity dam. In 1929, California passed a dam safety act that placed all dams within the state, except those owned by the federal government, under supervision of the state engineer. The supervision included design, construction, operation, alteration, and repair.[39] Although other states followed California's lead, their efforts were relatively modest by comparison.

Engineers responded to the safety issue in new dam construction by attempting to improve engineering practices. Beginning in 1929 and continuing into the 1940s, attention was given to developing a theoretical method of slope analysis for embankment dams and to further studying slope stability and compaction of embankments. Additional attention was paid to compaction, moisture control, and liquefaction. Statistical methods were employed to estimate the flood potential of watersheds. H. M. Westergaard published an important paper in 1933 on earthquake effects on dams.[40] Nevertheless, safety problems periodically surfaced in the 1930s and early 1940s, although not on a par with the St. Francis Dam disaster. Seismic activity was discovered at Lake Mead (Nevada and Arizona) in the mid- to late 1930s (the first shocks were felt in September 1936), and after a period of debate, many agreed that there was a connection between the reservoir and the seismic activity.[41]

Despite the increased study of dam safety measures, each case of failure posed some unique problems and often led to a variety of assessments. The safety issue in the Big Dam Era was not used as a rationale for slowing the construction of dams or questioning their value to society. Building new, large dams—while most often incorporating, or at least taking into account, the latest safety research—remained a greater priority than making safety modifications to existing dams.[42]

Despite legal and professional efforts taken to ensure the dams would be built to be safe and secure, dam building in the mid- and late twentieth century remained an art dependent upon the skills and judgments of human beings. This was brought home in a forceful—and tragic—manner on June 5, 1976, when the Bureau of Reclamation's newly completed Teton Dam (1976), in southeastern Idaho, failed during the first filling of the reservoir. Built to provide hydroelectric power and increased irrigation supply for the Upper Snake River Valley around Idaho Falls and Rexburg, Teton Dam was a 305-foot-high, 3,000-foot-long earthfill dam built across the Teton River. The central core-zoned earthfill dam failed and released 80 billion gallons of water that roared downstream in a 20-foot-high wave taking eleven lives, thousands of head of cattle, thousands of buildings, and tons of topsoil. At least 25,000 people were forced from their homes.[43] The failure occurred late on a Saturday morning, and fortunately many downstream residents were successfully warned of the impending disaster. The death toll could clearly have been much higher had the collapse taken place in the late evening or early morning hours.[44] Donald Pisani has argued the failure severely embarrassed the Bureau of Reclamation and signaled that "the boom years were over" for western water development.[45]

In the aftermath of the Teton Dam failure, intensive studies were undertaken to determine the cause. Those studies were hampered by the fact that the rush of water down the canyon washed away geological evidence that would speak to the condition of the foundations and the actual effect of measures taken (for example, the injection of a cement "grout curtain" wall into the cracked and relatively porous rock foundation) to prevent water from seeping through the foundation and to prevent erosion at the interface between the foundation and the earthen structure. After a six-month-long investigation, an independent panel of engineers appointed under the auspices of both the U.S. Department of the Interior and the State of Idaho reported that "because the failed section was carried away by the flood waters, it will probably never be possible to resolve whether the primary cause of leakage in the vicinity of Sta. 14+00 was due to imperfect grouting of the rock . . . or cracking in the key trench-fill, or possibly both." Specifically, the independent panel reported that:

> The fundamental cause of failure may be regarded as a combination of geological factors and design decisions that, taken together, permitted the failure to develop. The principal geologic factors were (1) the numerous open joints [i.e., cracks] in the abutment joints, and (2) the scarcity of more suitable materials for the impervious zone of the dam than the highly erodible and brittle windblown soils. The design decisions included among others (3) complete dependence for seepage

control on a combination of deep key trenches filled with windblown soils and a grout curtain . . . and (4) inadequate provisions for collection and safe discharge of seepage or leakage which inevitably would occur through the foundation rock and cutoff systems. . . . In final summary, under difficult conditions that called for the best judgment and experience of the engineering profession, an unfortunate choice of design measures together with less than conventional precautions was taken to ensure the adequate functioning of the Teton Dam, and these circumstances ultimately led to its failure.[46]

If nothing else, the Teton Dam failure served—and continues to serve—as a compelling reminder that every dam, and every damsite, presents a set of technological problems that must be addressed and solved on an individual basis in order to provide for a safe and enduring water storage structure. The failure also resulted in several acts and a number of federal programs, including at the Bureau of Reclamation, designed to better insure future dam safety.

A FISH STORY—CONFLICTS OVER RESOURCE DEVELOPMENT

Along the Columbia River, in particular, dam building came into direct conflict with fish habitats. Today, one-third of the original Columbia Basin salmon habitat is blocked by dams.[47] Anadromous fish, including Pacific salmon and steelhead trout, must return to their spawning grounds to reproduce and depend on the free flow of rivers to accomplish that goal. The building of Bonneville and Grand Coulee Dams, in particular, intensified the growing debate over the effects of dams on migratory fish and their spawning sites. Contemporary conservationists and several historians have claimed that few people, particularly the dam builders, gave much thought to the plight of the salmon and steelhead and that high dams virtually eliminated them from much of the Columbia and other rivers. While there is little doubt that the new high dams caused great loss to the fish population, the story is somewhat more complex.

The growing debate over dams impeding the migration of fish was not so much couched in environmental terms in the Big Dam Era but in terms of competing resources. As an economic resource, rather than as an essential component of the riverine ecology of the Columbia River and other rivers, anadromous fish gained significance in the eyes of the federal dam builders of the era.[48] In addition, dams were only one cause, albeit a major cause, of declining fish populations along the Columbia and other rivers. On this latter point, several forms of resource exploitation—mining, cattle grazing, lumbering—created water pollution problems on the Columbia and Snake Rivers because of runoff, which adversely affected fish stocks. Irrigated agriculture increased demand for water and killed salmon with its diversion dams and unscreened ditches. Small dams, going back to the late nineteenth century, also were destructive to fish populations. By the 1930s, vast areas of spawning grounds had already disappeared, and catches had declined dramatically through intensive commercial harvesting and canning operations. Efforts at conservation had been meek at best.[49]

The multipurpose dams, without a doubt, raised the stakes for anadromous fish in the Pacific Northwest and elsewhere. Fear of the eradication of salmon and other migratory fish became a galvanizing issue in the early fight for fish and wildlife conservation. Nascent conservation groups, such as the Izaak Walton League (founded in 1922) and later the National Wildlife Federation (formed in 1936), battled for the protection of aquatic habitats throughout the country. In 1934, the Fish and Wildlife Coordination Act required the builders of federal or federally licensed dams to consult with the Fish and Wildlife Service to prevent loss or damage to wildlife resources. This was the first law intended to protect wildlife in water projects.[50]

Along the Columbia River, the most concern focused on the fate of the salmon; the issue was especially the survival of a vital industry and a fragile resource. Those directly benefitting from the survival of the salmon—sportsmen, canners, Native Americans—loudly objected to the potential effects of the high dams on fish migration. And conservationists chimed in to support those interests. In 1938, an article in *Nature Magazine* made the following claims, not entirely accurate, on the heels of the construction of Bonneville Dam: "The sad part of projects of this sort [dams and inland waterway and irrigation projects on the Columbia, Willamette, and Snake Rivers] is that the surveys upon which they are based are concerned only with the feasibility of the construction. Little or no attention is paid to what resources may be destroyed in the process.... On the destruction side, the Columbia and Willamette dams mean the eventual destruction of the salmon industry.... [The industry] supports thousands of families and keeps them off the relief rolls."[51] The development of fishways at Bonneville, designed to allow the fish to migrate around the dam, was viewed by many as a workable solution to the problem, but it, nonetheless, led to some controversy. While the U.S. Army Corps of Engineers recognized the need for passages to protect anadromous fish well before Bonneville's construction, the rush to begin the work to provide unemployment relief resulted in a lag in refining details of a fish-passage plan.[52] In the end, Bonneville included three concrete fish ladders and two sets of fish lifts.

Some were impressed with the success of these measures. A study in

1951 proclaimed that "perhaps the most amazing feature to the tourist is not Bonneville's powerhouse or even its giant lock, but the amazing fish ladders."[53] Others were cautiously optimistic that the ladders and locks would have some benefit to the now struggling fisheries industry.[54] Still others were dubious, arguing either that the cost per fish was too high to merit success or the innovative technology failed to deliver on its promise. Assistant Chief of Engineers Thomas Robins (North Pacific Division engineer in the 1930s, when Bonneville was being constructed), among others, defended the corps against charges that juvenile fish mortality in dam turbines was high and thus threatened the salmon population. More problems arose, he argued, when juvenile fish were flushed down spillways, where they encountered water saturated with nitrogen gas that could cause gas bubble disease.[55] While more intensive study continued on fish ladders and locks, juvenile fish and turbines, and other threats to anadromous fish, uncertainty remained as to the effectiveness of the plan at Bonneville to protect the salmon and the fisheries industry and still to produce hydroelectric power.[56]

Grand Coulee Dam posed a related, but different, problem for the salmon and the fisheries industry. The Bureau of Reclamation, which had taken charge of the dam project in 1933, faced the same sort of scrutiny over its fish policy as had the corps at Bonneville. Critics claimed that the Bureau of Reclamation cared little about salmon if there was a choice to be made between fish and other economic contributions of the project. However, the Bureau of Reclamation initially recommended the development of a flume and a mechanical elevator to carry fish around the dam. The plan proved unsatisfactory because Grand Coulee would be too high. Alternatives were considered but without resolution. Temporary fish ladders were authorized during the early construction of the dam, but finally, in 1939, an emergency plan for capturing chinook and blueback salmon was announced. In May, fish traps at Rock Island began operating and the first trucks carrying salmon motored around the damsite. Focus turned to hatcheries, and in August 1941, 50,000 chinook salmon raised at a hatchery in Leavenworth were released into the Entiat River. Although the Bureau of Reclamation announced that the salmon transplant experiment was a success, many remained skeptical.[57]

The dams on the Columbia River had caused significant ecological changes, such as increasing the temperature of the water, and had, at the very least, accelerated the decline of the salmon runs. At Grand Coulee, which now sealed off the Upper Columbia to salmon, a makeshift solution to preserving the fish and the fisheries had replaced the natural migration with questionable results. The diversion of salmon to other locations may have preserved some salmon, but above the dam the species could not survive as before.[58]

THE ECHO PARK CONTROVERSY

Until some years after World War II, concern about the environmental implications of dams had focused largely on site-specific issues: flooding and silting; dam failures as opposed to general attention to dam safety; and salmon
on the Columbia and Snake Rivers. Questioning the inherent value of dams
and their impact on the environment rarely entered the discourse. The Echo
Park controversy changed this. It helped move along a process that inevitably
resulted in fracturing a rather uneasy consensus on the conservation value of
dams, polarizing the sides, and increasingly casting the U.S. Army Corps of
Engineers and the Bureau of Reclamation as antienvironmental. The controversy also saw the coming of age of several environmental organizations and
suggested that the public could become involved in environmental issues as
never before.

At the heart of the Echo Park controversy was the effort to save national
parks and national monuments from inundation and resource exploitation.
Echo Park became the biggest battle over wilderness preservation since the
one in Valley, California, in Hetch Hetchy in the 1920s. By the 1950s, the old
conservation movement was maturing, broadening its perspective to embrace a range of issues, including wilderness preservation, wildlife habitat
protection, outdoor recreation, a burgeoning interest in pollution, and the
perpetuation of national parks and monuments. The Izaak Walton League
was the largest and most politically active group. The National Wildlife Federation was linked closely with hunters and fishermen. The Audubon Society broadened its scope to embrace wildlife conservation in general, and the
Wilderness Society, which had begun in the East, became known for its advocacy of wilderness protection in the West. The Sierra Club, along with the
Wilderness Society, was beginning to develop a reputation as an outspoken
critic of government dam builders, among others, and to expand its interests
well beyond its California roots.[59]

Big dams became the harbinger of a threatened public landscape. At first,
a dam at Echo Park—located at the point where the Yampa River joins the
Green River along the border of Utah and Colorado—was just another proposed project for the Bureau of Reclamation. It was part of the Colorado
River Storage Project initiated in the 1940s to make additional water available for rural and urban residents in four states—Wyoming, Colorado, New
Mexico, and Utah—in the Upper Colorado River Basin. It also was part of a
major "participating project," the Central Utah Project. The construction of
the dam, however, would inundate Echo Park, a scenic valley upstream from
the proposed dam, and miles of nearby Lodore and Yampa Canyons, all of
which lie within Dinosaur National Monument. In 1915, President Wood-

row Wilson had designated 80 acres of the area, where dinosaur bones had been discovered, as a national monument. In 1938, President Franklin Roosevelt expanded the site to 210,000 acres.[60]

The Green River, a major tributary of the Colorado, narrowed as it passed through the cliffs at the core of Dinosaur National Monument, immediately below Echo Park, and offered an attractive damsite for generating hydroelectric power for the surrounding states. Since the national monument was located in a remote spot on the Colorado Plateau and had seen few visitors, the dam builders saw no reason why the National Park Service (NPS), which had jurisdiction over Echo Park, would object to the proposed construction. During World War II, before the Bureau of Reclamation made a formal claim to the site, the NPS displayed no strong reaction to the idea. However, the issue became a jurisdictional and a political matter after the war. The Bureau of Reclamation had enthusiastic support for the dam from the Upper Basin states of New Mexico, Colorado, Utah, and Wyoming, but the NPS refused to support it. Secretary of the Interior Oscar Chapman now had to mediate the dispute, and if he agreed with the Bureau of Reclamation, legislation could be written incorporating the new dam and then sent off to Congress for its approval. After public hearings in April 1950, Chapman was persuaded that the proposal had merit and approved the building of Echo Park Dam.[61]

The decision to build Echo Park Dam produced energetic opponents, none more vocal and committed than preservationist groups. It is not a cliche to suggest that the controversy exposed a clash of environmental values, resulting in the galvanizing of a preservationist coalition that would continue to question the river management policies of the Bureau of Reclamation and the U.S. Army Corps of Engineers. Echo Park Dam would not violate the Bureau of Reclamation's commitment to resource conservationism. To the contrary, the new dam would help to tame an unruly river and to maximize the use of riverine resources in the region. Preservationists were particularly concerned that building the dam would not only destroy a unique wilderness area but would set a terrible precedent for exploiting resources in America's national parks and monuments. They had reason to be alarmed because between 1945 and 1950, Olympic National Park, Grand Canyon National Park, Glacier National Park, Jackson Hole National Monument, Superior National Forest, and the Adirondack Forest Preserve had been threatened by various economic interests. But at Echo Park, a federal bureau was making plans to "invade" a national monument.[62] Ulysses S. Grant III, a former general officer with the U.S. Army Corps of Engineers and president of the American Planning and Civic Association, chided the Bureau of Reclamation for the decision to build the Echo Park Dam and Split Mountain Reservoir: "The Trojan Horse in our national park system, model

1950, is now driven by electricity supplied from water power impounded behind great dams."[63] Bernard DeVoto, then a writer for *Harper's Magazine*, wrote an exposé in the July 22, 1950, issue of the *Saturday Evening Post* about the decision to build the Echo Park Dam. The headline asked, "Shall We Let Them Ruin Our National Parks?" DeVoto served on the secretary of the interior's advisory board and was privy to a debate over the building of the dam between the Bureau of Reclamation Commissioner Michael Straus and Park Service Director Newton Drury. Since Drury could not take his feelings public, DeVoto decided to air the issue and also attacked the Bureau of Reclamation and the corps for their proposals to put dams in national parks.[64] The article and the decision to go ahead with the dam mobilized wilderness advocates. Eventually, the leaders of thirty-two opposition organizations created a lobbying group, the Citizens Committee on Natural Resources, to take the battle to Washington.[65]

Political allies "proved vitally necessary" to the campaign to save Echo Park because neither the modern regulatory apparatus for environmental protection nor access to a wide array of media outlets were available to wilderness advocates during the mid-twentieth century. Allies would have to be courted in eastern, midwestern, and southern states, where skepticism was high about the viability of hydropower to pay for multipurpose projects. In addition, concerns were deep about adding more acreage to the agricultural economy. On another front, California might be counted on for opposition to the dam because of its claims on Colorado River water. Other potential allies, but equally strange bedfellows, were fiscal conservatives opposed to federal public works and private utility companies fearing public power. In Congress, the strongest opposition to Echo Park came from the House of Representatives.[66]

For much of the first half of the 1950s, the future of the Echo Park Project was uncertain as government officials vacillated amid a blizzard of reports. Opponents stepped up their protests, and lawmakers squabbled. Bending to pressure, Secretary of the Interior Chapman reversed his previous pronouncement and established a task force in November 1951 to explore alternative sites to Echo Park. When he left office in January 1953, newly appointed Secretary of the Interior Douglas McKay would have to decide where the Dwight Eisenhower administration would stand on the issue. McKay did not favor withholding natural resources from economic development, even if they were in national parks and monuments. However, before taking a position on the specific proposal of Echo Park, he dispatched Undersecretary of the Interior Ralph Tudor (a former U.S. Army Corps of Engineers officer) to the Dinosaur National Monument site to reevaluate the Bureau of Reclamation's calculations about the rates of evaporation at the proposed reservoir.[67] Such figures were vital to determine the ability of a damsite to store a maximum amount of water at a reasonable cost. Tudor reported that the Echo Park site was vastly better than alternatives. Based on the findings, McKay approved Echo Park Dam as part of the Colorado River Storage Project in December 1953.[68]

Congress took up the authorization of the project, with the inclusion of Echo Park Dam, in 1954, and with bipartisan support the chances for passage seemed good. However, protests of the proposed legislation elevated the issue to national status, and the intensity of the debate that started several years before had not been quelled. Fred M. Packard, executive secretary of the National Parks Association, a leading conservationist group, strongly asserted that "the issue is clear-cut, in spite of the fog of technical data and irrelevant side issues that have confused its comprehension by Congress and the public."[69] Probably the most devastating critique came from Sierra Club Executive Director David Brower, who challenged the Bureau of Reclamation's evaporation figures. Using rather elementary math and a few charts, he proved to a congressional subcommittee that Echo Park was not likely to save as much water as supporters argued. Also other evidence was surfacing that the Colorado River Storage Project was more of a power-generation project than a water storage project as argued by the Bureau of Reclamation. In this context, power anticipated from Echo Park would be expensive, making the site even less economically desirable.

All this, plus aesthetic arguments about the inundation of a national monument, worked against support for Echo Park in Congress. The final straw, however, may have been the threat by the wilderness groups that they would fight the project as a whole if Echo Park was not removed from the proposed legislation. An open letter to the "Strategy Committee" of the Colorado River Storage Project, written by the Council of Conservationists, stated: "We want you to know that we will fight with every honest device at our command if the Upper Colorado bill continues to include, or require— now or at some later date—a dam at Echo Park, or elsewhere in a national park or monument." What had been a loose-knit group of local and regional conservation groups had acquired a loud, national voice. On April 11, 1956, President Dwight Eisenhower signed Public Law 485, authorizing the Colorado River Storage Project—without Echo Park Dam.[70]

The conventional wisdom has it that the price the preservationists paid for saving Echo Park was a concession on the Glen Canyon Dam, which would substitute for it in the project. From the start, however, Echo Park Dam and Glen Canyon Dam had been interconnected in the Bureau of Reclamation's plans to develop the Colorado. In addition, the aesthetics of Glen Canyon were not well known in the 1950s, and after all, opponents of the

Echo Park Dam clearly focused on saving Dinosaur National Monument from intrusion. In the debate over evaporation, Brower had made the strong case against a high dam at Echo Park, believing a high dam at Glen Canyon—a site barely within the Upper Colorado River Basin—was one more argument against building a dam at Echo Park and a low dam at Glen Canyon because the Upper Basin states wanted a site "safely within their territory" to protect their water rights. A dam at Glen Canyon would likely supply power downstream to Arizona and California rather than in the Upper Basin, but with the addition of the Echo Park Dam, California would not be viewed as singularly benefiting from the project. In Congress, the Bureau of Reclamation could make that case and likely garner broader support for the overall project.[71]

The Bureau of Reclamation did not get all it wanted in Congress, but neither did the wilderness advocates. Although the Echo Park case was a major victory for national park and monument preservation and a galvanizing event in the burgeoning modern environmental movement, regrets remained over Glen Canyon. Storage produced by the dam sometimes intruded into the Rainbow Bridge National Monument. A new round of litigation and debate followed, caustic enough to create major tensions within the environmental community over what compromise may have been struck in 1956 and the potential loss of scenic lands.[72] David Brower certainly had regrets, believing that he was partly responsible for the "death" of Glen Canyon.[73] There were to be no clear victories for either side.

DAMS AND THE MODERN ENVIRONMENTAL MOVEMENT

As the Big Dam Era was coming to an end in the 1960s, controversy surrounding dam building took a decidedly different tone. The substantive issues around which debate had occurred prior to that time largely remained the same—flooding, silting, and salinity; dam safety; dam siting and displacement of people and threats to natural environments. But the context was different. Wallace Stegner noted in 1965 that, "water, once paramount, has become secondary. The questionable dams are never simple water holes. What dictates the damsite is as often as not the power head: efficient generation of power calls for a higher dam, and hence a bigger lake, than a simple waterhole does."[74]

Redefining "risk" in an increasingly sophisticated and complex environmental era meant greater challenges to building and utilizing dams, not simply criticisms of specific dams. The act of dam building was increasingly coming into question, with trade-offs that were much more general in perception than the displacement of a special group of people or the inundation of a particular valley. Dam building was being questioned for threatening wild rivers and endangered species, for overbuilding structures at the expense of natural sites, and for placing too much emphasis on unrelenting economic growth. In addition, as some historians have noted, "beginning in the 1960s, an increasingly urbanized, educated society focused more on recreation, environmental preservation, and water quality than on irrigation, navigation, or flood control."[75]

In this setting, the Bureau of Reclamation and the U.S. Army Corps of Engineers were increasingly scrutinized. Beginning in the late 1960s, it became more common to question their organization, their mission, and their cost-benefit ratios. Elizabeth B. Drew, in a 1970 issue of the *Atlantic*, expressed the opinion that the corps was unwilling to change with the times, and she quoted its chief, Lieutenant General F. J. Clarke, as saying, "with our country growing the way it is, we cannot simply sit back and let nature take its course." She added that despite the rigidity of corps policy, few politicians were willing to criticize the corps publicly because "almost all of them want something from it at some point—a dam, a harbor, a flood-control project." A *Nation* article in 1966 branded the corps as "the pork-barrel soldiers" with antienvironmental aims.[76] How would dam builders respond to new challenges in an era when dams and reservoirs were no longer praised unreservedly for harnessing untamed rivers?

What made the modern environmental movement so remarkable was the speed with which it gained national attention in the late 1960s. Nothing epitomized that appeal better than Earth Day. The idea began as a "teach-in" based on the model of an anti-Vietnam War tactic. In *Earth Day—The Beginning*, the staff of Environmental Action (formerly Environmental Teach-In, Inc.) declared that "on April 22, [1970] a generation dedicated itself to reclaiming the planet. A new kind of movement was born—a bizarre alliance that spans the ideological spectrum from campus militants to middle Americans. Its aim: to reverse our rush toward extinction."

Across the country, on 2,000 college campuses, in 10,000 high schools, and in parks and various open areas, as many as 20 million people celebrated what was purportedly "the largest, cleanest, most peaceful demonstration in America's history." In form, Earth Day was so much like a 1960s-style peace demonstration that the Daughters of the American Revolution insisted that it must be subversive. In fact, however, it was pitched at moderate activists, somewhere between the New Left and the older conservationist groups, such as the Sierra Club and the Audubon Society. As a symbol of the new enthusiasm for environmental matters and as a public recognition of a trend already well underway, Earth Day served its purpose.[77]

The Richard Nixon administration gave its blessings to Earth Day. In his first State of the Union address, the president declared, "clean air, clean water, open spaces—these should be the birthright of every American." On January 1, 1970, four months earlier, Nixon signed the National Environmental Policy Act (NEPA) of 1969. While opposing the bill until it cleared the congressional conferees, the administration ultimately embraced it as its own. By identifying administration with environmentalism, Nixon wanted to address the issue on his own terms. Many people trumpeted their approval of the president's gesture; others reserved judgment or remained cynical.[78]

The NEPA was far from "the Magna Carta of environmental protection" that some people proclaimed, but it nonetheless called for federal bureaus and agencies to consider environmental effects, and ways of reducing those effects, before funding, approving, or carrying out projects. The NEPA did not mandate particular results, but it did arguably promote efforts to preserve and enhance the environment. It particularly emphasized the application of science, disclosure, and public participation in the decision-making process and in the search for solutions. With respect to integrated river basin management, the NEPA encouraged the Bureau of Reclamation and the U.S. Army Corps of Engineers to give more attention to environmental considerations and also gave environmental agencies more say in the process.[79]

The NEPA, in addition, required federal agencies to prepare environmental impact statements (EISs) for those projects that would significantly impact the environment. These provisions, for instance, stipulated that early public notifications should be given that an EIS was being prepared and that citizen comments should be part of the final statement. An EIS could lead to decisions to place limits on construction and could result in the resiting of structures. The new law gave opponents of dams a tool to slow down or impede construction.[80] According to one source, by the mid-1970s seven corps projects were halted as the result of environmentalist litigation. Of the remaining sixty-one environmental suits being litigated, twenty-seven involved alleged violations of the NEPA.[81]

The NEPA provided substantial opportunity for citizen participation, especially through the review of EISs and other environmental documents. It established the Council on Environmental Quality (CEQ) to review government agencies pertaining to the environment, to develop impact statement guidelines, and to advise the president on environmental matters.[82] The CEQ was essentially a presidential instrument, and governmental environmental programs remained widely dispersed. In early 1970, the CEQ recommended the establishment of a Department of Natural Resources and the Environment to centralize several departments and bureaus into one agency, but the departments of the Interior, Agriculture, and Commerce resisted such a consolidation of programs.

In June it was announced that pollution control programs and the evaluation of impact statements would be the responsibility of a new body—the Environmental Protection Agency (EPA), which began operations in December 1970 under the direction of William Ruckelshaus. Initially, it included divisions of water pollution, air pollution, pesticides, solid waste, and radiation. Other natural resource and environmental programs remained in other agencies, especially the Departments of Commerce and the Interior. More significantly, the EPA did not have single overall statutory authority for environmental protection; it simply administered a series of specific statutes directed at particular environmental problems.[83]

Despite some of the tentative steps of the NEPA and limits in the EPA's authority, national environmental policy was undergoing a substantial change in the 1970s. As early as the late 1940s and 1950s, social scientists and others already had begun to attack government agencies and their conservation programs. They found them self-serving and denied that governmental experts had special knowledge of what constituted "the public interest." The practice of delegating discretionary authority to administrative elites in the Progressive Era was questioned severely. In its place, calls came for greater political accountability among government bureaucrats, more congressional control, public access through the courts, and the opening of the decision-making process to any affected interest.[84]

By the mid-1970s, environmentalism was a solidly fixed national movement. Mainstream environmental groups responded by taking greater initiative in helping to draft new legislation, pressing for the implementation of existing legislation, focusing on the environmental impact review process, and monitoring government agencies. Demand rose to strengthen conservation laws for managing resources and to step up efforts in nature protection. Criticism rose against the traditional government role of promoting economic growth at the expense of resource depletion. In addition, the courts became an important battleground as more litigation tested key regulatory provisions. Inevitably, such extensive changes in environmental policy making brought about significant changes in the relationship between the environmental community and agencies like the U.S. Army Corps of Engineers and the Bureau of Reclamation.[85]

Not surprisingly, the Bureau of Reclamation and the U.S. Army Corps of Engineers balked at the rising environmental criticism of their efforts in the 1960s and 1970s, often resisting the conclusion that the context in which water and dam projects found themselves had changed. Justifying new dams on the grounds of economic growth, traditional flood-control concepts, recreational opportunities, and so forth had much less resonance in an era when charges of pork-barrel projects and environmental degradation of natural landscapes were increasingly heard not only from environmental interest groups but by a public increasingly suspicious of federal programs of any kind. Supporters of the the Bureau of Reclamation and the corps, however, claimed that the agencies made real efforts to adjust and to change in the face of intensifying criticism. For example, researchers Daniel Mazinanian and Mordecai Lee asked the following question of the corps: "Can Bureaucracies Change?" Their conclusion was that they can. Their assessment was that the corps was aware of its "lack of capacity" to confront broad ecological questions as early as the mid-1960s. In response, it established an Environmental Resources Branch within the Planning Division in 1966.[86]

In April 1970, the chief of engineers established the Environmental Advisory Board (EAB) to examine policies and programs, to identify problems, and to recommend changes. The board was unique in the sense that it was not established as an in-house body, but it was composed of members of environmental groups, albeit relatively moderate groups, outside the U.S. Army Corps of Engineers. Among the EAB's activities was recommending the establishment of the Environmental Reconnaissance Inventory, a comprehensive resource inventory initially implemented in four locations in the mid-1970s.[87] The board concept certainly had limits, however. Not surprisingly, consensus on issues was not easy to reach as the EAB periodically found itself divided on policy. Also, attention to pressing immediate issues, such as lawsuits or congressional deadlines, impeded effort at long-range planning.[88] The relationship between the corps and the environmental community remained cautious and often adversarial in the 1970s despite the internal changes in the bureau. Environmentalists often discovered that projects stopped by court injunctions were ultimately under construction after revised EIS reports were prepared. As historian Jeffrey Stine has observed, in the 1970s, "the Corps . . . regarded the environmental legislation as a mandate not to stop building, but to build in the best possible way."[89] Like the corps, the Bureau of Reclamation had work held up by environmental protests and lost some political support in Congress, but it managed to continue developing some important projects in the 1970s.[90] Neither agency, however, rose to the heights of the Big Dam Era.

FLOOD CONTROL AND NONSTRUCTURAL ALTERNATIVES

As much as the environmental context had changed beginning in the mid-1960s, and as much as the Bureau of Reclamation and the U.S. Army Corps of Engineers seemed willing to, or were forced to, bend to changing national environmental policy, divisive issues over the impact of dams remained. Familiar issues, however, were colored and flavored by growing resistance to the value of big dams promoted by an array of critics. The corps continued to argue in favor of flood-control projects as beneficial to local communities.

But increasing pressure was being exerted on the corps to consider nonstructural alternatives to dams and levees as flood-control devices. Suggestions were made for the development of detention ponds for floodwaters or for expanding green belts along floodplain lands near streams. Section 209 of the Flood Control Act of 1970 promoted "multiobjective planning," a form of planning that recognized noneconomic values such as environmental quality along with economic interests.[91]

WATER QUALITY AND OTHER ENVIRONMENTAL IMPACTS

A substantial context for change in dealing with repercussions of dam building focused on water quality and related issues in the new environmental era. Sentiment grew that dams were "the least reversible form of river alteration" and resulted in deleterious physical changes in the nation's river basins.[92] Whereas issues of silting and salinity received at best modest attention before the mid-1960s, a variety of more direct questions arose after that time about the quality of water resulting from dam and reservoir construction, the buildup of silt behind reservoirs, and the residual impacts of intense irrigation. As Donald Pisani noted, "environmentalists saw clear limits to economic growth and worried about such problems as siltation, alkali buildup, and the poisoning of groundwater with herbicides and pesticides."[93]

By their very nature, dams and reservoirs changed the riverine ecology.[94] Certainly, reservoirs can improve water quality for many users, and dams of different design and operation can produce different effects downstream. "The ability of large dams to compensate for the unpredictability" of nature, one study noted, "is what makes them so attractive."[95] However, changes occur from a free-flowing environment to a standing or lake environment, drowning a variety of native flora and fauna, ruining forests, altering or destroying riparian vegetation and habitat, encouraging evaporation that concentrates salts, and sometimes creating mud flats. Water released from dams is likely to be low in oxygen, thus threatening river life. In deep reservoirs, the water column can stratify by temperature. Little oxygen or light can reach the lower strata, and the upper stratum becomes warmer. This change can create a forbidding environment for cold water fish and can allow for the habitat to be taken over by other species. Dams can alter water temperature in other ways as well. At Glen Canyon Dam, for example, water released into the Colorado River is approximately twenty degrees colder than would be natural, which destroys many native organisms. Much of the river cannot produce algae, which in turn disrupts the food chain.[96] On the other hand, such situations sometimes result in flourishing trophy cold water fisheries.

While having constant, predictable in-stream flows has been valuable for irrigators and other water users, artificially regulated flows produce a number of problems. Native river animals and plants have a difficult time adjusting to constant flows and constant temperatures when the natural rhythms of rivers are altered. Without high flows, silt does not get flushed from the streambed gravel, harming many species of fish and insects that depend on clean, oxygenated gravel for their eggs and larvae. Artificially and naturally low flows can cause back channels and sloughs to dry up, thus destroying primary spawning areas for trout. In 1987, a low flow from Palisades Dam (1957) on the Snake River killed approximately 600,000 cutthroat and brown trout, mostly juveniles, along with much of the aquatic food chain.[97] In spite of this problem the Snake River does support a blue ribbon trout fishery in the area.

Intensive irrigation has led to serious salinity problems in many agricultural regions. As Donald Worster stated, "what nature has taken geological eons to achieve, the leaching of salts from the root zone of plants, the irrigator under takes to do in a matter of decades." Intensive irrigation can lead to a rising water table, bringing dissolved salts to the root zone or to the surface. Growers in the Imperial Valley in Southern California faced this daunting prospect, and by the early 1970s spent more than $66 million on the drains and canal linings to capture saline runoff and to discharge it elsewhere. They also faced shifting to salt-tolerant crops, even though they yielded less income. An alternative was to consume more water, if possible, to flush the salt deposits.[98]

The salinity issue took on international proportions in the Colorado River Basin. In 1944, a treaty had guaranteed Mexico 1.5 million acre-feet, but the agreement did not address water quality. Over time, Mexico was receiving heavy saline drainage from irrigated fields in the United States. In 1961, the Wellton-Mohawk Irrigation District, along the Lower Gila River in Arizona, discharged drainage water rich in salt into the Colorado River, immediately above Mexico's diversion canal, and essentially doubled the average annual salinity of the flow across the border. The United States denied that its treaty included any obligation on water quality issues, but fresher water was released from American dams and a channel was built to divert the drainage around the Mexican intake in 1965. This proved to be a temporary solution, and finally, in 1973, both countries signed an agreement to settle the dispute. Realizing that similar disagreements could break out again, Congress passed the Colorado River Basin Salinity Control Act in 1974. All along the Colorado River, use and reuse of the water diminished the flow and contributed to degradation of the quality of water not only as it crossed the border into Mexico but also in the Imperial Valley and the Metropolitan Water District of Southern California.[99]

The environmental repercussions of dam building are complex and not easily resolved—some have argued they are irreversible. One solution was to cease building dams on the remaining free-flowing rivers in the country. River preservation was given a boost by the Wild and Scenic Rivers Act of 1968. While not giving natural features legal standing per se, it provided an alternative to resource development by protecting the shorelines of designated rivers from federally permitted development. The act was an important sign that the perception of rivers as a commodity in the traditional sense was changing. Yet by the 1990s, the mileage preserved in the system was less than one percent of the nation's natural river courses.[100]

DECAYING DAMS—THE IMPENDING CRISIS IN DAM SAFETY

In the years since the mid-1960s, concern about the safety of specific dams turned into uneasy anxiety about the safety of all existing dams. Those built since midcentury, especially federal dams, had a good safety record overall, but there was an increasing likelihood of potential disasters. Some had uncorrected safety problems that had been detected but not addressed. In addition, of the 49,422 large dams (twenty-five feet or more in height and impounding more than 16.3 million gallons), 39,000 dams had never been inspected by state or federal engineers. The largest percentage of these dams were nonfederal structures, where the regulatory gap was the greatest. Before the mid-1970s indicators of bigger problems could be found in deterioration and corrective actions required at dams. For instance, in 1965, Lahontan Dam (1915), a Bureau of Reclamation dam in western Nevada, was found to have crumbling concrete in its spillways. While this was a serious problem that did not alone threaten the safety of Lahontan Dam, it took twelve years for the Bureau of Reclamation to work with the local irrigation district that managed the dam to produce a formal proposal to rectify it. Navajo Dam, a Bureau of Reclamation structure in northwestern New Mexico, was completed in 1963 and was found to leak as much as 1.8 million gallons per day by 1977. Even though all dams leak, this was considered to be excessive and dangerous and required corrective action. Canyon Lake Dam in Rapid City, South Dakota, failed in June 1972; Walter Bouldin Dam, an Alabama earth-fill structure, failed by erosion in February 1975; Bear Wallow Lake Dam, an embankment dam in North Carolina, failed in February 1976. A small and antiquated earthen dam at Toccoa, Georgia, regarded as a serious hazard, failed in 1977, overwhelming Toccoa Falls Bible Institute and taking thirty-nine lives. And there were others.[101]

These dam failures, accentuated by the failure of Teton Dam, even more so than the St. Francis Dam disaster of 1928, were a wake-up call about the deteriorating condition of dam inventories as well as the safety of dams due to design and construction flaws. Dam safety engineering had led to improved approaches to embankment dam analysis in the 1960s, studies of embankment liquefaction (after the San Fernando earthquake in 1971), and to the National Dam Inspection Act in 1972.[102] After the Teton Dam disaster, federal agencies reviewed safety practices and established an interagency committee to coordinate dam safety programs, which evolved into the Interagency Committee on Dam Safety. It issued management guidelines for planning, design, construction, operation, and regulation of dams in the United States. The U.S. Army Corps of Engineers began seismic investigations and established the Dam Safety Assurance Program in 1977. In 1978, the Bureau of Reclamation began its Safety Evaluation of Existing Dams Program, independent of other offices in the Bureau of Reclamation, to determine if it needed to move into a modification program to make a dam safe. The National Dam Inspection Program developed an inventory of about 76,000 dams, classified according to the potential for loss of life and property. Between December 1977 and October 1981, approximately 8,800 "high hazard" dams were inspected and specific actions were recommended, ranging from additional inspections to emergency repairs. Subsequent inspections, investigations, and remedial work became the responsibility of the owners of the dam.[103] In 1979, the government published *Federal Guidelines for Dam Safety* to encourage high standards among federal agencies. A presidential executive order in July 1979 placed responsibility for coordinating dam safety in the Federal Emergency Management Agency.[104]

With the end of the Big Dam Era, dam safety was not so much a queson of carefully monitoring new construction as it was being vigilant about the deterioration of a large and an increasingly aging inventory of dams and reservoirs. While the U.S. Army Corps of Engineers and the Bureau of Reclamation moved to shore up safety programs for federal dams, they did not have jurisdiction over the thousands of nonfederal dams throughout the country. A related question, which extended beyond specific considerations of safety, was: what is the useful life of these dams? This was both an engineering and an environmental issue.

TWO FISH STORIES—PACIFIC NORTHWEST SALMON AND THE TELLICO SNAIL DARTER

In the wake of the big dam development along the Columbia and Snake Rivers, the U.S. Army Corps of Engineers invested more than $60 million in fisheries research in an effort to have salmon and steelhead populations coexist with the multipurpose projects. In 1955, the large Fisheries-Engineering Research Laboratory was constructed at Bonneville, further committing the corps to addressing the issue of adult fish passage beyond the dams. Research efforts also went into studying degradation of habitats and fish diseases, such as gas bubble disease, which had become a serious problem after the corps completed the dams on the Lower Snake River in the 1960s and 1970s. One estimate suggested that gas supersaturation killed 70 percent of the fish migrating downstream in the Lower Snake. By 1971, the corps organized the Nitrogen Task Force to confront the problem.[105]

Criticism of both the corps' dams and its research continued. While the corps' research in the 1950s focused on adult fish populations, issues involving juvenile fish were often neglected. For example, dams continued to be built without much information about their impact on young salmon. By the late 1960s, the corps was involved in cooperative studies with the National Marine Fisheries Service and state fisheries to improve bypasses for juvenile fish, and, in the 1970s, it developed a new transportation program for juvenile passage. Critics believed these efforts at barging and trucking fish were ineffective and too manipulative of natural migrations. These complaints and accusations were superimposed over rivalries between Native American and commercial fishermen concerning the taking of fish, disagreements with fisheries agencies over the best methods of protecting salmon and steelhead, and resistance from those who opposed the building of additional dams.

Dealing with a new generation of environmentalists proved particularly vexing for the U.S. Army Corps of Engineers. Its response to criticisms of conservationists in the wake of Bonneville had been to help preserve a precious natural resource—anadromous fish—while developing other benefits, such as water for irrigation, hydropower, and flood control. The subsequent research programs that the corps fostered or participated in were largely to meet that end. Now criticisms were being raised about keeping anadromous fish in their natural habitat—a concern shared by Native American groups—so as not to create "aquarium fish" or "token zoo runs." There were objections to building any additional dams because they could threaten fish habitats at a time when runs were disappearing from many rivers. In addition, a change in tone in the modern environmental era respecting "the water rights of fish" seemed to have changed the context of the debate.[106]

The substantial change in the environmental regulatory apparatus in the 1970s transformed fish from the victims of dam building into a weapon to fight dam construction. The Tellico Dam controversy is the most notable example. The Tellico Project, on the Little Tennessee River south of Knoxville, was originally suggested in 1936 as part of the TVA system. Initial appropriations from Congress were not approved until 1966; construction began the next year. At the time, opponents questioned the project at congressional hearings, pointing out that the river had unique natural characteristics and had cultural and historic value because of archeological artifacts left by the Cherokee and predecessor groups and had been the site for the early European occupation of Tennessee. Congress, however, had turned a deaf ear to pleas to remove the dam's authorization.

Armed with more substantial weaponry in 1971, opponents filed a suit in federal court contending that the TVA had not prepared an adequate EIS on the project. Two years later, the TVA completed an EIS that never provided nonreservoir alternatives. Still, the project forged on, but this time opponents attempted a novel approach to stop the dam. In August 1973, biologist David Etnier of the University of Tennessee discovered *Percina tanasi*—the snail darter—a species of fish found in the Little Tennessee River. Under provisions of the Endangered Species Act—the nation's first comprehensive law to protect species from extinction—the U.S. Fish and Wildlife Service listed the snail darter as an endangered species in 1975 and in 1976 listed the Little Tennessee River as a critical habitat for the fish. Proponents of the dam were outraged, and the issue made its way to court.

In 1978, the Supreme Court heard the case, at which time Attorney General Griffin Bell belittled the effort to protect such an insignificant fish in the face of a major TVA project. The Court, however, upheld the Endangered Species Act, remarking that if Congress was unhappy with the decision it could change the law. The TVA began studying alternatives to Tellico, but Congress did take up debate over the Endangered Species Act and ultimately passed amendments to exempt Tellico from it. The dam was completed in 1979.[107]

The snail darter was not the central issue in this story. And despite the fact that the dam was built, it was becoming clearer that opponents of big dams now had potent means, in the form of new environmental laws, of challenging dam builders. That these challenges were made indicated little willingness by some or no tolerance by others for multipurpose projects. The economic and conservation justifications of the past carried little weight in the 1960s and 1970s.

ENVIRONMENTALISM COMES OF AGE—RAMPART DAM AND THE GRAND CANYON DAMS

That a variety of other battles over dams continued to rage in the 1960s and 1970s is further testament to a complete change in context about dam and reservoir construction since the waning of the Big Dam Era. Marc Reisner argued that "the battle over the Grand Canyon dams was the conservation movement's coming of age."[108] This most lively controversy was certainly a crucial bridge between the dispute over Echo Park and the wily use of new environmental legislation as manifested at Tellico. During the 1960s, substantial energy in the conservation community went into campaigns involving the Central Arizona Project. Among other things, the plan called for the building of two storage dams in Bridge Canyon and Marble Canyon, along the Colorado River. Both were meant to produce hydroelectric power. The major concern was that Bridge Canyon Dam would back up water into Grand Canyon National Park's Inner Gorge, in what appeared to be clear violation of the 1919 law establishing Grand Canyon National Park, which provided for future federal dams if development did not compromise other purposes of the park. Opponents of the new hydroelectric dams recommended that coal-fired steam plants and nuclear plants be constructed instead. (This was trading one environmental threat for another, of course, and some conservationists ultimately protested this alternative.) The Grand Canyon dams were proposed as part of the Bureau of Reclamation's Central Arizona Project, which was considered essential to providing water and power for Arizonans. Arizona had been locked in a protracted struggle with California and the Upper Basin states over water rights to the Colorado River. Commissioner Floyd E. Dominy had branded opponents as "status quo conservationists" whose arguments were "frantic flak." David Brower, executive director of the Sierra Club, in turn called Dominy and the Bureau of Reclamation "the dam-it-all reclamationists." Ultimately, the project was authorized (1968), because of its local and regional significance, but without Bridge Canyon and Marble Canyon Dams.[109]

Although the fight against Rampart Dam did not have the vivid symbolism or emotional power of the fight over the Grand Canyon dams, it represented an extension of the battle over big dams for the first time beyond the lower forty-eight states. In the early 1960s, the U.S. Army Corps of Engineers' Rampart Dam was proposed to be built on the Yukon River, ninety miles northwest of Fairbanks, Alaska. It was to be a 525-foot structure that would impound a body of water larger than Lake Erie. In the context of the Cold War, one congressional supporter urged construction on the grounds that it would be bigger than anything the Russians had built. Conservation organizations opposed the dam, protesting the inundation of about 11,000 square miles in the interior of Alaska, of which 8,000 square miles were waterfowl-producing habitat, and the blocking of salmon migration into a third or more of the Upper Yukon watershed.

Rampart could provide electricity for six million people—but Alaska had only 253,000 people at the time, and the damsite was 2,000 miles away from the lower forty-eight states. In pre-energy-crisis America, such electrical power production seemed excessive. An article in *Natural History* stated

CHAPTER FIVE

Private Water

THE CURIOUS CASE OF SAN JOSE'S WATER SUPPLY

PRIVATE MUNICIPAL WATER SUPPLIES

San Jose, California, is an anomaly. Throughout an extended era when public water systems prevailed in the United States, a major portion of the city's water supply came from and still comes from a private company. This was not a burning issue for me growing up in what was at the time a relatively modest-sized city in Santa Clara County in the 1940s and 1950s. Many years later—now living in Houston—when I was plotting the outline for *The Sanitary City*, I initially intended to utilize four major case studies to tell my story of water supply, wastewater, and solid waste in the United States. San Jose was going to be one of those case studies, and, in fact, I spent a whole summer plus a few other shorter research trips gathering data on my hometown's sanitary services. In time I junked the idea of four detailed case studies and turned to a broader approach to structure the book. For several years, the rather extensive data I collected on my trips back to the Pacific Coast gathered dust in an out-of-the-way file cabinet.

A couple of years before I began working on this present collection of my works, I was asked to contribute to a book—*Cities and Nature in the American West*—honoring friend and colleague Hal Rothman, who had died much too young from ALS.[1] It seemed that to truly honor him I needed to write something fresh, rather than to revise some previous work. Soon my attention turned to that file cabinet with the San Jose documents. Hal was, among other things, a Western historian who wrote on many subjects, including water, and thus a piece on a growing and vital western city seemed appropriate.

The history of the waterworks was most interesting, and potentially most enlightening, in the San Jose records I collected. Since having completed the research in California back in the late 1980s and early 1990s, I remained curious about what appeared to be the quirkiness of a major city in the United States remaining committed to a private water system. Having written more widely since then about all the reasons why public responsibility trumped private service delivery in American cities since the latter nineteenth century, the chance to understand why San Jose bucked the trend was a major challenge.

This chapter lays out my analysis of why private service persists in San Jose. In a recent conversation with an insider of the San Jose Water Company (originally called the San Jose Water Works until 1983), he confirmed that I was on the right track, providing some additional material that I may want to incorporate into the story some day.

While the case of San Jose does not suggest the reversal of a powerful trend toward municipal service in the United States, particularly in the area of water supply and distribution, or presage the recent privatization movement, it does suggest that under the right circumstances an alternative to public service is possible. In this case, politics and timing seem more important than some prevailing ideology about the superiority of the private over the public. Other factors may be equally important. The active interest of Santa Clara Valley Conservation District in improving or protecting local access to water proved crucial.

In essence, an informal public and private partnership made the task of the San Jose Water Company easier in maintaining its role as the major provider of the city's water. Municipal ownership of the waterworks never seemed to be as crucial to locals as good service, and the ability to have access to adequate supplies of water—with the conservation district's help—insulated the private company from a potential takeover. Those who sought to turn the water supply into a public utility in San Jose always faced uphill battles through an array of intervening circumstances.

Delving into the details of San Jose's waterworks, therefore, reveals a level of complexity—economic and political—that needs to be understood to avoid some pat answer about the success of privatization in the delivery of an essential city service. This complexity suggests how and why San Jose resisted the national trends in the public sector dominance of water service in the United States. That the more recent global privatization movement in the field of water supply has developed slowly in the United States also suggests how difficult it will be to reverse the trend in municipal ownership that has dominated the urban landscape since the mid-nineteenth century.

PRIVATE WATER

San Jose, located in Santa Clara County, California—the Valley of Heart's Delight and then Silicon Valley—became an incorporated city in 1850, the same year that California entered the Union. San Jose was the state's first capital and now is the third largest city in the state and the tenth most populous in the country. For the first several years of its history, San Jose depended on artesian wells for its water. Beginning in 1866, the San Jose Water Works established the first citywide water supply system, and to this day a large portion of the city's water is provided by a private company.

The persistence of a private water company in San Jose—regarded as the oldest investor-owned water utility in California—bucked the trend in providing water in urban America from public systems since the 1830s. This a very big deal because municipalities in the United States from the nineteenth century to quite recently coveted public control of many city services— water being the greatest prize. In the last decade or so efforts to privatize water supply systems in the United States—a trend more popular in western Europe and elsewhere—largely have failed to occur. The resolute belief that water supply service is a mainstay of municipal power and municipal revenue has been difficult to undermine. Yet San Jose, and a very few others, have viewed this issue differently.

What accounts for the long history of a private water company in San Jose? What did it take to resist the historical forces that shifted many private services to public ones in the nineteenth and twentieth centuries? And what does the relationship between San Jose Water Works and the city of San Jose tell us about the development and evolution of this community?

PUBLIC OWNERSHIP OF WATERWORKS
IN THE UNITED STATES[2]

While the fear of fire always loomed, the startling impact of an epidemic increased public pressure for improved water supplies in nineteenth-century American cities. Fear alone, however, was insufficient to lead towns and cities to abandon traditional sources of water and familiar methods of acquiring it (water carriers, wells, and cisterns). A community needed a political commitment, fiscal resources, and access to new technology. Most American cities and towns drew their supplies from wells, springs, or ponds, and did not have extensive distribution systems, if any.

While community-wide water supply systems developed slowly, in 1801 Philadelphia became the first to complete a waterworks and municipal distribution system sophisticated even by European standards. The necessary health, economic, and technical factors converged to produce what became a model for future systems.[3] The Philadelphia waterworks, however, was an anomaly, since it did not spark an immediate nationwide trend. Inexperience in dealing with such a major project helps to explain why urban population growth exceeded construction for so many years. In 1800 there were seventeen waterworks for an urban population of 322,000; in 1830 there were forty-five waterworks for 1,127,000 urban Americans. The great majority of the waterworks were located in the Northeast, with considerably fewer in the Old Northwest and Upper South.[4]

In absolute terms, the number of waterworks multiplied at an accelerated rate from 1830 to 1880. During the 1850s and 1860s, however, the number did not keep pace with the chartering of new cities. Urban population rose at a faster rate than the number of waterworks until 1870, when the trend began to reverse itself. Some communities experiencing modest growth continued to rely on wells and other local supplies or expected private companies under franchises to provide water service. Yet even cities undergoing rapid expansion were leery of the capital investment required for citywide systems. By the 1870s the trend toward more public water supplies was evident. There was a slow shift from private to public ownership in the period (9 of 45 existing waterworks were public in 1830) with relative parity by 1880 (of 599 waterworks, 293 were public and 306 private).[5]

The desire for adequate supplies of water to meet the needs of a variety of consumers—and to protect the public health—meant that city leaders in the largest urban areas wanted centralized systems, ultimately under their direct control. Boosterism was widespread, since an effective water system promoted a city's amenities. Many water companies had been profitable, but capital investment in modern systems and rising operating costs threatened profits and also weakened private companies from withstanding public takeovers. In addition, since public control of the water supply enhanced the power and prestige of city governments, municipalities had great incentive to pressure private companies to sell out. The increasing ability in the late nineteenth century for cities to incur debt—and thus acquire more capital through bonds for infrastructure projects—made takeover of private companies or the building of new systems possible.[6]

In developing citywide water supply systems in this era, substantial public investment proved difficult for all but the largest and most fiscally sound cities. If the legislature was not withholding extension of greater authority, the city council was debating the wisdom of increasing the municipality's bonded indebtedness or engaged in partisan debate. Going back at least to 1855, the percentage of public water systems tended to vary with the general financial health of the cities, at least until the 1880s when other issues also influenced decisions. In addition, municipal indebtedness had steadily grown in order to finance several improvements, including water supply. By 1860, municipal debt was three times the federal debt and almost equal to the aggregate state debt. Liberalization of charters and other fiscal changes also provided opportunity for cities to finance water supply systems, especially beginning in the 1860s. In most cases, a combination of local circumstances and the experience of other cities influenced the shift from private to public.[7]

Water supply became the first important public utility in the United States and the first municipal service that demonstrated a city's commitment to growth. Officials and urban boosters promoted a variety of improvements in competition with rival communities. Along with sanitarians and municipal engineers, they supported services to improve health conditions and to secure bragging rights about the cleanliness of their cities.[8] City leaders concluded that control of the sanitary quality of water service would be difficult if the supply remained in private hands. The push for municipal ownership, therefore, had as much to do with the desire to influence the growth of cities as to settle disputes with private companies over specific deficiencies. The "political nature" of water was fundamental.[9]

Major cities tended to support public systems earlier than other classes of cities. In 1890, more than 70 percent of cities with populations exceeding 30,000 had public systems. In 1897, forty-one of the fifty largest cities (or 82 percent) had public systems. Since most of the urban population was located in the larger cities, it was not surprising that while only 43 percent of all American cities had public waterworks in 1890, 66.2 percent of the total urban population was served by public systems. The Midwest showed the greatest propensity to adopt public systems by the end of the 1890s, which coincided with its efforts at reform of business regulation. Emerging industrial states along the Great Lakes showed strong support for public systems, as did agrarian states. For the East, the total was 42 percent, the South 38 percent, and the West 40 percent.[10]

Several factors account for the political and economic climate that favored public systems in the late nineteenth century: improved fiscal status of cities, cooperation between large cities and state legislatures in developing or expanding services, skepticism of private companies to deliver services, and broadening regulatory power with respect to public utilities. Most importantly, between 1860 and 1922 municipal debt increased from $200 million to more than $3 billion. Legislatures were more lenient in allowing cities to float water bonds than incurring other forms of public indebtedness, since they were stable and demonstrated a good payment record.[11]

Public systems became more widespread as criticism of private companies mounted. In some cases, a change in political environment worked against private companies, especially if reform-minded leaders criticized the franchisee as a source of corruption. In other cases, poor performance by the private company set off reconsideration of service delivery. Initially, waterworks franchises extended for long durations, offered tax exempt status for the company, and did little to regulate price. By World War I, fourteen states limited the length of a contract under provision of general law, but eighteen states still allowed perpetual franchises.[12]

While as many as 850 new waterworks franchises were let during the 1880s, they were not as generous as those in the past. The length of the franchise was usually a central point of debate, since a perpetual contract gave officials virtually no control over the waterworks company. Other key concerns included the ability to manage rates and the option to purchase the waterworks if the company did not live up to its obligations. Cities had unique leverage with respect to rates. During the 1890s, rates charged by private companies were 40 to 43 percent higher than rates charged by municipal works. Unlike private companies, cities could take a loss on operations and use taxes to make up the difference. Rate flexibility sometimes gave cities an advantage in keeping private companies from overcharging and often made the threat to terminate the franchise quite real.[13]

As public systems became more competitive, sensitivity to liberal water contracts often resulted in a call for municipal ownership. In some cases, a concern about local control was more persuasive than a demand for municipal ownership. Fresno, California, had considered municipal ownership since 1876 and reconsidered it after a major fire in 1882. But the city did little more than install public wells and hydrants in the 1880s, and the private

TABLE 5.1

Public vs. Private Ownership of Waterworks, 1830–1924

Year	Number of Works	Public	Private	Percent Public	Percent Private
1830	45	9	36	20	80
1840	65	23	42	35.4	64.6
1850	84	33	51	39.3	60.7
1860	137	57	80	41.7	58.3
1870	244	116	128	47.5	52.5
1880	599	293	306	48.9	51.1
1890	1,879	806	1,073	42.9	57.1
1896	3,197*	1,690	1,490	52.9	46.6
1924	9,850	6,900	2,950	70	30

* Includes 17 undocumented systems

Source: Waterman, Elements of Water-Supply Engineering, 6.

Fresno Water Works continued delivery to residential areas. In 1889, a small group petitioned the city board of trustees to shift to municipal ownership, but the majority of Fresnans favored small government and low taxes and had not lodged major complaints against the private company. When the local water and power companies went bankrupt, they were reorganized in 1902 by a local utility magnate and were purchased by national corporations in the 1920s. Only then did the demand for municipal ownership intensify.[14]

A few cities, such as San Francisco, resisted municipal ownership. The widespread belief that the city's water supply was clear and wholesome checked the demand for a change in control. Nearby San Jose also obtained most of its water from a private company and continued to do so to the present.[15]

During the 1890s, a combination of factors shifted momentum decisively toward municipal ownership in most major cities. These included dissatisfaction with private companies, questions concerning the quality of the supplied water, high rates, and local interest in controlling services. By then cities had increased authorization to erect, lease, purchase, and operate waterworks, lighting plants, and in some cases, street railways. Opportunities to issue bonds beyond previous authorized limits and tax-granting status produced additional capital. Progressive Era reforms were employed to sanction purchases or to grant new franchises. Between 1891 and 1901 permission to own, erect, and purchase water or lighting plants had been extended to municipalities in twenty-four states. California and Kansas passed very general laws allowing for municipal ownership. Several cities had ownership clauses in their new charters.[16]

The trend toward public water systems in the United States persisted throughout the twentieth century. Figures in 1990 indicated that almost 84 percent of all American cities relied on public systems.[17] Contrarily, the global trend toward privatization of water supplies and water supplies management that exploded in recent years has yet to occur in the United States. In 2003, only 5 percent of American cities had privately owned systems.[18]

SAN JOSE AND PRIVATE WATER

Between the time that Spanish settlers established Pueblo San Jose in 1777 and the 1850s, the area depended on acequias—irrigation ditches or canals—by building small dams across creeks to supply water. In 1854, the first artesian well was drilled, and groundwater became a mainstay of the first capital of California. Foundry owner Donald McKenzie and two partners founded the San Jose Water Works on November 21, 1866, taking advantage of the abundant artesian water that others had first tapped. The company was granted an exclusive franchise by the city of San Jose and the town of Santa

Clara (until 1895 when it built its own waterworks) one year earlier. Under its provisions, the franchise ran for twenty-five years but allowed the city to purchase the service and its assets after the expiration date. The San Jose Water Works was obligated to provide water for fire protection, and rates were to be set by the city council.

Demand for service rose rapidly, and the company reincorporated on December 12, 1868, with a substantial increase in capital stock. By the 1870s the company was becoming profitable and began to expand access to water sources beyond artesian wells to include surface water. The artesian wells provided abundant water through the late 1860s, but during dry periods several wells failed. The company continued to purchase water rights, and soon the Santa Cruz Mountains became important to watershed development and Los Gatos Creek, in particular, became a focus of attention. By 1880, the total area of the watershed available was fifty square miles, with a capacity of 500 million gallons in the receiving reservoir. The system was thus supplied with water by gravity from the mountains in the area of Las Gatos and by pumping from wells.[19]

On January 26, 1888, President Edward Williams of the waterworks assured the mayor and city council that despite the fact that consumers "have been accustomed to use [water] lavishly and without regard for the season of the year . . . it is a fact that there has always been a sufficient supply of water, which is ready at any moment—in case of fire." He added that "with our present increased reservoir capacity, and pumping machinery, and our source of supply—we can *truthfully* say that no city on the Pacific Coast, of the same size, is so well protected, and no where is there such a splendid supply of pure water for domestic purposes."[20]

Despite Williams' assurances that it could provide necessary water supplies to the city, the San Jose Water Works also began to move in on competitors to increase its control of the water market, buying Los Gatos Manufacturing Company (which owned Los Gatos Water Company) in 1890 and later Mountain Spring Water Company in 1899.[21] There were some, as early as the turn of the century, who feared the emerging "water octopus." This was an interesting turn of events considering that the company was regarded as well run and had cordial associations with prominent citizens and the city government.[22] Others not so well connected to the powers that be obviously were wary of the local company.

Indeed, the water company was never free of critics and rivals during its long and virtually unprecedented existence as a private water company. In 1903, for example, Bay Cities Water Company wanted to divert artesian water from Santa Clara Valley (Smith Creek, Ysabel Creek, and Bonita Creek) into the watershed of Coyote Creek for use by its customers in Oakland.

Crippled by the blows of the School Board and the Fire Commission, the Water
Octopus Still Holds San Jose in Its Clutches.

FIGURE 5.1. The Water Octopus.
From *The Sketch* (October 28, 1899), 31.

In this so-called Coyote Creek Battle of 1903–1905, San Jose Water Works joined forces with local ranchers and the *San Jose Herald* in opposing the effort of outside companies to control water rights to Coyote Creek.[23] A *San Jose Herald* editorial claimed that, "The diversion of this water will ruin farms and orchards; destroy real estate values in city and country; impoverish city and county treasuries; drive merchants and manufacturers out of business and throw wage workers out of employment."[24] More cynically, a story in the *San Jose News* asserted that, "compared to the San Francisco monopoly the San Jose Water Works is of as much consequence as a bunch of tar weed tied to the tail of a kite on a windy day, but nevertheless the local dictators of the price of aqua pura have apparently defied competition from any source."[25] Ultimately, an injunction against Bay Cities was upheld in the California Supreme Court, which also upheld San Jose's rights to the water in Coyote Creek.[26]

Competitors for the water supply were one source of concern to the water company, the other were attacks by those favoring municipal ownership of water services. Historical accounts suggest that a serious antifranchise and municipal ownership campaign was not mounted until 1938. Yet, contemporary sources suggest that such pressure was chronic, especially by those claiming that the company charged excessive rates for water. In the *Union Label* (July 1905), Louis Montgomery, secretary of the Municipal Ownership League, attacked the notion of a franchise as an opportunity for a few to make "large fortunes" at the expense of the municipality. "There is no value to a stream of water, no matter how pure or great if there is no one to use it," he stated. "It follows therefore that the value lies in its use and control. . . . The people exclusively use it, they should have the exclusive control."[27]

Trust, therefore, rested with municipal government to provide better and cheaper service than an avaricious private company—an argument stated time and again throughout the country in this period. An ironic twist in the Coyote Creek Battle of 1903–1905 was Bay Cities' claim that San Jose Water Works (and the San Francisco firm, Spring Valley Water Company, who also coveted water in Santa Clara Valley) was a monopoly who intended to impede competitors![28]

In the 1920s the controversy over municipal ownership of the waterworks intensified as a result of several pending changes in the water supply and administration of water resources in Santa Clara Valley. Application for a rate increase by San Jose Water Works in 1924 (the first since 1914) appears to have precipitated another round of debate over the "water monopoly."[29] Councilman D. M. Denegri, who opposed the rate hike, proposed that the city own its own water distribution system, connecting it with the Hetch Hetchy project. Hetch Hetchy Valley in Yosemite National Park was drained by the Tuolumne River—a water source that San Francisco had designs on for several years. After a bitter environmental struggle, O'Shaughnessy Dam on the Tuolumne was completed in 1923 with its water serving San Francisco, San Mateo, Alameda Counties, and parts of the San Joaquin Valley. In 1924 officials in San Jose were queried about their interest in obtaining Hetch Hetchy water. However, the city did not yet have a pressing need for imported water as was the case with San Francisco and its neighbor to the south, Los Angeles, which had tapped the Owens Valley.[30]

The debate over a new water supply—and a municipally owned waterworks—spilled over into the 1930s.[31] The consistent stance of the San Jose Water Works continued to be that they provided excellent service, abundant water, and were strongly linked to the community. A flyer appearing in the Los Gatos Star on January 1, 1925, affirmed that 75 percent of the stockholders lived in Santa Clara Valley and 95 percent lived in California. "It is not often," it stated, "that the control of a public utility is so closely confined to the place where it operates. This unusual condition makes San Jose Water Works, very distinctively, a Santa Clara County institution."[32]

By the end of the decade talk of a municipal system and the selling of the company remained in the air. But the city was not the only interested party. The San Jose Water Works was acquired by General Water Works and Electric Company in October 1929, as part of an effort by eastern utility holding companies to buy water companies and other utilities. Consummated amid the Wall Street Crash of 1929 (October 24, 1929 was "Black Thursday"), its purchase was typical of business consolidations through holding company acquisitions happening in several areas in the 1920s. There was to be no change in local management in San Jose, but the assertions of the value of a hometown company providing necessary services was certainly weakened by the purchase.[33]

Equally, if not more significant for San Jose Water Works in 1929, was the formation of the Santa Clara Valley Water Conservation District (SCVWCD, later the Santa Clara Valley Water District) that was established to manage some of the water resources of the area. The falling water table and problems of subsidence were noted in the 1920s, which was bad news particularly for local growers. An engineering report in 1921 stated that construction of dams to percolate water back into the aquifer was the solution—a rather bold idea for the time. Voters turned it down twice. But in 1929, the California legislature passed the Jones Act—named after Herbert C. Jones, a major figure in California water history—that set up a new type of water district that omitted provisions for bonds (later added to a 1931 law), and the SCVWCD was subsequently approved.[34]

Improvements were to take the form of several dams, reservoirs, and pumping stations. Economic growth, more than conservation, likely made the formation of the district popular with city and county officials.[35] One historian has noted that the San Jose Water Works "probably welcomed the creation of a water conservation district" because it kept the company from having to develop new sources of water on its own. The "mutually beneficial business relationship" between the new public agency and the private company, she concluded, allowed the waterworks to continue to grow and prosper.[36] Indeed, pressure to provide adequate capital expenditures had weakened the ability of private water companies throughout the country to stave off municipal ownership. In San Jose, the SCVWCD may very well have helped the waterworks avoid public takeover in the long run, since the company—wittingly or unwittingly—was becoming integrated into a water system not totally dependent on a single entity, public or private.

Despite the perceived advantages of the conservation district to the waterworks' future, the 1930s represented the most intense battles over public ownership in the company's history. What had changed? The makeup of the city council? The eroding of the waterworks' political clout? Poor service delivery? The answer is not readily apparent, although the fact that the waterworks was now owned by a New York company certainly played some role. Forces in favor of municipal ownership continually charged that the water rates for the city were too high. There was also, of course, competition for available water supplies from the potent agricultural interests in the Valley of Heart's Delight, which still dominated the economy. In 1932, the city council instructed the city manager and city attorney to initiate condemnation proceedings against the water company and to obtain a valuation of its property to force a sale to the city. In response, the waterworks voluntarily reduced rates on January 1, 1933, and stated that it was willing to "talk price" with the city. However, the water company refused the city's offer, and the council dropped plans for a water purchase bill from the subsequent ballot.[37]

In 1934, the city council, having momentarily turned away from direct purchase of the waterworks, contracted with Water Properties Company, Ltd. of Arizona to supply San Jose with water from the American River along with thirty-nine other cities and towns in California. The plan called for the participating communities to become joint proprietors in the company after purchasing water for thirty years.[38] This amounted to a run around the waterworks to accomplish municipal ownership in a new way. Voters were presented with the contract in a ballot on May 7, 1934. Proponents raised the specter of the New York interests: "Keep Wall Street Profits for San Jose" without raising taxes or issuing bonds. "Water Properties Company, Ltd. gives to the City of San Jose its water distribution system to own and operate for ever."[39]

From the point of view of San Jose Water Works: "The proposed contract would for thirty years turn over the water destiny of San Jose to a group unfamiliar with local needs and conditions. It would subordinate San Jose's interests to the factions, disputes, and litigation sure to arise from the proposed jumbling of forty cities' water projects in this scheme." It added that other cities had not found the project acceptable, and that Water Properties Company, Ltd. was neither "a public enterprise nor a public corporation subject to adequate regulation."[40] State engineer Edward F. Hyatt sided with the waterworks, viewing the plan "not financially feasible." Somewhat ironically opponents of the scheme (especially directors of the waterworks) branded Water Properties as "a foreign private corporation" in much the same way that supporters of the plan had characterized San Jose Water Works.[41] Voters rejected the proposal by a thin margin (240 out of a total of 11,758 ballots), which in itself did little to clarify public sentiment over public ownership.[42]

But there was to be no stopping the city council from exploring municipal ownership of the water system in San Jose throughout the decade, including the possible purchase of Hetch Hetchy water from San Francisco.[43] In a letter from city manager C. B. Goodwin to the city council on November 4, 1935, Goodwin outlined five reasons why municipal ownership was necessary: water rates were too high; water was too hard; interest rates were currently low, thus favoring a purchase of the waterworks; San Jose was the largest city in the state in which the water system was not publicly owned; and there was some danger of inflation that would increase the rate base. The options he presented to the council included acquiring the whole system, acquiring part of the system, or building a new system for San Jose alone. He believed that the best option was to acquire the whole system, "if the right price could be agreed upon."[44]

In 1935 plans to build a municipal system through federal grants was considered and then dropped. Once again, in that year, the cost of a municipal system was explored to determine a purchase price, and again the waterworks had no interest in selling.[45] The sparring continued into 1936 and 1937.[46] A test poll conducted by the San Jose Mercury Herald (sometimes San Jose Mercury) in early 1937 indicated an overwhelming majority for municipal ownership—78 percent by the close of the poll.[47] The poll seemed to reinvigorate the city council to move on the waterworks again, but all the communities in the central Santa Clara Valley—especially San Jose and Los Gatos—were not in agreement on what kind of plan would suit their needs. H. G. Mitchell, orchardist and secretary of the East Side County Water District argued that a takeover of the waterworks by San Jose might leave areas outside the city limits (currently served by the San Jose Water Works) "obliged to accept any sort of service or rates that might be imposed upon them." He concluded that if the waterworks was to become a community owned service, "it should be through the means of a Metropolitan Water District."[48] But a plan for a San Jose–Los Gatos municipal utility district was defeated at the polls largely because of opposition by the voters of San Jose.[49]

The debate over municipal ownership was getting significantly complicated in 1937—communities in Santa Clara Valley were increasingly at odds over the benefits of municipal ownership, the waterworks was predictably opposed to a change, and groups like the Citizens' League on Government and Taxation of Santa Clara County (Citizens' League), questioned a potentially arbitrary bond election without clear knowledge of the company's value and also questioned what the league believed to be unfounded assumptions about the inferior quality of the current supply or the level of the rates.[50]

But after a rancorous campaign, the latest effort to take over the waterworks failed when a bond issue to be used to purchase it went down to defeat in 1938. By a vote of 14,402 to 2,394 (six to one) voters turned away the latest and most vigorous effort by the city council to purchase the waterworks. As a San Jose Evening News editorial noted (the Evening News opposed the bond issue), "the surprise in yesterday's election was not that the water bonds were beaten, but that the majority against them was so large." The editorial suggested that recent bond proposals had met a similar fate, and that "this is not a good time to submit bond measures." The larger issue, it suggested, was that the voters were not asked directly to vote on municipal ownership. Whether by confusion or impulsive preparation for the election by the city manager and the council, there was not enough inertia in the bond issue vote to turn voters in a new direction.[51]

Harold Gilliam in the *San Francisco Chronicle* viewed the defeat as politics, pure and simple, with well-financed antimunicipal ownership forces creating a "buzz saw" that voters would not challenge.[52] The Citizens' League—beyond its firmly held belief that "political management is rarely, if ever, as efficient and economical as private management"—may have had its finger on the concrete issues that swayed the voters when it noted the following circumstances: the bond issue came "despite the lack of any widespread demand for public ownership," rates had been lowered rather than raised by the waterworks, supplies seemed adequate, bonded debt would only add to the current tax burden, the current "serious business recession" did not favor public ownership, and the potential for inconvenience if the city decided simply to duplicate the waterworks system instead of absorb it.[53]

In addition, as Leslie Parks suggested, another factor working against the bond issue was that citizens of Santa Clara Valley had recently voted for the construction of five new conservation dams and had little reason to be concerned about their water supply at the moment. Also, Ralph Elsman, elected as chairman of the board and president of the San Jose Water Works in 1937 (who also became president and general manager of the state's largest privately owned water utility, California Water Service Company in 1939), was effective in working behind the scenes through a variety of community contacts. Particularly important was Parks' observation that since the mid-1930s at least a close relationship existed between pro-growth forces that dominated city government (increasingly identified with new city manager Anthony P. "Dutch" Hamann, who became the most aggressive force for annexation in the city's history) and the directors of the water company—both benefiting from San Jose's rise as an urban industrial center out of its days as a center for agriculture and related activities. By the time General Water, Gas, and Electric liquidated its controlling interest in the San Jose Water Works since 1945, company stock increasingly returned to local ownership. Local stockholders obviously would support the continuation of the private company.[54]

Yet circumstances change. As droughts and fears of droughts challenged comfortable beliefs about existing supplies, as new residents poured into the valley, and as pro-growth advocates reconsidered the value of a municipal water system, controversy was on the horizon again in the 1950s. The years 1948 and 1949 were two of the driest years in California history. Farmers, in particular, began to get nervous. The advantage of tapping Hetch Hetchy water again found supporters. City council considered bringing waterworks employees under civil service in case the waterworks came under city control. The antimunicipal ownership individuals defeated this measure, but the upcoming city council campaign in 1950 pitted pro- and antimunicipal ownership candidates against each other over the water issue.

Alden Campen, a property manager, and Robert Doerr, a high school teacher, ran for city council on a municipal ownership platform and gained support particularly among agricultural interests. Ralph Elsman stated publicly that there was no water shortage to be concerned about, but Campen and Doerr printed a pamphlet stating that "Ralph Elsman—Water Works Czar—Pumps Water YOU OWN Into Million Dollar Profits." In turn, Campen and Doerr were charged by the Committee for the Preservation of the American Way of Life in good 1950s fashion as "sowing the seeds of Socialism in our midst." The results of the election were ambivalent for public ownership. Campen was defeated, but Doerr was elected.

The idea of a public waterworks was not just the platform for "left-leaning" proponents, therefore. Some pro-growth advocates in city council—even before the 1950 campaign—saw public ownership of the water system as enhancing the city's financial status, as it would lower rates and possibly become profitable in its own right. Dutch Hamann would mount his own campaign to purchase the waterworks. It was somewhat ironic that the pro-growth notions that had supported Elsman's claim of the value of private water were being turned on their heads in favor of public water. The council had pro and anti elements in the 1950s, however, and little changed.

In 1960 the proposed annexation by the town of Los Gatos of some 10,345 acres—much of which included the Santa Cruz Mountain watershed—raised concern, leading Doerr to propose a study on the purchase of the waterworks. The purchase was deemed feasible. Hamann ultimately supported ownership of the waterworks after Los Gatos achieved its annexation goal. But proposed changes in the city charter to help make public ownership possible were defeated in 1961 and 1962 thanks in part to the waterworks' opposition.[55]

Complicating matters was the question of supply for the fast growing Santa Clara County in these years. The SCVWCD provided wholesale supplies, but there were a variety of retail dealers in the area—but not necessarily working within county lines. Cities to the north of San Jose were using Hetch Hetchy water from San Francisco, but San Jose was barred from it (under federal law) as long as it maintained a privately owned water company that sold water for a profit. County supervisors believed that they were the party most able to provide imported water and favored utilizing state water from an aqueduct close to San Jose, while the water district wanted federal water via another route into the valley. A compromise was reached in the 1960s that would allow state and federal water to be imported, cities in the northern part of the county would continue to get Hetch Hetchy water, and a new Santa Clara Valley Water District would accept input from the county supervisors and the old water district. Most importantly, the compromise recognized the regional nature of water supply, although it did little to help resolve the fate of private water in San Jose.[56]

In 1961, San Jose "got its foot in the door" with the purchase of the Evergreen Water Company, which was a small, private firm serving a few hundred people in the Evergreen area. The city almost sold the company to the waterworks the next year but held on to it by a thread. Hamann tried to use the momentum of the purchase to get the council to support municipal ownership, but he failed. The pro-municipal ownership forces in place in 1958 were no longer in control of council, and he faced the opposition of the *San Jose Mercury* as well. Despite the fact that municipal systems (other than Evergreen) were selling water cheaper than San Jose Water Works, public support for municipal ownership was missing. It seemed that a comfort level existed with the privately owned company that time and opposition had been unable to overturn—despite many efforts. This was not a concrete reason, perhaps, but certainly a product of historical momentum. Helping to maintain that position was a large number of pro-growth advocates within and without government who saw little value in a public system, and they certainly possessed political leverage that the water company had courted for years.[57]

The year 1966 saw another attempt at a municipal system. Yet, the same opposition parties, public ambivalence, and especially high interest rates foiled the effort. Financial consultants Stone and Youngberg stated that it was not feasible for the city to make the purchase with current interest rates up to 1.5 percent above normal.[58] Another challenge was made in 1972, three years after pro-growth Dutch Hamann had retired. But there was no new strategy on either side, and the story played out as expected. The dwindling of pro-growth supporters on city council certainly dimmed enthusiasm for a public water system, and other city priorities shifted the battleground to other issues.[59] The passage of Proposition 13 in 1978 certainly was influential.[60] Through this "People's Initiative to Limit Property Taxation," the maximum amount of any ad valorem tax on real property could not exceed one percent of the full cash value of the property. By limiting revenue to the state, public sector initiatives faced little chance of success. A new bond issue to pur-

chase the water system was now out of the question. In the approching years
of the Reagan era, publicly sponsored programs would face "out-sourcing"
and "privatizing"—not congenial for promoting municipal ownership.

Yet the story of the San Jose Water Works does not end with a clear private sector victory. By 1974, there were three, albeit small, municipal water
systems operating in the city of San Jose: Evergreen, North San Jose, and Alviso. Evergreen Water System served an area of about 18 square miles in that
year. North San Jose served about 4 square miles, and Alviso about 20 square
miles, compared with about 138 square miles in metropolitan San Jose served
by the San Jose Water Works.[61] The name changed in 1983 from San Jose Water Works to San Jose Water Company, and since the 1990s at least, it also has
been constrained by slow or no-growth realities in its service area. As a *San
Jose Mercury News* story stated in December 1992, the company "has survived financial panics, eathquakes, depression, drought, takeover attempts
and political challenges. Now, it is threatened by slow strangulation."[62] The
combination of significant decline in water use plus limits to the physical
expansion of the city forced the San Jose Water Corporation (SJW Corp)—
the holding company formed in 1985 of which San Jose Water Company is
a wholly owned subsidiary—to attempt to obtain a percentage of California
Water Service Company, which is the state's largest investor-owned water
company. In addition SJW Corp has diversified to move into real property
and other investments. This strategy was deemed necessary since there was
little area within its existing territory for expansion.[63]

So what does this long history of San Jose and its private water company
tell us about this historical anamaly—private municipal water in a publicly
dominated world? In some respects, San Jose Water Works and later San Jose
Water Company survived because of a sustained period of economic and
physical growth in the Santa Clara Valley. The area's population explosion,
it's unyielding physical expansion, and its relentless transformation from a
valley of orchards to Silicon Valley offered consistent opportunities for the
water company to seek and serve customers and maintain its financial sol-
vency for more than a hundred years. But the company did not persevere
without challenges to its control and to its very existence.

At a distance it appears that San Jose Water Company had no real competitors and survived in an environment of content consumers. A closer
look suggests that the challenge of municipal ownership was unremitting
since the nineteenth century. But why did municipal ownership fail here
when it succeeded in an overwhelming number of other places in the United
States? There are several reasons. First, the company never lost its customer
base to rival private companies or from bad management and practices. Even

when rates were regarded as high, the company responded by lowering rates or asserting that rates were fair. Since the franchise required that the city council and then the railroad commission set rates, it removed—or at least softened—a political issue that had hurt other private companies, that is, a third party between consumers and retailers was responsible for determining the value of the commodity. Second, when water supplies were challenged by dry spells and growing demand, new sources were discovered or the company convincingly argued that supplies were plentiful. Ironically, the formation of a public entity, the SCVWCD, helped to undergird potentially dwindling supplies by providing new infrastructure—dams and reservoirs—and financing new sources available to the citizens of San Jose and the valley, thus relieving the company of constant pressure to seek new water supplies on their own. Third, groundwater never became so scarce or so threatened by pollution or competitors to remove this option from use. Bay Cities tried to capture groundwater, but the local water company—aided by the city and other supporters—fended them off. Again, public enitites came to the aid of a private company—if even unwittingly. In addition, the SCVWCD's plan for recharging the aquifers directly benefitted the water company. Fourth, support also was readily available within government circles and the business community, helping to shield the water company from takeover. As stated earlier, the political nature of water was important.

The momentum of successful service, plentiful supply, complementary support from a public entity like the SCVWCD, and continued political engagement made the San Jose Water Company difficult to take down. Timing was everything—recession, depression, high interest rates, and Proposition 13 worked against public ownership. And certainly public perception played a role as well; the company was never successfully portrayed as a "water monopoly" in the eyes of the public—at least not an unwelcomed one. The moniker never stuck long enough for the voting public to abandon the water company in any bond election. The image of the San Jose Water Company usually focused on success not failure—either by its backers or detractors. It was rarely if ever viewed as weak or moribund.

The historical context in which the San Jose Water Company found itself from 1866 to the present trumped the national swing toward municipal ownership in the nineteenth and twentieth centuries. Whether changing circumstances will lead to a new era of privatized water in the United States in the next several years remains to be seen. San Jose Water Company, however, bucked a long-standing trend, although it did so through a maze of issues not easily replicated by others.

CHAPTER SIX

The Historical Significance of Houston's Buffalo Bayou

URBAN WATER ARTERIES

This chapter grew out of a project in coordination with the National Park Service (NPS) to seek the designation of a National Heritage Area for Buffalo Bayou, the water artery running through Houston, Texas. According to the NPS: "National Heritage Areas are designated by Congress.... For an area to be considered for designation, certain key elements must be present. First and foremost, the landscape must have nationally distinctive natural, cultural, historic, and scenic resources that, when linked together, tell a unique story about our country."[1]

Those of us involved in the project are convinced that Buffalo Bayou would make an excellent addition to the list of existing National Heritage Areas.[2] In a broader sense, however, Buffalo Bayou represents an urban water artery not unlike those in other cities that link together the past and present history of a community. Such links include the location where early settlement occurred, a place marking key historical moments, an essential means of transport and commerce, and a recreational focal point. Buffalo Bayou has been all of those things and more.

As the locus of the Houston Ship Channel (HSC) it represents a truly significant national site. In a recent conversation, historian John McNeill asked me if I realized that the ship channel and the Panama Canal opened in the same year, 1914. He suggested, and I agree, that in its own way the HSC has made an incredible mark on the world economy and our energy history—a mark rivaling many of the accomplishments of the Panama Canal.

Indeed, the HSC was most responsible for making Houston a world-class "energy capital." Such places can be defined as cities or regions with strong ties to energy industries and with strong roles in energy production, energy distribution, or energy technology. When we think about energy capitals we often think about them as centers for financial capital accumulation—profit centers—generating wealth for corporate entities or governments that draw that wealth from the production and sale of energy, and then they distribute it beyond the community where it was generated. This perspective, however, is too narrow. Energy-led development has shaped the evolution of many cities and regions, influencing metropolitan growth while changing patterns of energy consumption and concentrating the environmental impacts of energy production locally as well as in areas of consumption far removed from production facilities.[3]

Buffalo Bayou's role in shaping Houston's economic life is possibly the most dramatic but not necessarily the only way that a water artery can influence the development of cities and regions. The broader function—including its political, social, and cultural roles—is presented here, and with respect to the themes of water as a public utility versus a private commodity, this chapter focuses more directly on real estate speculation, commerce and navigation, and industrial development.

THE HISTORICAL SIGNIFICANCE OF HOUSTON'S BUFFALO BAYOU

Buffalo Bayou—running through the new city of Houston—was designated as the "National Highway of the Republic" in 1840. While this label was a bit of hype, the bayou would soon live up to the name as a major artery serving the Gulf Coast and the Texas hinterland. Many years later, Houston became known as the "Energy Capital of the World," due in large part to its location along Buffalo Bayou. Also a bit of hype, this moniker again demonstrated the historical importance of this modest stretch of water.

In 1836, the city of Houston was founded on land adjacent the banks of Buffalo Bayou. The waterway also was the site for a wide array of other historically significant events and activities in the nineteenth and twentieth centuries that shaped the state of Texas and influenced the nation as a whole. The most notable of these was the building of the HSC in 1914. But also important was the Battle of San Jacinto—fought along the bayou's shores—that played the pivotal role in the struggle for Texas independence leading to the establishment of the Republic of Texas in 1836. Of additional note was the maritime activity along the bayou and naval engagements in Galveston Bay during the Civil War that led to blocking essential supplies sent from Texas to the rest of the Confederacy during the crucial last stages of the conflict. Two other somewhat disparate themes of regional importance—one related to the area's social and cultural heritage and the other to city building—took place in the vicinity of Buffalo Bayou. The first was the Camp Logan Riot of 1917, which pointedly illustrated the seriousness of race problems in the United States during wartime and the persistence of segregation in the American South. The second was the development of activated sludge water treatment facilities that set technological precedents nationally and internationally for water purification.

BUFFALO BAYOU—THE RISE OF SHIPPING AND COMMERCIAL DEVELOPMENT

The rise of shipping and commercial development along Buffalo Bayou in the nineteenth century was an essential precedent for the construction of the HSC and the emergence of Houston as an international focal point for oil production, refining, and petrochemicals in the twentieth century and beyond. Buffalo Bayou flows for sixty-five miles west to east from outside Katy in Fort Bend County to its mouth as a tributary of the San Jacinto River at Lynchburg. The river continues the journey into Galveston Bay and then to the Gulf of Mexico.[4]

Although little is known about Native American settlement along Buffalo Bayou, modest non-Indian settlement occurred in the 1820s. In 1824, Mexican grants of land were issued near the mouth of the San Jacinto River, on the lower end of Buffalo Bayou, and at the junction of Brays Bayou and Buffalo Bayou. John P. Austin's land grant of July 21, 1824 contained the location of the city of Houston. He died in Brazoria on August 11, 1833 from illness, but his wife, Elizabeth, inherited the grant jointly with Austin's brother William. The Austin family then sold the grant to brothers John Kirby and Augustus Chapman Allen in 1836.

Other land grants along Buffalo Bayou belonged to Luke Moore (August 3, 1824), John R. Harris (August 16, 1824), M. Callahan and Allen Vince (August 3, 1824), William Vince (July 21, 1824), John Brown (August 19, 1824), Ezekiel Thomas (August 9, 1824), W. P. Harris and Robert Wilson (January 3, 1832), Samuel C. Herons (July 25, 1831), Thomas Earle (July 7, 1824), and Arthur McCormick (August 10, 1824).[5]

In 1826, John Richardson Harris established the town of Harrisburg at the confluence of Buffalo and Brays Bayous (just below the present-day turning basin of the HSC), and he also set up the first industry—a steam sawmill—on Buffalo Bayou. The first house in Harrisburg was constructed in 1833. The new town served as a port of entry and trading center for early settlers in the region prior to the Texas Revolution. On April 19, 1836, two days before the Battle of San Jacinto, Santa Anna's Mexican army looted and burned Harrisburg.[6]

Persuaded that Harrisburg was an attractive location for a port, but unable to acquire property in the vicinity, Augustus Chapman Allen and John Kirby Allen decided to settle approximately fifteen miles upstream near present-day Main Street in Houston at the confluence of Buffalo and White Oak Bayous. On August 30, 1836, the Allen brothers ran an advertisement in the *Telegraph and Texas Register* about real estate available in the new town of Houston. While their glowing claims about the wonders of the townsite (named after the Texas Revolution's hero, Sam Houston) were clearly overstated, they persuaded the Texas Congress to designate it as the temporary capital of the new republic. The Allens laid out a street grid, set about selling lots (the first lot in the new town was sold to Benjamin Brown on January 1, 1837 for $700), built a meeting place for political leaders, made reservations for a school and churches, and promoted commerce along the bayou that was not yet effectively navigable.[7]

While Houston ceased to be the republic's capital after 1839, it grew and prospered as a shipping and commercial center. From these beginnings the city continued to grow, ultimately into the largest city in the state and one of the most important in the nation, and Buffalo Bayou was the focal point for the establishment of the new city of Houston.

A prosperous and productive shipping industry and commercial trade was established along the shores of Buffalo Bayou with local, regional, national, and international impacts. "The commerce of the republic [of Texas]," geographer D. W. Meinig stated, "very largely followed the flows of nature downriver to the Gulf." Galveston Bay provided the best access to the rich agricultural lands to its northeast, and with few rivers navigable for long stretches, access to those agricultural lands via Buffalo Bayou ultimately made Houston the state's chief inland port.[8] Marilyn McAdams Sibley added, "by the time Texas became a state, Buffalo Bayou was the only stream in Texas that was dependably navigable, and Houston was permanently established as a way station where water and land routes met."[9] As such, Buffalo Bayou became an economic access point into the hinterland of the Southwest and a corridor to the Gulf of Mexico and beyond. Barges and riverboats from Buffalo Bayou could load cargoes onto seagoing ships in Galveston and, in turn, pick up goods to deliver inland.

Until the 1830s, Buffalo Bayou was barely navigable. Nonetheless, nothing had to change to make the bayou an important commercial highway. When the Allen brothers surveyed potential sites for development, they searched for "the head of navigation" along Buffalo Bayou. Among the sites they considered were Morgan's Point, the Township of Harrisburg, and the junction of Buffalo and White Oak Bayous. The brothers decided on the junction of the two bayous because it was for sale, and it had a clear title. The brothers also sounded out the bayou to determine that the river to the site for their proposed township was at "the head of navigation." Finding that the water was six feet at the shallowest points, the Allens advertised that ships could sail to the new town in all seasons and in all kinds of weather and that steamboats "of the largest classes" could make a trip from Houston to Galveston in eight to ten hours.[10]

Buffalo Bayou quickly became a significant water highway for shallow-draft steamboats running between Houston and Galveston, and it was viewed as a potentially important access route to the Brazos River and the inland cotton trade, as well as an important point of transshipment for a wide variety of goods that entered or left the state and an avenue of passage for travelers and immigrants.[11] In December 1830, the *Ariel* became the first steamboat on Texas waters, traveling up Buffalo Bayou via Galveston Bay. The steamboat *Laura* was the first to dock at Houston's port in 1837.

Many had not readily believed the Allens' claim that a steamboat, or any kind of ship for that matter, could reach Houston. In order to prove this claim, the brothers arranged for the steamer *Laura* to make the trip up the bayou to the town to prove that it could be done. Unknown to many, the ship was the smallest steamboat in Texas. As the *Laura* made her way up the bayou, all of the passengers and crew cleared fallen trees and snags to make a path for the ship.[12] Once the *Laura* docked, regular steamboat service commenced from Houston to Galveston and other points in Galveston Bay.[13]

Francis Richard Lubbock, a merchant and later a Civil War governor of Texas, was one of the passengers aboard the *Laura* when it made the first voyage to Houston. According to his account, the townsite was so under-developed that the ship steamed passed it into White Oak Bayou. Recognizing the mistake, Lubbock and the others reversed their course and discovered a road leading off from the bayou. Following it, they realized that they had discovered the town site.[14]

The place where the *Laura* docked was called Allen's Landing, and it is located on the south bank of Buffalo Bayou and a fork of White Oak Bayou in central Harris County, where most of Houston is found. The city of Houston officially established the port in June 1841, and in 1910 the federal government approved funding for the dredging of a ship channel from the Gulf of Mexico to the present turning basin four miles to the east of Allen's Landing. A historical marker was placed at the site when it was dedicated as Allen's Landing Memorial Park in 1967.[15]

Buffalo Bayou's advantage over other waterways such as the Brazos River was that it ran east and west. It also was relatively wide and deep at its mouth along the San Jacinto River to Brays Bayou, although narrower and more difficult to float from Brays to White Oak Bayou. However, at the entrance to

Galveston Channel, vessels had to traverse a twelve-foot bar and then run over a shell reef (Red Fish Bar) stretching across the middle of the bay. It was not uncommon for ships to run aground at this juncture as they traveled toward Buffalo Bayou. Where the waters of the San Jacinto River entered Galveston Bay (opposite Morgan's Point) ships faced another bar (Clopper's Bar). Light-draft vessels traveled easiest along the bayou at this point.

In 1841, as stated above, the Houston City Council established the Port of Houston and levied wharfage fees to help finance dredging and port improvements. A "landing place" at the foot of Main Street had been provided in 1837, and a wharf along the waterfront from Main to Fannin Street was constructed in 1840.[16] The city council established the port at Allen's Landing in 1841. This waterfront coincided with the area between Main and Fannin Streets, and this area was specifically reserved for larger boats and steamships. Smaller ships "were assigned to other positions." In 1869, the Buffalo Bayou Ship Channel Company initiated major dredging and widening of the bayou.[17]

Soon ships were bypassing Galveston wharves to enter the bayou. As a way of avoiding the high port charges at Galveston, the Houston Direct Navigation Company (chartered in 1866) loaded and unloaded ocean vessels in the channel and carried the cargoes by barge along the bayou. The first federal survey for a ship channel running from Buffalo Bayou to Galveston Bay (completed in 1871) stated that the bayou was at least seventy feet wide and could be navigated to Houston by vessels drawing less than four feet.[18] Some stretches had been much deeper (fifteen to twenty feet), but urbanization as early as 1870 had encouraged shoaling and thus substantially reduced the depth despite previous efforts at dredging.[19]

Cotton from the western plantations found its way to the Houston port, as did sugar, cattle, and other commodities from the rich Brazos agricultural region. In the nineteenth century, "cotton was king" in Texas, and in the 1870s Houston was the center for exporting cotton to textile mills in the northeastern United States and Great Britain. In 1839, one observer stated that only 8 bales of cotton were shipped from Houston; by 1843, the figure reached 4,336 bales. In 1845, the Telegraph and Texas Register claimed that Houston had received more than 14,000 bales. The bayou also served as a source of power for grist mills and sawmills. In 1860, five sawmills along Buffalo Bayou were utilizing local timber. During the 1890s the mills were producing 400,000 board feet of lumber per day. Not unlike cotton, Houston was "the capital of the Texas lumber industry." By 1875, the ship channel along the eastern stretch of the bayou was widened and straightened, allowing most oceangoing vessels to deliver goods to the Houston area. Oceangoing ships docked at the wharves at Allen's Landing, as this area was specifically reserved for steamboats and larger ships. This practice continued until the turning basin was finished in August 1914, although smaller ships did navigate past the turning basin.[20]

Until the major competition of railroad lines in the late 1870s, the southwestern Gulf area depended on water transportation for access to inland markets, and Buffalo Bayou played a major role in offering such access. During these years, Buffalo Bayou helped Houston become a major port city.[21]

The chartering of the Buffalo Bayou, Brazos, and Colorado Railway (BBB&C) in February 1850 not only established Buffalo Bayou as the site for the state of Texas' first railroad, but it also acknowledged the emergence of the next great wave of commercial and passenger transportation in the southwestern Gulf area. The BBB&C only operated between Harrisburg and Stafford's Point by 1853 (twenty miles) and extended to East Richmond on the banks of the Brazos River (an additional twelve and a half miles) by 1856. However, by 1861, five railroads radiated from Houston. The Civil War halted further railroad development for a time, but Houston soon emerged as the leading railroad hub in the region, virtually eliminating the economic potential of Galveston as a rival urban center and helping to usher in a new era of ground transportation. Even with the extensive railroad network, Buffalo Bayou remained important, especially in the transportation of bulky cargo. As David McComb stated, "the usefulness of roads and railways, however, depended, at least in part, on a third commercial artery—Buffalo Bayou, Houston's link to the outside world until the rail connections of 1873."[22]

THE OIL BOOM COMES TO TEXAS:
THE SPINDLETOP STRIKE AND AFTER

Gigantic oil strikes in 1900 and 1901 west of the Mississippi River, especially in the Southwest and California, were transforming events in United States history. Beginning as a regional phenomenon, the discovery of rich oil fields in Texas, Oklahoma, and California created a new form of wealth in what would become the American Sunbelt and accelerated the process of industrialization across the nation. The supply of crude available on the market soared, and new companies promoted oil as the preeminent fuel for locomotives, ships, and, eventually, automobiles. In this way, oil became more directly competitive with coal.[23]

When a top official of Standard Oil allegedly boasted that he could drink all the oil found west of the Mississippi, he had no idea what a foolish statement that was. The discovery of the Gulf of Mexico, Midcontinent, and California oil fields signaled a major turning point in the production of crude in the United States with repercussions throughout the world.

A dramatic symbol of this historic moment was the 1901 strike at Spindle-top, ninety miles east of Houston. While Texas was only one of several states to challenge Pennsylvania's dominance (others included California, Okla-homa, and Kansas), Spindletop became synonymous with the birth of the twentieth-century oil industry in the United States. The *Year Book of Texas* reported how the famous well blew out on January 10, 1901: "At exactly 10:30 a.m., the well that made Beaumont famous burst upon the astonished view of those engaged in boring it, with a volume of water, sand, rocks, gas and oil that sped upward with such tremendous force as to tear the crossbars of the derrick to pieces, and scattered the mixed properties from its bowels, together with timbers, pieces of well casing, etc., for hundreds of feet in all directions."

The world's largest producing well, outside of the Baku field in Russia, was the result of eight frustrating years of effort by Pattillo Higgins, a Beau-mont local who insisted that oil lay under a swamp near the Neches River, and Captain Anthony F. Lucas, an Austrian mining engineer who Higgins took as a partner in 1899. The venture's financial woes brought in outside funds, and with replenished backing—and a new rotary rig—Lucas struck oil at 1,160 feet, almost exactly where Higgins predicted.

Newspapers everywhere announced the Lucas strike, and the little town of Beaumont was soon overrun with promoters, speculators, and swindlers. Beaumont became the "Queen of the Neches," where you could see "a gusher gushing." In three months the population tripled to 30,000, as six trains daily pulled in from Houston. Shacks and shanties dotted the town, saloons and bawdyhouses provided the entertainment. It was a time for legendary fortunes to be made, for even grander tall tales to be circulated.

The field itself was the most extraordinary story. By the end of 1902, al-most 400 wells were bunched together on Spindletop; by 1904, about 1,200. The first 6 wells drilled there accounted for more oil than all the world's other wells. In 1905, the Humble field, also near Houston, began producing oil, and by 1919, two other major fields were tapped. Approximately three-fourths of Gulf Coast oil was pumped from these fields. Between 1901 and 1950, crude-oil production in Texas accounted for about 33 percent of the all-time production of the United States and 21 percent of world production.[24]

The strike at Spindletop produced a variety of results. It meant new fi-nancial resources for the state of Texas. It led to the exploitation of other salt-dome fields near the coast, including Sour Lake, Goose Creek, Humble, Jennings, and Batson. The boom ultimately spread across the state, from the Gulf of Mexico to the Panhandle, and throughout the Southwest. Businesses servicing the oil industry, such as Hughes Tool Company, brought an industrial capacity to Texas like never before. Oil's effect on the development of major cities was no less significant: first Beaumont, then Houston, and then Dallas and Fort Worth all benefited from oil wealth.

On a broader scale, Spindletop signaled the permanent establishment of the oil industry in the Southwest, which provided important precedents for technique and growth. Most importantly, it produced a new group of rivals to challenge Standard Oil's control of the industry—Gulf, Texas (Texaco), Shell, Sun, and others. Having spawned several major oil companies and many smaller ones, Spindletop irreparably altered the oil industry in the twentieth century.[25]

THE CONSTRUCTION OF THE HOUSTON SHIP CHANNEL

Along with the discovery of oil at Spindletop, the construction of the HSC made Houston—and its location along Buffalo Bayou—the center of the oil and gas industry. Other parts of the country can boast of significant oil-producing and oil-refining areas, most notably the original oil-field development in Pennsylvania, the important refining complex in the Cleveland area inspired by John D. Rockefeller, Southern California's concentration of refineries in Long Beach, and the refining region in southern Louisiana. However, none of these areas represents such an important confluence of oil refining, petrochemical production, industrial capacity, and oceangoing commercial trade as the HSC.

Indeed, the ship channel altered Houston's commercial future in many ways. According to Lynn M. Alperin, as we have seen, "the goal of a ship channel from the Gulf to the head of navigation on Buffalo Bayou predates the inception of the city of Houston in 1836 and the boisterous era of the Texas Republic."[26] Not until the 1870s, however, was a concerted effort made to actually complete such a channel. The U.S. Army Corps of Engineers' 1870 survey had recommended a hundred-feet-wide and six-feet-deep channel, but without sufficient appropriations little was done.

Charles Morgan, who was involved in Gulf shipping and eager to by-pass Galveston's wharfage costs, bought the Bayou Ship Channel Company in 1874. Within two years he had dredged a channel from Galveston Bay to present-day Clinton in proximity to Houston (Clinton was to the southeast of the turning basin). He also stretched a chain across the channel at Morgan's Point in order to collect tolls, making Buffalo Bayou a nautical tollway. Morgan soon turned to railroading, and the United States government ultimately gained responsibility for the channel in 1892 in order, as McComb stated, "to liberate the stream" by removing the chain. Through the efforts of men such as Houston Congressman Thomas H. Ball—a member of the Rivers and Harbors Committee—appropriations became available to expand upon Morgan's channel improvements. This was particularly important since Galveston was developing plans for deepening the bar to allow ocean-going vessels access to the local wharves. Congress also authorized the channel to be deepened to twenty-five feet and a terminus to be located at Long Reach, later called the turning basin. By 1909, however, the channel had only been deepened to eighteen and a half feet.[27]

A delegation from Houston, led by Mayor Horace Baldwin Rice, traveled to Washington urging Congress to accept the "Houston Plan" for the channel, which would provide half of the cost of the remaining dredging. Events then moved quickly: Congress accepted the plan with assurances that the facilities would remain in public hands; the Texas Legislature enabled Harris County to establish a navigation district; and the citizens of the county approved a bond issue. In September 1914, the dredging was completed, and the channel was officially opened on November 10. This was the same year as the opening of the Panama Canal, and some would say that it was just as momentous in its own way.

Deepwater capacity along the ship channel was delayed until after World War I. In 1919, the *Merry Mount* became the first oceangoing vessel to ship cotton directly from Houston to Europe.[28] Within a decade, Houston was the leading cotton port in the United States, matching its role as the largest spot cotton market in the world and the second leading port in the country in the volume of cotton orders handled.[29] Oil would soon rival cotton as the HSC's most important cargo.[30]

PETROLEUM, PETROCHEMICALS, AND BUFFALO BAYOU

With the development of the HSC along Buffalo Bayou, and its proximity to one of the world's great concentration of oil fields, Houston was on the map as the "Energy Capital of the World" by the 1930s. At that time, half of the world's production of oil was located within 600 miles of Houston, and it could boast of 4,200 miles of pipeline reaching outward to hundreds of oil fields. While Beaumont was close to the major oil fields, it did not have the railroads, banking system, or the port facilities that Houston had already developed.[31]

One observer noted in 1918 that, "the future of the Houston Ship Channel appears to lie in the direction of industrial developments as its banks furnish very favorable locations for industries which would thus be given the advantage of water transportation."[32] The utilization of Buffalo Bayou as a major commercial conduit for cotton, timber, and other commodities established an important precedent that allowed the Port of Houston to build an industrial capacity that would surpass its nineteenth- and early-twentieth-century enterprises. In addition, before the dominance of oil and gas, Houston and the Gulf Coast also were the site of other extractive enterprises beyond timber, namely sulphur, salt, lime, and other minerals.[33]

The oil strike at Spindletop opened the way for oil, natural gas, and petrochemicals to dominate the Gulf Coast trade and industrial production centered along the bayou. In a reciprocal way, transporting oil and other petroleum-related goods added incentive for additional channel improvements.[34] Oil was transformed into many products; it created thousands of jobs in production, transportation, sales, refining, and distribution; it led many oil companies to establish headquarters in Houston and the surrounding area; and it became home to many oil-related businesses such as Hughes Tool Company (started by Howard R. Hughes) and Cameron Iron Works.[35] Between 1929 and 1945, oil and related industries replaced cotton as the central feature of the Houston economy. In 1935, almost half of all Texas oil was shipped through the Port of Houston. *Fortune* magazine asserted that "without oil Houston would have been just another cotton town."[36] Petroleum remains the top import and export, along with other petroleum products, crude fertilizers and minerals, and organic chemicals, and "Buffalo Bayou has been transformed from a meandering stream into a vast industrial complex."[37] With the Spindletop strike, oil companies began to extend pipelines to the ship channel, and the protected watercourse offered an excellent location for refineries and other oil- and gas-related businesses. By 1930, more than fifty businesses had developed along the channel.[38]

Oil refining became a trademark of the Houston area. As oil historian Joseph A. Pratt stated, "throughout the twentieth century, the Gulf Coast of the United States had been one of the largest centers of petroleum refining in the world." He added, "although all phases of the industry were important, refining left its mark most prominently on the region." While the Gulf Coast refining region, writ large, extended from New Orleans to Corpus Christi (with almost 35 percent of the nation's refining capacity in 1970 and providing a substantial share of refined goods going to the Northeast), Pratt argued that the "historical and geographic center" was focused along a hundred-mile coastline from Houston to Port Arthur, which contained the greatest concentration of refineries. Houston itself was at the core of the extensive expansion of refining, which further enhanced its reputation as a major energy center. The large, integrated oil companies—several of which were based in Houston—were most influential in shaping refining development along the Gulf Coast.[39]

As early as 1916, refineries had already come on line in the region, but initially they were not as important as oil production or pipeline development for oil transport. With the construction of pipelines from a variety of oil fields in Texas, Louisiana, and Oklahoma, oil continued to flow to the Gulf

Coast despite the subsiding of the Spindletop boom.[40] The turning point for Houston as the center of refining along the Gulf Coast came several years after the completion of the ship channel. With the end of World War I, refineries slowly began to be attracted to the area, but it was in the 1920s that large plants were constructed in earnest.

By 1927, eight refineries with a capacity of approximately 125,000 barrels of crude a day were operating along the ship channel. The early leader was Humble Oil and Refining Company's huge Baytown refinery—the largest on the Gulf Coast for several decades. In 1920, Sinclair Oil Company built a large plant in Houston, and Crown Central built another in Pasadena in 1924.[41] A variety of smaller refineries also dotted both sides of the ship channel. In the late 1920s and 1930s, Houston saw increasingly rapid expansion in refining capacity—Shell's plant in Deer Creek (1929), Pan American's in Texas City (1934), Republic's also in Texas City (1932), and the Eastern States Petroleum facility in Houston (1937). The refining capacity in the Houston area increased by more than 360 percent between 1931 and 1941, even greater than in the Port Arthur area, which had dominated years earlier.[42]

Emerging as a major economic force in World War II, the production of petrochemicals added to the importance of petroleum and natural gas to the Houston area in general and to the ship channel in particular. In 1920, there were only two active petrochemical companies in the United States. In the 1920s and 1930s, Union Carbide and Standard Oil of New Jersey were pioneers. World War II brought significant changes in the industry, especially with the need for aviation fuel, synthetic rubber, and other petroleum-based products necessary for the war effort. In fact, half of the synthetic rubber used in the war came from Texas. Pratt asserted that "petrochemicals were the catalyst for a second spurt of regional growth in the modern era, which repeated in many ways the refining-led expansion of the period from 1901 to the 1930s. By 1970 six billion dollars had been invested in the petrochemical industry in Texas." Houston, in particular, was at the heart of petrochemical production, especially because the Gulf Coast refineries were a major source of the raw material—the feedstock—for petrochemicals. By 1950, there were twenty-seven chemical plants along the ship channel. By the 1980s, the Houston area had more than half of the petrochemical capacity in the country.[43] One of the prices that the region has paid for the high concentration of petroleum and petrochemical facilities, however, has been high levels of air, land, and water pollution to accompany its economic bounty.

THE BATTLE OF SAN JACINTO AND TEXAS INDEPENDENCE

On the base of the San Jacinto Monument commemorating the Battle of Jacinto the following is enscribed: "Measured by its results, San Jacinto was one of the decisive battles of the world. The freedom of Texas from Mexico won here led to annexation and to the Mexican War, resulting in the acquisition by the United States of the states of Texas, New Mexico, Arizona, Nevada, California, Utah, and parts of Colorado, Wyoming, Kansas, and Oklahoma. Almost one-third of the present area of the American nation, nearly a million square miles, changed sovereignty."[44] While the statement attributes too much to this battle, or almost any one military engagement, the Battle of San Jacinto (April 21, 1836) did save the Texan cause from what seemed like defeat at the hands of Santa Anna's superior forces. While independence was not assured immediately, progress in that direction quickened.[45]

The banks of Buffalo Bayou were the site for the Battle of San Jacinto. In the war for Texas independence in the 1830s, General Sam Houston and his Texas army retreated eastward in the direction of Harrisburg after defeats at the hands of the Mexican army at the Alamo and Goliad. General Santa Anna and his Mexican troops sought to trap the members of the Texas government at Harrisburg, believing Houston would flee across the Sabine River a distance away from there. After burning Harrisburg, Santa Anna's troops pursued the Texas government officials first to New Washington and then turned toward Galveston, where the Texan leaders sought refuge. On the evening of April 19, Houston's army crossed Buffalo Bayou below Harrisburg, and they skirmished with the Mexicans on April 20. In a surprise attack the following day, the Texans overwhelmed the Mexicans, slaughtering them and eventually capturing Santa Anna. The Mexican general was forced to sign the Treaties of Velasco in which he recognized Texas's independence.

The defeat of the Mexican army was a pivotal event of the Texas Revolution and led to fulfillment of Texas independence that had been declared on March 2, 1836. The peace fostered increased colonization of the state and region, inflamed the issue of slavery in the South, and added to the expansionist furor of the age.[46]

The San Jacinto Monument, in San Jacinto Battleground State Park, sits at the site of the battle. The 570-feet-tall monument, taller than the Washington Monument, was completed in 1939. It had been part of the Texas Centennial celebration of 1936, albeit a belated dedication. Also in the park is the USS *Texas*, the last remaining World War I dreadnought in the world. It had been launched from Newport News, Virginia, in May 1912, and then commissioned two years later. The ship was considered the most powerful warship afloat at the time.[47]

BUFFALO BAYOU AND THE CIVIL WAR

Although not crucial to the prosecution of the Civil War, activities along Buffalo Bayou were closely linked to Texas participation. By the end of the first year of the war, commercial traffic on Buffalo Bayou was constrained due to the federal blockade at Galveston. Furthermore, Houstonians prepared for the potential invasion by adapting many buildings for war use. For example, John Kennedy's building on Travis Street was leased to the Confederacy for use as an ordnance depot.

The Union had captured Galveston in October 1862, and nominally held part of the Texas coast near Galveston and Sabine Pass, but Texans continued to attack Union soldiers and skirmish with federal ships by employing numerous vessels. In the Battle of Galveston, "cottonclads" *Neptune* and *Bayou City*—Galveston-bound steamboats loaded with cotton bales but also hiding artillerymen—engaged the U.S. gunboat *Harriet Lane* on December 31, 1862, in Galveston Bay. While the *Neptune* was sunk, the *Bayou City* captured the *Harriet Lane,* and the federal ship *Westfield* also ran aground during the battle. Confederates claimed several hundred prisoners from the two ships. The *Bayou City* returned up Buffalo Bayou and was greeted with great fanfare, while about 350 federal prisoners were marched along Main Street and were locked up in a warehouse on the north side of the bayou near present-day University of Houston-Downtown.

The Union forces were stunned by the resistance, but as the war dragged on "the Texas Coast remained in a state of anxiety," as Richard Francaviglia suggested, "its economy suffering severely and its residents on edge from nearly constant harassment of maritime trade by blockading Union vessels, the outright capture of some ports, and the incessant rumors of possible invasion by Union troops from the sea."[48]

The naval engagements in Galveston Bay and the trade activity along Buffalo Bayou in the largest sense were significant to the western campaign of the Civil War. The keys to strategy in the west for the Union forces were twofold: capturing Chattanooga in order to cut off the near Southwest from Richmond; and capturing Vicksburg to gain command of the Mississippi and to cut off Texas from the rest of the Confederacy. The blockade along the Texas coast was meant to limit food and munitions that were making their way from Texas to the Confederate troops to its east. When Vicksburg was taken in 1864, Texas was severed from the Confederacy, and the Union forces thus had gained clear advantage by being able to cease watching their backs so closely. The agricultural bounty that was available in the Texas hinterland could no longer find its way out of Buffalo Bayou, into Galveston Bay, and thus into the hands of southern forces.[49]

THE CAMP LOGAN RIOT OF 1917

The Camp Logan Riot in 1917 highlighted deep racial discrimination in the United States during World War I and the persistence of segregationist practices in the twentieth-century South. One of two military installations built in Harris County during World War I, Camp Logan was situated near Buffalo Bayou in the northwest outskirts of Houston. The relatively mild climate and the recently opened HSC made the site of the camp logical. The Illinois National Guard was to train there. The Third Battalion of the Twenty-fourth United States Infantry—a black unit with white officers—was brought in to guard the construction site for the camp in July 1917. Many of the troops were from the South and were not surprised to face racial discrimination when they were in town. As servicemen, however, they expected better treatment at the hands of the Houstonians.

Around noon on August 23, 1917, police arrested a black soldier for allegedly interfering with their arrest of an African American woman in the Fourth Ward. When a black military police officer with the battalion sought out the local police to determine what happened to the soldier, an argument broke out, the military police officer was hit, he was shot at when he fled, and eventually brought to police headquarters. A rumor that the military police officer had been killed led a group of soldiers from Camp Logan to march on the police headquarters to seek his release. The agitation made black soldiers in the camp skittish, and fears of a white mob storming the camp led some to fire rifles toward the phantom mob. Order could not be restored. More than one hundred armed black soldiers moved on downtown Houston, killing fifteen white people, four of whom were policemen, and also Captain Joseph Mattes of the Illinois National Guard, who was mistaken for a policeman, and seriously wounding twelve more. In the melee, four black soldiers died as well (two accidentally shot by their own men). The soldiers then returned to camp, where the leader of the group Sergeant Vida Henry shot himself.

The Army sent the Third Battalion back to its point of origination, Columbus, New Mexico. Seven of the mutinying soldiers, granted clemency, testified against the others. In three separate court-martials between November 1917 and March 1918, 118 soldiers were indicted; 110 were found guilty of mutiny and rioting; 19 of the soldiers were hanged; and 63 received life sentences. Two white officers who faced court-martial were released, and none of the white civilians participating in the riot went to trial.[50]

The Camp Logan Riot—or Houston Riot of 1917—was a grim reminder of the state of race relations in the United States at the time. It was sufficiently complex to make it difficult to draw clear conclusions about fault or innocence, but the underlying causes went deeper than the apparent tensions over the fate of one black soldier arrested for a somewhat ambiguous crime.

A BOON FOR CLEAN WATER: ACTIVATED SLUDGE

In the early twentieth century, Buffalo Bayou claimed a very different type of notoriety by building the first large-scale wastewater treatment plant to use the activated sludge method. According to the City of Houston Engineering Department 1922 end of the year report, the North Side Sewage Treatment Plant, "was the first large scale attempt to operate on the scattered sludge principal."[51] The North Side facility remained the largest plant of its kind in the world in 1922, some three years after it was first put into operation. The technique employed there gained international usage and has become a standard practice for effluent treatment and water purification worldwide.

Growing out of the study of sewage aeration processes, Dr. Gilbert J. Fowler (and his associates) of Manchester, England, reported that sewage inoculated with oxidizing bacteria could be clarified and free from bacteria within a few hours of aeration. The first use of the activated sludge process at a treatment facility took place in Salford, England, in 1914. The first American installation was completed in San Marcos, Texas, in 1916, and soon was followed by a facility in Milwaukee, Wisconsin. However, Houston's application of the activated sludge process was much larger. While the San Marcos plant treated 120,000 gallons per day and the Milwaukee plant 2 million gallons per day, the North Side Sewage Treatment Plant built in 1917 along Buffalo Bayou treated 5.5 million gallons per day. The southern facility in Houston, completed the following year, treated 5 million gallons per day. The Houston plants were uncontested until 1925 when Milwaukee constructed a plant that treated 45 million gallons per day using the activated sludge process.[52]

The historical importance of Buffalo Bayou is particularly rich. Most Houstonians likely recognize it as a familiar site where the Allen brothers planted the seed of the sprawling city of more than six hundred square miles and about four million people. However, the historical record suggests that Buffalo Bayou truly produced institutions and events of national significance, the most dramatic being the base of the twentieth-century's "Energy Capital of the World." Producing, refining, and shipping petroleum, natural gas, and petrochemicals via the HSC is central to the very modernity of our culture. That Buffalo Bayou also was the site of a battle that helped secure the independence of the Republic of Texas, contributed to the Confederates' role in the Civil War, highlighted the deeply serious problem of racial segregation, and contributed an innovative technology for wastewater treatment worldwide suggests its meaningful role beyond city and state borders. Buffalo Bayou truly represents how a water artery has transformative influence in many, albeit some unanticipated, ways on a region, state, and nation.

CHAPTER SEVEN

Houston's Public Sinks

WATER AND WASTEWATER SERVICES—LOCAL
CONCERNS TO REGIONAL CHALLENGES

WATER WELLS AND PUBLIC SINKS

The original version of this chapter appeared in *Energy Metropolis: An Environmental History of Houston and the Gulf Coast* (2007), edited by me and my colleague Joseph Pratt. The overriding purpose of the book was to demonstrate how cities by their very nature are energy intensive—in some instances generators of energy sources but certainly major consumers of energy. In the case of Houston, the concentration of oil refining and petrochemical industries in the twentieth century not only greatly affected its economic life, but also degraded its air and water quality. Less well understood is how the emergence of a world energy capital like the Bayou City was responsible for transforming—or at least modifying—the urban infrastructure along with its nature and scale. Modern Houston is a sprawling automobile city, dependent on air conditioning for its very daily functioning. In many respects, the city's physical characteristics are a reflection of the demands of the oil industry for transportation arteries and myriad services. Reinvestment of capital from the oil and petrochemical businesses also led to other major enterprises in Houston, such as the gigantic Medical Center, the Johnson Space Center, and real estate ventures like Friendswood Development (to its south) and the Woodlands (to its north). Houston's sanitary services are the result of a public and private partnership, where such services emerged out of the dynamics of unrelenting demand from its citizenry as well as from its commercial and industrial sectors. In and of itself this is not unusual, but that private business relies so much on public systems in a place that prides itself on individual initiative and market-

144

driven projects tells a quite different story than in the case of many other cities nationwide. And it certainly presents an alternative to the public and private co-operation in San Jose, California, in more recent years.

Despite the attempts to portray Houston as a "free enterprise city" and to remind us that it is the largest city in the United States without zoning, the de-velopment of its sanitary services has been remarkably typical of its counterparts throughout the country. Prior to World War II, however, the Bayou City commit-ted itself to singular approaches to providing water (wells), wastewater service (sanitary sewers), and solid waste disposal (incinerators), which has not been typical of other cities. In time, Houston utilized a variety of approaches, none of which were necessarily out of line with other municipal practices, but nonethe-less a shift from prior approaches. Like other urban areas, especially those with the opportunity to sprawl uncontrollably, local services got tangled up with ju-risdictions beyond the city limits, encroached into areas far removed from its borders in search of water, and contributed to environmental problems on a re-gional scale. In those respects, the potency of its oil-led economic development provided a key subtext.

For a city that celebrated the free market, embraced the American Dream, and apparently saw no limits to individuals rising above their economic sta-tion, sanitary systems in Houston were deeply imbedded in the public service model, albeit consistently in demand by the private sector. People might com-plain that the city too often devoted too little to providing adequate water supply and wastewater service—the city's massive flooding problems have been testa-ment to that as has its uneven distribution of the services among the haves and have-nots—but outsourcing these services has never been taken very seriously. At least in terms of structure, if not always performance, Houston has remained committed to public sanitary services for a variety of constituencies—public and private.

HOUSTON'S PUBLIC SINKS

Sanitary services—particularly water supply and wastewater—form the cir-culatory system of a city. Not only do they transport vital resources in and carry unwanted materials out, but they play a significant role in preserv-ing health. The timing of and commitment to establishing and maintaining sanitary services in Houston was not particularly unique. In most respects, city authorities followed a pattern of development inline with many cities in nineteenth-century America. These patterns were shaped by population growth, onset of epidemic diseases, inadequate maintenance of private wells and privy vaults, and newfound municipal authority and taxing power.

The perspective of Houston as a free enterprise city, eschewing public spending not directly benefiting profit-seeking business leaders, does not

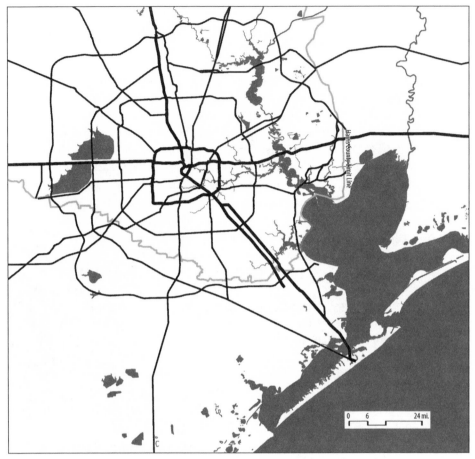

FIGURE 7.1. Roadway infrastructure of Houston.
Map by Maria Oran and Donna Kacmar, FAIA.

seem to apply here.[1] For the most part, the city invested in a water supply system and underground sewers irrespective of the vagaries of the business climate. Houston, however, was not a leader in offering adequate sanitary services to all citizens in a timely manner, and city authorities certainly took into account the value of services vis-à-vis the economic vitality of the community.

Despite its apparent unremarkable history, the development of Houston's water and wastewater infrastructure provides insight into the nature of the city's growth from a small nineteenth-century town deep in unsettled southeastern Texas to the fourth largest city in the United States. Houston's population in 1837 was a modest 1,500. Maturing as an important regional

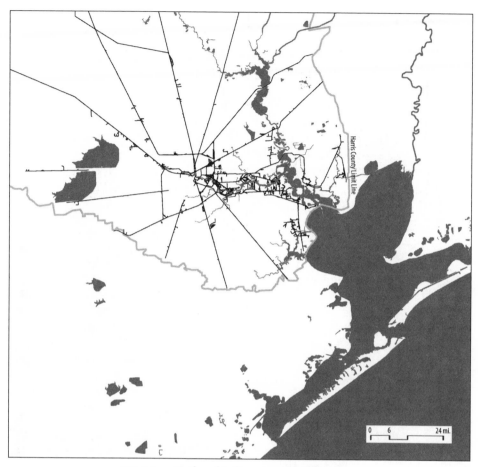

FIGURE 7.2. Railroad infrastructure of Houston.
Map by Maria Oran and Donna Kacmar, FAIA.

commercial and industrial center, spurred on by World War I and especially
World War II, Houston's population reached approximately 700,000 by
1945 and the city covered an area of about 17 square miles. By the late twentieth century, Houston clearly had arrived as a major American city topping
2 million people within the city limits and extending over more than 600
square miles. Beyond those gross statistics the Bayou City had long achieved
world-class status as the "Energy Capital of the World," a major international center of medicine and medical care, and an archetype of the modern Sunbelt city.

The development of the city's sanitary infrastructure is an important un-
derpinning to the city's evolution. Prior to World War II, the expansion of

water and wastewater systems was guided by localized issues, namely Houston's modest population growth and its physical assets and liabilities. After the war, the city's rampant physical growth, its population explosion, and its rising economic status produced a metropolis whose regional impact was immense and whose sanitary services were linked inextricably to southeastern Texas and the Gulf Coast. This was particularly the case in seeking new water supplies, and in producing runoff that polluted Galveston Bay.

Especially with respect to sanitation systems, there have been two Houstons: a pre–World War II emerging city where local concerns and interests dominated the delivery of services and a post–World War II metropolis, where those services reached beyond the city limits to have broad environmental and political impacts on the region.

ORIGINS AND IMPLEMENTATION OF WATER AND WASTEWATER SYSTEMS, 1876–1945

Before the 1870s, sanitary services in Houston were primarily the responsibility of the individual. The city did not develop its first public water supply and sewerage system until it emerged as a commercial center in the 1870s and 1880s. The establishment of citywide systems was spurred by growth demands, fire protection, and health questions—typical for most cities. However, the types of systems developed in this period—especially in the case of water supply—depended heavily on the geologic and climactic conditions of southeast Texas. Potable water came primarily from extensive aquifers beneath the city.

The new citywide sanitary systems obviously were meant to serve local, immediate needs and requirements. They did so unevenly, however, by giving preference to commercial districts and incorporated areas, with modest attention to the less affluent and to marginal land uses. The new services also proved inadequate in the wake of the aggressive physical expansion of the city and the great economic boom that followed World War II. As Houston became a regionally dominant metropolis its sanitary services had significant influence on places beyond its borders. Local needs would clash with regional effects and impacts—political and environmental.

WATER SUPPLY

Water supply was the first important public utility in the United States, and the first municipal service that demonstrated a city's dedication to growth. In the early nineteenth century, most American cities relied on streams, ponds, and wells; by 1900, public systems were the major source for residential and commercial consumption and fire protection.[2] During its frontier days, Houston depended upon underground brick cisterns, overhead cypress tanks, and private wells for drinking water and for fire protection. Water from the bayous was considered good for drinking. When fires broke out in residential areas bucket brigades tapped cisterns and shallow wells. Between 1838 and 1895, volunteer firemen provided the only fire protection.[3]

Houston developed its first public water supply system in 1876. By national standards, the Bayou City's commitment to a centralized water source and distribution network was typical for a city of its age, size, and location. The system was unique insofar as the city relied exclusively on groundwater from countless wells from 1887 until the 1940s. The water was drawn from the Chicot and Evangeline aquifers running southeast to northwest from the Gulf Coast through Harris County's western half and into Montgomery and Grimes counties.[4] Until it sought to develop surface water in the 1940s, Houston was the largest city in North America to rely exclusively on well water.

The public uproar over a major fire that scorched the business district in February 1859, led to the installation of the first public cistern in downtown Houston. After a second major fire broke out in March 1860, the city constructed additional public cisterns.[5] For nearly two decades little was done to upgrade the modest water supply service. In January 1878, Mayor James T. D. Wilson noted the pressing need for waterworks and sewers. Dependence on cisterns for fire protection had become unworkable as demands for water by a growing population intensified.

Episodic health problems linked to the water supply also raised questions about the need to change the source. In the wake of a yellow fever epidemic in 1869, Mayor J. R. Morris called for a survey of Houston's water supply and concluded that the city should change sources. He investigated using the nearby Brazos River west of the city, but engineers believed the water was impure. He also considered the San Jacinto River to the east for diversion into White Oak and Buffalo Bayous, but the Panic of 1873 derailed further action.[6]

Throughout the early 1870s, several northern companies approached the city council offering to install a water supply system, but the city's shaky financial status as a result of the Panic of 1873 precluded issuing a franchise. When the financial picture improved, the council entered into a twenty-five-year contract with James M. Loweree of New York and his associates on November 30, 1878. Loweree's credentials as an experienced engineer and builder of several other waterworks won him the franchise.[7]

The Loweree group organized itself into Houston Water Works Company on April 15, 1879, and began operations in August. The original waterworks consisted of a pumping plant, which drew water from Buffalo Bayou and pumped it directly into distributing mains. The water supplied was used primarily for fire purposes. Many people found the company's water unsuitable for drinking and continued to depend upon private cisterns. Some of the larger manufacturing companies dug their own wells. Shortly after the start of operations, a major fire broke out downtown, and the new system provided sufficient water at adequate pressure to fight the blaze. A grateful council immediately granted the company a permanent franchise.[8]

Despite advancements in fire fighting, Buffalo Bayou proved to be a poor source of supply particularly after a fire or after the mains had been put under pressure. Sand and mud often clogged the mains, clouding the water and reducing the flow. Company officials vowed to enhance the system, but improvements came slowly.[9]

In 1884, local business interests headed by former mayor and wealthy property holder Thomas H. Scanlan purchased the Houston Water Works Company, and in 1888, it drilled its first artesian well. While the water company and others appreciated the relative ease in obtaining fresh water from a source other than the bayous, they did not know that Houston sat atop what was one of the largest artesian reservoirs in the United States.[10]

The new supply was immediately heralded as the solution to Houston's long-term water needs. Between 1888 and 1891, the company operated fourteen wells, which supplied an area of seven square miles.[11] The 1890–1891 *City Directory* noted that, "Houston is the only city but one supplied through her system of water works with artesian water, the purest, clearest and best water to be found. . . . Houston's supply of artesian water is considered inexhaustible, as she has now nearly one hundred wells, spouting up cool, pure water."[12] The water company soon discovered that a supposedly bottomless pool of pure water did not solve all of the problems of operating a water system. Bayou water often was pumped into the city reservoir to meet increased demand when fires broke out, making it unfit to drink for several days. In 1904, the U.S. Supreme Court ordered the company to cease pumping bayou water into the mains, and artesian wells thus became the sole source for the Houston distribution system.[13]

As the population grew, the Houston Water Works Company sank more wells. The legal constraints on the use of bayou water left it with few alternatives, since no provisions had been made for tapping surface water. Some existing wells began to produce at very low pressure or failed to produce at all, resulting in short-term water famines. In some cases, sand clogged the strainers, obstructing the flow of water. As complaints multiplied about water quality, poor fire protection, or minimal efforts to extend distribution mains, officials tolerated few excuses from the water company.[14]

While confidence in the artesian water supply was wholehearted, faith in the company faded. In Houston as elsewhere, municipal leaders increasingly argued that cities could run their services more efficiently and effectively than private firms who were driven simply by profits.[15] The Houston Water Works Company, however, was unwilling to extend service without a new franchise. Mayor Horace Baldwin Rice concluded that while he had been doubtful of public ownership of utilities, "when it comes to the question of water, the very life and essence of a community, it would be far better for the City of Houston to own and operate its own water system."[16]

On October 6, 1906, the city purchased the waterworks, reflecting the editorial judgment of the *Houston Post* that "so vital an element of life as the water supply of a city should be in possession of the whole people. It should not be a source of revenue to any person or corporation."[17] City officials were quick to congratulate themselves for rescuing the waterworks from inefficiency and inadequate service. An August 1909 issue of *Progressive Houston* proclaimed, "some are expending millions of dollars and pushing pipe lines scores upon scores of miles out into the country, perhaps into the mountains, in efforts to procure such water as Houston is daily turning into every yard of the city."[18]

The debate over municipal ownership ignored the viability of a water system based solely on artesian wells, but the optimism about improved quality of service had some merit. The city soon addressed problems of water source and pumping capacity and then turned to extension of the distribution system. Although laying new mains favored downtown consumers and the affluent, aggregate mileage of the distribution lines increased significantly from 69 to 105 miles between 1907 and 1912. In the 1910s, the miles of water main doubled from approximately 98 to 200—slightly more rapidly than population growth for the period.[19] The extension of service also meant a greater draw on supply, and questions persisted about available water pressure and rates of withdrawal—problems that played a role in the company's loss of its franchise. In addition, Houston's system was a single network of mains, while some cities had two sets—one with high pressure exclusively for firefighting. This meant that in order to maintain balance between both services, less pressure for firefighting was available in Houston than in other cities.[20]

Dependence on well water went unabated, despite the city takeover of the system. Until 1915, the largest percentage of the wells in Houston was "free flowing," meaning that pressure decreased when withdrawal was heavy. Adding more wells did not address the issue of reduced pressure. Pumps had to be installed at the wells to discharge water into the pipelines leading to the reservoir.[21] Theoretically, the underground supply was abundant for many future generations; realistically, demand on the system increased so rapidly that productive wells were depleted or ceased to be free flowing. Population growth accounted for much of the escalating demand, but agricultural and industrial uses also were important. After the opening of the Houston Ship Channel (1914), pressure on the aquifer from industrial use rose dramatically. By 1940, groundwater sources supplied more than 140 million gallons per day distributed as follows: rice fields, 45 million gallons per day; metropolitan district and fringe areas, 81 million gallons per day; and the ship channel, 35 million gallons per day.[22]

The immediate response to growing demand was to sink new wells, to add pumps to existing wells, to build new pumping plants, and to extend distribution lines—all of which increased supply but did nothing to discourage demand.[23] Metering water use at the point of consumption was an early way to control demand, prevent waste, and limit development of new supplies. Meters were unpopular with citizens but nonetheless became important tools nationwide in administering the water supply in publicly managed systems by the turn of the century.[24] In Houston, these devices were first introduced in 1909, with the municipal water system completely metered by about 1914. Between 1906 (with flat rates) and 1914 (with metered rates), the average daily pumpage decreased from 11 million gallons to 5.5 million gallons—despite a 65 percent increase in the population served. To complement the meter system, the city had to implement better methods of detecting leaks.[25]

Metering did not create a conservation-minded public, although satisfaction with the artesian supply continued into the late 1930s. Periodically a cautionary note was voiced about the city's growth outstripping its well capacity, but many held out hope that Houston could continue to develop additional artesian wells rather than utilize surface water.[26] The satisfaction with the water supply, however, tended to mask structural deficiencies in the system. By the mid-1930s, it was essentially a collection of water plants and distribution mains pieced together by expansion into subdivisions along the fringes of the city and through modest annexation.[27]

Poor fiscal policy only aggravated the problems caused by expansion. Improvements were made through bond issues, since department net revenues went directly into the general fund. The result was a serious lag in improvements. In the mid-1930s, two important organizational changes occurred: in 1935 the Water Department separated from the Department of Public Works, and through a 1934 Texas Supreme Court decision revenues of the Water Department could only be used to pay for the operation and maintenance of the water system, any fixed obligations, and improvements to the water system.[28]

Despite the corrective actions, neglect of public health responsibilities was marked. Between 1915 and 1929, the Texas State Department of

Health and the United States Public Health Service conducted surveys of the Houston water system. Purity of the artesian water at the well head was not questioned, but there were several potential threats before it reached the consumer. In 1928, the city had been given only "provisional certification" contingent on making recommended sanitary improvements. Cross-connections had to be eliminated or at least regulated because they allowed water from any source to enter the city's system. Other precautions included providing laboratory control over water quality, replacing or eliminating tile sewers and privies close to wells or on water plant property, and chlorinating the water.

Little action was taken until after a major flood struck in May 1929. Buffalo Bayou left its banks due to heavy rains, and twenty feet of water inundated the Central Water Plant. The loss of the plant caused a severe water shortage, requiring pumpage from private wells. State and federal authorities slapped Houston's supply with "prohibitive status," and the city had to initiate emergency chlorination. In June, city officials signed a "sanitary improvement agreement" declaring that Houston would carry out recommendations made the previous year. In July, Houston received "provisional certification," and in 1933 "full certification."[29]

The increasing challenges to the water system began to erode the city's heretofore unshakable confidence in the groundwater supply. Artesian well pressure had begun to decline as early as 1910, and for several years the water level dropped by an average of five feet annually. During the early years of the Great Depression the quantity of water withdrawn declined by 10 percent. With increased industrial pumping along the ship channel for cooling and other purposes, the static level (depth to retrieve water) of the wells worsened. The deterioration of the wells—plus the lack of a wholesale rate for water—caused many industries and owners of commercial buildings to drill more of their own wells. By 1941, the public supply furnished less than 40 percent of the total demand of the metropolitan area.[30]

The decline in well productivity, in addition to growing independent action of commercial and industrial enterprises, led several experts to view the problem as nearing a critical stage. In the 1930s and early 1940s, as many as forty reports on the water supply's condition were issued, but they were often contradictory and inconclusive. In 1938, the Mayor's Advisory Board (in concurrence with the National Board of Fire Underwriters) recommended that a new well field be developed west of Houston and that implementation of a separate industrial supply be postponed.[31]

Alternatively, Alvord, Burdick & Howson—a Chicago engineering firm retained by the city—issued a report in February 1938 that favored the use of the San Jacinto River as a single, inexpensive, and reliable water source.

The San Jacinto was the nearest surface supply with a drainage area of 2,840 square miles above the ship channel. A reservoir site was available only fifteen miles from the city's industrial district.[32] The study painted a poor picture of the existing system that was lacking in capacity in wells, storage facilities, reservoirs, mains, and fire hydrants. "Houston," it stated, "presents an unusually aggravated example of uncoordinated efforts to solve the rapidly expanding water requirements of a thriving community without any comprehensive plan or continuing policy." Comparing the Bayou City with other cities, it noted that "Houston, located in the greatest well water field of the world and within a maximum distance of fifty miles of the four rivers draining two-fifths of all Texas, has a water supply system everywhere deficient, from source to its ultimate distribution to the consumer." The report added that the Houston system "is virtually a group of small town supplies without the distribution facilities or interconnections essential to the delivery of water for either fire or domestic use." Financially, the Houston waterworks existed on a "hand to mouth" basis, and the city's investment in it was less than one-third that of the average city of its size. Insurance costs were at least $180,000 per year above what they would be with an adequate waterworks.[33]

While the debate over Houston's water needs persisted, the Water Department decided on a middle course between those advocating drilling more wells and those supporting a shift to surface water. In May 1937—before the Alvord, Burdick & Howson report was made public—the engineering staff recommended filing an application with the State Board of Water Engineers to appropriate water from the San Jacinto River to complement the groundwater withdrawal. G. L. Fugate, chief engineer of the Water Department, pursued the combined groundwater and surface water program into the 1940s, viewing the damming of the San Jacinto as a source principally to supply industrial demand.[34]

The onset of World War II finally pushed Houston toward surface supply. On September 10, 1941, the city filed an application with the Federal Works Administration for financial support to improve the water supply system and to obtain a supplemental supply from the San Jacinto River. Wartime exigencies directed the federal government's interest in the project to the eastern portion of the city around the ship channel, designated as a "defense area." The industries there would employ an estimated 90,000 workers during the war.[35]

Fugate conducted a study in July 1942, that concluded a dual supply from groundwater and a single dam on the San Jacinto would be preferable to drawing on the Colorado River (although federal engineers disagreed about the potential of the Colorado). That same month the War Production Board authorized the San Jacinto River Conservation and Reclamation District to build a reservoir. Construction of Sheldon Reservoir (located on Carpenter's Bayou, a tributary of Buffalo Bayou) began in December 1942 for delivery of water to industries at Baytown and in the Pasadena area in 1943.[36]

Political wrangling ensued among federal, state, and local governments over the construction project. The city protested a grant of authority to an outside agency to construct water supply facilities in its jurisdiction. Because of the urgent need for the water, the War Production Board suspended the decision-granting authority to the district in August 1942 and declared that the agency showing the best ability to deliver water to industries in the Baytown area would be favored. Neither the city nor the district would permit a grant to the other, and the federal government announced its intention of constructing the facility itself.

Ironically, since the city's preliminary plans and surveys were well advanced, the Federal Works Administration adopted the city's program and, in November 1942, employed the city as its architect-engineer with Fugate as contract engineer. Actual construction of the dam began in December 1942 by Brown & Root for delivery of water to industries at Baytown and in the Pasadena area (to the east of the city of Houston) in 1943. Two open canals from the river were constructed to serve the ship channel: the West Canal leading to Pasadena and the East Canal terminating at the Humble Refinery in Baytown (both east of Houston). Despite the increase in available supply from the San Jacinto, distribution facilities still did not reach remote sites along the ship channel, and as a result wells served the increasing demand from new industries.

In June 1944, Houstonians voted for a $14 million bond issue to increase the amount of groundwater supply and for more mains, but they also approved it to buy the West Canal from the federal government in order to build a dam across the San Jacinto River north of Sheldon and to construct a filtration plant. Because of the need for additional funding, Lake Houston Dam on the San Jacinto—which would replace Sheldon Lake as the city's prime source of surface water—was not placed into operation until 1954. The new public water supply provided water for the city of Houston, the industrial complex from Houston to Baytown, and also supported local irrigation for various products including rice.[37]

The debate over water in the 1930s, coupled with the acquisition of wartime industries along the ship channel, began Houston's transition from a city totally dependent on groundwater to one eventually dependent on a dual supply. From its early years, residents and industries alike relied heavily on the underground aquifers located in or near the city. While this pure, inexpensive, and abundant source of water contributed to significant urban

growth, the almost blind faith in its ability to sustain the city diverted attention from weak links in the supply system, especially the extent and reliabil-
ity of the distribution network, and the need to anticipate future demand by
exploring new sources, sources that flowed primarily beyond the city limits.
New supplies meant new possibilities but also new challenges that would
force Houstonians to deal with jurisdictional and environmental issues not
encountered before World War II.

SEWERAGE SYSTEM

The development of an underground sewerage system in pre–World War
II Houston took into account issues of public health, but gave only passing
attention to chronic problems of heavy rainfall and flooding. Houston had
developed a sewerage plan in the late 1860s, but construction of a citywide
sewerage system did not begin until a quarter of a century after the public
water supply. Such a delay was not unusual. Northeast and Midwest cities
began constructing sewerage systems in the mid-nineteenth century, but
not until after World War II did all large cities have complete networks. Prior
to the installation of underground sewerage systems, urbanites disposed of
their wastewater by throwing it on the ground or in a gutter (which doubled
as a carrier of stormwater). Human wastes were deposited in cesspools or
privy vaults.

With rising population growth and the piping of water into homes and
businesses in the mid- to late nineteenth century, old methods of disposal
proved impractical and unsanitary. The great volumes of water used in
homes, businesses, and industrial plants had to flow out as well as in. Without ample sewers, wastewater flooded cesspools and privy vaults, inundated
yards and lots, and generally posed a major health hazard. Few cities simultaneously installed sewerage systems with their new water supply systems
because of the cost involved and the inability—or unwillingness—to foresee
the necessary interconnection of the two systems. Extensive construction of
municipal sewers did not commence in the United States until the 1880s.[38]

Houston confronted many of the same problems that non-sewered,
growing cities faced in their early years of development. Members of the
Board of Health voiced concern over good sanitation, and an 1866 ordinance
prescribed fines for citizens who did not keep their privies clean or randomly
emptied filth onto the sidewalks and streets.

Beside health concerns, southern cities like Houston faced severe drainage problems, exacerbated by frequent downpours. Soon after the Allen
brothers founded Houston in 1836, every structure in the new town flooded.
Runoff increased with more hard-surfaced streets, resulting in swelling
watercourses and flooding. Harold Platt noted in May 1868 that "the news-

paper had been quick to praise the horsecar venture for grading Main Street from curb to curb. But the first torrential storm replaced the street's 'metropolitan appearance' with sights of little boys floating down it on jerry-built rafts."[39] Between 1836 and 1936, Harris County experienced sixteen major floods, some cresting at more than forty feet, "turning downtown Houston streets into raging rivers."[40] Destructive floods in 1929 and 1935 raised serious public outcries. The 1929 flood caused staggering property damage of $1.4 million. The 1935 flood doubled that amount, resulted in the loss of seven people, and inundated twenty-five blocks of the business district and a hundred residential blocks. In addition, the Port of Houston was shut down for months because of submerged docks, destroyed railroad tracks, and a channel blocked up with tons of mud and debris. Finally, countywide flood-control action was taken in 1937 with the creation of the Harris County Flood Control District (HCFCD).[41]

Before and for a time after the water supply system was in place, building drainage ditches and sewers in Houston was piecemeal and unsystematic. Because of the cost and old habits, city leaders rationalized that relying on cesspools, privy vaults, and open ditches made underground sewers less vital than fire protection, a good water supply, or paved streets. Funds were allocated only for specific sewerage projects, not for an entire system, and those who could afford them constructed private sewers.

In 1866, civil engineer Colonel William H. Griffin developed the city's first sewerage plan under the auspices of the Board of Health. Griffin, who became city engineer the following year, made a case for three main sewer lines that would spill into Buffalo Bayou and drain the southern portion of the city focusing on the downtown area. While not an integrated system, the plan offered a practical starting point. City council supported it but directed Griffin to broaden the area of coverage. Two drainage ditches serving the downtown were completed immediately, and only the Caroline Street brick sewer—originally constructed for stormwater drainage and the first underground sewer to be constructed in the state—was completed in 1874. Attention turned to other city needs, and the call for a comprehensive system dropped down the list of priorities.[42]

By the mid-1880s, most Houston residents still relied on private cesspools. Tolerance for the lack of adequate sanitation was wearing thin, especially since Buffalo Bayou was being utilized simultaneously as a source for drinking water and as a sewage outlet. Citizens complained that "tar water" flowed out of the pipes, human waste floated in the bayou, and fish died because of the dumping of creosote. Diarrheic problems sent adults and children to the local doctors. The commitment to artesian wells for the city's water supply quelled immediate concern over the need for a source of pure water, but the question of increased incidence of wanton pollution of the bayou highlighted the need for adequate sewerage.[43]

In June 1887, city engineer W. M. Harkness drafted a proposal calling for the examination of sewerage plans in other cities. With the support of the Citizens' Committee—a businessmen's group interested in infrastructure and service improvements—Mayor Daniel C. Smith and the city council agreed in 1889 to develop a citywide system.[44]

Selecting the best approach was more than awarding a contract to the lowest bidder. The timing of Houston's decision came amid a national controversy over whether cities should adopt combined or separate systems. A combined system handled both household waste and stormwater in a single large pipe; a separate system utilized a small pipe for household waste and a large pipe or a surface ditch for stormwater. The debate over the systems actually began in Europe, where the first comprehensive sewerage systems were constructed. But in the United States, only combined systems were built in the 1860s and early 1870s, largely due to cost and the lack of a successful operating separate system. In the wake of the devastating yellow fever epidemic in the Mississippi Valley in 1878 and 1879, hard-hit Memphis chose a separate system in the hopes of avoiding a similar future disaster.

The scientific agriculturalist and drainage specialist turned engineer Colonel George E. Waring Jr. was the major proponent of the notion that "sewer gas" caused disease, and he recommended a separate system to insure the health of the city. Once implemented in Memphis, the "Waring system" provided only for house sewage, not stormwater. Nevertheless, the health of the people of Memphis improved markedly after its implementation, but the debate over the separate versus combined systems intensified rather than ended.[45]

The Citizens' Committee promoted the separate system concept in Houston, playing up Waring's work in Memphis and elsewhere. In November 1889, Wynkoop Kiersted, a hydraulic engineer from Kansas City, was hired as a consultant to help city engineer C. W. Jarvis devise a plan for the city. Among other things, Kiersted was selected because he had helped implement a Waring system in Kansas City in 1883. The Jarvis and Kiersted plan involved establishing sewerage districts and constructing sewer lines in several wards. The anticipated completion date was 1893, but it took substantially longer.[46] What infrastructure existed in Houston by World War I was, with a few exceptions, a rudimentary separate system on the Waring model. Jarvis and Kiersted's plan shifted the focus away from Griffin's emphasis on drainage—and thus flood control—toward sanitary sewers. Piecemeal development left many Houstonians with makeshift or incomplete sewerage or no sewerage at all.[47]

While most districts were connected with an intercepting sewer, the system was a hybrid of separate and combined pipes with insufficient storm sewerage.[48] The Board of Public Works, responding to the city's chronic drainage problems, exhorted the city council in September 1903 that a system of sanitary and storm sewers should be regarded "as being of the greatest importance to the City of Houston," and "in fact," it added, "we regard a more perfect drainage system as being of paramount importance to paving as under present conditions many of our paved streets ... become perfect canals after every heavy rain."[49]

Beyond the drainage problem, the pumping station and the disposal plant were inoperable, and other portions of the sewerage infrastructure were damaged. In 1904, the Sewer Department was made independent from the Engineering Department and the budget was increased, but additional defects were still being noted. In most respects, constructing an effective sewerage system proved much more difficult than developing a water supply. The 1904 annual report concluded that "there are some residences in the sewer district that are not connected with sewers, and in unsewered districts there are thousands of houses that cannot connect." Noting improvements in the following years, subsequent annual reports made it clear that rapid growth placed great demands on the city for more extensions. The 1922 annual report noted that in developing areas, private parties constructed three times the mileage installed by the city.[50]

Sanitary sewers appeared to be the most pressing need because of public-health concerns. Drainage ditches and the bayou system were regarded as sufficient for handling normal runoff. Because of its heavy rainfall and flooding problems, Houston faced more serious stormwater threats than cities of comparable size. Civic leaders were rightly proud of the Austin Street storm sewer in the eastern portion of the city (constructed in 1909), touted as the largest of its class in the nation, but the more typical practice in the city was "to carry off storm water, where it collects, by whatever sewer was near it," rather than to add more sewers specifically designed to handle stormwater. The storm sewer bond funds were only spent in parts of the city where major paving operations were located. Economics dictated construction practices and left the city less well protected from the chronic scourge of flooding.[51]

Despite Houston's commitment to new sanitary sewers, city leaders failed to give immediate attention to upgrading sewage disposal or developing a plan for sewage treatment. Disposal of sewage was first addressed in the mid-1890s, although more for the sake of local businesses than for residents. Buffalo Bayou had become a convenient depository for street runoff, stormwater, raw sewage, and dead animals. The battle over avoiding the bayou

as a water supply went hand in hand with concern over using it as a sink for
sewage.

A concerted effort to clean up the bayou did not occur until 1895, when
Major A. M. Miller of the U.S. Army Corps of Engineers was sent to Houston
to inspect the site for the proposed ship channel. He informed local leaders
that the city had to rid the bayou of its sewage and other pollutants if it expected federal aid for a ship channel. With support from the Houston Business League, the city council accepted the recommendation of consulting
engineer Alexander Potter to improve the sewerage system and construct a
filtration facility. Under the plan, wastewater would be delivered by pipe to
a central pumping station in the Fifth Ward, and then to filter beds four and
a half miles away. Heavy matter would dry on the surface and be removed,
and smaller material would be filtered through layers of stone, gravel, coke,
and sand. The final effluent—which Potter declared as "fit to drink"—would
then be dumped into the bayou.[52]

With prodding from the federal government, Houston was one of only
a few cities by the early twentieth century with a filtration program of this
type.[53] While filtration met immediate demands, pollution of the bayou persisted. The plan made no effective provisions for runoff or stormwater, and
surface polluters—such as grazing animals—were not deterred. In addition,
the upkeep on the filtration facility was dismal, the filter beds were often
clogged, and wastewater formed a standing lake.[54] Although the facility was
repaired, and new disposal plants added, an estimated 70 to 80 percent of the
sewage went into the bayou from public and private sewers in 1916.[55]

According to a 1915 state law, no untreated sewage was to be dumped
into watercourses beginning in January 1917. At that time Houston became
one of the pioneers in utilizing the activated sludge process, pioneered by
Dr. Gilbert J. Fowler in Manchester, England, which permitted conversion
of dry sewage into fertilizer, and built the first large-scale wastewater treatment plant to use the method. The technique gained international usage
and became a standard practice for effluent treatment and water purification
worldwide.

Despite better handling of dried sewage and the development of a relatively elaborate sanitary sewer system, wastewater treatment failed to allevi-
ate chronic water-pollution problems through the mid-twentieth century.[56]
Houston's aggressive annexation policy in particular resulted in the connection of several poor quality sewage disposal plants into the citywide system, which already was becoming outdated. Public health authorities feared
that the polio epidemics striking the city in the 1930s were traceable, among
other things, to the polluted condition of the drainage network. Surveys

TABLE 7.1.

Sanitary and Storm Sewers in Houston (in miles)

Year	Sanitary Sewers	Storm Sewers	Other	Total
1902	24.558	5.537	7.248	37.345
1914	94.03	21.721	—	115.751
1920	170.221	57.992	—	228.213
1925	282.868	88.013	—	370.881
1930	523.223	148.0	—	671.223
1937	616.353	175.498	—	791.851

Source: "Report of the City Engineer," City of Houston, Annual Report, 1904, 76, 90-91; City of Houston, First Annual Report of the City Engineer on Sewage Disposal (Feb. 1, 1916), 11-12; "Engineering Department," Municipal Book of the City of Houston, 1922, 110; "Report of the City Engineer," City of Houston, Annual Report, March 1, 1929, 18: "The Houston Sewage Program," American City 62 (February, 1947): 90.

of bayou pollution revealed serious contamination, and on December 19, 1946, the Houston Engineers' Council recommended that the city chlorinate all sewage, that it construct adequate main-sewer trunk lines and treating plants, that surface drainage connections be disconnected from sanitary sewers, and that plans be devised to contend with industrial waste.[57] The city's separate system also continued to place insufficient emphasis on storm sewers. As table 7.1 shows, construction of storm sewers lagged significantly behind sanitary sewers.

While storm sewers have a much larger carrying capacity than sanitary sewers, the disparity in miles constructed is not explained by that fact alone. Surface drains were called upon to carry some of the load, as were older combined sewers, and, of course, the bayous and the streets. Yet, the lack of balance in developing a sewer system that met both the needs of sanitation and runoff left Houston with a serious unresolved problem.

Like the artesian well system, Houston's sewerage system was a one-dimensional approach to the city's more complex disposal, drainage, and sanitation needs. Carrying the promise of improved health, it seemed to offer protection against the ravages of many communicable diseases, but it gave only secondary consideration to other significant environmental threats, especially water pollution and flooding.

SANITARY SYSTEMS AFTER WORLD WAR II

Between the years 1876 and 1929, Houston's leaders had settled upon clearly defined paths for its sanitary services: artesian wells for water supply and sanitary sewers for wastewater. By the 1930s, the resilience of those systems was sorely tested, and some of the inherent weaknesses were recognized. Confidence in the water and wastewater infrastructure was shaken by structural, economic, and environmental problems that plagued the sanitary systems. By the 1940s, the impact of war and pressures of growth—through annexation, in-migration, and natural increase in population—challenged the notion that the services were adequate for future needs.

Houston's history has always been defined by growth. In the post–World War II era, the Bayou City's emergence as a dynamic, regionally expansive metropolis not only transformed its politics, its economy, and its demographics, but placed its sanitary services in a new context. Aggressive annexations and unrelenting sprawl tested the integrity and functioning of its water supply and its wastewater system. Like never before, they were connected to and influenced by the functioning and safety of a variety of watersheds and to the Galveston Bay complex. Houston's sanitary services absorbed adjacent systems or at the very least influenced those systems beyond the city's grasp. In so doing, Houston's water and wastewater systems became regionalized, with noteworthy impact on the environment as well as on municipal responsibility for delivering adequate service.

Outward growth in Houston after World War II was made easier by the automobile culture stimulated by cheap gasoline and by a booming economy that attracted businesses and workers from around the country and the world. But Houston also benefited from negligible municipal competition along most of its periphery and a liberal annexation policy made possible by Texas law. The Municipal Annexation Act of 1963 was particularly significant, since it guaranteed space for future expansion for major cities statewide and encouraged orderly growth. The former succeeded, while the latter failed miserably.

Under the provisions of the law, Houston was granted extraterritorial jurisdiction (ETJ) over adjacent land that it could reserve for future growth, allowing the city to place all real property within five miles of its limits under ETJ. Only Houston was allowed to annex in this area and no settlements could incorporate themselves without permission from the city or without a change in state law. Houston could increase its city limits by 10 percent each calendar year. If less land was annexed, the difference could be added to a subsequent year's annexation as long as the city did not increase by more than 30 percent in a single year. By 1999, the policy allowed Houston to reserve 1,289 square miles for future annexation. Only in the southeastern portion of the city—the Pasadena area—was Houston blocked from expansion. With half the density of Los Angeles, Houston still held more than half of the population in its metropolitan statistical area within the city limits.[58]

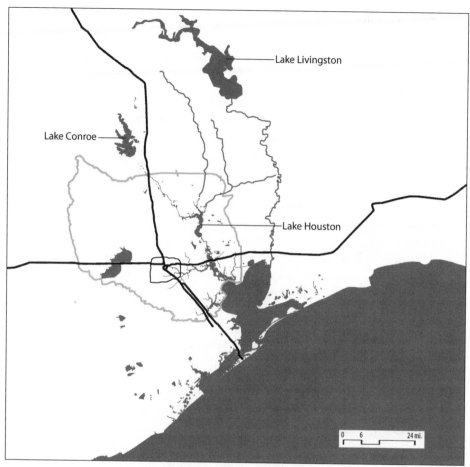

FIGURE 7.3. Surface water in Houston.
Map by Maria Oran and Donna Kacmar, FAIA.

WATER SUPPLY

Aside from unprecedented expansion, the major change in Houston's water supply service after World War II was the transition from a one-dimensional water system to a dual system increasingly dependent on surface water. Prior to the war, reliance on groundwater had already begun to expose the limitations of the once abundant resource. The shift to surface water raised new issues, not the least of which was potential environmental problems affecting the whole region of southeastern Texas.

The major forces leading to the increasing growth and dominance of surface supplies were many. Most persistent was the unrelenting drive for economic development that went hand in hand with rapid population growth. As a chamber of commerce report noted in 1954, "obviously, the community cannot attract new industries which require substantial quantities of water until such new supplies are assured."[59] Also significant was the growing disincentive to rely on groundwater because of severe land subsidence.

The development of the San Jacinto River to supply water for World War II defense industries along the ship channel resulted in a dual water system for urban, industrial, and agricultural users in the Houston metropolitan area. These systems consisted of: potable water for residential and commercial use, drawn primarily from underground aquifers with wells owned and operated by the city, municipal utility districts, and the private sector (including industry)[60]; and a separate industrial water system relying chiefly on raw—or untreated—water from the surface source owned and operated by the city.[61]

This pattern of water supply acquisition and delivery underwent substantial change over the years, with surface water becoming an increasingly important component of the city's water system. During the war, the industrial water supply from the San Jacinto River was taken from two reservoirs that sent the water to the ship channel through open canals (the East and West Canals). In 1945, the city acquired the pumping station on the San Jacinto and the West Canal; in the same year, the San Jacinto River Authority acquired the East Canal. With the completion of the Lake Houston Dam and implementation of the new East Water Purification Plant in 1954, a portion of the water from Lake Houston via the canal was diverted to the plant, and the treated surface water ultimately supplemented and was combined with groundwater in the municipal district system.[62] By 1970, treated surface water met about 40 percent of the demand of the municipal system. The remainder of the water went through the plant's Industrial Water Pump Station for delivery to ship-channel industries, although provisions were made for treated water to be diverted to the industrial area as needed.[63]

Despite satisfaction with the important role of the San Jacinto River to Houston's water needs, other sources, especially on the Trinity, Brazos, Colorado, and Neches Rivers, continued to be explored. After the completion of Lake Houston Dam, the City of Houston began developing a reservoir site on the Trinity River, which was initially meant to serve a nine-county industrial area (the Houston-Trinity Industrial Complex). Lake Livingston Dam along the Trinity was completed in 1968, with water rights owned by the Trinity River Authority (30 percent) and the City of Houston (70 percent). By the early 1980s, it represented more than 80 percent of the Houston area's available surface water supply. Lake Conroe Dam on the San Jacinto was completed in 1973, with the San Jacinto River Authority owning one-third of the water rights and the City of Houston owning two-thirds. San Jacinto River water supplied municipal and some industrial demand, while water from the Trinity was initially used to supply industrial needs only. Tapping the new surface supplies required attention to water conveyance, pumping, and all of the issues that had faced the San Jacinto River project. Continuing industrial demand for water led the Coastal Industrial Water Authority (CIWA), created in 1968, to develop a water conveyance system (the CIWA Conveyance System[64]), to acquire water from Lake Livingston for industrial use, and ultimately to replace water formerly delivered through West Canal for the industrial sector east of Houston.[65]

Within the city, a distribution grid delivers water to residential and commercial users. In the late 1940s, it consisted of a central plant with other plants located around it in a wheel pattern. The eight existing plants were interconnected by large or arterial mains (800 miles of mains and 300 miles of service lines). As the city grew the grid frequently had to be extended.[66] Outlying areas not incorporated within Houston often continued to rely on wells and might only be connected to the city's grid after annexation. A report of the Harris County Home Rule Commission optimistically noted in 1957 that, "the presence of the hitherto abundant groundwater helps to ease the water problem of the suburbs by making the technical problems of special water districts relatively simple; hence, the large number of districts in the Houston area."[67]

In reality, the ability to serve a city population that grew not only by in-migration but also by annexation was complex. Developers and subdividers, who were the essential players in Houston's growth politics, worked with city officials to acquire main extensions into their properties. While they would have liked the city to bear all the costs of furnishing and installing mains and hydrants, they usually had to share them. In the late 1960s, for example, the city was responsible for the design of the extension and contracts for installation on a fifty-fifty basis with developers within their property lines, and the city might also provide the pipe and hydrants. For short distances, the city usually furnished and installed the mains; for longer distances, the city could supply the hydrants, but the developer would be responsible for the remaining costs.[68]

The primary mechanism for establishing water service in suburban areas was the water district. After the disastrous Galveston hurricane of 1900—which inspired rethinking about ways to finance public building and rebuilding projects—an amendment to the Texas Constitution provided for taxing districts to be created for conservation and reclamation improvements, with provisions of the amendment liberalized in subsequent years to streamline the process. The special districts were granted unlimited bonded indebtedness and taxing power. Two types of districts were particularly important for suburban development: the Fresh Water Supply District (FWSD) created in 1919 and the Water Control and Improvement District (WCID) created in 1925.

The FWSDs were severely limited in issuing bonds for construction of drainage facilities, and thus were of little value in developing new communities. WCIDs, designed for irrigation purposes, demonstrated sufficient flexibility for water, sewer, and drainage improvements and could be formed prior to the development of a new suburban community. By the mid-1980s, there were more than 800 WCIDs in Texas, with approximately half in the Houston metropolitan area alone.[69] In the process of annexing parts of its ETJ, Houston also absorbed many special districts, and in so doing reduced their economic authority. Between 1949 and 1979, the city annexed fifty-three water districts and assumed their bonded indebtedness.[70]

Planning Houston's water needs before World War II amounted to calculating how many new wells would have to be sunk and when and where to extend mains within a relatively small area. During World War II, it became apparent that there was a "precarious situation confronting the water system," that was in desperate need of new wells to relieve extensive use of the groundwater supply, the building of a new purification plant, strengthening the existing grid, and contending with the problem of extending service to "fringe populations." Materials and monetary resources to accomplish these goals were constrained by the prosecution of the war, and yet the immediate postwar years did not produce radical change.[71] Outlying areas, especially in poorer neighborhoods, were not likely to get adequate service. The shift to surface water most immediately benefitted industry, rather than residential users. And the slow weaning from groundwater was made more urgent by growing concern over subsidence.

Subsidence occurs when too much groundwater is removed from a particular location, resulting in the surrounding clay collapsing and then compacting. On the surface land subsidence occurs and below the surface fresh water cannot replenish the structure. In addition, subsidence also may break pipes and clog sewers, encourage saltwater encroachment into the aquifer, and increase the potential for flooding. Areas where well fields and production facilities were concentrated experienced the most population growth in these years and also tended to incur the greatest subsidence.

There was little public notice of subsidence prior to the middle of 1953. But in the ten years between 1943 and 1953, there was already subsidence of about two feet: approximately half a foot in downtown Houston and as much as three-and-one-fourth feet in Pasadena. In roughly the same period, the problem of saltwater intrusion into the aquifers increased from a rate of one mile in seventy-five years (1940) to one mile in sixteen years (1952). In the late 1960s, it was estimated that subsidence lowered the ground level of Pasadena's north side and in Baytown by almost seven feet; by three feet south of Houston at Ellington Field; and by two feet along the shore of West Galveston Bay. By 1978 subsidence of up to ten feet was measured along the ship channel area. In the early 1980s, more than 20,000 acres in the Houston-Galveston area were below sea level, and even Lake Houston Dam sunk two feet since its construction in 1954.[72]

In time, the issue of subsidence became a central concern when planning for future expansion of the water supply system. Harris-Galveston Coastal Subsidence District was created in 1975 as a way to control regional subsidence through regulation of groundwater use and through formulation of plans to convert area water supplies to rely more heavily on surface water. A chamber of commerce task force concerned about potential constraints on the city's growth noted in 1983 that, "simply stated, Houston must, over the next 16 years, plan and implement water system expansion which equals the capacity of our existing system if we are to solve subsidence problems and assure a viable economic future for the Houston metropolitan area." But unease did not necessarily lead to effective action. The view that there was sufficient surface water to exploit was seen as a valuable countermeasure to past practices. However, continual dependence on groundwater in developing areas north and west of downtown—where access to surface water was limited—turned a blind eye to a problem that had plagued the area east of the city for years. Between 1878 and 1987, the area west of downtown experienced subsidence of one to three feet, due largely to aggressive land development. In the early 1990s, regulations meant to arrest subsidence overall required Houston to reduce dependence on groundwater from 43 percent of its total consumption in 1992 to 20 percent by the year 2020, along with expansion of surface supplies. This process has moved slowly.[73]

Other environmental problems arose in the development of the city's water supply system. The notion that dependence on groundwater protected the city from polluted sources of supply was unfounded and somewhat naive. Water quality and water pollution issues are a constant concern for any water system, anywhere. The confidence in the quality of Houston's groundwater supply had been tested in the past when well water was mixed with bayou water before distribution to customers. More recently, agricultural runoff, and especially runoff from developed land that is made impermeable, increased the flow and quantity of water draining off the land. Urban runoff, especially, carried large quantities of nonpoint pollutants—pesticides, oil and grease, salts, bacterial contaminants, hydrocarbons, and heavy metals—finding their way into various surface water and groundwater sources and seriously increasing flooding.[74]

Water-pollution regulation with respect to Houston's water supply has had a mixed record. While drinking water provided by the city regularly meets or exceeds the water-quality standards of the Texas Commission on Environmental Quality and the Environmental Protection Agency, a National Resources Defense Council report in 2003 showed Houston's drinking water with significant levels of contaminants, such as haloacetic acids, arsenic, and coliform. Wells in and around Houston sometimes show high radon levels. These problems are attributed to an aging infrastructure and dated technology.[75]

The shift to surface water engaged a different set of environmental issues from groundwater use. The controversy over the proposed Wallisville project is a good example. Authorized by Congress in 1962, construction began in 1966 on Wallisville Lake (or Reservoir) located approximately 40 miles east of Houston and 3.9 miles above the mouth of the Trinity River. The reservoir to be created by a 39,200-foot dam was meant to store 58,000 acre-feet of water. Its construction had support from the Galveston District of the U.S. Army Corps of Engineers, the Trinity River Authority, the Chambers-Liberty Counties Navigation District, and the City of Houston. Visualized as a multipurpose project, proponents claimed that it would increase the industrial water supply for Houston, control saltwater intrusion into the river, improve navigation, and enhance the habitat for fish and wildlife.[76]

The Wallisville project, including the construction of the Livingston Reservoir, had been proposed in response to drought conditions in the 1950s and was meant to maximize the ability to draw water from the Trinity. As one study aptly noted, "stripped of its bells and whistles . . . Wallisville is at its core a water supply project."[77] Almost 70 percent complete in 1973, opponents successfully stopped construction of Wallisville Lake. In close proximity to an environmentally sensitive coastline and fragile wetlands, the project made the U.S. Army Corp of Engineer's Galveston District a clear target for protest and litigation in a period of rising environmental awareness. Opponents of Wallisville (conservationist and environmentalist groups and the Texas Parks and Wildlife Department) employed a new weapon—the environmental impact statement (EIS) authorized under the National Environmental Policy Act (1969)—to further their cause.[78]

Criticism of Wallisville focused on several potential risk factors, many of which related to the link between the Trinity River and Galveston Bay. Opponents argued that the dam would reduce fresh water, sediment, and nutrients flowing to the bay. This would increase salinity, parasites, and pathogens harming the already weakened oyster fishery and could reduce shrimp harvests by as much as 65 percent. Exclusion of marine organisms from wetlands upstream from the dam and loss of Trinity delta wetlands also were possible. In the vicinity of the dam itself, approximately 13,000 acres of marsh, cypress swamp, and marine nurseries would be flooded. They added that other sources of water for Houston, such as the Toledo Bend Reservoir, had the capacity to meet long-term needs without constructing the Wallisville Reservoir.[79]

Wallisville proved to be a "legislative Lazarus" frequently resurrected by Congress and the courts.[80] In September 1971, environmental groups, including the Sierra Club and the Audubon Society, sued to halt the construction because the U.S Army Corps of Engineers had not filed a proper EIS. After the completion of the EIS, construction continued through 1972 but was stopped again in 1973 when the district court declared that an EIS for the entire Trinity River project had not been prepared. In 1974, a federal appeals court returned the case to the lower court, and additional review of the EIS created more gridlock. In 1977, the Galveston District announced alternative plans to the original Wallisville proposal, including a reduction in the size of the reservoir from 19,700 acres to 5,600 acres, and another plan that would install a temporary, nonimpoundment barrier on the river. Not until 1981 was the EIS mandated by the court released, but with an accompanying report dropping navigation and fish and wildlife enhancements as benefits of the project. The new EIS spawned another round of heated debate, which intensified when the U.S. Army Corps of Engineers added back the omitted benefits (navigation and fish and wildlife enhancements) in its 1982 Supplemental Information to the Post Authorization Change Report (SIPACR).[81]

One observer stated that the SIPACR became "perhaps the most controversial document ever produced by the District" by reinstating the benefits without explaining why they were added back and by not circulating the report for public review.[82] Despite the brouhaha and the continuation of the court injunction against the project, Congress appropriated funds for the scaled-down Wallisville plan in 1983. In their turn, the district court continued the injunction in 1986. But in a stunning reversal, the Fifth Circuit Court of Appeals in New Orleans ruled that the project could proceed after the fifteen-year delay—now as a single-purpose water supply project.[83]

In 1989, under the Houston Water Master Plan, Wallisville Reservoir was identified as the best of four alternatives for supplying water to Houston through the year 2030 (the other three were an inflatable saltwater barrier on the Trinity River, Toledo Bend Reservoir, and Brazos River Water Transfer). While litigation and environmental concerns continued to delay the project until 1991, it was completed in 1999. The Wallisville Saltwater Barrier put in place mechanically blocks upstream movement of saltwater from Trinity Bay during conditions of low flow from the river.[84]

The Trinity River Authority more recently has taken the position that from its inception the Wallisville Project was "constructed for the purpose of controlling the intrusion of saltwater from Trinity Bay during low river flow conditions," rather than the multipurpose aspirations of supporters evident in the documents going back to the 1960s. From that time forward, opponents consistently viewed the building of the reservoir as posing environmental risks. The most strident among them labeled the project "a fraud," "a monumental rip-off," "an economic blunder," and "a slowly growing cancer."[85]

Although regarded by proponents as a ready answer to the growing demand for water in the Houston area, and as a serious environmental misstep by opponents, the Wallisville controversy exposed the difficulty and sometimes the peril of sustaining urban development. A shift to surface water had been inevitable for Houston in the wake of its breathtaking growth. In the case of Wallisville, a public battle was waged that produced at best a temporary solution to the city's water needs, but at a price that some people were not willing to pay. Even in seemingly water-rich East Texas, water wars raged as if the engagement had taken place in water-poor West Texas. The question remains: how many more times would such controversies emerge as the city of Houston continued to grow? The panacea of surface water did not magically solve the problems of subsidence and groundwater depletion, but it shifted the challenge of meeting water demand from below the ground to above and from a local concern to a regional issue.

WASTEWATER

Houston faced an additional challenge in its effort to upgrade its existing sewerage system to meet the demands of growth. As with water supply, wastewater issues were regionalized after the war. The difficulty in providing adequate sanitary sewerage with effective delivery to treatment plants and maintaining greater control of drainage was constant in the central city. As sprawl increasingly typified the Houston metropolis, providing these services became more ominous. Not only were new customers to be served, but a relatively centralized urban sewerage system did not extend into the city's periphery. Unease over adequate treatment and problems of runoff had to take into account the flow of effluent into Galveston Bay. To a greater extent than before, stormwater exacerbated flooding problems beyond the residential and commercial property of the urban core.

The storm-sewerage issue was emblematic of a serious problem the city

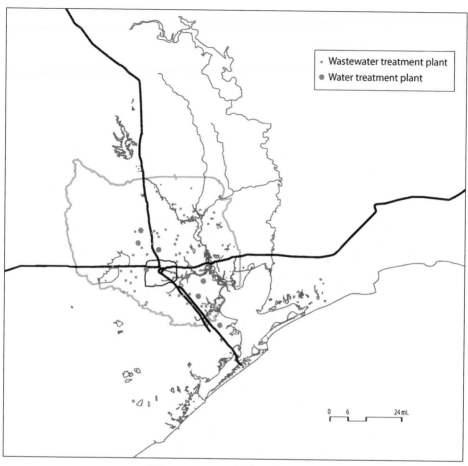

FIGURE 7.4. Water treatment infrastructure in Houston.
Map by Maria Oran and Donna Kacmar, FAIA.

faced by not constructing necessary infrastructure to keep up with rapid
growth and by not heeding the vagaries of Houston's weather. The Bayou
City's forty-eight inches or more of rain each year seemed to be reason
enough to taking storm sewerage and flooding seriously. The expansive-
ness of the city's impervious surfaces due to development also directly affected the rate of runoff even more than the volume of rain. In addition, the
increased rate of runoff made the response to potential flooding much more
difficult.[86]

The traditional approach to deal with runoff, stormwater, and flooding
in Houston was to include natural features (drainage basins, floodplains,
and the rivers and bayous) into the drainage system alongside human-made

features (channels, streets, roadside ditches, storm sewers, and, eventually, detention facilities). Great faith was placed in the natural features like the bayous as well as the streets to offset the shortfall in storm drains and detention facilities. Despite effort at flood damage reduction by the HCFCD since its inception in the late 1930s, almost thirty serious floods occurred in the area, resulting in millions of dollars in costs. However, after the 1940s, Harris County did not suffer massive regional flooding again until June 2001. In 1939, the HCFCD developed a flood-control master plan and cooperated with the U.S. Army Corps of Engineers in a flood-control program, beginning with the building of the Barker and Addicks Reservoirs in west Harris County and part of Fort Bend County in the 1940s. These were the first and largest flood-control detention facilities in the county. At this time the eleven independent drainage districts in Harris County were merged under the HCFCD.

The primary focus of the HCFCD and the U.S. Army Corps of Engineers' flood-control program was more than 2,500 miles of cement-lined channels built along the bayous between the 1940s and 1970s. Unstable Brays Bayou was canalized and lined with concrete between 1955 to 1960. White Oak Bayou became the last bayou in Harris County to be completely concrete lined.[87]

Relentless development and an increasingly aging and overburdened sewerage system worked against effective stormwater control, as did periods of extensive flooding. In June 1976, almost ten inches of rain fell in six hours in the Brays and Sims Bayou watersheds. The Texas Medical Center was most seriously damaged (exceeding $20 million in losses), as well as damage to Rice University, the University of Houston, and the Houston Museum of Fine Arts. The cause of the flooding was not attributed to the overflow of Brays Bayou but to a lack of capacity in the storm-sewer system. Urbanization on the west side of Houston exceeded design estimates and was a central contributor to the ineffectual flood-control technologies in place.[88] In 1980, the HCFCD initiated a "no downstream impact" policy for new developments, resulting in greater use of onsite detention facilities. In 1985, consultants recommended construction of four regional detention facilities on Brays and Sims Bayous and flow diversion channels for Keegar Bayou. Cost and politics scuttled the plan. Luckily, since 1983, Brays Bayou did not flood, but it did experience "near misses" in 1992, 1994, 1997, and 1998. New studies and additional flood-control projects continued through the period.[89]

In June 2001, Tropical Storm Allison—which proved to be "one of the most devastating rain events in the history of the United States"—dumped more than thirty-eight inches of rain on the Greater Houston Area between June 5 and June 9, causing twenty-two fatalities and more than $5 billion in property damage, including damage to 95,000 automobiles and trucks and 73,000 residences. Approximately 30,000 stranded people were housed in shelters. Allison went on to spread devastation in thirty-one counties in Texas, as well as in Louisiana, Florida, Mississippi, and Pennsylvania. In Houston and Harris County the rate and amount of runoff overwhelmed the drainage system. The storm sewers and roadside ditches in the area were designed to handle a rainfall rate of approximately one or two inches per hour (the streets are designed to carry at least four inches of water flowing slowly), far less than experienced during Allison but also less than many other major floods in Houston's history.[90] With resignation, one observer noted, "Harris County doesn't have earthquakes . . . doesn't have blizzards . . . doesn't have avalanches. We have flooding."[91]

While such an extraordinary event as Allison made an adequate response almost impossible, lesser storms demonstrated the vulnerability of the drainage system. Between 1980 and 1994, Houston suffered extensive flooding nine times, with many more localized events. The Comprehensive Storm Drainage Plan proposed in the 1990s—before Allison—was meant to evaluate the flooding patterns and stormwater generation.[92] Allison helped add additional resolve to that evaluation, but solutions—or at least serious mitigation of the effects of flooding—remain far from being achieved.

The Wastewater Treatment System Task Group of the Houston Chamber of Commerce concluded in 1983 that, "the major deficiency in the City's wastewater system is the lack of capacity in both its collection network and its treatment facilities."[93] This observation applies to much of Houston's history. After World War II, it was clear that the sewer system was not keeping up with Houston's aggressive building program. As American City noted, "in few cities is complete sewage treatment more seriously needed." By the late 1940s, a new sewage treatment plant and new sewer lines were under construction. It was the goal to consolidate the six existing plants—only one of which was satisfactory—into two larger ones. The one adequate plant was to be retained and a new facility, the Sims Bayou Plant, completed in 1948.[94]

In the 1950s, there was no centralized sewerage system in Harris County. Outside of the central city, sanitary sewerage came mostly from privies, septic tanks, and a variety of other collection systems that were public and private. Septic tanks were prevalent in parts of Houston, in nearby villages, and particularly in unincorporated areas. Some engineers noted that the privies and septic tanks with drain fields did not provide adequate sewage disposal, "and with this increase in suburban building tremendous amounts of disease-laden sewage in our roadside ditches, on the top of the ground, and in the yards of homes could easily be visualized if these methods of sewage disposal continued to be used." The problem with septic tanks in use was that they failed to function well due to the heavy rainfall, the low absorption rate of the soil, the high water table, and poor drainage. The same engineers who criticized privies and septic tanks were encouraged that subdividers and home builders in several larger subdivisions were installing new sewerage systems and favored increasing the number of treatment plants by the late 1950s.[95] This was not a strictly voluntary response. The Harris County Health Unit would not approve an individual sewage disposal method, and hence any subdividers who expected to acquire Federal Housing Authority—and later Veterans Administration—approval for building homes had to connect those homes to an existing system or construct their own. Some developers soon realized that they could profit from operating the utilities themselves.[96]

Coverage varied greatly in the county, however. Bellaire, an incorporated enclave within the Houston city limits, was completely sewered, as was Jacinto City. South Houston was over 80 percent sewered, and Baytown and La Porte were 95 percent sewered. Storm sewering, like in the central city itself, was less well-developed along the periphery. In fact, areas annexed by Houston in 1949 and 1956 were without storm drainage. Disposal of sewage in Harris County was uncoordinated, often using the bayous as receptors for effluent. Because the county did not provide sewerage service, developers and individual citizens utilized their own devices or sometimes relied upon the formation of FWSDs or WCIDs that had the power to finance, construct, and operate sewerage facilities. Homeowners who simply bought land from developers, but were not part of a large subdivision, could be left unsewered as could people who did not own their homes. In the metropolitan area, there were sixteen sewage disposal plants in 1945, with thirteen operated by cities, one by a water district, and two by private individuals. Estimates suggest that each plant served 39,400 people in 1945, improving to 10,000 people per plant in 1956—in large measure due to the existence of ninety-seven sewage treatment plants then in operation in the county. In 1945, the sewered population of the cities in Harris County was 60,000, increasing to 176,000 by 1956.[97]

The decentralized sewage treatment system met with serious criticism. Breakdowns in the plants could result in no sewage treatment for homes and businesses dependent on them. Little help was available because of the lack of any backup system or larger facility with a wider coverage area.[98] By the mid-1970s, criticism of the city and county's decentralized sewer system was unabated. In 1974, the city of Houston had forty-two wastewater treatment plants, two major sludge disposal plants, 179 pump stations, and approximately 3,600 miles of collection and conveyance lines. Much of the system was built by the city with the remainder acquired through annexation or purchase.

While the statistics give a sense of wide-scale city service, a closer look reveals shortcomings. The average treatment plant in the 1970s served approximately 30,000 people (several of them had very low capacity) and were unable to support a growing population in several parts of the city. In addition, many of the plants were antiquated, could not meet modern water-quality standards, and exceeded permissible odor levels. By comparison, a single plant served the entire population of Fort Worth and its suburbs. Dallas had three treatment plants for the whole city. A 1974 Environmental Protection Agency (EPA) EIS suggested that a way to offset the problems of Houston's decentralized wastewater system was to regionalize wastewater facilities.[99]

The inadequacy of Houston's sewerage system and wastewater treatment in the early 1970s is best expressed in the sewer moratorium. Because of insufficient sewage-treatment capacity, Houston was forced to develop a plan to avoid an EPA citywide moratorium on new sewer connections. The city chose a compromise in 1974 that protected downtown development, while curtailing new building over approximately 70 percent of the city. Connections in the ETJ were not covered by the plan. With the completion of Plan 208 in 1977—which outlined a long-term strategy for the watersheds of the Houston area—the moratorium was lifted.[100]

What regionalization actually meant in practice was fairly muddled. For a city strongly committed to growth, some leaders took particular notice of assessments like a 1975 Houston-Galveston Area Council report that argued, "with the completion of major interstate highway segments . . . sewerage facilities are becoming the prime determinant of the location of new development." There was, however, a cautionary observation in the report about the impact of wastewater system development as a growth tool:

> The capacity of the interceptor line (the major line that connects collector systems to treatment plants) has a major impact upon land use. There is a tendency to overdesign these systems in order to accommodate future development, and the oversizing contributes directly to the amount of development that can and probably will occur. When these large interceptor sewers are designed to run for long distances between the existing service area and the treatment plant, vast amounts of land are then opened up to sprawl between towns. The low-cost of land on the urban fringe encourages developers to move to the end of the new line, which results in leapfrog fill-in development patterns. Haphazard construction of sewerage facilities, therefore, increases the difficulty

of properly planning the timing and size of other public facilities and spreads the urban area out in a pattern that is wasteful of land and resources.[101]

Regionalization of the wastewater system, therefore, could be mistaken for future growth and not understood as a tool to more effectively deliver service to the citizenry of the metropolitan area. Confusing the two was common.

By the end of the 1980s, there was unease about the number of small wastewater treatment plants in the metropolitan area and the ETJ. These plants produced "a low quality effluent," that aggravated water-pollution problems in the region and were less cost effective than large regional facilities. Remedial action led to the construction of new plants or enlarging older ones. Between 1964 and 1989, seventy-one small sewage treatment plants were abandoned. In 1986, the Greater Houston Chamber of Commerce—a powerful force in the city's growth machine—prepared a report entitled "Wastewater Regionalization Plan for Houston" calling for the development of larger treatment plants in the ETJ prior to annexation. It was endorsed by the Developers Council, the Association of Consulting Municipal Engineers, members of the legal community, some local interest groups, and the city's Departments of Public Works and Health and Human Services.

In 1987, Mayor Kathy Whitmire formed the City Wastewater Regionalization Task Force with the mission of developing a wastewater regionalization program. In 1988, the city council approved a wastewater regionalization plan for the ETJ. The step away from a historic focus on decentralization occurred without seriously questioning Houston's plans for future growth, using sewers as a kind of stalking horse.[102] Since state law required Houston to provide water and sewer service to at least 75 percent of the residents in previously annexed areas and in all new areas within four and a half years of annexation, growth had a price.[103]

Despite the flurry of interest in sewage treatment in the ETJ, capital planning and system maintenance in the developed portions of the metropolitan area came under question as well. The city's growth in the 1970s and early 1980s led to substantial expansion of the wastewater system but with significant diversion of funds from system maintenance. Overflows became more common when stormwater began seeping into leaky pipes in the older parts of the system. In 1987, the EPA and the Texas Water Commission required the city to address the "infiltration and inflow" problems—a major contributor to water pollution in the city—resulting in Houston having to spend more than $1 billion over the next five years for system improvements.[104] In a 1991 Public Works Department report, management was criticized for insufficiently focusing on long-range issues and simply delegating responsibility to "consulting engineers." The result was inadequate treat-ment plant facilities, a poor collection system, and limited investment in preventive maintenance.[105]

Pollution from effluents was a chronic problem in the Bayou City only partially improved by greater attention to the water-treatment system. Sludge—an unwieldy semisolid precipitated by sewer treatment—proved to be the most difficult constituent. Despite the successful prewar operation of a sludge-drying plant and lagoons for the disposal of raw sludge, the problem remained after World War II. The lagooning method had begun in 1916, but by 1945 there was little available space for expansion. The existing open-air system also proved increasingly odiferous for residents and dissuaded com-mercial development.[106] Finally, in 1950, a sludge disposal plant—designed to serve more than 776,000 people—was completed utilizing the heat-drying method to produce dried sewage sludge for fertilizers. An enlarge-ment program was completed in 1960 with further expansion in sludge disposal in subsequent years.[107]

While the city confronted its sludge problem forthrightly, it faced more serious difficulty with bayou and stream pollution. The Engineers' Council of Houston, on December 19, 1946, adopted a resolution that read in part: "It is well known that the sanitary conditions of the bayous and streams in and around the City of Houston are intolerable. They are, in fact, in some in-stances on a par with those found in China and India. Their bacterial index count generally exceeds several million per 100 cc. This condition is due es-sentially to the lack of modern treating plants." The council continued, stat-ing that, "the main sanitary sewer trunk lines and gathering systems are so inadequate in capacity throughout the city that during and after almost ev-ery heavy rain raw human sewage flows freely through the manholes onto our streets." The Engineers' Council submitted its resolution to member societies for their approval with the intention of petitioning the mayor, city manager, councilmen, and engineers of the city to remedy the situation through new construction, chlorination, and better handling of residential sewage and industrial wastes.[108]

The resolution outlined an aggressive and comprehensive plan to sig-nificantly upgrade the city's sewerage system. Meeting the challenge was hard fought and only slowly addressed. Reference continued to be made to the chronic problems of sewage and chemical pollution derived from the cit-ies of Houston, Baytown, and other nearby communities as well as the ship channel industries. On June 28, 1948, on the heels of a polio outbreak that raised concerns about water pollution as a contributing factor, the *Houston Chronicle* noted that "pollution of both types—sewage and chemical—in

the bayous, the Ship Channel and the bays has been serious for a long time."
A headline in the newspaper on February 1, 1952, seemed to sum up the pace
of change: "City Attacks Sewer Stink, But Slowly."[109]

A Houston Chamber of Commerce report in 1972 reflecting back on the
wartime and postwar history of water pollution in Houston noted that the
city in the 1970s "found itself unable to keep pace with requirements for
sewage collection and disposal."[110] The war effort several decades earlier had
complicated the city's ability to keep up "with the requirements imposed by
the population growth," and set before the city "the Herculean task of cleaning up a massive backlog of urgently needed municipal improvements, not
the least of which was that of sewage collection and disposal." Public health
authorities had suspected polio epidemics of the 1930s and 1940s as related
in some way to the pollution in the bayous during those years, and continued
concern about the correlation between polio and bayou pollution led directly
to surveys of the bayou conducted by consulting engineer Frank Metyko and
delivered to the Harris County Commissioners Court in 1947.

Early postwar efforts at pollution control had been stalled, some believed, because of a cut in the city tax rate in 1944, at a time when population
was on the rise. The municipal government, the report noted, made progress in correcting the sewage disposal problem with the passage of a bond
program in 1946—most likely induced by the polio scare, increased population pressure on the existing system, and efforts at federal water-pollution
legislation—and especially through a "massive program" in the 1960s "to
eliminate the city as a principal polluter of the bayous and, thus, the Ship
Channel."[111]

Debate and controversy over the contribution of ship-channel industries
to the water pollution problem—as well as the city's role—persisted for several years. In 1974, the Texas Water Quality Board called for further cleanup
of the Houston Ship Channel, but the City of Houston and several industries
requested greater latitude in the amount of pollutants they could discharge
into the channel. About the same time, the State District Court ordered
Houston "without delay" to solve a sewage problem in several East End subdivisions that had not been addressed for forty-seven years.[112]

The inability of the city to upgrade and expand its sewerage system during a period of rapid growth in the 1970s and 1980s gave rise to a host of
problems in the 1990s. A 1988 report concluded that sanitary sewer overflow caused by infiltration and inflow, that is, intrusion of stormwater and
groundwater into the sewer pipes, was a major cause of water pollution in
the Houston area. Other studies came to conflicting conclusions and placed
the onus on improperly operated wastewater facilities. Nevertheless, many
agreed that the sewerage system had badly deteriorated and that, among

other things, increased water-quality standards would make improvements more expensive. Lakewood Heights subdivision on Lake Houston, for example, saw regular sewage discharges into the lake after a heavy rain.[113] Plans to spend $7 million in the early 1990s to improve sewage collection in the subdivision was only a small fraction of what some believed to be $2 billion needed to improve the whole system. Through an agreement with the Texas Water Commission and the EPA, Houston had until 1997 to complete the improvements that were necessary because of what one EPA official called "policies of benign neglect."[114]

The 1994–1998 City's Capital Improvement Plan included projects to provide service to unsewered areas and to reduce infiltration and inflow through extensive repairs. Under Mayor Bob Lanier, the massive $1 billion Greater Houston Wastewater Program was underway but not without concerns that there were flaws in testing and inspection of the system.[115] The battle over providing an adequate sewerage system that operated as designed and did not pollute adjacent watercourses continued.

A July 8, 2001, story in the *Houston Chronicle* bemoaning the state of the city's infrastructure began as follows: "Every time Houstonians turn on a faucet, flush a toilet, walk under a streetlight or drive down the city's mangled streets, they are at the mercy of the Department of Public Works and Engineering." The piece went on to question how the city's aging systems would fare in the future and if public works officials and city leaders were up to the task to provide necessary leadership.[116] Such concerns and criticisms plague almost every large city, but Houstonians are nevertheless justified in expecting their municipal services to deliver the promised benefits. Growth has been a relentless adversary in providing adequate sanitary services, and long-range planning for growth often has been missing in action. Whether the shortcomings of service delivery were problems of foresight, problems of scale, or the product of fiscal conservatism are not absolutely clear.

The initial development in the late nineteenth and early twentieth centuries of a citywide water supply system and underground sanitary sewers were positive steps in meeting service needs in the Bayou City. Banking on groundwater to provide the sole source of water and building sanitary sewers without similar attention to stormwater and runoff were exposed as inadequate once the city grew into a metropolis.

The regionalization of urban expansion also regionalized the operation of Houston's sanitary services. Rapid urban growth, as several municipal leaders argued, not only constrained the ability of the city to "keep up" in maintaining its service infrastructure but changed the rules of the game, and the impacts of those services went well beyond the city limits. Developing an adequate water supply for Houston now meant seeking sources of water many miles from the urban core and creating delivery systems that impinged on areas outside of Houston. Constructing sewer lines and sewage-treatment facilities to handle voluminous effluents was not sufficient to protect areas of outfall all the way to Galveston Bay. The bay also became the depository for staggering amounts of runoff from Houston's ever-increasing property development. Aside from the sanitary systems themselves, finding solutions to service needs also challenged traditional political institutions, demanding more attention to multiple jurisdictions and multiple interests.

In essence, the transformation of Houston's water and wastewater systems from local concerns to regional issues was a dramatic reflection of how the city was changing since its modest beginnings in the nineteenth century. The environmental implications of Houston's transformation were particularly striking, suggesting an even greater need for clear planning goals in the future. The mental leap is as significant as the evolving services themselves.

CHAPTER EIGHT

Privatization of Water

U.S. AND WORLDWIDE IMPLICATIONS

PUBLIC GOOD OR PRIVATE COMMODITY

The privatization movement with respect to municipal water supply confronts some practical issues and one that is more esoteric. From a practical standpoint, does a privatized approach to water delivery offer a better, more cost-effective, and efficient means of providing potable water to customers than public service? Is privatization simply a way to encourage economic development with players from within and without a region who see a public system as an impediment to such growth? From a broader perspective, does privatization undermine the idea of water as a public good?

Answering these questions is incredibly difficult. Imbedded in the first is the degree to which cities—and nation-states for that matter—are giving up too much control of a service that is essential to life and also historically has been a revenue generator rather than a drag on annual budgets. Also at stake is the degree to which local control of water supply service is eroded or altogether lost by the move to privatize, especially through water corporatism and the rise of multinational water companies. As to the second, do organizations like the World Bank and the International Monetary Fund push for privatized water to encourage economic expansion in developing countries, discouraging governments from actively controlling their own resources? And thus is privatizing water systems really about water at all?

On a more abstract level, recent debates over water corporatism suggest that privatizing water systems is nothing more than giving in to the idea that water is a commodity to be bought and sold. In this way, the right to fresh water—and thus the right to health and well-being—falls out of the equation not only for people in the developed world but especially in the developing world, where access to water is at best precarious for millions of people. The question of the right to clean water is fundamentally a basic environmental question—most precisely a survival question—as well as a social justice issue for those without the means to acquire water at whatever price is set for it, if indeed access to water is even possible.

If there is a positive side to the question of water as a commodity—and this greatly depends on your vantage point—it has to do with the need to ask: Have we placed so little monetary value on water throughout history that we treat it as if the supply were endless? Does giving water status with gold, let alone petroleum, lead us to use the available fresh water more conscientiously? For those with ready access to water, the issue has to be: what is a fair price? For those with limited or no access to clean water, the question transcends cost.

WATER—THE TWENTY-FIRST CENTURY'S OIL

It is very likely that fresh water will be the most contested commodity of the twenty-first century, like oil had been in the twentieth.[1] Central to this concern is who *does* and who *should* own, manage, and allocate fresh water in the present and in the future. Depending on who you ask, privatization— "non-state actors involved in water delivery where the transfer of ownership and/or decision making responsibility to private interests occurs"—is the solution to what some have called the "crisis in public service."[2] In many cases privatization has followed the so-called French model that suggests public-private partnerships (PPPs), where the state continues to own the assets but a private entity operates and plans water service.[3] Others regard privatization of water supplies and water management as simply a corporate opportunity to take advantage of water scarcity, anemic political leadership, and the lack of successful grassroots opposition.

Definitions of privatization can become complicated, and answering the question of who owns, manages, and allocates fresh water sources are an explanatory morass. Nevertheless, it is quite clear that the privatization movement of the 1990s and beyond emerged out of circumstances much different from those in earlier times. Particularly significant is the globalization of the water industry that has changed the organizational structure of water service in many parts of the world and presents a major challenge to local or regional approaches to water delivery.

Temporal circumstances always have made the difference in turning water service from private to public or vice versa. As we have seen in earlier chapters, the scale of urban growth, the persistent fear of fire, increasing demand for water, and vague notions connecting waste with sickness led to the construction of citywide water supply systems in the United States beginning in the early nineteenth century. Political leaders, especially in large cities, concluded that control of water service was increasingly necessary to protect the quality of the supply and to deliver sufficient water to fight fires. They also—quite significantly—came to believe that a public water supply could generate revenue for municipal government and would keep a valuable resource from being controlled by businessmen.

While several water companies had been profitable, capital investment in the modern systems escalated, and operating costs rose. Many private companies, therefore, found themselves accused of being inefficient or charging excessive rates. Yet, the push for municipal ownership had as much to do with the desire to influence the growth of cities as to settle disputes with private companies over specific deficiencies. Thus, private owners increasingly were under pressure to sell their assets as several communities gradually phased out private service. Major cities tended to support public systems earlier and more uniformly than any other class of cities in the United States. They also tended to invest more heavily in water supply and distribution than had the privately owned companies. Simply put, in a local setting in nineteenth-century America, modest-sized, private companies became no match for municipal governments whose power was on the rise.

As chapter 5 demonstrated, however, other contingencies kept San Jose from following the path of public service for its water supply—including a favorable political climate and partnership with a countywide entity. In Paris, France, the long history of private firms delivering water in a centralized state also resulted from circumstances that resisted a change in control, where the leverage of the private company could defend against public takeover. As we will see, several factors in recent times have opened up the opportunity for water privatization to take hold in key parts of the world and not in others—among them the scale of the companies themselves and the vulnerability of local governments to oppose them. The implications of such a change raise serious questions about control of the precious commodity of the twenty-first century.

Essential to an understanding of the impact of privatization writ large are four important and converging issues:

The "fresh water crisis"

Commodification of water

The "crisis in public service"

Water corporatism

This chapter will explore these four issues with an eye to assessing the United States and the worldwide implications of the privatization of water.

THE "FRESH WATER CRISIS"

Some have raised the specter of a "fresh water crisis" in recent years in much the same way as an "energy crisis" was proclaimed in the 1970s. In an article published in 2000, social ethics professor John M. Swomley predicted that a water crisis "looming on the horizon" could reach "dire proportions within the next ten to thirty years." It is unclear on what basis he made such a presumption (or if he has the expertise and information to do so).[4] An article in a 2002 issue of the *Nation* also sounded an alarm:

> The world is running out of fresh water. Humanity is polluting, diverting and depleting the wellspring of life at a startling rate. With every passing day, our demand for fresh water outpaces its availability and thousands more people are put at risk. Already, the social, political and economic impacts of water scarcity are rapidly becoming a destabilizing force, with water-related conflicts springing up around the globe. Quite simply, unless we dramatically change our ways, between one-half and two-thirds of humanity will be living with severe freshwater shortages within the next quarter-century.[5]

These predictions may seem unnecessarily dire, but the reality is that global water use continues to expand faster than population growth. One set of statistics suggests that over the past one hundred years the world population has tripled while water withdrawals have increased six times. Population upsurge explains a great deal about increase in fresh water use but not the whole story. In 1700, about 90 percent of withdrawals went for irrigation, mostly in Asia. One estimate suggests that by 1990, fresh water use was as much as forty times greater than in 1700. While 66 percent still was utilized for irrigation, urban expansion and industrial uses represented another 32 percent. And although water withdrawals in the twentieth century increased enormously over previous centuries, in more recent years it stabilized in more affluent parts of the world (probably more in Western Europe than North America) because of increased efficiencies and various forms of regulation. Asia, however, remained the hands down biggest consumer in the late twentieth century with withdrawals greater than on all other continents combined. This is due in large measure to its vast population and the presence of about one-third of the world's streamflow.[6]

To suggest that there has been stabilization of water use in richer parts of the world in recent years is not to imply that expanding demand and use of fresh water elsewhere translates into plentiful available supplies. By 2004, according to one source, thirty-one countries—mostly in Africa and the Near East—confronted water stress or scarcities. Seventeen additional countries (2.1 billion people) were water poor. In the Middle East, nine of fourteen countries experienced shortages. What had appeared to be a problem of scarcity in the twentieth century primarily affecting several developing countries has become globalized in the twenty-first century.[7]

Another estimate puts forth that for approximately one billion people there is inadequate and uneven access to clean water. But this is only the grossest way to determine shortages. For example, Israel only has 300 cubic meters per capita per year available to its citizens—compared with 1,693 cubic meters in the United States and Canada—but few suffer water shortages; while Nigeria is water rich, but more than half of the population has no access to water. To what uses water is put, who controls access, and the quality of the available water all play a role in determining scarcities and water crises.[8] Adequate sanitation directly relates to the quality of water available and protection of obtainable sources of water. Under World Health Organization standards, sanitation facilities that "break the fecal-oral transmission route" are regarded as adequate systems. For cities, adequate sanitation often is determined by connection to public sewers or household systems like pit privies, flush latrines, and septic tanks. In rural areas, pit privies, flush latrines, and septic tanks may be viewed as sufficient for sanitation purposes. Even by these measures, sanitation is severely limited or nonexistent in several parts of the world, and negatively affects water supply.[9]

Therefore, *crisis* is a loaded term that has to be used clearly and accurately. While shortages of fresh water have become more common, in many cases the question also has to do with unsustainable practices that deplete water supplies faster than they are replenished. Biologist and environmentalist Constance Hunt persuasively argues that, "The potential for a global water crisis is the result not of technological incapacity to sustain the global water cycle so much as of the weakness of political will to adopt sustainable technologies. The corporations that produce dams, irrigation equipment, sewage treatment systems, genetically altered crops, fertilizers, pesticides, barges and other water-related products are exerting a greater influence on governing bodies than are human communities which suffer because their water sources are destroyed."[10]

We have to guard against what geographer Eric Swyngedouw rightly calls "produced scarcity."[11] One report noted that most countries possess enough water to meet basic water requirements of their citizens, and only twelve countries have less than 1,000 liters of fresh water per person per day—enough for fundamental needs at least. What is missing in satisfying the billions of people who need access to reliable and safe drinking water, as well as sanitation, is "political will and priorities."[12] Producing this will and setting the right priorities, however, is too often easier said than done.

COMMODIFICATION OF WATER

Beyond the issue of scarcity there is growing unease that fresh water is being commodified, that is, being treated more as an economic as opposed to a social and environmental good.[13] From this vantage point, water is not just another commodity or consumer product, but—as one writer noted—it is "a shared resource and a public trust." In November 2002, the United Nations Committee on Economic, Social, and Cultural Rights adopted the General Comment No. 15 on the right to water. In referring to Articles 11 and 12 of the International Covenant on Economic, Social, and Cultural Rights, it stated that "the human right to water is indispensable for leading a life in human dignity. It is a prerequisite for the realization of other human rights." The United Nations also declared 2003 as the "International Year of Freshwater." The opening paragraph of the declaration affirmed that:

> Water is essential to human life—for basic health and survival, as well as food production and economic activities. Yet we are presently facing a global emergency in which over one billion people lack access to a basic supply of clean water and over two billion do not have access to adequate sanitation, the primary cause of diseases linked to water. It has frequently been argued in the international arena that the acknowledgement of water as a human right may prove to be the most important step in addressing the challenge of providing people with this most basic element of life.[14]

Others have echoed the notion that commodifying fresh water is ethically wrong. On a practical level, treating water simply as a product leads to choosing the most profitable markets for providing water service, leaving some areas—especially poor communities and those located on the urban margins—without adequate service.[15] Viewing water in moral terms and legal rights terms clashes with the age-old practice of treating water simply as a resource like any other. In this respect, the ethical argument carries less weight historically in some cultures than others where water has been treated as a tangible resource, where water has been commodified long before the onset of the twenty-first century. However, even in cultures that have treated water as a commodity to be bought and sold, the idea of water as a public good may exist side by side. Riparian water rights practiced in the United States and elsewhere, for example, deny ownership to sources of fresh water while allowing use of that very water. Regulations against water pollution recognize public as well as private value of water for a variety of uses from human consumption to transportation. And many economists argue that water itself and water rights most often are priced well below their value partly because, one would surmise, it is not always obvious what is being commodified and by whom.

It is clear, however, that while the debate between water as a right and water as a commodity has yet to be resolved, fresh water has become a significant medium for debate—and rightly so—in many instances falling within an environmental justice context. The environmental justice movement emerged in the United States in the late 1970s and early 1980s, bringing attention to environmental inequalities and environmental racism suffered by people of color in communities where they were exposed to toxic or hazardous materials or where they found themselves in workplaces with similar exposures. The term "environmental justice" is preferred by its advocates over "equity" or "environmental racism" in order to emphasize the right to safe and healthy surroundings for all people, and its definition has come to include ecological, physical, social, political, and economic themes. It has taken some time for the environmental justice or social justice moniker to catch on internationally as a term reflecting concerns growing out of various forms of environmental discrimination, but it is widely understood as such today.[16]

Water controversies in recent years have been brought under the banner of environmental justice issues. For example, the so-called Cochabamba Water Wars in Bolivia's third largest city in early 2000 brought international attention to protests against privatization of municipal water supplies and subsequent extraordinary rate hikes seriously affecting the poorer classes. In this case, privatization was reversed—"deprivatized"—but rates remain relatively high nonetheless.[17] Bechtel's reception of substantial contracts to "rebuild" Iraq in the wake of the U.S. attacks on that country led to, among other things, serious criticism of the failure to improve water supplies.[18]

Historically, changes in the control and ownership of lands due to conquest or other means often meant substantial changes in practices with respect to water. For example, the takeover of former Mexican lands by U.S. forces in the Upper Rio Grande watershed in current-day southern Colorado and northern New Mexico had a variety of impacts: transfers of land grant commons to private owners or the U.S. Forestry Service, replacement of communal acequia irrigation districts with market-oriented conservancy districts, replacement of a subsistence economy by a market economy or industrial development, and other actions all influencing water use.[19] After the Union of South Africa was formed in 1910, a variety of segregationist policies "determined how people related to each other, the state, the economy, and the environment," stated Nancy J. Jacobs, "although the last point is not often recognized."[20] In the municipality of Kuruman, for example, "environmental segregation involved the state taking from blacks well-watered parcels and sources of water and granting them to white people."[21]

In these cases, the real issue is not that water is now being commodified, but rather who is doing the commodifying. Water will always be an economic good whoever manages it. It seems that the truly radical—and quite worthy—notion that water is a human right has a long distance to go before it is widely accepted. To arrive at consensus on this point will be truly revolutionary.

THE "CRISIS IN PUBLIC SERVICE"

People, especially in industrialized nations, have come to expect water delivered to their homes and businesses efficiently and at low cost. Local governments and regional authorities, however, often face budgetary hardships—including reduced federal funding—and the increased cost of compliance with environmental regulations to the extent that many historically profitable water supply systems are difficult to maintain in the public arena.[22] Government leaders frequently must choose between maintaining services "in-house" that also may have political benefits versus substantial public spending that may have political costs. Given the predicament of many local authorities, private companies are increasingly pursuing opportunities to manage or to own local waterworks.[23]

In England and Wales, most water supply systems had been developed and managed by local governments until 1974. In that year, Parliament transferred responsibility for water (and sewage) service to publicly owned regional water authorities. This was a first step away from traditional local control there. Under the Margaret Thatcher government, the Water Act of 1989 privatized those authorities. The idea was that they would become more efficient and competitive in line with a general faith in market forces.[24]

In the United States, privatization most often means governments contracting with private companies to provide specific public services. For example, a PPP was established between Harrington Park, New Jersey, and United Water Resources through which the city maintained ownership of the water utility, while the company managed the facilities. Selling off assets or complete liquidation of public holdings also is possible in some instances.[25]

Not so many years ago, privatized municipal water systems seemed unthinkable in the United States. The historical context for maintaining public water service, however, has been sorely tested since the 1990s. In the wake of the so-called infrastructure crisis in the late twentieth century, water supply systems successfully avoided the direst predictions about decay and deterioration. In 1987, a report stated that a national water supply "infrastructure gap" of the magnitude that would require a substantial federal subsidy did not exist. Urban water supply systems as a whole, it concluded, "do not constitute a national problem."[26] This assessment was based on comparisons with other components of the nation's infrastructure. Water needs appeared modest when compared with highway repair and replacement estimated in the mid-1980s to reach a twenty-year "needs level" of approximately $2 trillion. Studies set price tags of $125 billion for water supply repairs, expansions, and improvements.

The relatively small, but hardly insignificant, number masked problems that had been building for years. Some experts, looking beyond the statistics, charged that many drinking water systems were outdated, faced massive leaks, were poorly maintained, and relied on pipes a hundred or more years old.[27] What seemed to be a somewhat achievable price tag for repairing water systems in the late 1980s was more unreachable as the nation slipped into recession by the mid-2000s. The documentary *Liquid Assets: The Story of Our Water Infrastructure* was broadcast on numerous public stations in 2008–2009, suggesting with alarm that "largely out of sight and out of mind, these aging systems [water supply, wastewater, and stormwater] have not been maintained, and some estimates suggest this is the single largest public works endeavor in our nation's history."[28]

Broadening federal regulatory authority over water pollution and the tightening of water-quality standards were first steps in recognizing the severity and complex nature of water pollution in the 1970s, but they also added additional financial pressures to managing water systems at the local and regional level.[29] Financing of water supply in the 1970s and 1980s largely remained at the local level. Statistics from the early 1980s indicate that state and local governments were primarily responsible for 83 percent of the expenditures for municipal water supplies. Federal funds for water projects were on the decline in the 1970s, and capital spending by all governments for water resources had fallen by 60 percent from the late 1960s to the late 1980s.[30]

Regionalization of the water industry in the United States attracted considerable attention, especially the Metropolitan Water District in California and the Metropolitan Sanitary District of Greater Chicago.[31] Moreover, efforts by several multinational companies to privatize water supply delivery and treatment globally were gaining significant attention as early as the

1990s. American waterworks remained largely public ventures managed on the local level by the first decade of the twenty-first century, but privatization was a trend to reckon with.[32]

From a business perspective, water supply systems often represent a "hot investment." Johan Bastin, with the European Bank for Reconstruction and Development in London, was reported as saying, "water is the last infrastructure frontier for private investors."[33] Thus, the most recent efforts of private water companies to penetrate the water market does not signal commodification of water per se but rather the rising expectations about new economic opportunities.

Underlying the assumption of a "crisis in public service" was also the notion that private enterprise was "necessarily more efficient than government-owned enterprises."[34] This view even crept into the public sector and became a clear justification for privatizing all manner of services. Yet, it sometimes was more of a justification emerging from budgetary woes and/or changing service priorities. There were times in the past, in periods when publicly managed enterprises were viewed as less corrupt, better capitalized, and more efficient than private ventures, when the argument about the superiority of privatization was turned on its head.

It also may be too simplistic to assume that a great wave of privatization is overtaking what once was a long, stable period of public sector management of water—a pendulum swinging in a totally new direction. As Charles Jacobson and Joel Tarr stated about the history of infrastructure and city services in the United States, "although it is widely believed that today's movement toward privatization represents the first major shift from public to private supply of infrastructure, history provides examples of many shifts in both directions." They added that "a simple distinction" between what is "public" and what is "private" does not really "encompass the range of arrangements that has existed with respect to the ownership, financing, and operation of facilities." These might include plans whereby a government agency builds and operates a facility, contracts out the construction, or contracts out the operation. Funding provisions might rely on user fees, taxes, and assessments to abutters, bonds, or a combination of some or all of these.[35]

Thus, it is important to be mindful of the variety of arrangement that have and will emerge and the variety of reasons for change. There is no simple international model and no uncomplicated set of reasons for public-to-private or private-to-public arrangements. Once again, the notion of a "crisis" is terribly misleading. Without any clear, broad trends, and without a careful understanding of local and regional circumstance, the desire to privatize in the recent environment may involve other motives than economic exigencies or some vague notion of efficient delivery of services. The historical record provides many examples of announcing a crisis as justification alone for change.

WATER CORPORATISM

Critics of privatization are skeptical of claims that privatizing water supplies could revitalize the water systems, make them more efficient, and deliver the product at a reasonable cost. They also are concerned as to whether the private market can deal with issues related to the public good in addition to focusing on profits—most likely to be taken out of the community. And they are particularly wary of multinational companies with no local ties that are most often the driving force behind recent efforts at privatization of water supply systems.[36] All of these are justifiable concerns. As Maria Alicia Gaura stated in the *San Francisco Chronicle* in 2002, "the transformation of water delivery from prosaic necessity to hot investment trend has startled many U.S. ratepayers, who never dreamed that stockholders in Europe would be wringing profits from their water bills."[37]

Globalization of fresh water service adds a significant layer of apprehension to the privatization trend in government. The rising influence of international water companies and their pursuit of local opportunities around the world do not take us full circle from individual and private water supplies in the past, to public utilities, and back again to private providers. They take us into a new era entirely.

Where public versus private competition over water supply, waterworks, and treatment plants has been largely a local matter in the past in many parts of the world, the potential impact of multinational—or transnational—water companies controlling vast numbers of systems represents a unique situation. Control over water supplies and water delivery is not a change from water as a public service to water as a commodity but a fundamental erosion of local authority well beyond more traditional tensions between city and region, city and state, and the city and national government.

At the turn of the new century, for example, privatization of water systems was much more widespread in Europe than in the United States. In 2003, only 5 percent of the water systems in the United States were privately owned, and only about 15 percent of the population was served by corporate water. Of the 94 percent of water systems that are publicly controlled (about 5,000), most are municipal.[38] Between 1997 and 2003, however, the number of publicly owned systems operated under long-term contracts by private companies increased from 400 to 1,100.[39] The Center for Public Integrity—a nonprofit advocacy group based in Washington, D.C.—estimated that before 2020, 65 to 75 percent of public waterworks in Europe and North

America would be controlled by private companies, with Africa and Asia not far behind.[40] Leading the way to this potential shift are approximately ten major corporations, several subsidiaries, and some smaller companies delivering water and wastewater services. Included here are Veolia Environment, Suez, Bouygues Saur, RWE-Thames Water, Bechtel-United Utilities, and several other smaller companies.

The prospect of a long-term contract to monopolize a key resource has attracted substantial corporate attention. For their part, the World Bank and the International Monetary Fund provided backing to many of the larger ventures, especially in developing countries. Since its inception, about 14 percent of the World Bank's budget has been earmarked for water development projects (including the building of many large dams in developing countries), and the World Bank has steadily supported the corporate role in water resource management.[41] As one source noted, "the World Bank is without doubt one of the most, if not the most important actor in the global water sector, be it in terms of financial aid or in terms of general policy-making in the developing countries."[42] Representatives of the World Bank argued that governments in developing countries are too poor and too much in debt to subsidize water and sanitation services with public funds. International trade accords—such as the North American Free Trade Agreement—also incorporated provisions for governments to turn over control of fresh water supplies to global trade institutions, helping private companies gain access to those supplies.

The bottled water industry (Culligan, for example, owned by Veolia) also must be included among water-for-profit enterprises, selling more than 90 billion liters of bottled water in 2002 alone (although compared to tap water sales this is relatively small). Total annual sales in 2006 were between $50 million and $100 million, with rapid growth in Asia and South America.[43] One report has noted that the annual profits of the water industry in recent years surpassed those in the pharmaceutical sector and is about 40 percent of the oil sector, although only about five percent of world's water is privately owned. It is not only this industry's rapid growth but the rising controversy over the energy-intensive and environmentally unfriendly nature the product that garners serious attention and criticism.

Two French companies have dominated the international water industry, Veolia Environment and Suez.[44] Veolia, formerly Vivendi Environment, grew out of Generale des Eaux, which had been established by Napoleon III in 1852, and is funded by Paribas. Its first contract called for supplying water to the city of Lyon. Suez has always been behind Lyonnaise des Eaux, which was founded in 1880 with the sponsorship of Credit Lyonnais. Both Generale des Eaux and Lyonnaise des Eaux established the tradition of private water delivery in France and benefited from years of protectionism, and now they have emerged as part of a powerful force on the world scene. Taken together, the two water giants—Veolia and Suez—provide service in more than a hundred countries with approximately 200 million customers. Only RWE-Thames comes close to them, benefiting from Margaret Thatcher's privatization of water in Great Britain in 1989. In many cases, low margins in the European water market have encouraged the multinationals to spread their financial risk into other parts of the world.[45]

Some American-based corporations attempted to challenge Veolia and Suez—most notably Azurix, which was a subsidiary of the now much maligned energy-trading company Enron. Enron had hoped to be a major player in the fresh water market on a scale equal to its core businesses in natural gas and electricity. It met with little success because it could not raise sufficient capital to operate effectively in both the water and energy markets.[46] In 1999, American Water Works Company was the leading water company in the United States serving 16 million customers in twenty-nine states, but its revenue was less than 10 percent of Veolia's. German conglomerate RWE AG purchased American Water Works for $8.6 billion, which further took American water companies outside the leadership of the industry. Through its ownership of U.S. Filter, Veolia has been the largest private wastewater firm operating in the United States.[47]

The water giants have not been without their failures as well as successes. The Buenos Aires water concession of Aguas Argentinas—a consortium that included Vivendi and Suez—had been noted regularly as a successful privatization venture.[48] However, allegations of corruption and unfair business practices regularly dogged them. Activities in developing countries generally have been less successful than elsewhere. In 1998, Bolivian authorities—under pressure from the World Bank—gave a contract for water service in the city of Cochabamba to a consortium of private investors (English, Italian, Spanish, American, and Bolivian), who promptly raised water rates by 35 percent. Water subsequently cost more than food. In 2000, a general strike and transportation stoppage ensued. Despite mass arrests and several deaths, the protesters continued to demand "deprivatization" of water, and ultimately the consortium abandoned the project—Suez cancelling half the investment value they had made—and the government revoked the privatization legislation. In neighboring Rio de Janeiro, an effort to auction off the state's water system was canceled by the Federal Supreme Court because of a clash between city and state authorities over ownership of the assets. In Argentina, government officials terminated a contract granted to the city of Tucuman after water rates doubled and water quality worsened. Veolia ultimately retired from the privatization effort there.[49]

In the wake of difficulties in developing countries, Suez retrenched, especially in Asia and Latin America, while Veolia proved more successful focusing on Eastern Europe and North America. The China market appeared promising but has yet to be effectively penetrated. And little attention is given to places such as sub-Saharan Africa where the need for water is great but where the business of water seems less profitable.[50]

A wholesale trend toward privatization of water supplies and water supplies management has yet to occur in the United States. However, in 1999 alone there were $15 billion in acquisitions in the U.S. water industry. For example, Suez purchased Nalco Chemical Company of Illinois—a water treatment group—for $4.1 billion and also acquired Calgon Corporation—the third largest water-conditioning company based in Pittsburgh—for $425 million. The Safe Drinking Water Act of 1996 and other federal and state laws requiring renovation or improvement of deteriorating water systems placed a financial burden on several cities, which afterwards were ready to explore a relationship with private water companies. Also, a 1997 executive order, tax-rule changes by the Internal Revenue Service, and privatization advocates in Congress opened up the possibility of more shifts from public to private service. Cities such as Indianapolis, Milwaukee, and Gary, Indiana, contracted with private companies to manage their waterworks.[51]

In the United States as elsewhere, the global water company juggernaut has not always prevailed. Atlanta officials struck a twenty-year operations and maintenance contract with United Water, Inc. (a subsidiary of Suez) in 1998, which paid the company $21.4 million per year. What had been one of the first large privatization awards in the United States was terminated in 2003, ostensibly because of faulty contract provisions but also because of poor service and the protest (and lawsuits) of environmentalists over the construction of suburban reservoirs. As one journalist noted, "the decision, in many ways, takes Atlanta back to square one."[52] While the action was a setback for privatization of water, and cities such as New Orleans (before Katrina), Louisiana, and Stockton, California, were rethinking plans to privatize (or to further privatize in the case of New Orleans), Atlanta's decision was not likely to have long-range implications for water privatization in the United States.[53]

The water industry is not remaining static. It is consolidating and also evolving. One estimate suggests that global water service is a $260 billion market growing at a rate of 6 percent per year. However, public water companies in 2005 still were providing about 95 percent of water and wastewater services globally. Nevertheless, since the 1990s private management has expanded significantly. In 1990, private companies provided water to 51 million people; by 2002, the number ballooned to 300 million.[54] Water corporatism has become a way of life in some parts of the world. Trends indicate more privatization, but how universal the trends will become remains uncertain.

Many environmental activists have encouraged the public to "think globally, act locally." Multinational water companies have taken up that call but for much different ends. Water corporatism certainly is on the rise internationally, and the loss of local control over water management and even water supplies is increasingly daunting. What has not changed is the fact that water long has been a commodity to be bought and sold, to be fought over, to be won and lost. The difference is that the tension between water as a public good and water as economic gain is being played out on a global scale, as is a growing interest in water as a human right. This latter point changes the debate from a question of resource use (and sustainability for that matter) to a moral issue with broad policy implications.

In addition, if there is a worldwide water crisis, it is too simplistic to equate it with physical water scarcity alone. Focusing only on geographic water scarcity suggests—inaccurately—that there is little that can be done to rectify the problem. A larger concern must be water allocation. Providing equity of access to water incurs several pitfalls and tensions, many of them associated with political decision making in a world where local needs and global realities have yet to be reconciled. Allocation is one of those issues that speak not only to economics but to power. Controlling water supplies and the ability to maintain water purity are sturdy political and social tools. Giving up such power for the sake of the "public good" goes to the heart of modern privatization efforts and the very nature of the obligations of public service.

Conclusion

THE QUESTION OF CONTROL

This book provides historical perspective on public and private responsibility for water as a resource, be it water supplies for drinking and washing, river and dam development, or water as an urban artery. The contested nature of water is a powerful indicator of its central importance. Just how it is controlled and by whom can make the difference between economic failure and success, an inhabitable or barren physical environment, and life or death itself. In extreme cases, state control of water, on the one hand, and private monopoly of water, on the other, can be wielded as a kind of weapon. As one study stated: "Control of water has, in many places and moments of history, been equated with the control of society. Water can provide and sustain political power."[1]

There is, as some authors suggest, a certain historical "spectrum of control" between the polar positions, with several permutations from public to private or vice versa.[2] Particular control mechanisms really tell us more about the vital character of the resource than adequately explaining the motives and methods of control. Oftentimes, the significance of control has less to do with the ownership of water than the choices made concerning its use. The building of dams, for example, may only temporarily impede much of the water in a river—although markedly changing the river to be sure—and still allow for existing water rights to be sustained downstream. How the impounded water—and the power of the flowing water—are utilized means everything.

The allocation of the supply for a variety of uses makes all the difference in the world. This is particularly true for municipal water supplies. Where the pipes travel from a primary pumping station and where they end is crucial. Is there equal access to water for all citizens, all businesses? Should cities provide water service beyond their political borders and at what cost? Ultimately, decisions over allocation demonstrate control to a greater extent than rights of possession.

This book has been about choices made in the use and allocation of water, from "improving" rivers and building dams to supplying water and wastewater service in cities. Many of the chapters ended with some ambiguity in addressing those issues. To what extent did water law, for instance, preserve individual rights to the use of river water? Were dams simply physical obstructions on rivers or technologies that sealed the choices in the use of those rivers? In the chapters on water supply and wastewater systems, it may be unclear if public or private control better served public needs for pure water and pollution abatement. The degree to which Buffalo Bayou in Houston was transformed from a transportation artery into an access and exit point serving a massive industrial complex fails to answer the question as to whether this was a better use of the waterway. Even the chapter on privatization, which presented the controversial nature of the move toward water corporatism, gives only a glimpse of the implications of that change.

In most respects, however, the book as a whole was not meant to answer those larger questions in detail. Instead, *Precious Commodity* was designed to alert readers to the centrality of control of a vital resource and how such control influenced choices made about using water in the past. Stephen Graham and Simon Marvin in their influential book, *Splintering Urbanism*, attempted to deconstruct several urban networked infrastructures—including transport, telecommunication, energy, and water—to better understand the functioning of cities. They write that their "starting point . . . is the assertion that infrastructure networks are the key physical and technological assets of modern cities."[3] However, Graham and Marvin recognized that building, maintaining, and using these infrastructures is not simply a physical process, but one imbued with social, cultural, economic, and political meaning. Thus by "unbundling" the networks they attempt to explain or reconceptualize the relationship among them and thus better understand the functioning of cities.[4] My present effort hardly brings the rigor of *Splintering Urbanism* to the study of water use in the United States, but it is useful to think about the processes of privatizing water supplies, building public systems, and managing rivers as human acts that place water in new relationships with people. Again, control of water is not exclusively about ownership but also about choice.

For American cities, the trend for municipal ownership and management of water supplies remains strong. In 2000, 85 percent of the U.S. population received its drinking water supply from publicly owned waterworks, up from 62 percent in 1950. Figures for 1996 show that wastewater treatment facilities served 71.8 percent of the population.[5] While overall use of water in the United States stabilized during the last several years, a disproportionably large amount was not consumed in cities but in irrigation and in

the production of thermoelectric power. Because of irrigation, western water use tended to be greater than in the East (60 percent higher in the West),
especially in states like California and Texas.[6]

Without a doubt, jurisdictional issues have complicated the control
of water in the United States. Cities, counties, special districts, water and
sewer authorities, state governments, and the federal government all compete for the management and/or regulation of water systems—more so
than any time in American history. Yet, as we have seen, current trends in
financing water supply and wastewater systems demonstrate the continuing local nature of these services. While the federal government developed
water-quality standards and regulations, it provided only a small portion of
funding for constructing water supply systems and wastewater treatment
facilities.[7] Within this context, inroads for privatization will be slow despite
the faltering economy of the last few years.

As several of the chapters have shown, however, understanding the issue
of local water control is not simply determining if the pendulum will swing
back to privatization after years of public management and ownership. Most
importantly, the modern privatization movement has developed in a very
different context than public and private contention in the past, as chapter
8 attempted to demonstrate. Furthermore, the idea that municipalities operate with pure public or pure private systems defies the evidence. San Jose
relied heavily on the work of the Santa Clara Valley Conservation District to
undergird the development of an adequate water inventory to maintain its
own market. The oil and petrochemical industries in Houston relied on the
municipal water and wastewater system and public efforts to expand water
supplies via new surface sources of water (the San Jacinto River initially),
rather than to directly usurp the management of water supplies as might
have been expected in a "free enterprise city." And beyond cities, big dam
construction was a public venture, but largely it was undertaken for the economic benefit of farmers, industries, and cities requiring water and power.
In light of the historical examples, it might be best to inquire as to the extent
of public and private participation in water service delivery and why, rather
than to rely upon an arcane polarity such as public versus private conflict. Of
course, questions of control become a great deal messier but such is the burden of historical analysis.

On the broader scale of global water issues, concern over a "fresh water
crisis," water corporatism, water as a human right, and gross inequalities
in access to water supplies remain in play. Added to that list can be efforts
to increase fresh water supplies through technologies such as desalination;
environmental implications, such as several forms of pollution and wet-
land destruction; and chronic concerns over floods and droughts. However,

at least three less well-considered issues have captured recent worldwide attention: water and terrorism, water and energy, and climate change. All three are equatable with water issues because terrorism, energy, and climate change are the big issues of the day, and as we have seen, it is difficult to separate questions concerning water from almost any social, political, or economic discourse.

According to Peter H. Gleick, "the chance that terrorists will strike at water systems is real. Water has been used as a political or military target or tool for over four thousand years."[8] This might be said for other resources as well, especially those upon which we are most dependent and which might be least easy to protect. In the case of water, attacks on infrastructure and chemical and biological assaults come quickly to mind. Gleick fuses terrorist attacks, however, with what he views as a long history of violent conflicts over water, ranging from destroying a reservoir because it might be a health hazard to military attacks on water facilities.[9] In several of these cases, the comparisons seem strained, with the definition of terrorism stretched to its limits. In some curious way, Gleick connects the perils of the day with a concern over the vulnerability of an essential resource—water—reinforcing its centrality to society's long-term needs. This is reminiscent—but certainly more substantive—than the 1950s and 1960s scare about water fluoridation, which some on the Far Right argued was an insidious Communist plot. Equating fear of terrorism with protection of water clearly fits a pattern of societal concerns long attached to this precious commodity, but there is a need to separate a potential terrorist act from a water conflict with other motives.

The case of the relationship between water and energy also has grown out of a contemporary preoccupation, but the interconnection is more obvious. We have become increasingly aware that a central use for water is producing energy—going back at least to water mills and later hydroelectric power generation. In 2000, 4 percent of the nation's electricity was used for moving and treating water and wastewater, with about 80 percent of municipal water processing and distribution costs going for electricity. Pumping groundwater requires substantial amounts of electrical power as well. In California, the California State Water Project is the largest single user of energy in the state; delivering water from San Francisco to Southern California requires 2 percent to 3 percent of all electricity consumed in the Golden State. In 2005, it took approximately 32 billion kilowatt hours of electricity for public agencies nationwide to supply fresh water to their customers—and the numbers are rising.[10] Concerns about heavy withdrawals of water from the Great Lakes to produce biofuels are raising questions about the economic value of such action. Other correlations between water use and energy production are beginning to attract more attention. Unlike the potential implications of water terrorism, the intersection of water issues and energy indicates that current debates over increasing oil production, alternative fuels, and energy efficiency have to be informed by a holistic look at the impact of energy production and consumption within a larger natural resource framework.

Climate change offers a more staggering problem with respect to water. Some of the most serious issues do not speak directly to fresh water, such as the rising levels of the oceans, but many do. In 2008, an Intergovernmental Panel on Climate Change technical paper on "Climate Change and Water" stated the following: "Climate, freshwater, biophysical and socio-economic systems are interconnected in complex ways. Hence, a change in any one of these can induce a change in any other. Freshwater-related issues are critical in determining key regional and sectoral vulnerabilities. Therefore, the relationship between climate change and freshwater resources is of primary concern to human society and also has implications for all living species."[11] It added that, "observed warming over several decades has been linked to changes in the large-scale hydrological cycle such as: increasing atmospheric water vapor content; changing precipitation patterns, intensity and extremes; reduced snow cover and widespread melting of ice; and changes in soil moisture and runoff."[12]

The report also made note of a laundry list of possible changes in the twenty-first century, including precipitation increases in high latitudes and in the tropics and decreased precipitation in some subtropical and some mid-latitude regions; increases and decreases in river runoff by region; increased risk of flooding and drought; decline in water supplies stored in glaciers; higher water temperatures; impacts on food availability; and impacts on the operation of existing water infrastructure such as irrigation systems and hydropower facilities.[13]

Such predictions for a not-so-distant era seem quite dire.[14] Yet, some people would prefer to put their hands over the ears, close their eyes, and recite a mantra, rather than face up to the possibility of an uncomfortable future marred by dwindling or changing water supplies and other resources. Most pertinent to our discussion—aside from such predictions—is an understanding of the degree to which water is imbedded in the world's life cycle; how decisions we make about protecting sources of water have long-term impacts; how providing access to water must meet myriad needs; and the importance of placing a value on water that transcends business transactions.

Precious Commodity can only hint at these profound issues. It can make some historical sense out of the quest to control water. And it can prod us to think more assertively about how water is used as a resource and as a source of power and control. Here's hoping it has done a little of that.

Further Reading

Introduction: Water—Truly a Precious Commodity

On broad issues related to water history, see Petri S. Juuti, Tapio S. Katko, and Heikki S. Vurinen, eds., *Environmental History of Water: Global Views on Community Water Supply and Sanitation* (London: IWA Pub., 2007); R. Coopey and T. Tvedt, eds., *A History of Water,* volume 2, *The Political Economy of Water* (London: I.B. Tauris, 2006); Marc DeVilliers, *Water: The Fate of Our Most Precious Resource* (Boston: Mariner Books, 2001); Marnie Leybourne and Andrea Gaynor, eds., *Water: Histories, Cultures, Ecologies* (Crowley, Western Australia: University of Western Australia Press, 2006); Alice Outwater, *Water: A Natural History* (New York: Basic Books, 1996); T. Tvedt and E. Jakobsson, eds., *A History of Water,* volume 1, *Water Control and River Biographies* (London: I.B. Tauris, 2006); T. Tvedt and T. Oestigaard, eds., *A History of Water,* volume 3, *The World of Water* (London: I.B. Tauris, 2006).

Many of the volumes produced by Resources for the Future Press deal with key questions with respect to management and control of water, resource economics, and water rights. Some current titles include Geoffrey Gooch and Per Stålnacke, eds., *Science, Policy and Stakeholders in Water Management: An Integrated Approach to River Basin Management* (Washington, D.C.: Resources for the Future, 2010); Rutgerd Boelens, David Getches, and Armando Guevara Gil, eds., *Out of the Mainstream: Water Rights, Politics and Identity* (Washington, D.C.: Resources for the Future, 2010); Ronald C. Griffin, ed., *Water Policy in Texas: Responding to the Rise of Scarcity* (Washington, D.C.: Resources for the Future, 2010); Kristiina A. Vogt, et al., *Sustainability Unpacked: Food, Energy and Water for Resilient Environments and Societies* (Washington, D.C.: Resources for the Future, 2010); Maggie Black and Jannet King, *The Atlas of Water: Mapping the World's Most Critical Resource,* The Earthscan Atlas Series (Washington, D.C.: Resources for the Future, 2010; 2nd ed.); José Esteban Castro and Léo Heller, eds., *Water and Sanitation Services: Public Policy and Management* (Washington, D.C.: Resources for the Future, 2009); *Water and Sanitation in the World's Cities: Local Action for Global Goals* (Washington, D.C.: Resources for the Future, 2003).

Chapter One. "Improving" Rivers in America:
From the Revolution to the Progressive Era

The historical literature on rivers has exploded in recent years. Many new books have taken their place alongside such classics as Donald Worster's *Rivers of Empire: Water, Aridity, and the Growth of the American West* (New York: Pantheon Books, 1985) and Richard White's *The Organic Machine: The Remaking of the Columbia River* (New York: Hill and Wang, 1995). For American rivers, in particular, the number of new studies has been remarkable. See, for example, John O. Anfinson, *The River We Have Wrought: A History of the Upper Mississippi* (Minneapolis: University of Minnesota Press, 2003); James M. Aton and Robert S. McPherson, *River Flowing from the Sunrise: An Environmental History of the Lower San Juan* (Logan: Utah State University Press, 2000); Robert Baron and Thomas Locker, *Hudson: the Story of a River* (Golden, CO: Fulcrum Pub., 2004); Frances F. Dunwell, *The Hudson: America's River* (New York: Columbia University Press, 2008); Calvin R. Flemling, *Immortal River: The Upper Mississippi in Ancient and Modern Times* (Madison: University of Wisconsin Press, 2005); Douglas E. Kupel, *Fuel for Growth: Water and Arizona's Urban Environment* (Tucson: University of Arizona Press, 2003); Tom Lewis, *The Hudson: A History* (New Haven: Yale University Press, 2005); Gregory Summers, *Consuming Nature: Environmentalism in the Fox Valley, 1850–1950* (Lawrence: University Press of Kansas, 2006); Donald Worster, *A River Running West: The Life of John Wesley Powell* (New York: Oxford University Press, 2001).

On western water conflicts and other issues, see William Ashworth, *Ogallala Blue: Water and Life on the High Plains* (Woodstock, VT: Countryman Press, 2006); Douglas E. Kupel, *Fuel for Growth: Water and Arizona's Urban Environment* (Tucson: University of Arizona Press, 2003); Char Miller, ed., *Fluid Arguments: Five Centuries of Western Water Conflict* (Tucson: University of Arizona Press, 2001); Donald J. Pisani, *Water and American Government: The Reclamation Bureau, National Water Policy, and the West, 1902–1935* (Berkeley: University of California Press, 2002); Stephen C. Sturgeon, *The Politics of Western Water: The Congressional Career of Wayne Aspinall* (Tucson: University of Arizona Press, 2002); Evan Ward, *Border Oasis: Water and the Politics Ecology of the Colorado River Delta* (Tucson: University of Arizona Press, 2003); Daniel Tyler, *Silver Fox of the Rockies: Delphius E. Carpenter and Western Water Compacts* (Norman: University of Oklahoma Press, 2003); Ellen E. Wohl, *Virtual Rivers: Lessons from the Mountain Rivers of the Colorado Front Range* (New Haven: Yale University Press, 2001). A good study on the environmental movement germane to the discussion of rivers is Robert Gottlieb, *Forcing the Spring: The Transformation of the American Environmental Movement* (Washington, D.C.: Island Press, 2005).

See also Cynthia Barnett, *Mirage: Florida and the Vanishing Water of the Eastern U.S.* (Ann Arbor: University of Michigan Press, 2007); Mark Cioc, *The Rhine: An Eco-Biography, 1815–2000* (Seattle: University of Washington Press, 2002); Christof Mauch and Thomas Zeller, eds., *Rivers in History: Perspectives on Waterways in Europe and North America* (Pittsburgh: University of Pittsburgh Press,

2008); Jerry R. Rogers, ed., *Great Rivers History: Proceedings and Invited Papers for the EWRI Congress and History Symposium, May 17–19, 2009, Kansas City, Missouri* (Reston, VA: American Society of Civil Engineers, 2009).

Chapter Two. How Bad Theory Can Lead to Good Technology: Water Supply and Sewerage in the Age of Miasmas

Historical literature on water supply and wastewater services in the United States has grown impressively in the last decade. Among my own work, a more elaborate discussion of sanitary services can be found in the original edition of *The Sanitary City: Urban Infrastructure in America from Colonial Times to the Present* (Baltimore: Johns Hopkins University Press, 2000) and also in *The Sanitary City: Environmental Services in Urban America from Colonial Times to the Present* (Pittsburgh: University of Pittsburgh Press, 2008; abridged edition), and "Pure and Plentiful: The Development of Modern Waterworks in the United States, 1801-2000," *Water Policy* 69 (2000): 243–65 (excerpted in chapter 3). See also Louis P. Cain and Elyce J. Rotella, "Death and Spending: Urban Mortality and Municipal Expenditure on Sanitation," *Annales de Demographie Historique* 45 (2001): 139–54; Kate Foss-Mollan, *Hard Water: Politics and Water Supply in Milwaukee* (West Lafayette, IN: Purdue University Press, 2001); Matthew Gandy, *Concrete and Clay: Reworking Nature in New York City* (Cambridge: MIT Press, 2002); Charles Hardy, "The Watering of Philadelphia," *Pennsylvania Heritage* 30 (Spring 2004): 26–35; Gerard T. Koeppel, *Water for Gotham: A History* (Princeton: Princeton University Press, 2000); Harold L. Platt, *Shock Cities: The Environmental Transformation and Reform of Manchester and Chicago* (Chicago: University of Chicago Press, 2005); Michael Rawson, "The Nature of Water," *Environmental History* 9 (July 2004): 411–35; Joel A. Tarr and Terry F. Yosie, "Critical Decisions in Pittsburgh Water and Wastewater Treatment," in *Devastation and Renewal: An Environmental History of Pittsburgh and Its Region,* ed. Joel A. Tarr (Pittsburgh: University of Pittsburgh Press, 2003), 64–88; Werner Troesken, *The Great Lead Water Pipe Disaster* (Cambridge: MIT Press, 2006); Troesken, *Water, Race, and Disease* (Cambridge: MIT Press, 2004); Troesken, "Race, Disease, and the Provision of Water in American Cities, 1889-1921," *Journal of Economic History* 61 (2001): 750–76; and Julie Sze, *Noxious New York: The Racial Politics of Urban Health and Environmental Justice* (Cambridge: MIT, 2006). See also Jamie Benidickson, *The Culture of Flushing: A Social and Legal History of Sewage* (Vancouver: UBC Press, 2007); Steven Johnson, *The Ghost Map: The Story of London's Deadliest Epidemic* (New York: Penguin, 2006); Jouni Paavola, "Water Quality as Property," *Environment and History* 8 (2002): 295–318.

Chapter Three. Pure and Plentiful: The Development of Modern Waterworks in the United States, 1880–2000

See the introduction to chapter 2 for several recent books on municipal water supply and sewerage. See also William L. Andreen, "The Evolution of Water Pollution Control in the United States: State, Local and Federal Efforts, 1789-1972: Part

1," *Stanford Environmental Law Journal* 22 (January 2003): 145–200; Steven P. Erie, *Beyond "Chinatown": The Metropolitan Water District, Growth, and the Environment in Southern California* (Palo Alto: Stanford University Press, 2006); Robert Glennon, *Water Follies: Groundwater Pumping and the Fate of America's Fresh Water* (Washington, D.C.: Island Press, 2002); Thomas R. Huffman, "U.S. Water Pollution," in *Water and the Environment Since 1945: A Cross Cultural Perspective,* ed. Char Miller (New York: St. James/Gale, 2001); Charles D. Jacobson, *Ties that Bind: Economic and Political Dilemmas of Urban Utility Networks, 1800–1990* (Pittsburgh: University of Pittsburgh Press, 2000); Michael Rawson, *Eden on the Charles: The Making of Boston* (Cambridge: Harvard University Press, 2010); Jeffrey L. Jordan and Aaron T. Wolf, eds., *Interstate Water Allocation in Alabama, Florida, and Georgia: New Issues, New Methods, New Models* (Gainesville, FL: University Press of Florida, 2006); Christopher Sellers, "The Artificial Nature of Fluoridated Water," *Osiris* 19 (2004): 182–200.

On the Clean Water Act and its relation to environmentalism in the United States, see Paul Charles Milazzo, *Unlikely Environmentalists: Congress and Clean Water, 1945–1972* (Lawrence: University Press of Kansas, 2006).

Chapter Four. The Environmental Impact of the Big Dam Era

For recent studies on dam history and dam-related issues, see David P. Billington and Donald C. Jackson, *Big Dams of the New Deal Era: A Confluence of Engineering and Politics* (Norman: University of Oklahoma Press, 2006); Donald C. Jackson and Norris Hundley Jr., "Privilege and Responsibility: William Mulholland and the St. Francis Dam Disaster," *California History* 82 (Fall 2004): 8–47; William R. Lowry, *Dam Politics: Restoring America's Rivers* (Washington, D.C.: Georgetown University Press, 2003); Karen M. O'Neill, *Rivers by Design: State Power and the Origins of U.S. Flood Control* (Durham: Duke University Press, 2006); Keith Peterson, *River of Life, Channel of Death: Fish and Dams on the Lower Snake* (Corvallis: Oregon State University Press, 2001); Donald J. Pisani, *Water and American Government: The Reclamation Bureau, National Water Policy, and the West, 1902–1935* (Berkeley: University of California Press, 2002); Diane Raines Ward, *Water Wars: Drought, Flood, Folly and the Politics of Thirst* (New York: Riverhead Books Penguin Putnam, 2002); "Dams and Diversions," in *Something New Under the Sun: An Environmental History of the Twentieth-Century World,* ed. J. R. McNeill (New York: W. W. Norton, 2000), 157–82.

For some studies on dams and the environmental movement, see Mark Harvey, *A Symbol of Wilderness: Echo Park and the American Conservation Movement* (Seattle: University of Washington Press, 2000); Byron E. Pearson, *Still the Wild River Runs: Congress, the Sierra Club, and the Fight to Save Grand Canyon* (Tucson: University of Arizona, 2002); Robert W. Righter, *The Battle Over Hetch Hetchy: America's Most Controversial Dam and the Birth of Modern Environmentalism* (New York: Oxford University Press, 2005).

Chapter Six. Historical Significance of Houston's Buffalo Bayou

For other examples of other cities (especially including close neighbor New Orleans) and their urban water arteries from a variety of perspectives, see Douglas Brinkley, *The Great Deluge: Hurricane Katrina, New Orleans, and the Mississippi Gulf Coast* (New York: William Morrow, 2006); Craig E. Colten, *An Unnatural Metropolis: Wresting New Orleans From Nature* (Baton Rouge: LSU Press, 2005); Blake Gumprecht, "Who Killed the Los Angeles River?" in *Land of Sunshine: An Environmental History of Metropolitan Los Angeles,* ed. William Deverell and Greg Hise (Pittsburgh: University of Pittsburgh Press, 2005), 115–34; Ari Kelman, *A River and Its City: The Nature of Landscape in New Orleans* (Berkeley: University of California Press, 2003); Matthew Klingle, *Emerald City: An Environmental History of Seattle* (New Haven: Yale University Press, 2007), 203–64; Edward K. Muller, "River City," in *Devastation and Renewal: An Environmental History of Pittsburgh and Its Region,* ed. Joel A. Tarr (Pittsburgh: University of Pittsburgh Press, 2003), 41–63; Jared Orsi, "Flood Control Engineering in the Urban Ecosystem," in *Land of Sunshine: An Environmental History of Metropolitan Los Angeles,* ed. William Deverell and Greg Hise (Pittsburgh: University of Pittsburgh Press, 2005), 135–51; Jared Orsi, "Reclaiming the City: Water History in the Urban North American West," *Journal of the West* 44 (Summer 2005): 8–11; Marienka Sokol, "Reclaiming the City: Water and the Urban Landscape in Phoenix and Las Vegas," *Journal of the West* 44 (Summer 2005): 52–61.

On Houston as an "energy capital," see Martin V. Melosi and Joseph A. Pratt, eds., *Energy Metropolis: An Environmental History of Houston and the Gulf Coast* (Pittsburgh: University of Pittsburgh Press, 2007), which covers a wide range of topics from the Houston Ship Channel to air pollution and from air conditioning to urban sprawl. For some of the newest scholarship on Houston, see *Houston History,* published by the Center for Public History at the University of Houston and edited by Joseph Pratt.

Chapter Seven. Houston's Public Sinks:
Water and Wastewater Services—Local Concerns to Regional Challenges

In Summer 2009, *Cite: The Architecture-Design Review of Houston,* published a special issue guest edited by Thomas Colbert and Christof Spieler focusing on "The Hidden Machine." This issue meant to grasp in words, pictures, and maps the "complex infrastructure" of the City of Houston that we often take for granted. Lewis Mumford referred to these systems, building elements, and functions as the "hidden city." As Colbert and Spieler argue, "These networks are like umbilical cords that keep us nourished, but they are so woven into the fabric of the city in such great numbers that the umbilical cord metaphor immediately breaks down" (11). I contributed a piece on water, "Standing on Fishes: A History of Supplying Water to Houston" (16–17), but the issue also includes essays on the infrastructure of a typical street, the architecture of a nuclear power plant, the network of pipelines and reservoirs, "edge conditions," and a series of wonderful maps by Spieler on stormwater, drinking water, electricity, natural gas, and solid waste. In a closing essay, engineer John Lienhard discusses the city as organism, rightly observing that Houston is not the sum of its parts but something more than that (43–45).

Chapter Eight. Privatization of Water: U.S. and Worldwide Implications

A good deal of the literature on privatization remains polemic as several of these titles suggest. There are some good scholarly accounts, very few of which, however, have been written by historians. For studies on privatization, water corporatism, the water "crisis," and related topics, see Karen J. Bakker, *An Uncooperative Commodity: Privatizing Water in England and Wales* (New York: Oxford University Press, 2003); Maude Barlow, *Blue Covenant: The Global Water Crisis and the Coming Battle for the Right to Water* (New York: New Press, 2007); Maude Barlow and Tony Clarke, *Blue Gold: The Battle Against Corporate Theft of the World's Water* (Toronto: Stoddart, 2002); Frank Chapelle, *Wellsprings: A Natural History of Bottled Spring Waters* (Piscataway, NJ: Rutgers University Press, 2005); Tony Clarke, *Inside the Bottle: An Expose of the Bottled Water Industry* (Ottawa: Polaris Institute, 2007); Matthias Finger and Jeremy Allouche, *Water Privatisation: Trans-National Corporations and the Re-Regulation of the Water Industry* (London: Spon Press, 2002); Robert Jerome Glennon, *Water Follies: Groundwater Pumping and the Fate of America's Fresh Waters* (Washington, D.C.: Island Press, 2002); Constance Elizabeth Hunt, *Thirsty Planet: Strategies for Sustainable Water Management* (London: Zed Books, 2004); Nick Johnstone and Libby Wood, eds., *Private Firms and Public Water: Realising Social and Environmental Objectives in Developing Countries* (Cheltenham, UK: Edward Elgar, 2001); David A. McDonald and Greg Ruiters, eds., *The Age of Commodity: Water Privatization in Southern Africa* (London: Earthscan, 2005); Ken Midkiff, *Not a Drop to Drink: America's Water Crisis (And What You Can Do)* (Novato, CA: New World Library, 2007); Robert D. Morris, *The Blue Death: Disease, Disaster, and the Water We Drink* (New York: Harper Collins, 2007); National Research Council, *Privatization of Water Services in the United States* (Washington, D.C.: National Academies Press, 2002); Fred Pearce, *When the Rivers Run Dry: Water—The Defining Crisis of the Twenty-first Century* (Boston: Beacon Press, 2006); Elizabeth Royte, *Bottlemania: How Water Went on Sale and Why We Bought It* (New York: Bloomsbury, 2008); Fredrik Segerfeldt, *Water for Sale: How Business and the Market Can Resolve the World's Water Crisis* (Washington, D.C.: Cato Institute, 2005); Vandana Shiva, *Water Wars: Privatization, Pollution and Profit* (Cambridge: South End Press, 2002); Ann-Christin Sjolander Holland, *The Water Business: Corporations Versus People* (London: Zed Books, 2005); Alan Snitow, Deborah Kaufman, and Michael Fox, *Thirst: Fighting the Corporate Theft of Our Water* (San Francisco: Jossey-Bass, 2007); Ted Steinberg, "Big Is Ugly: Corporate Enclosure and the Global Water Supply," *Technology and Culture* 45 (July 2004): 618–23.

For studies on environmental and social justice as they relate to water, see Barbara L. Allen, *Uneasy Alchemy: Citizens and Experts in Louisiana's Chemical Corridor Disputes* (Cambridge: MIT Press, 2003); Jose Esteban Castro, *Water, Power and Citizenship: Social Struggle in the Basin of Mexico* (Houndmills, Basingstoke, Hampshire, UK: Palgrave Macmillan, 2006); Ian Ith, "The Road Back: From Seattle's Superfund Sewer to Haven Once More," *Pacific Northwest: The Seattle Times Magazine* (October 2, 2004): 22–29; Steve Lerner, *Diamond: A Struggle for Environmental Justice in Louisiana's Chemical Corridor* (Cambridge: MIT Press, 2005); and Erik Swyngedouw, *Social Power and the Urbanization of Water* (New York: Oxford University Press, 2004).

Notes

Introduction

1. Kathryn Cooper, "Water is the new oil," *Times Online,* June 8, 2008, http://www.timesonline.co/uk/tol/money/article4086457.ece. See also, Faisal Laljee, "Water is the New Oil," *Seeking Alpha,* October 1, 2006, http://seekingalpha.com/article/17769-water-is-the-new-oil; Mark Clayton, "Is water becoming 'the new oil'?," *Christian Science Monitor,* May 29, 2008, http://features.csmonitor.com/environment/2008/05/29/is-water-becoming-%E2%80%98t; and J. R. McNeill, *Something New Under the Sun* (New York: W. W. Norton, 2000), 121.

2. McNeill, *Something New Under the Sun*, 120.

3. Geoff Manaugh, "Water, the New Oil," *Next American City,* October 16, 2009, http://americancity.org/magazine/article/water-the-new-oil-manaugh. See also, Deborah Zabarenko, "As climate changes, is water the new oil?" *Reuters,* March 22, 2009, http://www.reuters.com/article/idUSN21529713; Adam Bluestein, "Blue Is the New Green," *Inc. Magazine,* November 2008, 118–22, 124, 126, 128.

4. See Martin V. Melosi, *Coping with Abundance: Energy and Environment in Industrial America* (New York: Knopf, 1985).

5. See Martin V. Melosi, *The Sanitary City: Urban Infrastructure in America from Colonial Times to the Present* (Baltimore: Johns Hopkins University Press, 2000).

6. Peter Rogers, *America's Water: Federal Roles and Responsibilities* (Cambridge: MIT Press, 1996), 75–81.

7. Ibid., 87.

8. Terje Tvedt and Terje Oestigaard, eds., *A History of Water,* vol. 3, *The World of Water* (London: I. B. Tauris, 2006), xiv–xvii.

9. Terje Tvedt and Eva Jakobsson, eds., *A History of Water,* vol. 1, *Water Control and River Biographies* (London: I. B. Tauris, 2006), ix.

Chapter One. "Improving" Rivers in America: From the Revolution to the Progressive Era

This chapter is a revised version of chapter 1 in David P. Billington, Donald C. Jackson, and Martin V. Melosi, *The History of Large Federal Dams: Planning, Design, and Construction* (Denver: U.S. Department of Interior, Bureau of Reclamation, 2005). Donald C. Jackson contributed a portion to some sections of this chapter.

1. Christof Mauch and Thomas Zeller, eds., *Rivers in History: Perspectives on Waterways in Europe and North America* (Pittsburgh: University of Pittsburgh Press, 2008), 1.

2. See McNeill, *Something New Under the Sun.*

3. Peter Rogers, *America's Water,* 1.

4. Joseph M. Petulla, *American Environmental History* (San Francisco: Boyd and Fraser, 1977), 24.

5. William L. Graf, "Landscapes, Commodities, and Ecosystems: The Relationship Between Policy and Science for American Rivers," in *Sustaining Our Water Resources: Water Science and Technology Board Tenth Anniversary Symposium,* National Resource Council, Water Science and Technology Board (Washington, D.C.: National Academies Press, 1993), 11–12. See also, E. J. Nygren, *Views and Visions: American Landscapes Before 1830* (Washington, D.C.: Corcoran Gallery of Art, 1986).

6. John Seelye, *Beautiful Machine: Rivers and the Republican Plan, 1175–1825* (New York: Oxford University Press, 1991), 8–9. See also Graf, "Landscapes, Commodities, and Ecosystems," 12.

7. Theodore Steinberg, *Nature Incorporated: Industrialization and the Waters of New England* (Amherst: University of Massachusetts Press, 1991), 16.

8. Melosi, *Coping with Abundance,* 17.

9. Ernest S. Griffith and Charles R. Adrian, *A History of American City Government, 1775–1870: The Formation of Traditions* (Washington, D.C.: University Press of America, 1983), 218.

10. Zane L. Miller and Patricia M. Melvin, *The Urbanization of Modern America: A Brief History,* 2nd ed. (San Diego: Harcourt Brace Jovanovich, 1987), 31–32, 48–49, 57.

11. Charles E. Brooks, *Frontier Settlement and Market Revolution: The Holland Land Purchase* (Ithaca, NY: Cornell University Press, 1996), 7–9.

12. Ben Moreell, *Our Nation's Water Resources–Policies and Politics* (Chicago: Law School, University of Chicago, 1956), 15–16.

13. Todd Shallat, "Water and Bureaucracy: Origins of the Federal Responsibility for Water Resources, 1787–1838," *Natural Resources Journal* 32 (Winter 1992): 5–6.

14. Richard N. L. Andrews, *Managing the Environment, Managing Ourselves: A History of American Environmental Policy* (New Haven: Yale University Press, 1999), 140.

15. Petulla, *American Environmental History,* 28–31; Ellis L. Armstrong, Michael C. Robinson, and Suellen M. Hoy, eds., *History of Public Works in the United States, 1776–1976* (Chicago: American Public Works Association, 1976), 7–8; Andrews, *Managing the Environment, Managing Ourselves,* 71. See also John Opie, *The Law of the Land: Two Hundred Years of American Farmland Policy* (Lincoln: University of Nebraska Press, 1987); Frank Gregg, "Public Land Policy: Controversial Beginnings for the Third Century," in *Government and Environ-*

mental Politics, ed. Michael J. Lacey (Washington, D.C.: Woodrow Wilson Center Press, 1989), 143.

16. Andrews, *Managing the Environment, Managing Ourselves,* 79–88; Peter S. Onuf, *Statehood and Union: A History of the Northwest Ordinance* (Bloomington: Indiana University Press, 1987), xiii–xvii, 40–42.

17. Armstrong, Robinson, and Hoy, *History of Public Works in the United States,* 7; Andrews, *Managing the Environment, Managing Ourselves,* 88–89.

18. John Lauritz Larson, "A Bridge, A Dam, A River: Liberty and Innovation in the Early Republic," *Journal of the Early Republic* 7 (Winter 1987): 354.

19. Martin Reuss and Paul K. Walker, *Financing Water Resources Development: A Brief History* (Washington, D.C.: Historical Division, Office of Administrative Services, Office of the Chief of Engineers, July 1983), 4–5. See also, Petulla, *American Environmental History,* 111–13.

20. Seelye, *Beautiful Machine,* 8–10.

21. Armstrong, Robinson, and Hoy, *History of Public Works in the United States,* 23–30. See also Petulla, *American Environmental History,* 114–18; Carol Sheriff, *The Artificial River: The Erie Canal and the Paradox of Progress, 1817–1862* (New York: Hill and Wang, 1996).

22. See Andrews, *Managing the Environment, Managing Ourselves,* 41–42.

23. The Industrial Revolution brought steam power that supplanted humans and animals. However, the origins of large-scale manufacturing, factory production, and resource extraction at first depended on fuelwood for iron production, and waterpower for integrated New England textile mills. Not until the 1880s did steam exceed water as an energy source for industrial expansion in the United States. See Louis C. Hunter, *A History of Industrial Power in the United States, 1780–1930, Volume One: Waterpower in the Century of the Steam Engine* (Charlottesville: University Press of Virginia, 1979), 139; Melosi, *Coping with Abundance,* 22–23.

24. Morton J. Horwitz, *The Transformation of American Law, 1780–1860* (Cambridge: Harvard University Press, 1977), 34.

25. Hunter, *Waterpower in the Century of the Steam Engine,* 54–55, 140.

26. Ibid., 115, 141, 151.

27. Steinberg, *Nature Incorporated,* 141.

28. However, since surface water was abundant, few conflicts over water rights needed to be resolved in the eastern state courts in the nineteenth century. See William F. Steirer Jr., "Riparian Doctrine: A Short Case History for the Eastern United States," in *Historic U.S. Court Cases, 1690–1990: An Encyclopedia,* ed. John W. Johnson (New York: Garland Publishing, 1992), 312.

29. Hunter, *Waterpower in the Century of the Steam Engine,* 33, 140–42, 145.

30. Horwitz, *Transformation of American Law,* 35–36.

31. The greatest departure from riparian principles occurred in Massachusetts, where "mill acts" had granted privileges to mill owners since the colonial period.

32. Horwitz, *Transformation of American Law,* 37, 40–42. See also Steinberg, *Nature Incorporated,* 146–47.

33. Horwitz, *Transformation of American Law*, 42.

34. Ibid, 43. See also Hunter, *Waterpower in the Century of the Steam Engine*, 141; Donald J. Pisani, *To Reclaim a Divided West: Water, Law, and Public Policy 1848–1902* (Albuquerque: University of New Mexico Press, 1992), 11–12.

35. See Opie, *Law of the Land*, 108–9.

36. Samuel P. Hays, *Conservation and the Gospel of Efficiency: The Progressive Conservation Movement, 1890–1920* (New York: Atheneum, 1972; orig. pub. 1959), 16–17. See also Robert G. Dunbar, *Forging New Rights in Western Waters* (Lincoln: University of Nebraska Press, 1983), 59–60.

37. Richard White has argued that appropriative rights in the West were "a local implementation of a larger national modification of the law, not a western innovation." This is a useful refinement, but does not contradict the point that the application of appropriative rights in the West had local roots. See White's *"It's Your Misfortune and None of My Own": A History of the American West* (Norman: University of Oklahoma Press, 1991), 401. See also Donald J. Pisani, "State vs. Nation: Federal Reclamation and Water Rights in the Progressive Era," *Pacific Historical Review* 51 (August 1982): 266–67; Patricia Nelson Limerick, *The Legacy of Conquest: The Unbroken Past of the American West* (New York: W. W. Norton, 1987), 72.

38. Donald J. Pisani, *From the Family Farm to Agribusiness: The Irrigation Crusade in California and the West, 1850–1931* (Berkeley: University of California Press, 1984), 30–31.

39. Walter Prescott Webb, *The Great Plains* (Boston: Ginn and Company, 1931), 3–44.

40. Keyworks include: Lawrence B. Lee, *Reclaiming the American West: A Historiography and Guide* (Santa Barbara, CA: ABC–Clio Press, 1980); Donald J. Pisani, "Deep and Troubled Waters: A New Field of Western History," *New Mexico Historical Review* 63 (October 1988): 311–31; and Lawrence B. Lee, "Water Resource History: A New Field of Historiography?" *Pacific Historical Review* 57 (November 1988): 457–67. Notable other books include Pisani, *From Family Farm to Agribusiness*; Pisani, *To Reclaim a Divided West*; Donald Worster, *Rivers of Empire: Water, Aridity and the Growth of the American West* (New York: Pantheon, 1985); Norris Hundley Jr., *Water and the West: The Colorado River Compact and the Politics of Water in the American West* (Berkeley: University of California Press, 1975); Norris Hundley Jr., *The Great Thirst: Californians and Water, 1770–1990* (Berkeley: University of California Press, 1992); Stanley Davison, *The Leadership of the Reclamation Movement: 1875–1902* (New York: Arno Press, 1979); and James Earl Sherow, *Watering the Valley: Development Along the High Plains of the Arkansas River* (Topeka: University Press of Kansas, 1990).

41. Useful histories include Worster, *Rivers of Empire*; Marc Reisner, *Cadillac Desert: The American West and Its Disappearing Water* (New York: Viking Press, 1986); William A. Warne, *The Bureau of Reclamation* (New York: Praeger Press, 1973); Michael Robinson, *Water for the West* (Chicago: Public Works Historical

Society, 1979); Karen Smith, *The Magnificent Experiment: Building the Salt River Project, 1870–1917* (Tucson: University of Arizona Press, 1986); Joseph Stevens, *Hoover Dam: An American Adventure* (Norman: University of Oklahoma Press, 1988). In addition, the role of the federal government in supporting the construction of the Los Angeles and Owens Valley has been described in William L. Kahrl, *Water and Power: The Conflict over Los Angeles' Water Supply in the Owens Valley* (Berkeley: University of California Press, 1982); Abraham Hoffman, *Vision or Villainy: Origins of the Owens Valley–Los Angeles Water Controversy* (College Station, Texas: Texas A&M Press, 1981).

42. The need for capital in hydraulic mining helped to promote the success of prior appropriation by the mid-1850s.

43. Those states are Alaska, Arizona, Colorado, Idaho, Montana, New Mexico, Nevada, Utah, and Wyoming. See Hundley, *Great Thirst*, 69–73; Dunbar, *Forging New Rights in Western Waters*, 61–63.

44. Hays, *Conservation and the Gospel of Efficiency*, 16–17.

45. Hundley, *Great Thirst*, 84–85.

46. Ibid., 88.

47. Pisani, *From Family Farm to Agribusiness*, 246–47. For a thorough discussion of the legal context for western water law from 1848 to 1902, see Pisani, *To Reclaim a Divided West*, 11–68.

48. According to Donald J. Pisani, "After the Desert Land Act was passed in 1877, it was impossible to assert riparian rights–at least not if someone had claimed water under prior appropriation before a final patent was issued to that land" (Donald J. Pisani to David P. Billington, February 15, 1998).

49. Hundley, *Great Thirst*, 95–97; Dunbar, *Forging New Rights in Western Waters*, 67–72; Pisani, *From the Family Farm to Agribusiness*, 246–47; Pisani, *To Reclaim a Divided West*, 35–36.

50. Pisani, *From the Family Farm to Agribusiness*, 248; White, *"It's Your Misfortune and None of My Own,"* 402; Dunbar, *Forging New Rights in Western Waters*, 78–98. In Utah, however, the appropriative rights developed by the Mormons were a little more unique. Based on the Mormons' "ecclesiastical brotherhood," they divided rights into primary and secondary categories. Within each category water was divided proportionately among the users. See Dunbar, *Forging New Rights in Western Water*, 82.

51. Dunbar, *Forging New Rights in Western Waters*, 99–132; White, *"It's Your Misfortune and None of My Own,"* 402.

52. Andrews, *Managing the Environment, Managing Ourselves*, 60–61.

53. Pisani, *To Reclaim a Divided West*, 31–32, 37–38.

54. Arthur A. Ekirch Jr., *Man and Nature in America* (New York: Columbia University Press, 1963), 81, 83, 88; G. Michael McCarthy, *Hour of Trial: the Conservation Conflict in Colorado and the West, 1891–1907* (Norman: University of Oklahoma Press, 1977), 15; Petulla, *American Environmental History*, 217–18; Roderick Frazier Nash, ed., *American Environmentalism* (New York: McGraw-Hill

Pub. Co., 1990), 36, 45; Craig W. Allin, *The Politics of Wilderness Preservation* (Westport, CT: Greenwood Press, 1982), 24–36. See also Roderick Nash, *Wilderness and the American Mind* (New Haven: Yale University Press, 1967).

55. Petulla, *American Environmental History*, 221–25.

56. See Carolyn Merchant, ed., *Major Problems in American Environmental History* (Lexington, MA: D.C. Heath and Co., 1993), 338; Robert Gottlieb, *Forcing the Spring: The Transformation of the American Environmental Movement* (Washington, D.C.: Island Press, 1962), 19–21; Petulla, *American Environmental History*, 217; Nash, *American Environmentalism*, 10–11; McCarthy, *Hour of Trial*, 3–4, 12.

57. See Ekirch, *Man and Nature in America*, 82. See also Elmo R. Richardson, *The Politics of Conservation: Crusades and Controversies, 1897–1913* (Berkeley: University of California Press, 1962), 2–3, 6.

58. W. Stull Holt, *The Office of the Chief of Engineers of the Army: Its Non-Military History, Activities, and Organization* (Baltimore: Johns Hopkins Press, 1923), 2.

59. Todd Shallat, *Structures in the Stream: Water, Science, and the Rise of the U.S. Army Corps of Engineers* (Austin: University of Texas Press, 1994), 2; Terry S. Reynolds, "The Engineer in Nineteenth-Century America," in Terry S. Reynolds, ed., *The Engineer in America* (Chicago: University of Chicago Press, 1991), 7.

60. Prior to 1750, the state was the primary employer of engineers throughout Europe. The growth of commercial operations and the acceleration in industrial development, however, enabled self-trained civilian engineers—especially in Great Britain—to practice their occupation. See Reynolds, "The Engineer in Nineteenth-Century America," 7–9; Shallat, *Structures in the Stream*, 14–15, 18.

61. Reynolds, "The Engineer in Nineteenth-Century America," 8–9.

62. Holt, *Office of the Chief of Engineers of the Army*, 2. See also Forest G. Hill, *Roads, Rails, and Waterways: The Army Engineers and Early Transportation* (Norman: University of Oklahoma Press, 1957), 5–7.

63. Reynolds, "The Engineer in Nineteenth-Century America," 16; Todd Shallat, "Building Waterways, 1802–1861: Science and the United States Army in Early Public Works," *Technology and Culture* 31 (January 1990): 22, 25–26; Edwin Layton, "Mirror-Image Twins: The Communities of Science and Technology in Nineteenth-Century America," *Technology and Culture* 12 (October 1971): 570; Hill, *Roads, Rails, and Waterways*, 12–19. See also Stephen E. Ambrose, *Duty, Honor, Country: A History of West Point* (Baltimore: Johns Hopkins Press, 1966), 22–23, 62–68, 90–92, 97–100, 100–103.

64. Martin Reuss and Charles Hendricks, "The U.S. Army Corps of Engineers: A Brief History" (draft), 1–2. The history is available under "history" on the U.S. Army Corps of Engineers Web site, www.usace.army.mil/.

65. Louis C. Hunter, *Steamboats on the Western Rivers: An Economic and Technological History* (Cambridge: Harvard University Press, 1949). See also Melosi, *Coping with Abundance*, 20–22.

66. Shallat, "Water and Bureaucracy," 5.

67. Reuss and Walker, *Financing Water Resources Development*, 6; Hill,

Roads, Rails, and Waterways, 25–26, 154–61; Isaac Lippincott, "A History of River Improvement," *Journal of Political Economy* (1914): 634.

68. Reuss and Walker, *Financing Water Resources Development*, 3; Allan H. Cullen, *Rivers in Harness: The Story of Dams* (Philadelphia: Chilton Co., 1962), 35.

69. Livingston and Fulton had died by that time.

70. Francis N. Stites, "A More Perfect Union: The Steamboat Case," in *Historic U.S. Court Cases, 1690–1990*, ed. Johnson, 187–93.

71. Stites, "A More Perfect Union," 190.

72. See Beatrice Hort Holmes, *A History of Federal Water Resources Programs, 1800–1960* (Washington, D.C.: Economic Research Service, Misc. Pub. No. 1233, June 1972), 3; Reuss and Walker, *Financing Water Resources Development*, 8; Shallat, "Water and Bureaucracy," 14–15; Shallat, *Structures in the Stream*, 125–27.

73. Michael C. Robinson, "The Relationship Between the Army Corps of Engineers and the Environmental Community, 1920–1969," *Environmental Review* 13 (Spring 1989): 3. See also Frank E. Smith, *The Politics of Conservation* (New York: Pantheon Books, 1966), 71.

74. Holmes, *History of Federal Water Resources Programs*, 3.

75. Robert W. Harrison, *History of the Commercial Waterways and Ports of the United States*, Vol. I (Fort Belvoir, VA: U.S. Army Engineer, Water Resource Support Center, 1979), 5; Reuss and Walker, *Financing Water Resources Development*, 6; Michael C. Robinson, *History of Navigation in the Ohio River Basin* (Alexander, VA: U.S. Army Engineer, Water Resource Support Center), 12; Holmes, *History of Federal Water Resources Programs*, 3; Charles F. O'Connell Jr., "The Corps of Engineers and the Rise of Modern Management, 1827–1856," in *Military Enterprise and Technological Change: Perspectives on the American Experience*, ed. Merritt Roe Smith (Cambridge: MIT Press, 1985), 97.

76. Holmes, *History of Federal Water Resources Programs*, 4; Aubrey Parkman, *History of the Waterways of the Atlantic Coast of the United States* (Washington, D.C.: Institute for Water Resources, January 1983), 43; Reuss and Walker, *Financing Water Resources Development*, 6; Reuss and Hendricks, "U.S. Army Corps of Engineers," 3.

77. Shallat, *Structures in the Stream*, 98. See also Reuss and Walker, *Financing Water Resources Development*, 6–7.

78. The board was in existence for eight years until the Corps of Topographical Civil Engineers were placed in a separate bureau. Its responsibilities included determining general possibilities for improvement of roads, canals, and railways on a national scale. See Hill, *Roads, Rails, and Waterways*, 63–66.

79. Holt, *Office of the Chief of Engineers of the Army*, 6–7; Reuss and Hendricks, "U.S. Army Corps of Engineers," 3; Hill, *Roads, Rails, and Waterways*, 56–57.

80. Robinson, *History of Navigation in the Ohio River Basin*, 13–14; Hunter, *Steamboats on the Western Rivers*, 193–98, 202. See also Hill, *Roads, Rails, and Waterways*, 164; Lippincott, "A History of River Improvement," 639.

81. According to Louis Hunter, "Bars acted as dams to hold back and conserve the water supply during the dry seasons. Their elimination would simply result

in the stabilization of the depth of water at a proportionately lower level, to the prejudice of navigation. To deepen the channel over a bar without increasing the 'expense' of water and draining the pool above, the [Board of Engineers] proposed the construction of dikes of timber and stone to concentrate the flow of water at a lower stage within a limited space. The flow of water thus concentrated would cut a deeper channel for the benefit of navigation. This was the hope, at any rate, and the act of 1824 provided for experiments on certain bars to determine the practicality of the scheme" (Hunter, *Steamboats on the Western Rivers*, 201).

82. The Italians and the French had experimented many years earlier with structures that would enlarge a channel's carrying capacity by increasing a stream's velocity. See Shallat, "Building Waterways, 1802–1861," 41–42; Shallat, "Water and Bureaucracy," 19–20.

83. Robinson, *History of Navigation in the Ohio River Basin*, 12–16; Hunter, *Steamboats on the Western Rivers*, 200–3.

84. Hunter, *Steamboats on the Western Rivers*, 205–7. See also Robinson, *History of Navigation in the Ohio River Basin*, 17–18.

85. In 1838, the Topographical Bureau was given the assignment of directing all river and harbor work. All new work was assigned to it and some works in progress also were transferred. However, the Corps of Topographical Engineers only remained an independent unit until 1863. See Hill, *Roads, Rails, and Waterways*, 177. See also Frank N. Schubert, ed., *The Nation Builders: A Sesquicentennial History of the Corps of Topographical Engineers, 1838–1863* (Fort Belvoir, VA: Office of History, U.S. Army Corps of Engineers, 1988).

86. Robinson, *History of Navigation in the Ohio River Basin*, 16–17; Hill, *Roads, Rails, and Waterways*, 173; Holt, *Office of the Chief of Engineers of the Army*, 8–10; Hunter, *Steamboats on the Western Rivers*, 203.

87. Parkman, *History of the Waterways of the Atlantic Coast*, 47. See also Holt, *Office of the Chief of Engineers of the Army*, 10–11; Shallat, *Structures in the Stream*, 106; Hill, *Roads, Rails, and Waterways*, 181–98.

88. Hill, *Roads, Rails, and Waterways*, 205; Robinson, *History of Navigation in the Ohio River Basin*, 22.

89. Parkman, *History of the Waterways of the Atlantic Coast*, 49; Reuss and Walker, *Financing Water Resources Development*, 12.

90. Robinson, *History of Navigation in the Ohio River Basin*, 23–25; Hunter, *Steamboats on the Western Rivers*, 210.

91. Robinson, *History of Navigation in the Ohio River Basin*, 25; Hunter, *Steamboats on the Western Rivers*, 209; Leland R. Johnson, *The Davis Island Lock and Dam, 1870–1922* (Pittsburgh: U.S. Army Engineer District, 1985), 34–35.

92. Robinson, *History of Navigation in the Ohio River Basin*, 26; Hunter, *Steamboats on the Western Rivers*, 212. For his movable dam, Merrill chose the design of Frenchman Jacques Chanoine. Invented in 1852, the Chanoine wicket consisted of a line of timbers bolted together into a rectangular panel hinged to a concrete foundation placed on the river bottom. Upon completion, the movable dam was 1,223 feet in length and contained 305 wickets. The wickets were raised by

a grapple on a maneuver boat and supported by an iron pole sloping downstream. When the river was high, the pole was removed and the wickets returned to the river bottom. The lock itself was 110 feet wide by 600 feet long. Both dam and lock were the largest of their kind in the world. The lock also was one of the first in the United States to use concrete instead of masonry. Although the new system, as a prototype, faced some problems, the critics were silenced since the Pittsburgh harbor increased in depth and large tows could be assembled there. See Robinson, *History of Navigation in the Ohio River Basin*, 26–27; Hunter, *Steamboats on the Western Rivers*, 211–12; Reuss and Hendricks, "U.S. Army Corps of Engineers," 5; Johnson, *Davis Island Lock and Dam,* 37–38. See also Francis H. Oxx, "The Ohio River Movable Dams," *Military Engineer* 27 (January–February 1935): 49–58.

93. Hunter, *Steamboats on the Western Rivers*, 212. See also John P. Davis, "Locks and Mechanical Lifts: State of the Art" (Paper prepared for the National Waterways Roundtable, Norfolk, Virginia, April 22–24, 1980), 6.

94. Roald D. Tweet, *History of Transportation on the Upper Mississippi and Illinois Rivers* (Washington, D.C.: Government Printing Office, 1983), 51–52; William Patrick O'Brien, Mary Yeath Rathbun, Patrick O'Bannon, and W. Christine Witacre, ed., *Gateways to Commerce: The U.S. Army Corps of Engineers' 9-foot Channel Project on the Upper Mississippi River* (Denver: National Park Service, 1992), 19.

95. John O. Anfinson, "Commerce and Conservation on the Upper Mississippi River," *The Annals of Iowa* 52 (Fall 1993): 387–88.

96. Hunter, *Steamboats on the Western Rivers*, 214.

97. Tweet, *History of Transportation on the Upper Mississippi and Illinois Rivers*, 54.

98. The first and largest project resulted in an experimental dam at Lake Winnibigoshish (completed 1883; reconstructed 1899), followed by dams at Pokegama Falls (completed 1885; reconstructed 1904), Leech Lake (completed 1884; reconstructed 1903), Pine River (completed 1886; reconstructed 1907), and Sandy Lake (completed 1895; reconstructed 1911). A sixth dam was completed in 1912 at Gull Lake. Jane Lamm Carroll, "Mississippi River Headwaters Reservoirs," *Historic American Engineering Record* Report No. MN–6: 2–8; Raymond H. Merritt, *The Corps, the Environment, and the Upper Mississippi River Basin* (Washington, D.C.: Historical Division, Office of the Chief of Engineers, 1981), 1.

99. Carroll, "Mississippi River Headwaters Reservoirs," 11–15. See also Anfinson, "Commerce and Conservation on the Upper Mississippi River," 389–90.

100. A commission in 1884 authorized to determine damages, recommended $10,000 in property damage and an annual additional payment of $26,800, but by 1886 even that paltry award was not paid. In 1890, the commission authorized a meager appropriation of $150,000 as full payment for damages. Some of the overflowed acres were ceded to the United States government, and all of the lands likely to be damaged were subject to construction and building of new dams and reservoirs. See Merritt, *The Corps, the Environment, and the Upper Mississippi River Basin*, 3–10.

101. Ibid., 13–19.

102. Ibid., 19–20. See also Philip V. Scarpino, *Great River: An Environmental History of the Upper Mississippi, 1890–1950* (Columbia: University of Missouri Press, 1985), 153.

103. See John R. Ferrell, "From Single- to Multi-Purpose Planning: The Role of the Army Engineers in River Development Policy, 1824–1930" (Washington, D.C.: Department of the Army, Office of the Chief of Engineers, February 1976; draft), 307.

104. Early irrigation by Native Americans is described in R. Douglas Hurt, *Indian Agriculture in America: Prehistory to the Present* (Lawrence: University Press of Kansas, 1987), 19–26. See also Hundley, *Great Thirst*, 16–24.

105. For more on Spanish irrigation in the Southwest, see Michael C. Meyer, *Water in the Hispanic Southwest: A Social and Legal History, 1550–1850* (Tucson: University of Arizona, 1984). For information on Old World irrigation, see J. A. Garcia-Diego, "The Chapter on Weirs in the Codex of Juanelo Turriano: A Question of Authorship," *Technology and Culture* 17 (April 1976): 217–34; and J. A. Garcia-Diego, "Old Dams in Extramadura," *History of Technology* 2 (1977): 95–124.

106. Mormon irrigation is discussed in detail in Charles H. Brough, *Irrigation in Utah* (Baltimore: The Johns Hopkins University Press, 1898); and George Thomas, *The Development of Institutions under Irrigation with Special Reference to Early Utah Conditions* (New York: MacMillan Company, 1920). See Leonard J. Arrington, *Great Basin Kingdom: Economics History of the Latter-Day Saints* (Lincoln: University of Nebraska Press, 1958) for a complete overview of Mormon economic development in the nineteenth century.

107. Leonard J. Arrington and Dean May, "A Different Mode of Life: Irrigation and Society in Nineteenth Century Utah," *Agricultural History* 49 (January 1975): 3–20; and Brough, *Irrigation in Utah*, 75.

108. For information on nineteenth-century irrigation colonies (and irrigation settlements in general) that were based upon private financing, see Pisani, *To Reclaim a Divided West*, 69–104.

109. See Smith, *Magnificent Experiment*, 4–5.

110. See Pisani, *From the Family Farm to Agribusiness*, 121–28.

111. W. Turrentine Jackson, Rand F. Herbert, and Stephen R. Wee, "Introduction," *Engineers and Irrigation: Report of the Board of Commissioners on the Irrigation of the San Joaquin, Tulare, and Sacramento Valleys of the State of California, 1873* (Engineer Historical Studies Number 5) (Fort Belvoir, VA: Office of History of the U.S. Army Corps of Engineers, 1990), 10–12.

112. Thomas G. Alexander, "The Powell Irrigation Survey and the People of the Mountain West," *Journal of the West* 7 (January 1968): 48–49; John Wesley Powell, *Report on the Lands of the Arid Region in the United States* (Washington, D.C.: Government Printing Office, 1879).

113. Historiographical analysis of the irrigation movement in this era can be found in Lee, *Reclaiming the American West*, 6–15.

114. The work of the Irrigation Survey is documented in *The Annual Reports of*

the U.S. Geological Survey from 1888–89 through 1892–93. For example, see John Wesley Powell, *Tenth Annual Report of the United States Geological Survey, Part II–Irrigation* (Washington, D.C.: Government Printing Office, 1890). See also Pisani, *To Reclaim a Divided West,* 143–68; Davison, *Leadership of the Reclamation Movement;* and Everett Sterling, "The Powell Irrigation Survey, 1888–1893," *Mississippi Valley Historical Review* 27 (1940): 421–34.

115. Powell, *Tenth Annual Report of the United States Geological Survey, Part II–Irrigation,* 22–29, describes the process of withdrawing lands from "sale, entry, settlement or occupation."

116. Pisani, *To Reclaim a Divided West,* 150–65.

117. S. T. Harding, *Water Rights for Irrigation: Principles and Procedures for Engineers* (Palo Alto: Stanford University Press, 1936), 130–31, describes and analyzes the requirements and legal procedures stipulated by the Act of March 3, 1891.

118. Davison, *Leadership of the Reclamation Movement,* 127–63.

119. For the views of a major proponent of sentimentalism, see William E. Smythe, *The Conquest of Arid America* (New York: Privately printed, 1900).

120. Pisani, *To Reclaim a Divided West,* 169–272.

121. Discussion of the Carey Act can be found in Lee, *Reclaiming the American West,* 12–13; and in Pisani, *To Reclaim a Divided West.*

122. Davison, *Leadership of the Reclamation Movement,* 245; Pisani, *To Reclaim a Divided West,* 285–94.

123. Pisani, *To Reclaim a Divided West,* 275.

124. For more on Chittenden's work in reclamation planning, see Gordon Dodds, *Hiram Martin Chittenden: His Public Career* (Lexington: University of Kentucky Press, 1973), 29–41. Pisani, *To Reclaim a Divide West,* 276–78, provides good discussion of Chittenden's project.

125. See Pisani, *To Reclaim a Divided West,* 279–85, for extended discussion of the politics that underlay the rejection of Warren's efforts to utilize "rivers and harbors" expenditures for irrigation work.

126. The collapse of the Bear Valley Irrigation Company in Southern California is noted in Davison, *Leadership of the Reclamation Movement,* 188–89.

127. For extended discussion of the Wright Act and the difficulties that accompanied its implementation, see Pisani, *From Family Farm to Agribusiness,* 252–80.

128. Smith, *Magnificent Experiment,* 6. Undeniably, there had been noteworthy successes. For example, by the beginning of the twentieth century over 110,000 acres were under irrigation in the greater region of Phoenix-Tempe-Mesa in Arizona Territory; in slightly more than thirty years the population of greater Phoenix had grown from almost nothing to more than 20,000 settlers. Nonetheless, no major storage dam had been built to capture the flood flow of the Salt River and the limits of irrigation based upon "natural flow" long since had been reached.

129. For biographical information on Newell, see his professional obituary: "Frederick Haynes Newell," *Transactions of the American Society of Civil Engineers* 98 (1933): 1597–1600.

130. Frederick Haynes Newell Papers; Diary entry for January 8, 1901; Manuscript Division, Library of Congress, Washington, D.C.

131. Davison, *Leadership of the Reclamation Movement*, 150–51.

132. Frederick Haynes Newell, *Irrigation in the United States* (New York, 1902), 1, 406.

133. Newlands has become prominently associated with federal reclamation thanks to his co-sponsorship of the National Reclamation Act. However, his contributions to the irrigation movement as a whole appear limited. For more on his career as a lawyer and politician, see William D. Rowley, *Reclaiming the Arid West: The Career of Francis G. Newlands* (Bloomington: University Press of Indiana, 1996).

134. See *The Works of Theodore Roosevelt: State Papers as Governor and President,* Vol. 15 (New York: C. Scribner and Sons, 1926), 81–135.

135. The full text and all amendments to the National Reclamation Act prior to 1919 appear in: Institute for Government Research, *The U.S. Reclamation Service: Its History, Activities and Organization* (New York: D. Appleton and Company, 1919), 104–24. See also Lee, *Reclaiming the American West*, 22–23; and Pisani, *To Reclaim a Divided West*, 306–10.

136. Between 1902 and 1907, the Reclamation Service operated as a part of the U.S. Geological Survey; in 1907, it became an independent agency within the Department of the Interior.

137. Cited in Leon Fink, ed., *Major Problems in the Gilded Age and the Progressive Era* (Lexington, MA: D.C. Heath and Company, 1993), 412.

138. In the Progressive Era, governmental technical expertise addressed forest depletion through selective harvesting and planting techniques, ranching problems through new forage mixtures, fencing, and the introduction of purebred stock; and water use through dam building and new irrigation systems. See Hays, *Conservation and the Gospel of Efficiency,* 1–2. In the cities, government officials passed antipollution laws, scientists established laboratories for testing water purity, engineers built elaborated sanitation systems, and reformers promoted programs of "civic responsibility." See Martin V. Melosi, ed., *Pollution and Reform in American Cities, 1870–1930* (Austin: University of Texas Press, 1980).

139. Ekirch, *Man and Nature in America*, 94; Guy-Harold Smith, ed., *Conservation of Natural Resources,* 4th ed. (New York: John Wiley & Sons, Inc., 1971), 7.

140. Petulla, *American Environmental History*, 267, 271–72.

141. Hays, *Conservation and the Gospel of Efficiency*, 5.

142. Ibid.

143. Reuss and Hendricks, "U.S. Army Corps of Engineers," 11–12; Ekirch, *Man and Nature in America*, 94.

144. Ferrell, "From Single- to Multi-Purpose Planning," 91.

145. Gifford Pinchot, *The Fight for Conservation* (Seattle: University of Washington Press, 1967; orig., 1910), 54.

146. Hays, *Conservation and the Gospel of Efficiency*, 100–102.

147. The Lakes-to-the-Gulf-Waterway.

148. Ferrell, "From Single- to Multi-Purpose Planning," 96–97.

149. For an interesting parallel argument about the corps and its views on stream flow, see Gordon B. Dodds, "The Stream-Flow Controversy: A Conservation Turning Point," *Journal of American History* 56 (June 1969): 59–69.

150. Ferrel, "From Single- to Multi-Purpose Planning," 103, 125–26.

151. Smith, *Politics of Conservation*, 89, 101, 106; Hays, *Conservation and the Gospel of Efficiency*, 102–5, 108–9; Ferrell, "From Single- to Multi-Purpose Planning," 105–6; Donald C. Swain, *Federal Conservation Policy, 1921–1933* (Berkeley: University of California Press, 1963), 96–98.

152. Quoted in Ekirch, *Man and Nature in America*, 94.

153. Hays, *Conservation and the Gospel of Efficiency*, 105–8; Ekirch, *Man and Nature in America*, 94–95; Ferrell, "From Single- to Multi-Purpose Planning," 115–17; Moreell, *Our Nation's Water Resources—Policies and Politics*, 37.

154. "Report from the Inland Waterways Commission, February 26, 1908," in *Conservation in the United States*, ed. Smith, 91.

155. See Ferrell, "From Single- to Multi-Purpose Planning," 125–30; Paul K. Walker, "Developing Hydroelectric Power: The Role of the U.S. Army Corps of Engineers, 1900–1978," (Washington, D.C.: Department of the Army, Office of the Chief of Engineers, draft, February 1979), 29.

156. Holmes, *History of Federal Water Resources Programs*, 6.

157. "Supplementary Report of Commissioner General Alexander Mackenzie," in *Conservation in the United States*, ed. Smith, 93–94. See also Reuss and Walker, *Financing Water Resources Development*, 15; Ferrell, "From Single- to Multi-Purpose Planning," 118–19.

158. Hays, *Conservation and the Gospel of Efficiency*, 109–14. Newlands was able to get his legislation for a new Inland Waterways Commission passed in 1917. However, President Wilson was too deeply involved in the war effort to appoint commissioners, and conservationists were too severely split to force the appointments. See Swain, *Federal Conservation Policy*, 97–98.

159. Holmes, *History of Federal Water Resources Programs*, 6; Ferrell, "From Single- to Mult-Purpose Planning," 123.

160. Hundley, *Great Thirst*, 170–74. James C. Williams, *Energy and the Making of Modern California* (Akron: University of Akron Press, 1997), 250–51; Stephen Fox, *The American Conservation Movement: John Muir and His Legacy* (Madison: University of Wisconsin Press, 1981), 139–40; Petulla, *American Environmental History*, 282.

161. Michael P. Cohen, *The Pathless Way: John Muir and American Wilderness* (Madison: University of Wisconsin Press, 1984), 280–81; Douglas H. Strong, *The Conservationists* (Menlo Park, CA: Addison Wesley Publishing Co., 1971), 91–104; Hundley, *Great Thirst*, 178–80; Peter Wild, *Pioneer Conservationist of Western America* (Missoula, MT: Mountain Press Publishing Company, 1979), 1–17.

162. Quoted in Cohen, *Pathless Way*, 330.

163. Strong, *Conservationists,* 110, 114–15; Hundley, *Great Thirst,* 176–84; Williams, *Energy and the Making of Modern California,* 251–52; Richardson, *Politics of Conservation,* 44–45.

164. Richard White, *"It's Your Misfortune and None of My Own,"* 413. See also Williams, *Energy and the Making of Modern California,* 251–52; Strong, *Conservationists,* 104, 111; Fox, *American Conservation Movement,* 111, 115, 130, 140–46.

165. Fox, *American Conservation Movement,* 141; Williams, *Energy and the Making of Modern California,* 252–53; Hundley, *Great Thirst,* 187–90; Petulla, *American Environmental History,* 282–83; Strong, *Conservationists,* 114–15.

166. Hunter, *Waterpower in the Century of the Steam Engine,* 513.

167. Ibid., 137–39, 388, 512.

168. Previous advances in equipment and materials for dam building made possible the construction of the high dams necessary for power production. See Reuss and Walker, *Financing Water Resources Development,* 36.

169. Reuss and Walker, *Financing Water Resources Development,* 138. See also Melosi, *Coping with Abundance,* 64, 81.

170. Reuss and Hendricks, "U.S. Army Corps of Engineers," 11–12; Reuss and Walker, *Financing Water Resources Development,* 36; Walker, "Developing Hydroelectric Power," 8–9.

171. Harold T. Pinkett, *Gifford Pinchot: Private and Public Forester* (Urbana: University of Illinois, 1970), 61–62; Andrews, *Managing the Environment, Managing Ourselves,* 142–44; Melosi, *Coping with Abundance,* 81–82; M. Nelson McGeary, *Gifford Pinchot: Forester–Politician* (Princeton: Princeton University Press, 1960), 73, 75, 77–78.

172. Reuss and Hendricks, "U.S. Army Corps of Engineers," 12; Reuss and Walker, *Financing Water Resources Development,* 36–37; Hays, *Conservation and the Gospel of Efficiency,* 114–19; Holmes, *History of Federal Water Resources Programs,* 7; Pinkett, *Gifford Pinchot,* 63; Melosi, *Coping with Abundance,* 81–82; Walker, "Developing Hydroelectric Power," 15, 21–22.

173. The corps did install a power station substructure at Lock and Dam No. 1 on the Upper Mississippi, however. See Reuss and Hendricks, "U.S. Army Corps of Engineers," 12; Reuss and Walker, *Financing Water Resources Development,* 36–37.

174. Smith, *Politics of Conservation,* 126, 141; Petulla, *American Environmental History,* 281; Arthur S. Link, *Wilson: The New Freedom* (Princeton: Princeton University Press, 1956), 128.

Chapter Two. How Bad Theory Can Lead to Good Technology: Water Supply and Sewerage in the Age of Miasmas

This chapter was derived from my book *The Sanitary City: Urban Infrastructure in America from Colonial Times to the Present* (Baltimore: Johns Hopkins University Press, 2000), and published in a slightly different version in Arthur Molella and Joyce Bedi, eds., *Inventing for the Environment* (Cambridge: MIT Press, 2003), 231–56.

1. Eric Lemelson, "Foreword," in *Inventing for the Environment,* ed. Molella and Bedi, ix.

2. "Preface" in *Inventing for the Environment,* ed. Molella and Bedi, xi.

3. Ernest S. Griffith, *A History of American City Government: The Conspicuous Failure, 1870–1900* (Washington, D.C.: University Press of America, 1983), 178.

4. Charles David Jacobson, *Ties That Bind: Economic and Political Dilemmas of Urban Utility Networks, 1800–1990* (Pittsburgh: University of Pittsburgh Press, 2000), 3.

5. Ibid., 3–11.

6. Ibid., 14. For an elaborate analysis of the development and functioning of networked infrastructure, see Stephen Graham and Simon Marvin, *Splintering Urbanism: Networked Infrastructures, Technological Mobilities and the Urban Condition* (London: Routledge, 2001).

7. Bryan D. Jones, *Service Delivery in the City: Citizen Demand and Bureaucratic Rules* (New York: Longman, 1980), 2.

8. Charles E. Rosenberg, *The Cholera Years: The United States in 1832, 1849, 1866* (Chicago: University of Chicago Press, 1987; orig. pub. 1962), 228.

9. Ibid., 7.

10. Ibid., 37, 38, 55–57, 59–62, 135–37.

11. Howard N. Rabinowitz, *Race Relations in the Urban South, 1865–1890* (Champaign: University of Illinois Press, 1980), 114–21.

12. David R. Goldfield, *Urban Growth in the Age of Sectionalism: Virginia, 1847–1861* (Baton Rouge: Louisiana State University Press, 1977), 152, 153, 160; William H. Pease and Jane H. Pease, *The Web of Progress: Private Values and Public Styles in Boston and Charleston, 1828–1843* (New York: Oxford University Press, 1985), 90, 93, 99.

13. Khaled J. Bloom, *The Mississippi Valley's Great Yellow Fever Epidemic of 1878* (Baton Rouge: Louisiana State University Press, 1993), 10, 11.

14. Charles-Edward Amory Winslow, *The Conquest of Epidemic Disease* (New York: Hafner, 1967), 266.

15. Howard D. Kramer, "The Germ Theory and the Public Health Program in the United States," *Bulletin of the History of Medicine* 22 (May/June 1948): 234, 235.

16. Several theories of disease transmission vied for acceptance in the middle of the nineteenth century. See J. K. Crellin, "The Dawn of the Germ Theory: Particles, Infection and Biology," in *Medicine and Science in the 1860s,* ed. F. Poynter (London: Wellcome Institute of the History of Medicine, 1968), 57–67, 71–74; J. K. Crellin, "Airborne Particles and the Germ Theory: 1860–1880," *Annals of Science* 22 (March 1966): 49, 52, 56, 57; Mazyck Ravenel, ed., *A Half Century of Public Health* (New York: American Public Health Association, 1921), 66, 67.

17. Erwin H. Ackernecht, "Anticontagionism between 1821 and 1867," *Bulletin of the History of Medicine* 22 (September–October 1948): 567.

18. Stanley K. Schultz, *Constructing Urban Culture: American Cities and City Planning, 1800–1920* (Philadelphia: Temple University Press, 1989), 132, 133.

19. C. E. A. Winslow to Lemuel Shattuck, "Introduction," *Report of the Sanitary Commission of Massachusetts 1850* (Cambridge: Harvard University Press, 1948), 237; John Duffy, *The Sanitarians* (Champaign: University of Illinois Press, 1990), 96, 97, 137; John H. Ellis, *Yellow Fever and Public Health in the New South* (Lexington: University Press of Kentucky, 1992), 7.

20. See Charles E. Rosenberg, *Explaining Epidemics and Other Studies in the History of Medicine* (Cambridge: Cambridge University Press, 1992), 126, 127.

21. John C. Trautwine Jr., "A Glance at the Water Supply of Philadelphia," *Journal of the New England Water Works Association* 22 (December 1908): 421.

22. See Michal McMahon, "Fairmount," *American Heritage* 30 (April–May 1979): 100, 101; Donald C. Jackson, "'The Fairmount Waterworks, 1812–1911,' At the Philadelphia Museum of Art," *Technology and Culture* 30 (July 1989): 635.

23. City of Philadelphia, Department of Public Works, Bureau of Water, *Description of the Filtration Works and Pumping Stations, Also Brief Historical Review of the Water Supply, 1789–1900* (Philadelphia: Department of Public Works, Bureau of Water, 1909), 57–59; Michal McMahon, "Makeshift Technology: Water and Politics in Nineteenth-Century Philadelphia," *Environmental Review* 12 (Winter 1988): 24.

24. Edward C. Carter II, "Benjamin Henry Latrobe and Public Works," *Essays in Public Works History* (Washington, D.C.: Public Works Historical Society, 1976); Jane Mork Gibson, "The Fairmount Waterworks," *Bulletin of the Philadelphia Museum of Art* 84 (Summer 1988): 9–12; Jackson, "'The Fairmount Waterworks, 1812–1911,'" 635; McMahon, "Makeshift Technology," 25–26.

25. Joel A. Tarr, "The Evolution of the Urban Infrastructure in the Nineteenth and Twentieth Centuries," in *Perspectives on Urban Infrastructure,* ed. R. Hanson (National Academy Press, 1984), 19; "Golden Decade for Philadelphia Water," *Engineering News-Record* 159 (September 19, 1957): 37.

26. The financial security of the waterworks took longer than popular acceptance of the water supply. See Martin J. McLaughlin, "Philadelphia's Water Works from 1798 to 1944," *American City* 59 (October 1944): 86, 87.

27. See Charles Jacobson, Steven Klepper, and Joel A. Tarr, "Water, Electricity, and Cable Television: A Study of Contrasting Historical Patterns of Ownership and Regulation," *Technology and the Future of Our Cities* 3 (Fall 1985): 9.

28. Letty Donaldson Anderson, "The Diffusion of Technology in the Nineteenth Century American City: Municipal Water Supply Investments" (PhD dissertation, Northwestern University, 1980), 102–4, 117; Letty Anderson, "Hard Choices: Supplying Water to New England," *Journal of Interdisciplinary History* 15 (Autumn 1984): 218; Tarr, "Evolution of the Urban Infrastructure," 30, 31; Griffith and Adrian, *History of American City Government, 1775–1870,* 198–217. In an important case study concerning the financing of physical improvements in Chicago, historian Robin L. Einhorn makes an impressive alternative case for privatization in this period. Utilizing special assessments, the city government operated through what she labeled the "segmented system," especially between

1845 and 1865. Einhorn argued that "what made this system 'segmented' rather than simply elitist was that a voice in decision making ... required the ownership of property that was 'chargeable' or 'interested' in the decision at hand. An owner had to show that he owned a lot that was liable to a particular special assessment before he could participate in the decision to levy that assessment." The segmented system, Einhorn concluded, did not disfranchise the propertyless, but was a way to distribute costs and decision-making power among the propertied class. Einhorn's analysis is especially persuasive with respect to public works projects such as street paving and bridge building. However, as she suggests, water and sewer systems could not be segmented "with the rigor of street projects or fire limit rules" because they required central planning and large initial investments. See Robin L. Einhorn, *Property Rules: Political Economy in Chicago, 1833–1872* (Chicago: University of Chicago Press, 1991), 16–19, 133.

29. See Anderson, "Diffusion of Technology," 108.

30. The water commission discovered that the Indians called Long Pond "Cochituate." The mayor proposed the name change to Lake Cochituate—thus the name of the aqueduct. For information on Boston's water supply, see Nelson Manfred Blake, *Water for the Cities: A History of the Urban Water Supply Problem in the United States* (Syracuse: Syracuse University Press, 1956), 172–98; J. Michael LaNier, "Historical Development of Municipal Water Systems in the United States, 1776–1976," *Journal of the American Water Works Association* 68 (1976): 174; John B. Blake, "Lemuel Shattuck and the Boston Water Supply," *Bulletin of the History of Medicine* 29 (1955): 554–62.

31. Fern L. Nesson, *Great Waters: A History of Boston's Water Supply* (University Press of New England, 1983), 6–12.

32. George C. Andrews, "The Buffalo Water Works," *Journal of the American Water Works Association* 17 (March 1927): 280; "History of the Buffalo Water Works," *Engineering Record* 38 (September 1898): 24, 363, 364.

33. James C. O'Connell, "Chicago's Quest for Pure Water," *Essays in Public Works History* 1 (Public Works Historical Society, 1976), 1–3; W. W. DeBerard, "Expansion of the Chicago, Ill., Water Supply," *Transactions of the American Society of Civil Engineers* CT (1953): 588–93; LaNier, "Historical Development of Municipal Water Systems in the United States," 176.

34. Bruce Jordan, "Origins of the Milwaukee Water Works," *Milwaukee History* 9 (Spring 1986): 2–5; Elmer W. Becker, *A Century of Milwaukee Water* (Milwaukee: Milwaukee Water Works, 1974), 1–3.

35. Despite its pioneering effort, Philadelphia's water supply system deteriorated in the middle of the nineteenth century. Shortages struck the system and pollution infested the Schuylkill and Delaware rivers, once sources of pure supplies. See Sam Bass Warner Jr., *The Private City: Philadelphia in Three Periods of Its Growth* (Philadelphia: University of Pennsylvania Press, 1987), 108, 109.

36. Richard Wade, *The Urban Frontier* (Cambridge: Harvard University Press, 1959), 297; LaNier, "Historical Development of Municipal Water Systems in the

United States," 176; Gurdon G. Black, "The Construction and Reconstruction of Compton Hill Reservoir," *Journal of the Engineers' Club of St. Louis* 2 (January 2, 1917): 4–8.

37. John Ellis and Stuart Galishoff, "Atlanta's Water Supply, 1865–1918," *Maryland Historian* 8 (Spring 1977): 6, 7; Ellis, *Yellow Fever and Public Health*, 29, 142.

38. Black, "Construction and Reconstruction of Compton Hill Reservoir," 4.

39. The cost of the tunnel would have been less had not the Civil War been raging, since some of the materials used were in great demand. See Louis Cain, *Sanitation Strategy for a Lakefront Metropolis: The Case of Chicago* (DeKalb: Northern Illinois University Press, 1978), 37–51; DeBerard, "Expansion of the Chicago, Ill., Water Supply," 593–97; Frank J. Piehl, "Chicago's Early Fight to 'Save Our Lake'", *Chicago History* 5 (Winter 1976–77): 223, 224; Samuel N. Karrick, "Protecting Chicago's Water *Supply*," *Civil Engineering* 9 (September 1939): 547, 548; John Ericson, *The Water Supply System of Chicago* (Chicago: Bureau of Engineering, 1924), 11–13.

40. Voters approved the project by a three-to-one margin, except in the sparsely populated northern part of the city that had good well water. See Larry D. Lankton, "1842: Old Croton Aqueduct Brings Water, Rescues Manhattan from Fire, Disease," *Civil Engineering* 47 (October 1977): 93.

41. Lankton, "1842," 94.

42. Ibid.

43. Ibid., 95, 96; Stuart Galishoff, "Triumph and Failure: The American Response to the Urban Water Supply Problem, 1860–1923," in *Pollution and Reform in American Cities, 1870–1930,* ed. Melosi, 36.

44. Ibid., 90.

45. Eugene Moehring, *Public Works and the Patterns of Urban Real Estate Growth in Manhattan, 1835–1894* (New York: Arno Press, 1981), 31, 32, 44–47, 50.

46. Blake, *Water for the Cities,* 199–218; Nesson, *Great Waters,* 11, 12. In 1878 the Sudbury system, drawing water from the Sudbury River, complemented the Cochituate.

47. William R. Hutton, "The Washington Aqueduct, 1853–1898," *Engineering Record* 40 (July 29, 1899): 190–93.

48. Cited in John B. Blake, "The Origins of Public Health in the United States," *American Journal of Public Health* 38 (November 1948): 1541.

49. Galishoff, "Triumph and Failure," 37, 38.

50. Michael P. McCarthy, *Typhoid and the Politics of Public Health in Nineteenth-Century Philadelphia* (Philadelphia: American Philosophical Society, 1987), 1.

51. Ibid., 1.

52. Galishoff, "Triumph and Failure," 37, 38.

53. The first efforts in water purification probably occurred in China and India several thousand years ago. It was common in China and Egypt to put alum in water to clarify it. Sir Francis Bacon wrote about water purification experiments, which were published one year after his death in 1627. The first known illustrated description of sand filters was published by the Italian physician Luc Antonio

Porzio in 1685. For filtration history, see "Community Water Supply" in *History of Public Works in the United States, 1776–1976,* ed. Armstrong, Robinson, and Hoy, 235, 236; M. N. Baker, "Sketch of the History of Water Treatment," *Journal of the American Water Works Association* 26 (July 1934): 904, 905; Harold E. Babbitt and James J. Doland, *Water Supply Engineering* (New York: McGraw-Hill, 1949), 4, 5; John W. Clark and Warren Viessman Jr., *Water Supply and Pollution Control* (Scranton, PA: International Textbook Co., 1965), 2–4; George W. Fuller, "Progress in Water Purification," *Journal of the American Water Works Association* 25 (October 1933): 1566.

54. Cited in Baker, "Sketch of the History of Water Treatment," 905.

55. Stein designed the first settling basin in the United States for Lynchburg in 1829. See "Community Water Supply," ed. Armstrong, Robinson, and Hoy, 236; Baker, "Sketch of the History of Water Treatment," 906–8; George E. Symons, "History of Water Supply 1850 to Present," *Water and Sewage Works* 100 (May 1953): 191; M. N. Baker, *The Quest for Pure Water,* vol. 1, *The History of Water Purification from the Earliest Records to the Twentieth Century* (Washington, D.C.: American Water Works Association, 1981; orig. pub. 1948), 127.

56. Baker, "Sketch of the History of Water Treatment," 908–10. See also Baker, *Quest for Pure Water,* 133, 135; City of Cincinnati, Water Commission, *Report of the Commission to Take into Consideration the Best Method of Obtaining an Abundant Supply of Pure Water* (Cincinnati: Water Commission, 1865), 3–9.

57. In 1878, professor William Ripley Nichols studied water purification in Europe for the Massachusetts State Board of Health. He published his findings on filtration and related matters in a state report, and five years later expanded his observations in a book, *Water Supply.* See George C. Whipple, "Fifty Years of Water Purification," in *A Half Century of Public Health,* ed. Ravenel, 163.

58. See Baker, *Quest for Pure Water,* 148.

59. Baker, "Sketch of the History of Water Treatment," 912–14; Baker, *Quest for Pure Water,* 136–38.

60. See J. Leland FitzGerald, "Comparison of Water Supply Systems from a Financial Point of View," *Transactions of the American Society of Civil Engineers* 24 (April 1891): 252–56.

61. Armstrong, Robinson, and Hoy, *History of Public Works in the United States,* 232, 233; Frederic Stearns, "The Development of Water Supplies and Water-Supply Engineering"; *Transactions of the American Society of Civil Engineers* 56 (June 1906): 455; Jean-Pierre Goubert, *Conquest of Water: The Advent of Health in the Industrial Age* (Princeton: Princeton University Press, 1986), 56–58; Anderson, "Diffusion of Technology," 10–14; Allen Hazen, "Public Water Supplies," *Engineering News-Record* 92 (April 17, 1924): 696; John W. Alvord, "Recent Progress and Tendencies in Municipal Water Supply in the United States," *Journal of the American Water Works Association* 4 (September 1917): 291–92.

62. Sam Bass Warner, *The Urban Wilderness: A History of the American City* (New York: Harper and Row, 1972), 202.

63. Wade, *Urban Frontier,* 294, 295; O'Connell, "Chicago's Quest for Pure

Water," 3; Tarr,"Evolution of the Urban Infrastructure," 14; Joel A. Tarr, James
McCurley, and Terry F. Yosie, "The Development and Impact of Urban Wastewater
Technology: Changing Concepts of Water Quality Control, 1850–1930," in *Pollution and Reform in American Cities,* ed. Melosi, 60.

Chapter Three. Pure and Plentiful:
The Development of Modern Waterworks in the United States, 1880–2000

This chapter is excerpted from "Pure and Plentiful: The Development of Modern
Waterworks in the United States, 1801–2000," *Water Policy* 2 (2000): 243–65,
which is based on Melosi, *Sanitary City.*

1. P. A. Gorringe, "Path Dependence—Causes, Consequences, and Policy,"
in *Economics for Policy: Expanding the Boundaries; Essays by Peter Gorringe,* ed.
Arthur Grimes, Alan Jones, Roger Procter, and Grant Scobie (Wellington, NZ:
Institute of Policy Studies, 2001).

2. "The Clean Water Act Turns 30," *Newspaper in Education,* Oct. 22, 2002,
http://www.cincinnati.com/nie/archive/10-22-02.

3. United State Environmental Protection Agency, Office of Water, *Report
to Congress: Implementation and Enforcement of the Combined Sewer Overflow
Control Policy,* EPA 833-R-01-003 (December 2001), ES2, 2–1.

4. Penn State Public Broadcasting, "Liquid Assets: The Story of Our Water
Infrastructure," http://liquidassets.psu.edu/the_film/index.html.

5. *Protosystem* is meant to connote an original system or "first in rank or time"
as opposed to the idea of a primitive system.

6. For a general discussion of municipal ownership as a public issue, see Griffith
and Adrian, *A History of American City Government, 1775–1870,* 86–87.

7. Ibid., 180; Committee on Municipal Administration, "Evolution of the City,"
Municipal Affairs 2 (Sept.1898): 726–27.

8. "Water-Supply Statistics of Metered Cities," *American City* 23 (Dec. 1920):
614–20; Allen Hazen, *Meter Rates for Water Works* (New York, 1917), 1–25.

9. See Kahrl, *Water and Power*; Hoffman, *Vision or Villainy.*

10. Earle Lytton Waterman, *Elements of Water Supply Engineering,* 2nd ed.
(New York: Wiley, 1938), 254.

11. Pittsburgh is an excellent example of a city that fought a prolonged battle
with typhoid but successfully combated it with filtration. See Mark J. Tierno, "The
Search for Pure Water in Pittsburgh: The Urban Response to Water Pollution,
1893–1914," *Western Pennsylvania Historical Magazine* 60 (Jan. 1977): 23–36;
"New Filtered Water Supply for the City of Pittsburgh," *Scientific American* 102
(June 25, 1910): 522; F. E. Wing, "Thirty-Five Years of Typhoid," *Survey* 21 (Feb 6,
1909): 933–39. See also Allen Hazen, *The Filtration of Public Water Supplies* (New
York, 1905), 4.

12. Baker, "Sketch of the History of Water Treatment," 902–38; Symons, "History of Water Supply, 1850 to Present," 191–94; Baker, *Quest for Pure Water,* 179; F.
E. Turneaure and H. L. Russell, *Public Water Supplies* (New York: John Wiley and
Sons, 1911), 502–3; Fuller, "Progress in Water Purification," 1568.

13. Turneaure and Russell, *Public Water Supplies* (1948), 124–26; Hazen, *Filtration of Public Water Supplies,* 1–2; William T. Sedgwick, "Water Supply Sanitation in the Nineteenth Century and in the Twentieth," *Journal of the New England Water Works Association* 30 (June 1916): 185–86.

14. Turneaure and Russell, *Public Water Supplies* (1911), 506–11; James H. Fuertes, *Water Filtration Works* (New York: John Wiley and Sons, 1904), 246–55.

15. William P. Mason, "Sanitary Problems Connected with Municipal Water Supply," *Journal of the Franklin Institute* 143 (May 1897): 354; Waterman, *Elements of Water Supply Engineering,* 38–39; Floyd Davis, "Impure Water and Public Health," *Engineering Magazine* 2 (Dec. 1891): 362; George A. Johnson, "The High Cost of Sanitary Ignorance," *American City* 14 (June 1916): 586; Baker, *Quest for Pure Water,* 228–52.

16. American Water Works Association, *Water Chlorination* (New York: AWWA, 1973), 3–4; N. J. Howard, "Twenty Years of Chlorination of Public Water-Supplies," *American City* 36 (June 1927): 791–94; Morris M. Cohn, "Chlorination of Water," *Municipal Sanitation* 2 (July 1931): 333–34; "Is the Chlorination of Water-Supplies Worth While?" *American City* 20 (June 1919): 524–25; George W. Fuller, "The Influence of Sanitary Engineering on Public Health," *AJPH* 12 (Jan. 1922): 16; Edward Meeker, "The Improving Health of the United States, 1850–1915," *Explorations in Economic History* 9 (Summer 1972): 370; C.A. Jennings, "Uses and Accomplishments of Chlorine Compounds in Water and Sewage Purification," *American City* 9 (Oct. 1918): 299.

17. John W. Alvord, "Recent Progress and Tendencies in Municipal Water Supply in the United States," *JAWWA* 4 (Sept.1917): 283–84; Symons, "History of Water Supply," 191–94; Baker, "Sketch of the History of Water Treatment," 922–24; Baker, *Quest for Pure Water,* 253–64.

18. Martin V. Melosi, "Hazardous Waste and Environmental Liability," *Houston Law Review* 25 (July 1988): 753.

19. George W. Fuller, "Water-Works," *Proceedings of the ASCE* 53 (Sept.1927): 1588; Turneaure and Russell, *Public Water Supplies* (1948), 9.

20. "Water Supply Statistics for Municipalities of Less than 5,000 Population," *American City* 32 (Feb. 1925):185–91; (March 1925): 309–23; (April 1925): 435–45; (May 1925): 555–65; (June 1925): 665–77; (July 1925): 47–59; Calvin V. Davis, "Water Conservation: The Key to National Development," *Scientific American* 148 (Feb. 1933): 92.

21. V. Bernard Siems, "The Advantages of Metropolitan Water-Supply Districts," *American City* 32 (June 1925): 644–45.

22. Armstrong, Robinson, and Hoy, *History of Public Works in the United States,* 228, 231–32; Roger Daniels, "Public Works in the 1930s," in *The Relevancy of Public Works History* (Washington, D.C.: Public Works Historical Society, 1975), 9; Public Works Administration, *America Builds* (Washington, D.C.: PWA, 1939), 170, 173–78.

23. "Water Supplies Will Be Widely Extended After the War," *Scientific American* 171 (July 1944): 18.

24. Fuller, "Progress in Water Purification," 1574–75; Harry E. Jordan, "Water Supply and Treatment," *Transactions of the ASCE CT* (1953): 573; Nicholas S. Hill Jr., "Twenty-One Years of Progress in Water-Supply and Purification Practice," *American City* 43 (Sept. 1930): 88–89; Eskel Nordell, "Water Treatment Today—and What of the Future?" *American City* 46 (June 1932): 71–73; American Water Works Association, *Water Quality and Treatment*, 2nd ed. (New York: AWWA, 1951), 255.

25. "Filtration versus Chlorination," *American City* 47 (July 1932): 7; Paul Hansen, "Some Relations Between Sewage Treatment and Water Purification," *American City* 36 (June 1927): 765–67; "The Unsolved Problems of Water Supply," *American City* 52 (Feb. 1937): 9.

26. Earle Lytton Waterman, "The Present Status of Public Water Supply," *American City* 53 (Oct. 1938): 9; Baker, "Sketch of the History of Water Treatment," 922–26.

27. Seth G. Hess, "Pollution—and the Pocketbook," *Municipal Sanitation* 10 (July 1939): 356–58; Cornelius W. Kruse, "Our Nation's Water," in *Advances in Environmental Sciences,* ed. James N. Pitts Jr. and Robert C. Metcalf, vol. 1 (New York: Wiley-Interscience, 1969), 44–45.

28. Turneaure and Russell, *Public Water Supplies* (1948), 133.

29. J. Frederick Jackson, "Stream Pollution by Industrial Wastes, and Its Control," *American City* 31 (July 1924): 23; Sheppard T. Powell, "Industrial-Waste Problems and Their Correction," *Mechanical Engineering* 61 (May 1939): 364; L. F. Warrick, "Relative Importance of Industrial Wastes in Stream Pollution," *Civil Engineering* 3 (Sept. 1933): 495; E. F. Eldridge, *Industrial Waste Treatment Practice* (New York: McGraw-Hill, 1942),1–4; Wellington Donaldson, "Industries and Water Supplies," *JAWWA* 22 (Feb. 1930): 203; Donaldson, "Industrial Wastes in Relation to Water Supplies," *American Journal of Public Health* 11 (March 1921): 193–94; Earle B. Phelps, "Stream Pollution by Industrial Wastes and Its Control," in *A Half Century of Public Health,* ed. Ravenel, 201; L. M. Fisher, "Pollution Kills Fish," *Scientific American* 160 (March 1939):144–46; Pitts and Metcalf, eds., *Advances in Environmental Sciences,* 1:43, 46, 48–50.

30. H. R. Crohurst, "Water Pollution Abatement in the United States," *AJPH* 36 (Feb. 1936):177.

31. P. Aarne Vesilind, "Hazardous Waste," in *Hazardous Waste Management,* ed. J. Jeffrey Peirce and P. Aarne Vesilind (Ann Arbor: Ann Arbor Science Pub., 1981), 26; Philip P. Micklin, "Water Quality," in *Congress and the Environment,* ed. Richard A. Cooley and Geoffrey Wandesforde-Smith (Seattle: University of Washington Press, 1970), 131; Joel A. Tarr, "Industrial Wastes and Public Health," *AJPH* 75 (1985): 1059, 1064.

32. Warrick, "Relative Importance of Industrial Wastes," 496; Monger, "Administrative Phases of Stream Pollution Control," 790; James A. Tobey, "Legal Aspects of the Industrial Wastes Problem," *Industrial and Engineering Chemistry* 31 (Nov. 10, 1939): 1322.

33. Donaldson, "Industrial Wastes in Relation to Water Supplies," 198; Edmund B. Besselievre, *Industrial Waste Treatment* (New York: McGraw-Hill, 1952), 325–44; Hervey J. Skinner, "Waste Problems in the Pulp and Paper Industry," *Industrial and Engineering Chemistry* 31 (Nov. 1939): 1332.

34. M. C. Hinderlider and R. I. Meeker, "Interstate Water Problems and Their Solution," *Proceedings of the American Society of Civil Engineers* 52 (April 1926): 606–8.

35. Harold W Streeter, "Surveys for Stream Pollution Control," *Proceedings of the ASCE* 64 (Jan. 1938): 6.

36. Edward T. Thompson, "The Worst Public-Works Problem," *Fortune* 58 (Dec. 1958): 58.

37. George P. Hanna Jr., "Domestic Use and Reuse of Water Supply," *Journal of Geography* 60 (Jan. 1961): 22.

38. John C. Bollens and Henry J. Schmandt, *The Metropolis,* 2nd ed. (New York: Harper and Row, 1970), 176; Thompson, "The Worst Public-Works Problem," 102; G. M. Fair, J. L. Geyer, and Daniel Alexander Okun, *Elements of Water Supply and Wastewater Disposal,* 2nd ed. (New York: Wiley, 1977), 14.

39. Babbitt and Doland, *Water Supply Engineering,* 40; Fair, Geyer, and Okun, *Elements of Water Supply and Wastewater Disposal,* 14.

40. U.S. Department of Commerce, Bureau of the Census, *Historical Statistics of the United States, Part 2* (Washington, D.C.: Department of Commerce, 1975), 619, 621.

41. Fair, Geyer, and Okun, *Elements of Water Supply and Wastewater Disposal,* 14.

42. Bollens and Schmandt, *Metropolis,* 176, 178.

43. Rodney R. Fleming, "The Big Questions . . ." *American City* 82 (June 1967): 94–95; Charles M. Bolton, "A Metropolitan Water Works Is Best;" *American City* 74 (Jan. 1959): 67–68; Water Resources Council, *The Nation's Water Resources* (Washington, D.C.: Water Resources Council, 1968), 5–1–3.

44. T. E. Larson, "Deterioration of Water Quality in Distribution Systems," *JAWWA* 58 (Oct. 1968): 1316.

45. Donald E. Stearns, "Expanding and Improving Water Distribution Systems," *Water and Sewage Works* 104 (June 1957): 256; William D. Hudson, "Studies of Distribution System Capacity in Seven Cities," *JAWWA* 58 (Feb. 1966): 157, 159, 161–63.

46. Kenneth J. Ives, "Progress in Filtration," *JAWWA* 56 (Sept. 1964): 1225, 1231; J. T. Ling, "Progress in Technology of Water Filtration," *Water and Sewage Works* 109 (Aug. 1962): 315–16.

47. Ling, "Progress in Technology," 317–19.

48. J. Carrell Morris, "Future of Chloridation," *JAWWA* 58 (Nov. 1968): 1475, 1481.

49. Larry E. Jordan, "Outstanding Achievements in Water Supply and Treatment," *Civil Engineering* 22 (Sept. 1952):137; "Water Supply," *AJPH* 37 (May 1947):

556; Herman E. Hilleboe, "Public Health Aspects of Water Fluoridation," *AJPH4* 41 (Nov. 1951): 1370–71.

50. "Fluoridation OK," *Newsweek* 38 (Dec. 10, 1951): 46; "Fluoridation of Public Water Supplies," *AJPH* 42 (March 1952): 339; "Fluoridation," *Bulletin of Atomic Scientists* 20 (Sept. 1964): 30; Armstrong, Robinson, and Hoy, *History of Public Works in the United States*, 240.

51. J. C. Furnas, "The Fight Over Fluoridation," *Saturday Evening Post* 228 (May 19, 1956): 37, 142–44; Fred Merryfield, "Water Supply Progress in 1956," *Water and Sewage Works* 104 (Jan. 1957): 12–13.

52. American Water Works Association, *Water Quality and Treatment*, 406.

53. Edward S. Hopkins, W. McLean Bingley, and George W. Schucker, *The Practice of Sanitation in Its Relation to the Environment,* 4th ed. (Baltimore: Williams & Wilkins, 1970), 131–32, 137.

54. Victor B. Scheffer, *The Shaping of Environmentalism in America* (Seattle: University of Washington Press, 1991), 50; Richard J. Frankel, "Water Quality Management," *Water Resource Research* 1 (June 1965): 173.

55. In the 1960s the federal standards were supplemented by the International Standards for Drinking Water (1963) sponsored by the World Health Organization and the American Water Works Association's Quality Goals for Potable Water (1968). American Water Works Association, *Water Quality and Treatment: A Handbook of Public Water Supplies* (New York: AWWA, 1971), 20–31, 69; Armstrong, Robinson, and Hoy, *History of Public Works in the United States*, 244.

56. Joel A. Tarr and Charles Jacobson, "Environmental Risk in Historical Perspective," in *The Social and Cultural Construction of Risk,* ed. Branden B. Johnson and Vincent T. Covello (Boston: Reidel, 1987), 329.

57. "What Stream Pollution Means Nationally," *American City* 67 (Jan. 1952):139; M. D. Hollis and G. E. McCallum, "Federal Water Pollution Control Legislation," *Sewage and Industrial Waste* 28 (March 1956): 308; David H. Howells, "We Need More Municipal Waste Treatment Works," *Civil Engineering* 33 (Sept. 1963): 54; Hanna Jr., "Domestic Use and Reuse of Water Supply," 22.

58. "Where We Stand on Pollution Control," *Engineering News-Record* 137 (Dec. 26, 1946): 78; Warren J. Scott, "Federal and State Legislation for Stream Pollution Control," *Sewage Works Journal* 19 (Sept. 1947): 884; W. B. Hart, "Antipollution Legislation and Technical Problems in Water Pollution Abatement," in *Water for Industry,* ed. Jack B. Graham and Meredith F. Burrill (Washington, D.C.: AAAS, 1956), 79–81; Allen V. Kneese, "Scope and Challenge of the Water Pollution Situation," in *Water Pollution*, ed. Ted L. Willrich and N. William Hines (Ames: Iowa State University Press, 1965), 56, 60.

59. J. Clarence Davies III, *The Politics of Pollution* (New York: Pegasus, 1970), 40–41; Federal Security Agency, USPHS, *Water Pollution in the United States* (Washington, D. C.: GPO, 1951), 36; "Advances in Sewage Treatment in the Decade Ending with the Year 1949," *ASCE Transactions* 115 (1950): 1262–63.

60. Davies, *Politics of Pollution*, 41; Howells, "We Need More Municipal Waste

Treatment Works," 54; Murray Stein, "Legal Aspects Stimulate Pollution Control Program," *Civil Engineering* 32 (July 1962): 50–51.

61. "Water Pollution: Federal Role Is Strengthened by Law Authorizing New Agency and Quality Standards," *Science* 150 (Oct. 8, 1965): 198–99; Micklin, "Water Quality," 133–34, 136–44.

62. National Council on Public Works Improvements, *The Nation's Public Works: Executive Summaries of Nine Studies* (Washington, D.C.: NCPWI, May 1987), 37–38.

63. Neil S. Grigg, *Urban Water Infrastructure* (New York: Wiley, 1986), 7–8.

64. Carol T. Everett, "So Is There an Infrastructure Crisis or What?" *Public Works Management and Policy* 1 (July 1996), 91; Jesse H. Ausubel and Robert Herman, eds., *Cities and Their Vital Systems* (Washington, D.C.: National Academy Press, 1988), 265.

65. Bernard .H. Ross and Myron A. Levine, *Urban Politics: Power in Metropolitan America* (Itasca, IL: F.E. Peacock Publishers, 1996), 261.

66. National Council on Public Works Improvement, *Nation's Public Works: Executive Summaries of Nine Studies,* 16; David Holtz and Scott Sebastian, eds., *Municipal Water Systems: The Challenge for Urban Resource Management* (Bloomington: Indiana University Press, 1978), 71; Grigg, *Urban Water Infrastructure,* 1, 85.

67. American Public Works Association, *Proceedings of the National Water Symposium* (Washington, D.C.: APWA, Nov. 1982), 11, 32.

68. J. Carrell Morris, "Chlorination and Disinfection-State of the Art," *JAWWA* 63 (Dec. 1971): 769, 772–73; Charles D. Larson, O. Thomas Love, and James M. Symons, "Recent Developments in Chlorination Practice," *Journal of the New England Water Works Association* 91 (Sept. 1977): 279; George E. Symons and Kenneth W. Henderson, "Disinfection: Where Are We?" *JAWWA* 69 (March 1977): 148–54; T. E. Stallworth Jr., "An Economic Assessment of the Impact of Present Shortages on the Water Industry," *JAWWA* 67 (April 1975): 171.

69. Carrell Morris, "Chlorination and Practice," *Proceedings of the Annual Public Water Supply Engineers' Conference* (1978): 31; Joseph T. Ling, "Research: Key to Quality Water Supply in the 1980s," *JAWWA* 68 (Dec. 1976): 659; National Council on Public Works Improvement, *Nation's Public Works: Report on Water Supply,* 3, 5.

70. John Cary Stewart, *Drinking Water Hazards* (Hiram, Ohio: Envirographics, 1990), 121–26; "The Fluoridation Controversy," *Health Matrix* 2 (Summer 1984): 66–76.

71. National Council on Public Works Improvement, *Nation's Public Works,* 10. Improvement most likely referred to conventional sources of pollution, not nonpoint pollution.

72. Robert B. Williams and Gordon L. Culp, eds., *Handbook of Public Water Systems* (New York: Van Nostrand Reinhold, 1986), 552; William H. Rodgers Jr., *Environmental Law: Air and Water,* vol. 1 (St. Paul: West, 1986), 230–37; Herman Koren, ed., *Handbook of Environmental Health and Safety,* vol. 1 (Boca Raton, Fla.:

Lewis Publishers, 1991), 472; George Tchobanoglous and Franklin L. Burton, eds., *Wastewater Engineering* (New York: McGraw-Hill, 1991), 5.

73. National Council on Public Works Improvement, *Nation's Public Works; Report on Water Supply*, 18; Sarah E. Lewis, "The 1986 Amendments to the Safe Drinking Water Act and Their Effect on Groundwater," *Syracuse Law Review* 40 (1989): 894.

74. Conservation Foundation, *State of the Environment: A View Toward the Nineties* (Washington, D.C.: Conservation Foundation, 1987), xlii, 96; Lewis, "The 1986 Amendments to the Safe Drinking Water Act," 897; Sally Benjamin and David Belluck, *State Groundwater Regulation* (Washington, D.C.: Bureau of National Affairs, 1994), 3, 7, 10; Carol Wekesser, ed., *Water* (San Diego: Greenhaven Press, 1994), 81; James J. Geraghty and David W. Miller, "Status of Groundwater Contamination in the U.S.," *JAWWA* 70 (March 1978): 162, 166; Joan Goldstein, *Demanding Clean Food and Water* (New York: Plenum Press, 1990), 113, 116; David E. Lindorff, "Ground-Water Pollution: A Status Report," *Ground Water*, vol. 1 of the *Proceedings of the Fourth NWWA-EPA National Ground Water Quality Symposium* (Jan.–Feb. 1979), 9–12; U.S. Congress, Office of Technology Assessment, *Protecting the Nation's Groundwater from Contamination* (Washington, D.C.: GPO, 1984), 7.

75. Laurel Berman, C. Hartline, N. Ryan, and J. Thorne, *Urban Runoff Water Quality Solutions* (Chicago: APWA Research Foundation, May 1991), 9–10; Vladimir Novotny and Gordon Chesters, *Handbook of Nonpoint Pollution* (New York: Van Nostrand Reinhold, 1981), 2–3, 7–9, 11; Ralph A. Luken and Edward H. Pechan, *Water Pollution Control* (New York: Praeger, 1977), 4.

76. Luken and Pechan, *Water Pollution Control*, 4.

77. National Council on Public Works Improvement, *Nation's Public Works: Report on Wastewater Management*, 57–58.

78. Paul B. Downing, *Environmental Economics and Policy* (Boston: Little, Brown, 1984), 5, 7–8.

79. Lewis, "The 1986 Amendments to the Safe Drinking Water Act," 898–99; Environment and Natural Resources Policy Division, Congressional Research Service, *Nonpoint Pollution and the Area-Wide Waste Treatment Management Program Under the Federal Water Pollution Control Act* (Washington, D.C.: GPO, 1980), 14; Wallis E. McClain Jr., ed., *U.S. Environmental Laws* (Washington, D.C.: Bureau of National Affairs, 1994), 2–1–1; Koren, *Handbook of Environmental Health*, 534, 540–41.

80. See J.P. Eberhard and A.B. Bernstein, eds., *Technological Alternatives for Urban Infrastructure* (Washington, D.C.: National Academies Press, 1985). Modular flexibility "concerns the degree to which the origin, destination, and distribution network are sufficiently independent that any one of them can be removed and its replacement simply 'plugged into' the system."

81. See Thomas P. Hughes, *American Genesis* (New York: Viking, 1989), 2–3.

Chapter Four. The Environmental Impact of the Big Dam Era

This chapter is a revised version of chapter 9, "The Environmental Impact of the Big Dam Era," in Billington, Jackson, and Melosi, *History of Large Federal Dams,* 383–419.

1. Peter Rogers, *America's Water,* 51.

2. Karen M. O'Neill, *Rivers by Design: State Power and the Origins of U.S. Flood Control* (Durham, NC: Duke University Press, 2006), 170.

3. Paul Zucker, *American Bridges and Dams* (New York: Greystone Press, 1941), 14.

4. Patrick McCully, *Silenced Rivers: The Ecology and Politics of Large Dams* (London: Zed Books, 1996), 281–311; Michael Collie, Robert H. Webb, and John C. Schmidt, eds., *Dams and Rivers: A Primer on the Downstream Effects of Dams* (Tucson: U.S. Geological Survey, Circular 1126, June 1996), 6–8; Hundley, *Great Thirst,* 359.

5. Collie, Webb, and Schmidt, *Dams and Rivers,* 2. In very general terms, the standard wisdom has it that public dams from the Mississippi River eastward (with the exception of TVA dams) were the purview of the U.S. Army Corps of Engineers; those in the West were under the jurisdiction of the Bureau of Reclamation. Like all general rules, there were exceptions.

6. Pacific Constructors, Inc., *Shasta Dam and Its Builders* (April 1945), 10.

7. Mark Harvey, "Symbols from the Big Dam Era in the American West," (Unpublished paper delivered at the ASEH conference, San Antonio, Texas, 1998), 3; Harvey, "The Changing Fortunes of the Big Dam Era in the American West," in *Fluid Arguments: Five Centuries of Western Water Conflict,* ed. Char Miller (Tucson: University of Arizona Press, 2001), 276–302. Theodore Steinberg in "'That World's Fair Feeling': Control of Water in Twentieth-Century America," *Technology and Culture* 34 (April 1993): 401–2, took a more strident position, suggesting that "the guiding philosophy behind this profusion of dams was the simple will to control and dominate the natural world." In addition, he argued, "perhaps never before has the will to conquer nature been so consciously and purposefully expressed, so matter-of-fact. What was being expressed here was arrogance by design."

8. Paul C. Pitzer, *Grand Coulee: Harnessing a Dream* (Pullman: Washington State University Press, 1994), 2; Steinberg, "'That World's Fair Feeling','" 402.

9. See quote in Clayton R. Koppes, "Efficiency/Equity/Esthetics: Towards A Reinterpretation of American Conservation," *Environmental Review* 11 (Summer 1987): 135–36. The debate over public power was fought on several fronts, however. See Hundley, *Great Thirst,* 224–25; Linda J. Lear, "Boulder Dam: A Crossroads in Natural Resource Policy," *Journal of the West* 24 (October 1985): 86, 88, 90–91; Wesley Arden Dick, "When Dams Weren't Damned: The Public Power Crusade and Visions of the Good Life in the Pacific Northwest in the 1930s," *Environmental Review* 13 (Fall/Winter 1989): 119, 122, 133–36; Mary Austin, "The Colorado River Controversy," *Nation* 125 (November 9, 1927): 511; Williams, *Energy and the*

Making of Modern California, 261–63; Lee, *Reclaiming the American West*, 40–41; "Who Benefits by Boulder Dam?" *New Republic* 63 (July 30, 1930): 310–12; Frank Bohn, ed., *Boulder Dam: From the Origin of the Idea to the Swing-Johnson Bill* (1927), 102; Warne, *Bureau of Reclamation*, 90–103; Paul L. Kleinsorge, *The Boulder Canyon Project: Historical and Economic Aspects* (Palo Alto: Stanford University Press, 1941), 281–300.

10. Dick, "When Dams Weren't Damned," 123–24, 127, 129–30, 132–33, 138–39; Harvey, "Symbols from the Big Dam Era in the American West," 2–3, 6–8, 12–15.

11. Tim Palmer, *Endangered Rivers and the Conservation Movement* (Berkeley: University of California Press, 1986), 1.

12. Michael L. Lawson, *Dammed Indians: The Pick-Sloan and the Missouri River Sioux, 1944–1980* (Norman: University of Oklahoma Press, 1982), xx–xxi; Lawson, "The Oahe Dam and the Standing Rock Sioux, *South Dakota History* 6 (Spring 1976): 203; Joy A. Bilharz, *The Allegheny Senecas and Kinzua Dam: Forced Relocation Through Two Generations* (Lincoln: University of Nebraska Press, 1998), xv; McCully, *Silenced Rivers*, 70–76; Philip L. Fradkin, *A River No More: The Colorado River and the West* (Berkeley: University of California Press, 1996), 172; Peter Iverson, *"We're Still Here": American Indians in the Twentieth Century* (Wheeling, IL: Harlan Davidson, Inc., 1998), 131; Sarah F. Bates, et al., *Searching Out the Headwaters: Change and Rediscovery in Western Water Policy* (Washington, D.C.: Island Press, 1993), 125; Roy W. Meyer, "Fort Berthold and the Garrison Dam," *North Dakota History* 35 (Summer–Fall 1968): 220–21; Elizabeth S. Helfman, *Rivers and Watersheds in America's Future* (New York: David McKay Co., Inc., 1965), 169–79; Richard L. Berkman and W. Kip Viscusi, *Damming the West* (New York: Grossman Publishers, 1973), 151–96.

13. See Dick, "When Dams Weren't Damned," 125–26; Eric B. Kollgaard and Wallace L. Chadwick, eds., *Development of Dam Engineering in the United States* (New York: Pergamon Press, 1988), 1038; F. Lee Brown and Helen M. Ingram, *Water and Poverty in the Southwest* (Tucson: University of Arizona Press, 1987), 3–4; Worster, *Rivers of Empire*, 210–11. See also Reisner, *Cadillac Desert*. Critics of federal water policy in this period often point to special interests who benefitted most, and sometimes unfairly, from the big dams—particularly irrigators. One criticism is that irrigators do not pay a fair share of the price of impounding water. See Tim Palmer, *The Snake River: Window to the West* (Washington, D.C.: Island Press, 1991), 59, 63; Palmer, *The Columbia: Sustaining a Modern Resource* (Seattle: The Mountaineers, 1997), 60–61; Edward Goldsmith and Nicholas Hildyard, *The Social and Environmental Effects of Large Dams* (San Francisco: Sierra Club Books, 1986), 51; Robert S. Devine, "The Trouble with Dams," *Atlantic Monthly* 276 (August 1995): 68.

14. Dick, "When Dams Weren't Damned," 118.

15. Karl E. Mundt, "Not All Dams Are Damnable!" *Outdoor America* 8 (December 1943): 4. See also Joseph C. Goodman, "Build a Dam, Save a Stream," *American Game* 20 (March–April 1931): 23, 28.

16. William L. Finley, "Salmon or Kilowatts: Columbia River Dams Threaten Great Natural Resource," *Nature Magazine* 26 (August 1935): 107.

17. Palmer, *Endangered Rivers*, 1–2; McCully, *Silenced Rivers*, 1–6; Collier, Webb, and Schmidt, *Dams and Rivers*, 1–2; Guy LeMoigne, Shawki Barghoutti, and Herve Plusquellac, eds., *Dam Safety and the Environment* (Washington, D.C.: The World Bank, 1990), 3; Worster, *Rivers of Empire*, 310–11; Dick, "When Dams Weren't Damned," 118, 147–48; Lear, "Boulder Dam," 91.

18. Richard Lowitt, *The New Deal and the West* (Bloomington: Indiana University Press, 1984), 82–83; Ralph B. Simmons, *Boulder Dam and the Great Southwest* (Los Angeles: The Pacific Publishers, 1936), 141; U.S. Department of the Interior, *The Story of Hoover Dam* (Washington, D.C.: U.S. Department of the Interior, 1953), 40–43, 51–53, 65–66; Kleinsorge, *Boulder Canyon Project,* 246–311; Stevens, *Hoover Dam*, 259–61.

19. Simmons, *Boulder Dam and the Great Southwest*, 84. See also David O. Woodbury, *The Colorado Conquest* (New York: Dodd, Mead & Co., 1941), 358.

20. Carl Abbott, *Urban America in the Modern Age: 1920 to the Present* (Arlington Heights, IL: Harlan Davidson, 1987), 2, 5; Howard P. Chudacoff and Judith E. Smith, *The Evolution of American Urban Society*, 4th ed. (Englewood Cliffs, NJ: Prentice-Hall, 1994), 4.

21. Carl Abbott, *The Metropolitan Frontier: Cities in the Modern American West* (Tucson: University of Arizona Press, 1998), xix.

22. See Miller and Melvin, *Urbanization of Modern America*, 184–85; Bollens and Schmandt, *Metropolis*, 17, 19; Alfred H. Katz and Jean Spencer Felton, eds., *Health and the Community* (New York: Free Press, 1965), 25; U.S. Department of Commerce, Bureau of the Census, *Historical Statistics of the United States, Colonial Times to 1970*, Part 1 (Washington, D.C.: Department of Commerce, 1975), 8, 11; Kenneth T. Jackson, *Crabgrass Frontier: The Suburbanization of the United States* (New York: Oxford University Press, 1985), 139–40.

23. See Bureau of the Census, *Historical Statistics of the United States, Colonial Times to 1970,* Part 2, 619–21; Water Resources Council, *Nation's Water Resources*, 4–1–1 and 4–1–2; Murry Stein, "Problems and Programs in Water Pollution," *Natural Resources Journal* 2 (December 1962), 395; Jack Hirshleifer, James C. DeHaven, and Jerome W. Milliman, *Water Supply: Economics, Technology, and Policy* (Chicago: University of Chicago Press, 1960), 2, 26.

24. Abbott, *The Metropolitan Frontier*, 6.

25. Paul C. Pitzer, *Grand Coulee: Harnessing a Dream* (Pullman, WA: Washington State University Press, 1994), xi–xii, 363; Robinson, *Water for the West*, 63–64; S. E. Hutton, "The Grand Coulee Dam and the Columbia Basin Reclamation Project," *Mechanical Engineering* 62 (September 1940): 651–52. See also Reuss and Walker, *Financing Water Resources Development*, 39–42. For World War II and hydropower, see Donald J. Pisani, "Federal Water Policy and the Rural West," in *The Rural West Since World War II,* ed. R. Douglas Hurt (Lawrence: University Press of Kansas, 1998), 119–38.

26. See Lowitt, *New Deal and the West*, 116; Richard White, *"It's Your Misfortune and None of My Own,"* 485–87; Pitzer, *Grand Coulee*, 364, 368. For figures on total installed hydropower by the early 1970s, see Peter H. Freeman, *Large Dams and the Environment: Recommendations for Development Planning* (A Report prepared for the United Nations Water Conference, Mar Del Plata, Argentina, March 1977), 3. See also Jan A. Veltrop, "Importance of Dams for Water Supply and Hydropower," in *Water for Sustainable Development in the Twenty-first Century,* ed. Asit K. Biswas, Mohammed Jellali, and Glenn E. Stou (Delhi: Oxford University Press, 1993), 102–15.

27. Steinberg, "'That World's Fair Feeling'," 403. See also Theodore Steinberg, *Slide Mountain: or the Folly of Owning Nature* (Berkeley: University of California Press, 1995).

28. Walker R. Young, "Boulder Dam Plays Its Part in Reclamation," *Reclamation Era* 27 (February 1937): 26–27.

29. U.S. Department of the Interior, *Story of Hoover Dam*, 36.

30. The 1928 Flood Control Act, which authorized the corps to use federal funds to unify the flood-control system for the whole alluvial valley of the Mississippi River, led directly to the 1936 legislation. Once flood control on the Mississippi became a federal responsibility, it was just a matter of time before all flood control became a federal activity on all navigable rivers. Armstrong, Robinson, and Hoy, *History of Public Works in the United States,* 250–52, 257–58; Keith Petersen, "The Army Corps of Engineers and the Environment in the Pacific Northwest" (May 1982), Records of the Office of History, Headquarters, U.S. Army Corps of Engineers, Alexandria, Virginia.

31. Martin Reuss, "Coping with Uncertainty: Social Scientists, Engineers, and Federal Water Resources Planning," *Natural Resources Journal* 32 (Winter 1992): 117–27.

32. "Dams and Wild Rivers: Looking Beyond the Pork Barrel," *Science* 158 (October 13, 1967): 235. See also Devine, "The Trouble with Dams," 66–67.

33. E. W. Lane and J. R. Riter, "The Life of Hoover Dam," *Reclamation Era* 34 (April 1948): 61. See also Young, "Boulder Dam Plays Its Part in Reclamation," 27–28; Simmons, *Boulder Dam and the Great Southwest*, 85; Donald Worster, *Under Western Skies: Nature and History in the American West* (New York: Oxford University Press, 1992), 68; U.S. Department of the Interior, *Story of Hoover Dam*, 46; Elmer T. Peterson, *Big Dam Foolishness: The Problem of Modern Flood Control and Water Storage* (New York: Devin-Adair Co., 1954), 69–85.

34. Goldsmith and Hildyard, *Social and Environmental Effects of Large Dams*, 94. See also Worster, *Under Western Skies*, 75–76; Lear, "Boulder Dam," 91–92; "Flood Control? Not by a Dam Site!" *Outdoor America* 16 (March–April 1951): 8.

35. LeMoigne, Barghoutti, and Plusquellac, *Dam Safety and the Environment*, 1, 9–10. See also Robert B. Jansen, *Dams and Public Safety* (Washington, D.C.: U.S. Department of Interior, Water and Power Resources Service, 1980), 94; "High Dams in the United States," *Reclamation Era* 26 (January 1936): 22.

36. Kollgaard and Chadwick, *Development of Dam Engineering*, 1035–36.

37. Kermit Pattison, "Why Did the Dam Burst?" *American Heritage of Invention & Technology* 14 (Summer 1998): 23–24; Peter Briggs, *Rampage: The Story of Disastrous Floods, Broken Dams, and Human Fallibility* (New York: David McKay Co., Inc., 1973), 21–22.

38. Pattison, "Why Did the Dam Burst?" 24–31; Briggs, *Rampage*, 22. See also Charles F. Outland, *Man-Made Disaster: The Story of St. Francis Dam* (Glendale, CA: Arthur H. Clark Co., 1963); Reisner, *Cadillac Desert*, 100–104.

39. Gaylord Shaw, "The Search for Dangerous Dams—A Program to Head Off Disaster," *Smithsonian* 9 (April 1978): 42–43; Pattison, "Why Did the Dam Burst?" 31; Kollgaard and Chadwick, *Development of Dam Engineering*, 1036–37: Jansen, *Dams and Public Safety*, 96.

40. Kollgaard and Chadwick, *Development of Dam Engineering*, 1038.

41. Goldsmith and Hildyard, *Social and Environmental Effects of Large Dams*, 104–6; "WPA Dam Fails at Kansas City," *Engineering News-Record* 119 (September 23, 1937): 495; "Large Slide in Fort Peck Dam Caused by Foundation Failure," *Engineering News-Record* 122 (May 11, 1939): 55–58.

42. For a good case on the politics of dam safety, see David M. Introcaso, "The Politics of Technology: The 'Unpleasant Truth About Pleasant Dam,'" *Western Historical Quarterly* 26 (Autumn 1995): 333–52.

43. Palmer, *Snake River*, 29; USCOLD, *Lessons from Dam Incidents, USA* (New York: ASCE, 1988), 191–95; Kollgaard and Chadwick, *Development of Dam Engineering*, 1041; Worster, *Rivers of Empire*, 308.

44. A description of the collapse and the human tragedy associated with Teton Dam is provided in Reisner, *Cadillac Desert*, 398–425.

45. Pisani, "Federal Water Policy and the Rural West," 139.

46. Independent Panel to Review Cause of Teton Failure, *Summary of Conclusions from Report to the U.S. Department of the Interior and State of Idaho on Failure of Teton Dam* (Washington, D.C.: U.S. Government Printing Office, December 1976), ix–x.

47. The issues of anadromous and controversial catadromous fisheries and the effects of dams upon them are exceptionally controversial. The literature, both technical and popular, is extensive and available for those who further wish to explore impacts on fisheries. Suffice it to say here that more detailed history could be done on the issues involved.

48. Palmer, *Columbia*, 47.

49. Cullen, *Rivers in Harness*, 116.

50. Richard White, *The Organic Machine: The Remaking of the Columbia River* (New York: Hill and Wang, 1995), 89–90; Lisa Mighetto and Wesley J. Ebel, *Saving the Salmon: A History of the U.S. Army Corps of Engineers' Efforts to Protect Anadromous Fish on the Columbia and Snake Rivers* (Seattle: Historical Research Associates, Inc., 1994), 7–8, 17–19, 30–32; White, *"It's Your Misfortune and None of My Own,"* 487; Harvey, "Symbols from the Big Dam Era in the American West," 31. See also Lisa Mighetto, "Salmon, Science, and Politics: Writing History for the U.S. Army Corps of Engineers," *Public Historian* 17 (Fall 1995): 21–22: Dick,

"When Dams Weren't Damned," 144–46; Joseph E. Taylor III, *Making Salmon: An Environmental History of the Northwest Fisheries Crisis* (Seattle: University of Washington Press, 1999).

51. Palmer, *Endangered Rivers*, 59–60.

52. "Dams and Destruction," *Nature Magazine* 31 (October 1938): 505. See also William L. Finley, "Salmon or Kilowatts: Columbia River Dams Threaten Great Natural Resource," *Nature Magazine* 26 (August 1935): 107–08.

53. Mighetto and Ebel, *Saving the Salmon*, 53–55. See also Frank N. Schubert, "From the Potomac to the Columbia: The Corps of Engineers and Anadromous Fisheries" (unpublished ms., December 1978), Office of History, Headquarters, U.S. Army Corps of Engineers, Ft. Belvoir, Virginia; Lowitt, *New Deal and the West*, 158.

54. Albert N. Williams, *The Water and the Power: Development of the Five Great Rivers of the West* (New York: Duell, Sloan and Pearce, 1951), 281.

55. Pitzer, *Grand Coulee*, 223–30. See also Lowitt, *New Deal and the West*, 159; "Dams and Destruction," 491; "Fish Stairways," *Literary Digest* 121 (May 30, 1936): 19.

56. Due to dam spillway design on the Columbia, some pools below dams became supersaturated with nitrogen, an issue that has been addressed by redesign of spillways to avoid entrainment of nitrogen.

57. Jim Marshall, "Dam of Doubt," *Collier's* 99 (June 19, 1937):19–22; Mighetto and Ebel, *Saving the Salmon*, 71, 81, 84–88, 103; "Dams Threaten West Coast Fisheries Industry," *Oregon Business Review* 6 (June 1947): 3–4; Harvey, "Symbols from the Big Dam Era in the American West," 31.

58. Pitzer, *Grand Coulee*, 223–30. See also Lowitt, *New Deal and the West*, 159; "Dams and Destruction," 491; "Fish Stairways," 19; R. G. Skerrett, "Fish Over a Dam," *Scientific American* 159 (October 1938): 182–85. See also Joseph T. Barnaby, "North Pacific Fishery Investigations to Director, Fish and Wildlife Service," May 25, 1945, Thomas M. Robins File, Office of History, Headquarters, U.S. Army Corps of Engineers; White, *Organic Machine*, 89.

59. Michael Robinson, "The United States Army Corps of Engineers and the Conservation Community: A History to 1969" (draft manuscript, November 1982), 64–68, Files, Office of History, Headquarters, U.S. Army Corps of Engineers, Alexandria, Virginia.

60. Robinson, "The Relationship between the U.S. Army Corps of Engineers and the Environmental Community, 1920–1969," *Environmental Review* 13 (Spring 1989): 1–41. Mark W. T. Harvey, *A Symbol of Wilderness: Echo Park and the American Conservation Movement* (Albuquerque: University of New Mexico Press, 1994), xi–xiii; Bates, *Searching Out the Headwaters*, 45.

61. Mark W. T. Harvey, "Echo Park Dam: An Old Problem of Federalism," *Annals of Wyoming* 55 (Fall 1983): 10; Robinson, *Water for the West*, 92.

62. Mark W. T. Harvey, "Echo Park, Glen Canyon, and the Postwar Wilderness Movement," *Pacific Historical Review* 60 (February 1991): 48; Jon M. Cosco, *Echo Park: Struggle for Preservation* (Boulder: Johnson Books, 1995), xii–xv; Wallace

Stegner, "Battle for the Wilderness," *New Republic* 130 (February 15, 1954): 13; Michael P. Cohen, *The History of the Sierra Club, 1892–1970* (San Francisco: Sierra Club Books, 1988), 143–44.

63. U.S. Grant III, "The Dinosaur Dam Sites Are Not Needed," *Living Wilderness* 15 (Autumn 1950): 17. See also "Dams or Wilderness Areas?" *Audubon Magazine* 52 (September–October 1950): 287.

64. Harvey, "Echo Park, Glen Canyon, and the Postwar Wilderness Movement," 48–50.

65. Robinson, *Water for the West*, 93; Worster, *Rivers of Empire*, 274. See also Elmo Richardson, *Dams, Parks, and Politics: Resource Development & Preservation in the Truman-Eisenhower Era* (Lexington: University Press of Kentucky, 1973), 57, 60–61.

66. Harvey, *A Symbol of Wilderness*, xiii, xviii. See also Robinson, *Water for the West*, 93; Harvey, "Echo Park: An Old Problem of Federalism," 13, 15; Rich Johnson, *The Central Arizona Project, 1918–1968* (Tucson: University of Arizona Press, 1977), 101–2; Norris Hundley Jr., "The West Against Itself," in Gary D. Weatherford and F. Lee Brown, eds., *New Courses for the Colorado River* (Albuquerque: University of New Mexico Press, 1986), 29.

67. Richardson, *Dams, Parks, and Politics*, 69.

68. Harvey, "Echo Park Dam," 10. See also Richardson, *Dams, Parks, and Politics*, 135, 142, 151.

69. Fred M. Packard, "Echo Park Dam? Not By a Damsite!" *National Parks Magazine* 29 (July–September 1955): 99.

70. "Echo Park Controversy Resolved," *Living Wilderness* 20 (Winter–Spring 1955–56): 23–25; Harvey, *Symbol of Wilderness*, 181–205; Harvey, "Echo Park Dam," 12; Hundley, *Great Thirst*, 307; Cohen, *History of the Sierra Club*, 154, 157, 165, 172. See also Russell Martin, *A Story that Stands Like a Dam: Glen Canyon and the Struggle for the Soul of the West* (New York: Henry Holt and Company, 1989), 50–74.

71. Harvey, "Echo Park, Glen Canyon, and the Postwar Wilderness Movement," 46–47, 52, 58–59.

72. Robinson, *Water for the West*, 93; Cohen, *History of the Sierra Club*, 161.

73. Eliot Porter, *Glen Canyon on the Colorado*, edited by David Brower (Salt Lake City: Peregrine Smith Books, 1988), 8; Cohen, *History of the Sierra Club*, 177–79; Harvey, "Echo Park, Glen Canyon, and the Postwar Wilderness Movement," 65–67; Hundley, "The West Against Itself," 29; Hundley, *Great Thirst*, 307. See also Martin, *Story That Stands Like a Dam*, 320–32.

74. Wallace Stegner, "Myths of the Western Dam," *Saturday Review* 48 (October 23, 1965): 29.

75. Reuss and Hendricks, "U.S. Army Corps of Engineers," 20.

76. Elizabeth B. Drew, "Dam Outrage: The Story of the Army Engineers," *Atlantic* 225 (April 1970): 51–52; Robert G. Sherill, "Corps of Engineers: The Pork-Barrel Soldiers," *Nation* (February 14, 1966): 180–83. See also Berkman and Viscusi, *Damming the West*, 73–77; Robinson, "The United States Army Corps of

Engineers and the Conservation Community," 84–88; Luther J. Carter, "Dams and Wild Rivers: Looking Beyond the Pork Barrel," *Science* 158 (October 13, 1967): 237–42; Martin Heuvelmans, *The River Killers* (Harrisonburg, PA: Stackpole Books, 1974), 15; "The Dam Shame: It's Still With Us," *Outdoor Life* 163 (June 1979): 84–89; Tim Palmer, "Saving the Stanislaus: Must We Wear Chains to Keep Rivers Free?" *Sierra Club Bulletin* 64 (September/October 1979): 10.

77. Martin V. Melosi, *Coping with Abundance*, 297. See also Gottlieb, *Forcing the Spring*, 105–14; Otis L. Graham Jr., *A Limited Bounty: The United States Since World War II* (New York: McGraw-Hill Co., 1996), 164.

78. Melosi, *Coping with Abundance*, 297–98. See also Gottlieb, *Forcing the Spring*, 109–10.

79. For an example of ecological effects of dams and endangered species, see John R. Ferrell, *Big Dam Era: A Legislative and Institutional History of the Pick-Sloan Missouri Basin Program* (Omaha: Missouri River Division, U.S. Army Corps of Engineers, 1993), 161–66.

80. McClain Jr., *U.S. Environmental Laws*, 9–1; Gottlieb, *Forcing the Spring*, 124–25; Melosi, *Coping with Abundance*, 298. See *Water Resources: Hydraulics and Hydrology: Interview with Alfred S. Harrison* (Alexandria, VA: Office of History, Headquarters, U.S. Army Corps of Engineers, 1997), 92–94. See also Valerie M. Fogelman, *Guide to the National Environmental Policy Act* (New York: Quorum Books, 1990), 1–2; Joseph Petulla, *Environmental Protection in the United States* (San Francisco: San Francisco Study Center, 1987), 47–48; Daniel H. Henning and William R. Mangun, *Managing the Environmental Crisis: Incorporating Competing Values in Natural Resource Administration* (Durham, NC: Duke University Press, 1989), 19–20; Dinah Bear, "National Environmental Policy Act of 1969," in *The Encyclopedia of the Environment,* ed. Ruth A. Eblen and William R. Eblen (Boston: Houghton Mifflin Co., 1994), 463–65; Lynton K. Caldwell, "National Environmental Policy Act (U.S.)," in *Conservation and Environmentalism: An Encyclopedia,* ed. Robert Paehlke (New York: Garland Pub., Inc., 1995), 449–51; Robert V. Bartlett, "Environmental Impact Assessment," in *Conservation and Environmentalism,* ed. Paehlke, 248–50; Daniel Mazmanian and Mordecai Lee, "Tradition Be Damned! The Army Corps of Engineers Is Changing," *Public Administration* 35 (March–April 1975): 169; William L. Kahrl, "Paradise Reclaimed: The Corps of Engineers and the Battle for the Central Valley," (manuscript, undated), 128–29, 142–43 Files, Office of History, Headquarters, U.S. Army Corps of Engineers, Alexandria, Virginia.

81. Mazmanian and Lee, "Tradition Be Damned! The Army Corps of Engineers Is Changing," 168–69. See also Holmes, *History of Federal Water Resources Programs,* 112–14; T. Michael Ruddy, *Damming the Dam: The St. Louis Corps of Engineers and the Controversy Over the Meramec Basin Project from Its Inception to Its Deauthorization* (St. Louis: U.S. Army Corps of Engineers, 1992), 68–72; *Water Resources: Hydraulics and Hydrology: Interview with Jacob H. Douma* (Alexandria, VA: Office of History, Headquarters, U.S. Army Corps of Engineers, 1991), 91–92.

82. Melosi, *Coping with Abundance*, 298; McClain Jr., *U.S. Environmental Laws*, 9–1; Gottlieb, *Forcing the Spring*, 128–29.

83. Richard N. L. Andrews, "Environmental Protection Agency," in *Conservation and Environmentalism,* ed. Paehlke, 256; Gottlieb, *Forcing the Spring*, 129; Petulla, *Environmental Protection in the United States*, 48–49; Melosi, *Coping with Abundance*, 298. See also Terrie Davies, "Environmental Protection Agency," in *The Encyclopedia of the Environment,* ed. Eblen and Eblen, 221–22; Stren, White, and Whitney, eds., *Sustainable Cities*, 192; Marc K. Landy, Marc J. Roberts, and Stephen Thomas, *The Environmental Protection Agency: Asking the Wrong Questions from Nixon to Clinton* (New York: Oxford University Press, 1990), 22–45; Alfred Marcus, "Environmental Protection Agency," in *The Politics of Regulation,* ed. James Q. Wilson (New York: Basic Books, Inc., 1980), 267–303; Edmund P. Russell III, "Lost Among the Parts Per Billion: Ecological Protection at the United States Environmental Protection Agency, 1970–1993," *Environmental History* 2 (January 1997): 29–51.

84. Richard N. L. Andrews, *Managing the Environment, Managing Ourselves*, 218–26. See also Martin V. Melosi, "Lyndon Johnson and Environmental Policy," *The Johnson Years, Volume Two: Vietnam, the Environment, and Science* (Lawrence: University Press of Kansas, 1987), 113–17.

85. Gottlieb, *Forcing the Spring*, 126, 129; Andrews, *Managing the Environment, Managing Ourselves*, 294–316; Jeffrey Kim Stine, "Environmental Politics and Water Resources Development: The Case of the Army Corps of Engineers during the 1970s," (PhD dissertation, University of California, Santa Barbara, 1984), 21–22, 34–35; Holmes, *History of Federal Water Resources Programs*, 9–10, 13, 17, 111.

86. Mazmanian and Lee, "Tradition Be Damned! The Army Corps of Engineers Is Changing," 171.

87. Mazmanian and Lee, "Tradition Be Damned! The Army Corps of Engineers Is Changing," 166–71. See also Holmes, *History of Federal Water Resources Programs and Policies,* 116–17; "The Corps of Engineers, Water, and Ecology," *Audubon Magazine* 72 (July 1970): 102.

88. Martin Reuss, *Shaping Environmental Awareness: The United States Army Corps of Engineers Environmental Advisory Board, 1970–1980* (Washington, D.C.: Historical Division, Office of Administrative Services, Office of the Chief of Engineers, 1980), 67–68. See also Stine, "Environmental Politics and Water Resources Development," 46, 100.

89. Stine, "Environmental Politics and Water Resources Development," 197. See also 94, 97–98, 101, 194–98; Carter, "Dams and Wild Rivers: Looking Beyond the Pork Barrell," 233.

90. Holmes, *History of Federal Water Resources Programs and Policies,* 140.

91. Reuss, "Coping with Uncertainty," 129–31; Brent Blackwelder, "In Lieu of Dams," *Water Spectrum* (Fall 1977), 41; Samuel Stafford, "Big Problem: Damming Up the Flood of Antipathy," *Government Executive* 1 (December 1969): 49.

92. John D. Echeverria, Pope Barrow, and Richard Roos-Collins, *Rivers at Risk:*

The Concerned Citizen's Guide to Hydropower (Washington, D.C.: Island Press, 1989), 4.

93. Pisani, "Federal Water Policy and the Rural West," 139. See also Reisner, *Cadillac Desert*, 48–95.

94. For additional information on water quality and dams, see the EPA's 1989 *Report to Congress: Dam Water Quality Study* (EPA 506/2-89/002).

95. Goldsmith and Hildyard, *Social and Environmental Effects of Large Dams*, 13.

96. Devine, "The Trouble with Dams," 72–73; Committee on Environmental Effects of the United States Committee on Large Dams, *Environmental Effects of Large Dams* (New York: American Society of Civil Engineers, 1978), 5; Echeverria, Barrow, and Roos-Collins, *Rivers at Risk*, 4; Worster, *Rivers of Empire*, 310; Palmer, *Snake River*, 67; Palmer, *Endangered Rivers*, 1–2; Goldsmith and Hildyard, *Social and Environmental Effects of Large Dams*, 52, 63; Collier, Webb, and Schmidt, *Dams and Rivers*, 83–84. See also John A. Dixon, Lee M. Talbot, and Guy J. M. Le Moigne, *Dams and the Environment: Considerations in World Bank Projects* (Washington, D.C.: World Bank, 1989), 2.

97. Devine, "The Trouble with Dams," 71–72; Palmer, *Snake River*, 20–21; Echeverria, Barrow, and Roos-Collins, *Rivers at Risk*, 6.

98. Worster, *Rivers of Empire*, 153–54, 240, 319–24. See also Goldsmith and Hildyard, *Social and Environmental Effects of Large Dams*, 134–63.

99. Hundley, "The West Against Itself," 37–39: Warne, *Bureau of Reclamation*, 117–21. See also Berkman and Viscusi, *Damming the West*, 34–41, 46–51; Cullen, *Rivers in Harness*, 120–23. For another significant case of water degradation, see Gene Rose, *San Joaquin: A River Betrayed* (Fresno: Linrose Pub. Co., 1992), 123, 125–30. For a general description of the impact of dams and reservoirs on water quality, see McCully, *Silenced Rivers*, 36–38, 40–41.

100. William Graf, "Landscapes, Commodities, and Ecosystems," 18–20; Joseph L. Sax, "Parks, Wilderness, and Recreation," in *Government and Environmental Politics,* ed. Michael J. Lacey (Washington, D.C.: Woodrow Wilson Center Press, 1989), 124. See also Palmer, *Endangered Rivers*, 2.

101. LeMoigne, Barghoutti, and Plusquellac, *Dam Safety and the Environment*, 1; Shaw, "The Search for Dangerous Dams—A Program to Head Off Disaster," 36, 38–39; Kollgaard and Chadwick, *Development of Dam Engineering*, 1040–41; Worster, *Rivers of Empire,* 309.

102. The 1972 act authorized the secretary of the army, acting through the chief of engineers, to initiate a national program of dam inspections. See Jansen, *Dams and Public Safety*, 96.

103. National Research Council, *Safety of Existing Dams: Evaluation and Improvement* (Washington, D.C.: National Academic Press, 1983), 4–5.

104. Kollgaard and Chadwick, *Development of Dam Engineering*, 1042. See also Shaw, "The Search for Dangerous Dams—A Program to Head Off Disaster," 44.

105. Mighetto, "Salmon, Science, and Politics," 22–25. See also Mighetto and Ebel, *Saving the Salmon*, 84; Darrell J. Turner, "Dams and Ecology: Can They Be Made Compatible?" *Civil Engineering* 41 (September 1971): 78; Keith C. Petersen,

River of Life, Channel of Death: Fish and Dams on the Lower Snake (Lewiston, Idaho: Confluence Press, 1995); Petersen, "Battle for Ice Harbor Dam," *Pacific Northwest Quarterly* 86 (Fall 1995): 178–88.

106. Mighetto, "Salmon, Science, and Politics," 24–26; Mighetto and Ebel, *Saving the Salmon*, 174–76. See also "Fish v. Dams," *Time* 71 (February 17, 1958): 89; Joel W. Hedgpeth, "The Passing of the Salmon," *Scientific Monthly* 59 (November 1954): 378; John E. Thorson, *River of Promise, River of Peril: The Politics of Managing the Missouri River* (Lawrence: University Press of Kansas, 1994), 182–84; Jeffrey F. Mount, *California Rivers and Streams: The Conflict Between Fluvial Process and Land Use* (Berkeley: University of California Press, 1995), 326–29; Senator Frank E. Moss, *The Water Crisis* (New York: Frederick A. Praeger, Pub., 1967), 137; McCully, *Silenced Rivers*, 41–43, 50–53; Reisner, *Cadillac Desert*, 187–88.

107. Robert K. Davis, "Lessons in Politics and Economics from the Snail Darter," in *Environmental Resources and Applied Welfare Economics: Essays in Honor of John V. Krutilla,* ed. V. Kerry Smith (Washington, D.C.: Resources for the Future, 1988), 213–18. See also William Bruce Wheeler and Michael J. McDonald, *TVA and the Tellico Dam, 1936–1979: A Bureaucratic Crisis in Post-Industrial America* (Knoxville: University of Tennessee Press, 1986); Daniel Deudney, *Rivers of Energy: The Hydropower Potential* (Worldwatch Paper 44, June 1981), 19; Ann Shalowitz, "Endangered Darters 'Endanger' Tellico Dam," *Conservation News* 40 (March 15, 1975): 7–8; Mighetto and Ebel, *Saving the Salmon*, 179.

108. Reisner, *Cadillac Desert*, 295.

109. Robinson, *Water for the West*, 93; "Grand Canyon Dams?" *Audubon Magazine* 67 (May 1965): 181; Arnold Hano, "The Battle of the Grand Canyon," *New York Times Magazine*, December 12, 1965, 56; "Canyon Dams: Dissents from Arizona Scientists," *Science* 157 (July 7, 1967): 46; "Damming the Grand Canyon for a Thirsty Southwest," *New Republic* 154 (April 30, 1966): 9; Cohen, *History of the Sierra Club*, 314–18, 357–64. See also Warne, *Bureau of Reclamation*, 99–103; Fradkin, *River No More*, 194–95, 228–34; Robert Dean, "'Dam Building Still Had Some Magic Then': Stewart Udall, the Central Arizona Project, and the Evolution of the Pacific Southwest Water Plan, 1963–1968," *Pacific Historical Review* 66 (February 1997): 92; "Water and Power for the Southwest," *National Parks Magazine* 39–40 (September 1965): 2; "'No Compromise' on Grand Canyon Dams: Sierra Club's Reply to Goldwater Plan," *U.S. News and World Report* 61 (December 12, 1966): 60–61; "Dam the Grand Canyon?" *Audubon Magazine* 68 (September 1966): 308–11; "Grand Canyon: Colorado Dams Debated," *Science* 152 (June 17, 1966): 1600–1605; "Canyon Controversy: Second Round," *Science News* 91 (April 1967): 302–3; John Ludwigson, "Dams and the Colorado," *Science News* 91 (February 1967): 167; "Grand Canyon Dams Go," *Science News* 91 (February 11, 1967): 135; "The Grand Canyon: Dam It or Not?" *Senior Scholastic* 90 (February 3, 1967): 6–7; "Grand Canyon Dams Blocked," *Audubon Magazine* 68 (November 1966): 462; "Good News on the Grand Canyon," *National Parks Magazine* 41 (March 1967): 289; Stephen Raushenbush, "A Bridge Canyon Dam Is Not Necessary," *National Parks Magazine* 38 (April 1964): 4–8.

110. See "Building the Bigger Dam," *Natural History* 72 (December 1963): 66; A Starker Leopold and Justin W. Leonard, "Alaska Dam Could Be Resources Disaster," *Audubon Magazine* 68 (May–June 1966): 176–78; Stephen H. Spurr, "Rampart Dam: A Costly Gamble," *Audubon Magazine* 68 (May–June 1966): 172–75, 179. See also "Fish and Wildlife Service Issues Unfavorable Report on Rampart Dam," *Izaak Walton Magazine* 29 (August–September 1964): 13; "Rampart Dam—Alaska Study," *Izaak Walton Magazine* 31 (May 1966): 12–13; "Rampart Dam," *National Parks Magazine* 41 (August 1967): 20; "Rampart Dam and the Perpetual Engineers," *Field and Stream* 71 (June 1966): 34, 36.

111. "Daniel Boone's Wilderness May Be Tamed by a Lake," *Smithsonian* 6 (September 1975): 56–58.

112. "Engineers' Dam Is Coup de Grace for Meramec," *Audubon Magazine* 75 (March 1973): 121–22.

113. See Thorson, *River of Promise, River of Peril*; Ferrell, *Big Dam Era*.

114. See also Richard C. Albert, *Damming the Delaware: The Rise and Fall of Tocks Island Dam* (University Park: Pennsylvania State University Press, 1987).

Chapter Five. Private Water: The Curious Case of San Jose's Water Supply

The original version of this chapter appears in Char Miller, ed., *Cities and Nature in the American West* (Reno: University of Nevada Press, 2010).

1. Char Miller, *Cities and Nature in the American West*.

2. The overall structure for this section comes from Melosi, *Sanitary City*.

3. John C. Trautwine Jr., "A Glance at the Water Supply of Philadelphia," *Journal of the New England Water Works Association* 22 (Dec. 1908): 421, 425; McMahon, "Fairmount," 100–101; McMahon, "Makeshift Technology," 24–26; Jackson, "'The Fairmount Waterworks, 1812–1911,'" 635; City of Philadelphia, Department of Public Works, Bureau of Water, "Description of the Filtration Works and Pumping Stations, Also Brief Historical Review of the Water Supply, 1789–1900" (1909), 57–59; Carter II, "Benjamin Henry Latrobe and Public Works"; Gibson, "The Fairmount Waterworks," 9–12; Armstrong, Robinson, and Hoy, *History of Public Works in the United States*, 232–33; "Golden Decade for Philadelphia Water," *Engineering News-Record* 159 (Sept. 19, 1957): 37; Martin J. McLaughlin, "Philadelphia's Water Works from 1798 to 1944," *American City* 59 (Oct. 1944): 86–87.

4. U.S. Bureau of Census, *Census of Population: 1960*, vol. 1, *Characteristics of the Population* (Washington, D.C.: Department of Commerce, 1961), pt. A, 1–14–15, table 8; Waterman, *Elements of Water Supply Engineering*, 6; Harrison P. Eddy, "Water Purification: A Century of Progress," *Civil Engineering* 2 (Feb. 1932): 82; J. J. R. Croes, *Statistical Tables from the History and Statistics of American Water Works* (New York, 1885), 4–69.

5. Waterman, *Elements of Water Supply Engineering*, 6.

6. Anderson, "Diffusion of Technology," 102–4, 117; Letty Anderson, "Hard Choices," *Journal of Interdisciplinary History* 15 (Autumn 1984): 218; Joel A. Tarr, "Evolution of the Urban Infrastructure," 30–31.

7. M. N. Baker, "Public and Private Ownership of Water-Works," *Outlook* 59 (May 7, 1898): 79; Anderson, "Diffusion of Technology," 108.

8. Tarr, "Evolution of the Urban Infrastructure," 26. Ellis and Galishoff, "Atlanta's Water Supply, 1865–1918," 5–22.

9. Cornelius C. Vermeule, "New Jersey's Experience with State Regulation of Public Water Supplies," *American City* 16 (June 1917): 602; Ernest S. Griffith, *A History of American City Government: The Progressive Years and Their Aftermath, 1900–1920* (1974; Washington, D.C.: UP of America, 1983), 86–87; Maureen Ogle, "Redefining 'Public' Water Supplies, 1870–1890," *Annals of Iowa* 50 (Spring 1990): 507–30; Gregg R. Hennessey, "The Politics of Water in San Diego, 1895–1897," *Journal of San Diego History* 24 (Summer 1978): 367–83.

10. Committee on Municipal Administration, "Evolution of the City," *Municipal Affairs* 2 (Sept. 1898): 726–27; Griffith, *History of American City Government: The Conspicuous Failure*, 180; Anderson, "Diffusion of Technology," 106; *The Manual of American Water-Works* (New York, 1897), f–g.

11. Anderson, "Diffusion of Technology," 106, 108, 112; Tarr, "Evolution of the Urban Infrastructure," 26, 30; Baker, "Public and Private Ownership of Water-Works," 78.

12. Anderson, "Diffusion of Technology," 122; Henry C. Hodgkins, "Franchises of Public Utilities as They Were and as They Are," *JAWWA* 2 (Dec. 1915): 743.

13. Anderson, "Diffusion of Technology," 115, 119, 121.

14. Todd A. Shallat, "Fresno's Water Rivalry," *Essays in Public Works History* 8 (1979): 9–13.

15. A. S. Baldwin, "Shall San Francisco Municipalize Its Water Supply?" *Municipal Affairs* (June 1900): 317–28; Clyde Arbuckle, *History of San Jose* (San Jose: Memorabilia of San Jose, 1986), 301, 486–87, 501–9.

16. "The Recent History of Municipal Ownership in the United States," *Municipal Affairs* 6 (Winter 1902–3): 524, 529; Anderson, "Diffusion of Technology," 122–23; M. N. Baker, "Municipal Ownership and Operation of Water Works," *Annals of the American Academy* 57 (Jan. 1915): 281.

17. Frits van der Leeden, Fred L. Troise, and David Keith Todd, *The Water Encyclopedia*, 2nd ed. (New York: Lewis Publishers, 1990), 351.

18. Martin V. Melosi, "Public Goods versus Privatization: The Development of Water Supplies in the United States" (unpublished paper).

19. Sharon Whaley, ed., *San Jose Water Company: 125th Anniversary* (San Jose: San Jose Water Company, 1991), 3–5, 8–9; U.S. Bureau of the Census, *Statistics of Power and Machinery Employed in Manufactures*, v. 17 (1880), 174; Doug Hayward, "The quiet giant–and your money: Water—does it belong to the people?" *East San Jose Sun* (December 28, 1965); Glory Anne Laffey, "Water Management and Urban Growth in San Jose, 1846–1870," (MA thesis, San Jose State University, June 1982), 47, 74–75; San Jose Water Works, *Nine Men and 100 Years of Water History: The Story of the San Jose Water Works* (San Jose: San Jose Water Works, March, 1967), Archives, San Jose Historical Museum; Philip Schuyler, "The San Jose Water Works," *Western Construction News* 2 (October 10, 1927): 44.

20. Edward Williams to the Mayor and Common Council, January 26, 1888, Box 02307, Archives, San Jose Historical Museum.

21. Whaley, *San Jose Water Company: 125th Anniversary*, 8–9; "Company Organized in 1866, Has Had Interesting Growth," *San Jose Evening News* (April 3, 1937), San Jose Water Works Notebooks, San Jose Water Company.

22. Leslie Sayoko Parks, "A History of the San Jose Water Company" (Unpublished MA thesis, San Jose State University, December 1983), 50–51. See also Arbuckle, *History of San Jose*, 501–9.

23. Whaley, *San Jose Water Company: 125th Anniversary*, 11–12.

24. Editorial, *San Jose Herald*, October 8, 1903, San Jose Water Works Notebooks, San Jose Water Company. See the notebooks for extensive newspaper coverage of this and other issues of interest to the water company.

25. "Water Company May Have Competition," *San Jose Evening News*, July 1906, San Jose Water Works Notebooks, San Jose Water Company.

26. Parks, "A History of the San Jose Water Company," 61–62.

27. "Advantages of Owning Our Own Water System," *The Union Label* 3 (July 24, 1905): 1. See also J. R. Lewis and Louis Montgomery to Mayor and Common Council of the City of San Jose, March 19, 1906, and City Attorney to Lewis and Montgomery, February 26, 1906, Box 02307, Archives, San Jose Historical Museum; "Appeal to Honest Stock Holders of Water Co.," *San Jose Times*, March 5, 1907, and "Mayor and Common Council: Are They Servants of the People, or Are They the Agents of the San Jose Water Company," *San Jose Times*, February 6, 1907, San Jose Water Works Notebooks, San Jose Water Company. Please note that Montgomery's comments do not necessarily reflect a pro-labor position on municipal ownership of the water works. For example, an article in the *Union*, Sept. 5, 1910 (on Labor Day) stated that "organized labor has a deep interest in the water supply and the members of the 63 labor bodies here rely upon the company that is supplying us with this great necessity."

28. "Claim Water Co. Is a Monopoly," *San Jose Evening News*, August 21, 1906, San Jose Water Works Notebooks, San Jose Water Company.

29. In 1912, regulation of water utility rates passed from San Jose City Council to the state Railroad Commission. In 1916, the original charter of incorporation for San Jose Water Company expired, and the name changed to San Jose Water Works with the new company assuming all franchises. See Whaley, *San Jose Water Company: 125th Anniversary*, 13. Missing from this official company history were many of the controversies surrounding the municipal ownership debate. See also Seonaid McArthur, ed., "Water in the Santa Clara Valley: A History," *Local History Studies* 27 (California History Center, DeAnza College, 1981), 14.

30. Glenna Matthews, "'The Los Angeles of the North': San Jose's Transition from Fruit Capital to High-Tech Metropolis," *Journal of Urban History* 25 (May 1999): 468; "San Jose Rate for Water Up," *San Francisco Chronicle*, October 30, 1924; editorial, *San Jose Evening News*, January 14, 1926; "Hetch Hetchy Water Urged for San Jose," *San Francisco Chronicle*, November 11, 1924; "San Jose Right

in Resisting Water Corporation's Demands," *San Jose Evening News*, April 26, 1924, San Jose Water Works Notebooks, San Jose Water Company.

31. "Efforts to Obtain Hetchy Water Here Being Opposed at Modesto," *San Jose Mercury*, June 19, 1930, San Jose Water Works Notebooks, San Jose Water Company.

32. "A New Year Endeavor," *Los Gatos Star*, January 1, 1925.

33. Whaley, *San Jose Water Company: 125th Anniversary*, 16; "N.Y. Company Is Declared Purchaser of Water System," *San Jose Mercury*, April 2, 1929; "Talk of Selling San Jose's Water System Brings Out Big Variety of Opnions," *San Jose Evening News*, March 15, 1929; "Water Purchase to Link S. J. with Big Utility Firm," *San Jose Mercury*, May 9, 1929; "$5,100,00 Sent Here to Close Water Co. Sale," *San Jose Mercury*, October 26, 1929, San Jose Water Works Notebooks, San Jose Water Company. In 1931, the San Jose Water Works was reincorporated with an increase in its authorized stock. "Local Water Co. Is Being Reorganized," *San Jose Evening News*, Oct. 24, 1931, San Jose Water Works Notebooks, San Jose Water Company.

34. Matthews, "'Los Angeles of the North,'" 468.

35. See Santa Clara Valley Water District, *The Story of the Santa Clara Valley Water District* (June 1978), California History Center, De Anza College, Cupertino, California; "Formation of Valley Water Conservation District Is Approved by Huge Majority," *San Jose Herald*, November 6, 1929, San Jose Water Works Notebooks, San Jose Water Company. See also McArthur, "Water in the Santa Clara Valley."

36. Parks, "History of the San Jose Water Company," 80, 85.

37. City Manager to City Council, May 15, 1933, City of San Jose, Box 1538; San Jose Water Company, *Annual Report, 1932*; "Our City Should Own Its Own Water Supply," *San Jose Evening News*, October 29, 1932; "Council Moves to Force Sale of S.J. Water Works to City," *San Jose Mercury*, Nov. 1, 1932; "Council Starts Action to Buy Water Company," *San Jose Mercury*, Dec. 20, 1932; "Water Works Asks City Delay Suit: Ready to Talk Price," *San Jose Evening News*, Janaury 6, 1933; "Water Works Will Refuse City's Offer," *San Jose Evening News*, May 15, 1933; "Council Drops Plan for Water Purchase Ballot," *San Jose Mercury*, May 23, 1933, San Jose Water Works Notebooks, San Jose Water Company.

38. "San Jose Signs 30-Year Contract for Municipal Water Purchase," *San Jose Mercury*, March 6, 1934; Louis Ashlock, "10,000 to Get Jobs by Huge Water Plan," *San Jose Evening News*, March 9, 1934, San Jose Water Works Notebooks, San Jose Water Company.

39. "Vote Yes" flyer (1934); P.C. Edwards, "San Jose Voters to Decide on Water Promotion Scheme Declared 'Gold Brick' Offer," *San Jose Evening News*, May 4, 1934, San Jose Water Works Notebooks, San Jose Water Company.

40. Letter to Pacific, Gas & Electric employees from H.S. Kittridge, President of San Jose Water Works, May 2, 1934, San Jose Water Works Notebooks, San Jose Water Company.

41. "Vote Down This Fantastic Water Scheme!" (1934), San Jose Water Works Notebooks, San Jose Water Company.

42. "City Rejects Water Supply Plan by 240; Re-Elect Cuncilmen," *San Jose Evening News*, May 8, 1934, San Jose Water Works Notebooks, San Jose Water Company.

43. "City Negotiates for Hetch Hetchy Water from San Francisco," *San Jose Mercury*, March 3, 1937; F. G. Cahill, Manager of Utilities, City and County of San Francisco to C. B. Goodwin, Oct. 12, 1937, City of San Jose, Box 1538.

44. C. B. Goodwin to City Council, November 4, 1935, City of San Jose, Box 1538.

45. "Municipal Water Plans Dropped by City Council," *San Jose Mercury*, Sept. 3, 1935; "Council Paves Way for Public Owned Utilities," *San Jose Mercury*, Oct. 8, 1935; "Move to Acquire S.J. Water Works Launched by City," *San Jose Mercury*, Nov. 5, 1935; "Water Works Won't Sell to City," *San Jose Evening News*, Nov. 21, 1935; "San Jose Bids $4,500,000 for Water Company," *San Jose Mercury*, Dec. 6, 1935; "Water Works Turns Down Offer," *San Jose Evening News,* Dec. 21, 1935, San Jose Water Works Notebooks, San Jose Water Company; J. Lester Miller, Citizen's League on Government and Taxation of Santa Clara County to Mayor and City Council, November 25, 1935, City of San Jose, Box 1538; H. S. Kittridge to C. B. Goodwin, November 21, 1935, City of San Jose, Box 1538.

46. T. A. Hopkins (Consulting Engineer) to C. B. Goodwin, January 21, 1936, and "Comparative Costs of Acquisition and Operation of Proposed Municipal Water System for the City of San Jose, California," City of San Jose, Box 1538; "City Gets Water Plans," *San Jose Evening News*, March 6, 1936; "Council Hears Pro and Con on Municipal Water System," *San Jose Mercury*, July 25, 1936; "Water Company Again Refuses City Sale Price," *San Jose Mercury*, Feb. 20, 1936; "Water Company Announces Rate Cut," *San Jose Evening News*, Nov. 10, 1936; "Does S. J. Want Water Works?" *San Jose Evening News*, Dec. 8, 1936; San Jose Water Works Notebooks, San Jose Water Company.

47. "Water Poll Vote 81 Percent in Favor of City-Owned System," *San Jose Mercury*, Feb. 1, 1937; "80 Percent Favor Municipal Ownership, Test Poll Shows," *San Jose Mercury*, Feb. 2, 1937; "Council Launches Move to Buy Water Works," *San Jose Mercury*, Feb. 9, 1937, San Jose Water Works Notebooks, San Jose Water Company.

48. H. G. Mitchell to San Jose City Council, April 3, 1937, City of San Jose, Box 1538.

49. "Utility District Defeated; City Water Plan Speeded," *San Jose Mercury*, Nov. 24, 1937; "East Side Opposes City's Buying Water Co.," *San Jose Evening News*, April 5, 1937, San Jose Water Works Notebooks, San Jose Water Company.

50. See J. Lester Miller to City Council, May 15, 1937; Miller to City Council, May 27, 1937; Ralph Elsman, Chairman of the Board, San Jose Water Works to Richard French, City Council and C.B. Goodwin, City Manager, Dec. 15, 1937; Elsman to French and Goodwin, March 9, 1937; M. J. Vertin, Los Gatos Chamber of Commerce to City Council, May 15, 1937, City of San Jose, Box 1538. See also San Jose City Council Minutes, Dec. 16, 1937, March 21, 1938.

51. "Election Results," *San Jose Evening News*, May 3, 1938. See also "Water

Bonds Out; Brooks Is Beaten," *San Jose Evening News*, May 5, 1938, San Jose Water Works Notebooks, San Jose Water Company.

52. Harold Gilliam, "San Jose—Worried City in a Thirsty Valley," *San Francisco Chronicle*, July 16, 1950, 1.

53. J. H. Jamison, Director of the Citizens' League to City Council, February 25, 1938, City of San Jose, Box 1538.

54. Parks, "History of the San Jose Water Company," 96–97, 111–17; Whaley, *San Jose Water Company: 125th Anniversary*, 19.

55. Gilliam, "San Jose—Worried City in a Thirsty Valley," 1–2, 11; Parks, "History of the San Jose Water Company," 119–41, John Spalding, "Buying Water Works Said 'Feasible' in City Report," *San Jose Mercury*, Sept. 12, 1961; Doug Hayward, "Water Works Grows and Prospers," *San Jose Sun*, Dec. 15, 1965. See also McArthur, "Water in the Santa Clara Valley," 75.

56. See Matthews, "'Los Angeles of the North,'" 469–70. According to Matthews, in 1996 42 percent of Santa Clara Valley's water came from local reservoirs, 23 percent from the federal Central Valley Project, 19 percent from a state project, and 16 percent from Hetch Hetchy water.

57. Parks, "History of the San Jose Water Company," 142–45.

58. "Interest Rate Balks Water Co. Purchase," *San Jose Mercury*, Aug. 23, 1966; "Water Works Series Brings Out Strong Views," *East San Jose Sun*, January 12, 1966; "San Jose Water Activity—Higher Rates and Too Many Districts Are Some of the Problems," *San Jose Sun*, Nov. 9, 1966; Parks, "History of the San Jose Water Company," 145–48.

59. Philp J. Trounstine and Terry Christensen, in *Movers and Shakers: The Study of Community Power* (New York: St. Martin's Press, 1982), discuss San Jose Water Company as one of the interlocking institutions and boards of directors in the San Jose political and economic community (see 73, 121–22). More on the political economy and water in Santa Clara Valley can be found in Richard A. Walker and Matthew J. Williams, "Water from Power: Water Supply and Regional Growth in the Santa Clara Valley," *Economic Geography* 58 (April 1982): 95–119.

60. See Parks, "History of the San Jose Water Company," 149–61; Stone and Youngberg, *Preliminary Report: Acquisition of San Jose Water Works* (Oct. 1971); "Danger of Jumping into the Water Works," *San Jose Sun*, August 8, 1973.

61. Operations Analysis Division, Office of Fiscal Affairs, *Physical Facility Narrative Profile: City of San Jose* (San Jose, Sept. 30, 1974), 20.

62. Ron Wolf, "San Jose Water Co. Charts an Unusual Course to Growth," *San Jose Mercury News,* December 7, 1992, 1E.

63. See ibid., 1E, 9E; SJW Corp, http://www.sjwater.com; Parks, "History of the San Jose Water Company," 165. On San Francisco, which also had a private system for many years, see Jacobson, *Ties That Bind*, 48–51.

Chapter Six. The Historical Significance of Houston's Buffalo Bayou

This chapter is based on a July 18, 2005, report commissioned by the National Park Service to help justify Buffalo Bayou as a National Heritage Area. Preparation of this report was conducted with the assistance of Thomas McKinney and Terry Tomkins-Walsh.

1. National Park Service, U.S. Department of the Interior, "National Heritage Areas FAQ," http://www.nps.gov/history/heritageareas/FAQ/INDEX.HTM.

2. As of the book's publication the proposal was before Congress.

3. See Martin V. Melosi, "Houston: Energy Capital," *New Geographies* 2 (2009): 97–102. In May 2010, the Center for Public History at the University of Houston, with funding from the National Science Foundation, sponsored "Energy Capitals: Local Impact, Global Influence." At the meeting historians presented papers on nine other "energy capitals" aside from Houston. They included Stavanger, Norway; Port Gentil, Gabon; Perth, Australia; Tampico, Mexico; Calgary, Canada; Los Angeles, California; Oakridge, Tennessee; Oklahoma City, Oklahoma; and Baton Rouge, Louisiana.

4. Texas State Historical Association, "Buffalo Bayou," *The Handbook of Texas, Online* (December 4, 2002), 1, www.tsha.utexas.edu/handbook/online/articles/view/BB/rhb28.html.

5. James L. Glass, *1836 Sesquicentennial [Galveston] Bay Chart; A Reconstruction Drawing Showing Settlements, Geographic Features and Land Grants to the Earliest Settlers of the Galveston Bay Area*, July 11, 1983, H–1836, Houston Metropolitan Research Center, Houston Public Library, Texas Room, Julia Ideson Building, Houston, Texas.

6. See Louis F. Aulbach and Linda C. Gorski, *Buffalo Bayou: An Echo of Houston's Wilderness Beginnings*, www.hal-pc.org; Marilyn McAdams Sibley, *The Port of Houston: A History* (Austin: University of Texas Press, 1968), 15; Buffalo Bayou Partnership and East End Area Chamber of Commerce, *Houston's Heritage Corridor: Buffalo Bayou East Sector Redevelopment Plan* (Houston: Buffalo Bayou Partnership and East End Area Chamber of Commerce, 1994), 13. See also R. M. Farrar, *The Story of Buffalo Bayou and the Houston Ship Channel* (Houston: Chamber of Commerce, November 1926).

7. David G. McComb, *Houston: A History* (Austin: University of Texas Press, 1981), 11–12; David G. McComb, "Houston, Texas," *The Handbook of Texas, Online* (Texas State Historical Association, December 4, 2002), 1, www.tsha.utexas.edu/handbook/online/articles/view/HH/hdh3.html; Charles E. Closmann, "Buffalo Bayou: Past, Present and Future" (Unpublished paper, Department of History, University of Houston, 1994), 5; Glass, *1836 Sesquicentennial [Galveston] Bay Chart.*

8. D. W. Meinig, *Imperial Texas: An Interpretive Essay in Cultural Geography* (Austin: University of Texas Press, 1969), 59.

9. Sibley, *Port of Houston*, 59.

10. Ibid., 31–34

11. Many of the shallow-draft boats used high-pressure, wood-burning steam engines and employed side paddle wheels that improved maneuverability. See McComb, *Houston: A History*, 34.

12. Sibley, *Port of Houston*, 37.

13. Farrar, *Story of Buffalo Bayou and the Houston Ship Channel*.

14. Ibid., 38.

15. "Allen's Landing, Texas," *Handbook of Texas, Online*, http://www.tshaonline.org/handbook/online.

16. Farrar, *Story of Buffalo Bayou and the Houston Ship Channel*.

17. Sibley, *Port of Houston*, 53, see also 16–17, 21, 32–33; Lynn M. Alperin, *Custodians of the Coast: History of the United States Army Engineers at Galveston* (Galveston: Galveston District, United States Army Corps of Engineers, 1977), 91–93; McComb, "Houston, Texas." See also Richard V. Francaviglia, *From Sail to Steam: Four Centuries of Texas Maritime History, 1500–1900* (Austin: University of Texas Press, 1998), 96–97, 182; Frederick Law Olmsted, *Journey through Texas; or a Saddle-Trip on the Southwestern Frontier* (New York: Mason Brothers, 1860), 361.

18. Hugh Rice's survey made no mention of how far one could freely navigate up Buffalo Bayou. He commented that the average depth was seven and a quarter feet and that the course of the bayou from Harrisburg to Houston was "very circuitous." See Hugh Rice, *Survey of Buffalo Bayou, San Jacinto River, and Galveston Bay from the City of Houston to the Gulf of Mexico* (Houston: Gray, Smallwood & Company, 1867).

19. The city council granted authority to improve the bayou to the Houston Direct Navigation Company on October 9, 1866. This was the first time improving the bayou was mentioned in the city's records. The construction of a ship channel was first mentioned in the city council minutes on April 18, 1867. However, the first state appropriation for improving the bayou came on February 7, 1853; $4,000.00 was given to cut a channel through Clopper's Bar. See Farrar, *Story of Buffalo Bayou and the Houston Ship Channel*; Alperin, *Custodians of the Coast*, 95.

20. Rice, *Survey of Buffalo Bayou*, 53.

21. Robert A. Calvert and Arnoldo DeLeon, *The History of Texas* (Arlington Heights, IL: Harlan Davidson, Inc., 1990), 169; Joseph L. Clark and Elton M. Scott, *The Texas Gulf Coast: Its History and Development*, vol. 2 (New York: Lewis Historical Publishing Co., 1955), 136–38; James P. Baughman, "The Evolution of Rail-Water Systems of Transportation in the Gulf Southwest, 1836–1890," *Journal of Southern History* 34 (August 1968): 357; Sibley, *Port of Houston*, 58–59; McComb, *Houston: A History*, 20.

22. In 1916, Houston had four passenger stations as well as numerous railroad yards and shops. There were no common facilities used by all of the rail lines that serviced the city, so rail activity was decentralized in nature. See City of Houston and the Houston Chamber of Commerce, *City Book of Houston 1916* (Houston: Cumming and Sons, 1916), 7–12; "Buffalo Bayou, Brazos and Colorado Railway," *The Handbook of Texas, Online*, 1–2, www.tsha.utexas.edu/handbook/online/articles/view/BB/eqb16.html; Andrew Forest Muir, "Railroad Enterprise in Texas, 1836–1841," *Southwestern Historical Quarterly* 47 (April 1944): 339–70; Muir, "Railroads Come to Houston, 1857–1861," *Southwestern Historical Quarterly*, 42; Vera L. Dugas, "A Duel with Railroads: Houston vs. Galveston, 1866–1881," *East*

Texas Historical Journal, 118; Calvert and DeLeon, *History of Texas,* 104; Sibley, *Port of Houston,* 72–73; McComb, "Houston, Texas," 3; McComb, *Houston: A History,* 26–31.

23. Melosi, *Coping with Abundance,* 43.

24. Ibid., 43–45. See also John S. Sproat, *The Road to Spindletop: Economic Change in Texas, 1875–1901* (Austin: University of Texas Press, 1955, 1970), 272–76; Beth Anne Shelton, Nestor P. Rodriguez, Joe R. Feagin, Robert D. Bullard, and Robert D. Thomas, *Houston: Growth and Decline in a Sunbelt Boomtown* (Philadelphia: Temple University Press, 1989), 11; James J. Parsons, "Recent Industrial Development in the Gulf South," *Geographical Review* 40 (January 1950): 73; David G. McComb, *Texas: A Modern History* (Austin: University of Texas Press, 1989), 117–19,

25. Melosi, *Coping with Abundance,* 45–46.

26. Alperin, *Custodians of the Coast,* 91.

27. Above Long Reach to Main Street—approximately six and a half miles—the channel after dredging was eight by forty feet in 1908. It was redredged by the city in 1914. That stretch continued to attract light-draft navigation only, although there was considerable local traffic. See Alperin, *Custodians of the Coast,* 113.

28. The turning basin was finished in August 1914 and marked the western terminus of the Houston Ship Channel at that time. The *Merry Mount* left from the wharves at the turning basin, as the draft of the ship was too deep to travel to the upper channel. While the turning basin remained the terminus for larger ships, boats with smaller drafts could still head up the bayou to the "upper channel." These smaller ships ferried cotton and other goods from cotton compresses and warehouses located along the bayou from the turning basin to the foot of Main Street. During the year ending December 31, 1925, 282,536 tons of goods were moved over the upper channel. See City of Houston and the Houston Chamber of Commerce, *City Book of Houston 1916,* 6; Farrar, *Story of Buffalo Bayou and the Houston Ship Channel.*

29. Currently the Port of Houston is made up of the Port of Houston Authority and more than 150 private industrial companies along the ship channel. In 2005, the port was ranked first in the United States in foreign waterborne commerce, second in total tonnage shipped, and sixth overall in the world. See the Port of Houston Authority, www.portofhouston.com.

30. Marilyn M. Sibley, "Houston Ship Channel," *The Handbook of Texas, Online,* 1–3, www.tsha.utexas.edu/handbook/online/articles/view/HH/rhh11.html; Sibley, *Port of Houston,* 102–45; Garvin Berry, "Promoters, Politicians Turned Shallow Bayou into Seaport," *Houston Business Journal* (November 22, 1893); Alperin, *Custodians of the Coast,* 95–101; McComb, *Houston: A History,* 65–68.

31. See Joe Feagin, *Free Enterprise City: Houston in Political-Economic Perspective* (New Brunswick: Rutgers University Press, 1988), 61.

32. R. C. Smead quoted in Alperin, *Custodians of the Coast,* 111.

33. Feagin, *Free Enterprise City,* 52–56.

34. Alperin, *Custodians of the Coast*, 111.

35. Feagin, *Free Enterprise City*, 58. See also Joseph A. Pratt, *The Growth of a Refining Region* (Greenwich: JAI Press, 1980).

36. Quoted in Shelton, Rodriguez, Feagin, Bullard, and Thomas, *Houston: Growth and Decline in a Sunbelt Boomtown*, 15.

37. Ibid., 114.

38. Barry J. Kaplan, "Houston: The Golden Buckle of the Sunbelt," in *Sunbelt Cities: Politics and Growth Since World War II,* ed. Richard M. Bernard and Bradley R. Rice (Austin: University of Texas Press, 1983), 197; Walter L. Buenger and Joseph A. Pratt, *But Also Good Business: Texas Commerce Banks and the Financing of Houston and Texas, 1886–1986* (College Station: Texas A&M University Press, 1986), 73, 109; Walter Rundell Jr., *Early Texas Oil: A Photographic History, 1866–1936* (College Station: Texas A&M University Press, 1977), 136; McComb, *Houston: A History*, 78–79.

39. Pratt, *Growth of a Refining Region,* 3–7.

40. Ibid., 33.

41. The Sinclair Plant was located just outside the Houston City Limits, along the La Porte Road (State Highway 228). The Eastern States plant was also located along the channel. Most of the large refineries were constructed along the channel once the turning basin was finished in 1914, with a few exceptions. The ship channel area was classified as a special tax district by the City of Houston in an effort to encourage industrial development. Thus, many of the refineries located there for the tax advantage.

42. Pratt, *Growth of a Refining Region,* 72–75. See also Feagin, *Free Enterprise City*, 62, 65–66; McComb, *Texas*, 125; Kaplan, "Houston: The Golden Buckle of the Sunbelt," 197; Sibley, *Port of Houston*, 161; Parsons, "Recent Industrial Development in the Gulf South," 74.

43. Pratt, *Growth of a Refining Region*, 105. See also Shelton, Rodriguez, Feagin, Bullard, and Thomas, *Houston: Growth and Decline in a Sunbelt Boomtown*, 16–17; Parsons, "Recent Industrial Development in the Gulf South," 76–77; Randolph B. Campbell, *Gone to Texas: A History of the Lone Star State* (New York: Oxford University Press, 2003), 407–8; Kaplan, "Houston: Golden Buckle of the Sunbelt," 198; McComb, *Texas,* 143; Feagin, *Free Enterprise City*, 66, 71; McComb, *Houston: A History*, 81, 128–29; Clark and Scott, *Texas Gulf Coast*, 234; Warren Rose, *Catalyst of an Economy: The Economic Impact of the Port of Houston, 1958–1963* (Houston: Center for Research in Business and Economics, University of Houston, August 1965), 7.

44. Quoted in James W. Pohl, *The Battle of San Jacinto* (Austin: Texas State Historical Society, 1989), 48.

45. Rupert N. Richardson, Adrian Anderson, Cary D. Wintz, and Ernest Wallace, *Texas: The Lone Star State* (Upper Saddle River, NJ: Prentice Hall, 2001), 122.

46. L. W. Kemp, "Battle of San Jacinto," *The Handbook of Texas, Online*, 1–3, www.tsha.utexas.edu/handbook/online/articles/view/SS/qes4.html. See also Stephen L. Moore, *Eighteen Minutes: The Battle of San Jacinto and the Texas Inde-

pendence Campaign (Dallas: Republic of Texas Press, 2004); Stephen L. Hardin, *Texian Iliad: A Military History of the Texas Revolution* (Austin: University of Texas Press, 1994); Richardson, Anderson, Wintz, and Wallace, *Texas: The Lone Star State,* 120–22; Sibley, *Port of Houston,* 29–30; McComb, *Texas,* 44–46.

47. Doris Estis Knepper, "San Jacinto Monument and Museum," *The Handbook of Texas, Online,* 1–3, www.tsha.utexas.edu/handbook/online/articles/view/SS/lbs1.html; Betty T. Chapman, "USS Texas Rests in Houston as a Reminder of Decades of Service," *Houston Business Journal* (July 12–18, 2002).

48. Francaviglia, *From Sail to Steam,* 205, see also 189–220; Louis F. Aulbach and Linda C. Gorski, "Buffalo Bayou 'Cottonclads' and Dick Dowling's Irish Guards, Houston's Civil War Heroes," *Buffalo Bayou: An Echo of Houston's Wilderness Beginnings,* www.hal-pc.org; Marguerite Johnston, *Houston: The Unknown City, 1836–1946* (College Station: Texas A&M University Press, 1991), 64–66; Edward T. Cotham Jr., *Battle on the Bay: The Civil War Struggle for Galveston* (Austin: University of Texas Press, 1998), 1–6; Ralph A. Wooster, *Texas and Texans in the Civil War* (Austn: Eakin Press, 1995), 63–71.

49. J. G. Randall and David Donald, *The Civil War and Reconstruction* (Lexington, MA: D.C. Heath and Co., 1969), 406.

50. See Robert V. Haynes, "Houston Riot of 1917," *The Handbook of Texas, Online,* 1–2, www.tsha.utexas.edu/handbook/online/articles/view/HH/jch4.html; Haynes, *A Night of Violence: The Houston Riot of 1917* (Baton Rouge: Louisiana State University Press, 1976).

51. Norman H. Beard, ed., *The Municipal Book of the City of Houston, 1922* (Houston: The City of Houston, 1922), 110.

52. Melosi, *Sanitary City,* 172, 249, 253–54; Debbie Winikates, "A History of Houston Bayou Technology," in Stephen Cruse, Michael Moore, Mark Rothfeld, and Debbie Winikates, *Willow Street Pumping Station Preservation Project* (Houston: Institute for Public History, Spring 1993), 1–1, 1–2, 1–8, 1–9, 1–24.

Chapter Seven. Houston's Public Sinks:
Water and Wastewater Services—Local Concerns to Regional Challenges

The original version of this chapter appeared in Martin V. Melosi and Joseph A. Pratt, eds., *Energy Metropolis: An Environmental History of Houston and the Gulf Coast* (Pittsburgh: University of Pittsburgh Press, 2007), 109–47. Material on Houston's sanitary services prior to 1945 was drawn from Martin V. Melosi, "Sanitary Services and Decision-Making in Houston, 1876–1945," *Journal of Urban History* 20 (May 1994): 365–406. I also would like to acknowledge Tom McKinney for gathering important data for the post-1945 sections of the chapter.

1. Feagin's *Free Enterprise City* best embodies this interpretation of Houston.

2. See Melosi, *Sanitary City,* 74, 117–48. For Galveston's water supply system, see Janice Ranee Clark, "Fresh Water for Galveston: The Development of a Supply System from the Texas Mainland" (MA thesis, University of Houston, 2000).

3. Bud A. Randolph, "The History of Houston's Water Supply," *Texas Commercial News* (June 1927): 43.

4. Planning and Development Department, *Public Utilities Profile for Houston, Texas* (Summer 1994), III–15.

5. Charles D. Green, *Fire Fighters of Houston, 1838–1915* (Houston: Dealy-Adey Co., printers, 1915), 13, 21; Houston Fire Museum, Inc., *The History of the Houston Fire Department, 1838–1988,* text by Thomas A. McDonald and F. Scott Mellott (Houston: Taylor Publishing Co., 1988), 8; H. H. Page, comp., *Houston and Harris County Facts* (Houston: Facts Publishing Co.,1939), 98.

6. "First Survey of Houston's Water Supply Was Prompted by 1869 Yellow Fever Epidemic," *Houston Chronicle* (October 26, 1933); Page, *Houston and Harris County Facts,* 98.

7. Harold L. Platt, *City Building in the New South: The Growth of Public Services in Houston, Texas, 1830–1910* (Philadelphia: Temple University Press, 1983), 67.

8. T. Lindsay Baker, "Houston Waterworks: Its Early Development," *Southwest Water Works Journal* 56 (July 1974), 37; Andrew Morrison, *The City of Houston* (St. Louis: Englehardt, 1891), 15–17; City of Houston, Water Department, *Report of Director for Year 1942,* 2; "History of the Houston Water System," in City of Houston, Department of Utilities, *Water Service in Houston,* prep. by Edna D. Wood (October 1953), 19; Platt, *City Building in the New South,* 67; David McComb, *Houston: A History,* 87–89.

9. "History of the Houston Water System," 19; Green, *Fire Fighters of Houston,* 126.

10. See Morrison, *City of Houston,* 16; Platt, *City Building in the New South,* 67; Randolph, "The History of Houston's Water Supply," 43; Houston Fire Museum, *Houston Fire Department,* 13; McComb, *Houston: A History,* 88–89.

11. Ibid., 89.

12. *Directory of the City of Houston, 1890–91,* 5.

13. "History of the Houston Water System," 19; Water Department, *Report of Director for Year 1942,* 3; City of Houston, *Public Water Supply System* (January 1948), 2; Baker, "Houston Waterworks," 37; Platt, *City Building in the New South,* 197–99.

14. See Houston, "City Council Minutes," Book M, June 16, 1902, 52–57; January 12, 1903, 336–37; Book N, April 5, 1904, 426–27; April 25, 1904, 458, 462–63; May 23, 1904, 537; April 17, 1905, 372–73; "Report of Chief of Fire Department," City of Houston, *Annual Report, 1903,* 105; Green, *Fire Fighters of Houston,* 126.

15. The trend toward municipal ownership was well underway in the United States in the 1870s; by 1899, 205 waterworks changed from private to public systems. See Anderson, "Diffusion of Technology," 104, 106; Tarr, "Evolution of the Urban Infrastructure," 30–31; B. M. Wagner, "The Acquisition of Private Water Plants by Municipalities," *Journal of the American Water Works Association* 2 (March 1915): 25–41.

16. "Mayor's Message," City of Houston, *Annual Report, 1905,* 8–9.

17. Quoted in Water Department, *Report of Director for Year 1942,* 6.

18. "Report of Water, Light and Health Committee," City of Houston, *Annual*

Report, 1908, 23; "Water Supply and Works," *Progressive Houston* 1 (August 1909): 1.

19. See "Report of Water Committee," City of Houston, *Annual Report, 1912,* 24.

20. Houston Fire Museum, Inc., *Houston Fire Department,* 28; Green, *Fire Fighters of Houston,* 127.

21. City of Houston, *Public Water Supply System,* 4.

22. G. L. Fugate, "Development of Houston's Water Supply," *Journal of the American Water Works Association* 33 (October 1941): 1768–69.

23. "Report of Water Committee," City of Houston, *Annual Report, 1909,* 24.

24. See Melosi, *Sanitary City,* 123–26.

25. City of Houston, Department of Utilities, *Water Service in Houston,* 20; Water Department, *Report of Director for Year 1942,* 7–8; "Report of Water Committee," City of Houston, *Annual Report, 1909,* 25–31; "Report of Water Committee," City of Houston, *Annual Report, 1910,* 19, 22; "Report of Water Committee," City of Houston, *Annual Report, 1912,* 18–21, 23; *Progressive Houston* 4 (June 1912).

26. "Report of Water Commissioner," *City Book of Houston, 1914,* 106; "Mayor's Message," City of Houston, *Annual Report, 1905,* 80–81; *City Book of Houston, 1925,* 41; Randolph, "The History of Houston's Water Supply," 122.

27. In 1900, the incorporated area covered nine square miles; in 1937, seventy-three square miles. By the 1940s, the Houston public water supply consisted of six interconnected water systems, each having its own wells and storage reservoirs, supplying a particular portion of the distribution network. See Clyde R. Harvill, et al., "Maintenance of Chlorine Residual in the Distribution System," *Journal of the American Water Works Association* 34 (December 1942): 1797–98.

28. The decision grew out of the Allred case. James V. Allred, Texas attorney general, refused to approve a 1933 bond issue passed by the Houston City Council because he believed it violated state law and a bond agreement entered into by the city in 1926. The city brought suit against the attorney general to compel him to approve the bonds, but the Supreme Court sided with Allred. See also Clyde R. Harvill, "The Houston Water System," *Southwest Water Works Journal* (October 1935): 20–21; City of Houston, Department of Utilities, *Water Service in Houston,* 20; Water Department, *Report of Director for 1942,* 9–10.

29. City of Houston, Department of Utilities, *Water Service in Houston,* 21. See also Page, *Houston and Harris County Facts,* 99. Regular chlorination of the water supply began in 1929; chloramination was instituted in 1933.

30. Fugate, "Development of Houston's Water Supply," 1770–71.

31. The National Board of Fire Underwriters supported continuation of ground-water withdrawal, but its report stressed the "very poor" quality of the overall water system because of inadequate fire protection capability and deficiency in mains and fire hydrants in many large residential areas. See "Spending $4,000,000 to $6,000,000 on Water System Urged," *Houston Chronicle,* September 2, 1937.

32. Ibid., 1772–74; "Water Supply for City Said to Be Ample," *Houston Chronicle,* October 17, 1932; George B. Waters, "Controversy Over River Water and Well Supply Rages," *Houston Press,* June 8, 1938; "City Urged to Tap San Jacinto to

Insure Adequate Water Supply," *Houston* (March 22, 1938), 1; Committee Report to Houston Water Board, September 12, 1938.

33. Alvord, Burdick, and Howson, "Report on an Adequate Water Supply for the City of Houston, Texas" (Chicago, February 1938), 1–3, 75–76.

34. "New Plan for Water Supply to Be Offered," *Houston Chronicle*, February 3, 1939. See also Fugate, "Development of Houston's Water Supply," 1175–78.

35. J. M. Nagle, "Houston Gets Needed Water," *American City* 60 (February 1945): 77.

36. The district was created by the legislature in 1937 and empowered to develop the San Jacinto watershed and its tributaries under supervision of the Texas Board of Water Engineers. Harris County, in which most of Houston was located, was omitted from the district because of possible conflicts with the authority of the Harris County Flood Control District. See William W. McClendon, "The San Jacinto River Conservation and Reclamation District's Proposed Plan of Full Scale Development," *Slide Rule* (March 1945): 11; Water Department, *Report of Director for Year 1942*, 12–16; "Water Supply Dam to Be Built on San Jacinto," *Houston Post* July 14, 1942; City of Houston, Utilities Department, *Engineering Report for Water Works Improvements*, January 17, 1944. The war years also exposed weaknesses in the existing water supply system, and the growing population made effective service for "fringe populations" more difficult. See Water Department, *Report of Director for Year 1942*, 26–27.

37. Lake Houston, the site of the dam, is a reservoir on the San Jacinto River located twenty-five miles east-northeast of downtown Houston. Water Department, *Report of Director for Year 1942*, 16; McComb, *Houston: A History*, 146; Nagle, "Houston Gets Needed Water," 77; "Houston's Greater Water Supply Near," *Houston* 23 (August 1952): 8–9; "Its First Water Filter Plant," *American City* 67 (March 1952): 102; Water Supply and Conservation Committee, Houston Chamber of Commerce, *Water for the Houston Area* (Houston: Houston Chamber of Commerce, December 1954), 3; U.S. Department of the Interior, U.S. Geological Survey, "Characteristics of Water-Quality Data for Lake Houston, Selected Tributary Inflows to Lake Houston, and the Trinity River Near Lake Houston, August 1983–September 1990," *Water-Resources Investigations Report 99-4129* (1999), 2, 4; "'Water ... Water ... Everywhere!'" *Houston* 37 (May 1966): 75.

38. Melosi, *Sanitary City*, 90–99; Joel A. Tarr, "Sewerage and the Development of the Networked City in the United States, 1850–1930," in *Technology and the Rise of the Networked City in Europe and America,* ed. Joel A. Tarr and Gabriel Dupuy (Philadelphia: Temple University Press, 1988), 159–66.

39. Platt, *City Building in the New South*, 40.

40. Harris County Flood Control District, "Harris County's Flooding History," http//www.hcfcd.org/hcfloodhistory.html.

41. Ibid. See also "History: Houston and Brays Bayou" and "History: Flooding and Flood Policies," Rice University/Texas Medical Center, Brays Bayou Flood ALERT System, January 12, 2006 and http//www.floodalert.org/BraysFAS/index.php?sPageID=History&sRadar=KHGX.

42. Elisabeth O'Kane, "'To Lift the City Out of the Mud': Health, Sanitation and Sewerage in Houston, 1840–1920," (Paper read at the American Society for Environmental History Conference, Houston, 1991), 5–9; Platt, *City Building in the New South*, 40; "Report of the City Engineer," City of Houston, *Annual Report, 1902*, 40.

43. McComb, *Houston: A History*, 89.

44. See O'Kane, "'To Lift the City out of the Mud'," 11–13; McComb, *Houston: A History*, 89.

45. Joel A. Tarr, "The Separate vs. Combined Sewer Problem: A Case Study in Urban Technology Design Choice," *Journal of Urban History* 5 (May 1979): 308–12, 317–30; Melosi, *Sanitary City*, 153–61.

46. *Directory of the City of Houston, 1892–93*, 7; O'Kane, "'To Lift the City Out of the Mud,'" 15–18.

47. Cost savings often was a consideration of the city council. See, for example, Houston, "City Council Minutes," Book J, November 9, 1896, 164.

48. An evaluation of the work to be done in several sewer districts indicated little uniformity. The 1902 *Annual Report*, 52, showed the following distribution of sewer lines in the city:

First Ward (northwest of downtown): Sanitary, 9,750 linear feet
Second Ward (east of downtown): Sanitary, 15,300; Combined, 4,000; Storm, 5,100
Third Ward (downtown): Sanitary, 77,600; Combined, 1,734; Storm, 12,500
Fourth Ward (west of downtown): Sanitary, 35,100; Storm, 3,400
Fifth Ward (north of downtown): Storm, 16,200; Force Main, 9,500
Sixth Ward (west of downtown): Sanitary, 2,000; Combined, 5,000

49. Houston, "City Council Minutes," Book N, September 14, 1903, 101–2.

50. *Directory of the City of Houston, 1912*, 3; City of Houston, *First Annual Report of the City Engineer on Sewage Disposal* (February 1, 1916), 11–12; "Report of the City Engineer," City of Houston, *Annual Report, 1902*, 38–43; "Mayor's Message," City of Houston, *Annual Report, 1904*, 11; "Report of the City Engineer," City of Houston, *Annual Report, 1904*, 76; "Report of Sewer Inspector," City of Houston, *Annual Report, 1904*, 90–91; "Report of the Water, Light, and Health Committee," City of Houston, *Annual Report, 1905*, 24–25; "Report of the Water, Light, and Health Committee," City of Houston, *Annual Report, 1906*, 22–23; "Report of the City Sewer Inspector," City of Houston, *Annual Report, 1906*, 127; "Report of City Engineer," City of Houston, *Annual Report, 1908*, 73; "Engineering Department," *Municipal Book of the City of Houston, 1922*, 109.

51. "Report of City Engineer," City of Houston, *Annual Report, 1902*, 40–41; "Report of City Engineer," City of Houston, *Annual Report, 1909*, 110; "Report of Consulting Engineer," City of Houston, *Annual Report, 1909*, 135; "The Austin Street Reinforced Concrete Sewer," *Progressive Houston* 1 (December 1909); "Austin Street Sewer," *Progressive Houston* 1 (May 1909).

52. McComb, *Houston: A History*, 89–91; O'Kane, "'To Lift the City Out of the Mud,'" 18–26.

53. See Tarr, "Sewerage and the Development of the Networked City in the United States," 169–70.

54. The Willow Street Pump Station, completed in 1902, was the first lift station in Houston. See Mark Rothfeld, "History of the Willow Street Pump Station," in *Willow Street Pumping Station Preservation Project Report,* Stephen Cruse, Michael Moore, Mark Rothfeld, Debbie Winikates (Unpublished report, Institute for Public History, University of Houston, 1993), III–3–III–4; G. L. Fugate, *Division of Sewage Pumping and Disposal Plants: Report of Operation to December, 1923* (Houston: City of Houston, Texas, Engineering Department, Division of Sewage, 1924), 7–9.

55. McComb, *Houston: A History,* 89–91; "Engineering Department," *Municipal Book of the City of Houston, 1922,* 110; "Engineering Department," City of Houston, *Annual Report, February 28, 1915,* 14.

56. "The Houston Sewerage Program," *American City* 62 (February 1947): 90.

57. E. E. Rosaire, "Engineer's Council Raps at City Water Pollution," *Slide Rule* (February 1947), 8; Houston Chamber of Commerce and Gordon H. Turrentine, *Clean Air and Water—A Trust: A Review of Houston Chamber of Commerce Efforts in Behalf of Effective Abatement of Pollution, 1941–1972* (1972), 1–3, 6–8, 10, 15.

58. Martin V. Melosi, "Community and the Growth of Houston," in *Effluent America: Cities, Industry, Energy, and the Environment* (Pittsburgh: University of Pittsburgh Press, 2001), 193–95.

59. Water Supply and Conservation Committee, Houston Chamber of Commerce, *Water for the Houston Area, I–II.*

60. A survey indicated that seventeen of thirty-four private water systems within the city had been connected to the Houston system by the end of 1950. Four separate systems also were purchased from the Texas Water Company. See Department of Utilities, City of Houston, *Consolidated Progress Report of the Department of Utilities* (1950), 32.

61. Metropolitan Harris County, *A Report of the Harris Home Rule Commission* (1957), 59–60; Regional Service Systems Task Force, Water Supply System Task Group, Houston Chamber of Commerce, *A Water Supply System Plan for the Greater Houston Region* (October 1983), 2; Metropolitan Water Systems, Division of Public Works, *City of Houston, Texas, Resume* (1979), 1.

62. The project on the San Jacinto called for half of the supply reserved for municipal use and half allocated to industries. The total yield of water was approximately 150 million gallons per day. See Water Supply and Conservation Committee, Houston Chamber of Commerce, *Water for the Houston Area,* 4.

63. Turner, Collie & Braden, Inc., Consulting Engineers, for the City of Houston, Department of Public Works, Water Division, *Fifth Quadrennial Engineering Report on Physical Condition and Adequacy of the Water System* (November 1970), 6; Metropolitan Water Systems, Division of Public Works, *City of Houston, Texas, Resume,* 3; "Welcome to Lake Houston" (no date), 2; City of Houston, Texas, *Public Water Supply System* (January 1948), 17; Water Supply and Conservation Com-

mittee, Houston Chamber of Commerce, *Water for the Houston Area*, 3; Nagle, "Houston Gets Needed Water," 77.

64. The Coastal Industrial Water Authority Conveyance System consists of a pumping station on the Trinity River about seven miles downstream from Liberty, Texas, in the headwaters of the Wallisville Reservoir; a canal system terminating at a point north of the Houston Ship Channel at Lynchburg; and a distribution system to the industrial area along the ship channel. See Metropolitan Water Systems, Division of Public Works, *City of Houston, Texas, Resume*, 9.

65. "Water . . . Water . . . Everywhere!" *Houston* 37 (May 1966): 75; Coastal Industrial Water Authority, *The CIWA Waterway: Houston's New River* (no date); Alison Hart Hill, "Water Supply in Houston," (University of Houston, unpublished paper, 1993), 9–10; "What Is Houston's Real Water Picture?" *Houston* 28 (April 1957): 27; "Ground Water . . . A Rich Resource," *Houston* 32 (September 1961): 15; Regional Service Systems Task Force, Water Supply System Task Group, Houston Chamber of Commerce, *A Water Supply System Plan for the Greater Houston Region*, 1, 5; U.S. Department of the Interior, U.S. Geological Survey, "Characteristics of Water-Quality Data for Lake Houston, Selected Tributary Inflows to Lake Houston, and the Trinity River Near Lake Houston, August 1983– September 1990," 2–3.

66. City of Houston, Texas, *Public Water Supply System* (January 1948), 9; Turner, Collie & Braden, Inc., Consulting Engineers, for the City of Houston, Department of Public Works, Water Division, *Fourth Quadrennial Engineering Report on Physical Condition and Adequacy of the Water System* (April 1966), 2–3.

67. Metropolitan Harris County, *A Report of the Harris Home Rule Commission* (1957), 55.

68. Turner, Collie & Braden, Inc., Consulting Engineers, for the City of Houston, Department of Public Works, Water Division, *Fourth Quadrennial Engineering Report on Physical Condition and Adequacy of the Water System* (April 1966), 9.

69. Virginia Marion Perrenod, *Special Districts, Special Purposes: Fringe Governments and Urban Problems in the Houston Area* (College Station: Texas A&M University Press, 1984), 14–34.

70. Metropolitan Harris County, *A Report of the Harris Home Rule Commission* (1957), 57, 59, 62; Tax Research Association, *Water Districts in Harris County: A Survey of Water District Finances* (February 1969); Metropolitan Water Systems, Division of Public Works, *City of Houston, Texas, Resume* (1979), 11; Turner, Collie & Braden, Inc., Consulting Engineers, for the City of Houston, Department of Public Works, Water Division, *Fourth Quadrennial Engineering Report on Physical Condition and Adequacy of the Water System* (April 1966), 7, 24–26; Tax Research Association, *Water Districts in Harris County: A Survey of Water District Finances* (Houston: Tax Research Association, February 1969), 4, 6–7, 9–11.

71. City of Houston, Water Department, *Report of Director for Year 1942*, 26–27; J. M. Nagle, "Houston Gets Needed Water," *American City* 60 (February 1945),

77; Water Supply and Conservation Committee, Houston Chamber of Commerce, *Water for the Houston Area* (December 1954), I–II, 9.

72. See Regional Service Systems Task Force, Water Supply System Task Group, Houston Chamber of Commerce, *A Water Supply System Plan for the Greater Houston Region* (October 1983), 3; "Houston," in *Twentieth Century Cities*, 121–24; W. H. Gaines, A. G. Winslow, and J. R. Barnes, *Water Supply of the Gulf Coast Region*, Bulletin 5101 (Washington, D.C.: Geological Survey, U.S. Department of the Interior, January 1951), 5; Water Supply and Conservation Committee, Houston Chamber of Commerce, *Water for the Houston Area* (December 1954), 6–8; Water Supply and Conservation Committee, Ground Water Division, Houston Chamber of Commerce, *Ground Water Resources of the Metropolitan Houston Area* (June 1961), 16–17; "Water for Houston: Blessing and Challenge," *Houston* (May 1968): 81–82; Metropolitan Water Systems, Division of Public Works, *City of Houston, Texas, Resume* (1979), 4; Citizen's Environmental Coalition, *2004 Environmental Resource Guide*, 19; Harris-Galveston Coastal Subsidence District, *Subsidence '81*, 1–2, 7, 10–11; Perrenod, *Special Districts, Special Purposes*, 87–98.

73. U.S. Department of the Interior, U.S. Geological Survey, "Characteristics of Water-Quality Data for Lake Houston, Selected Tributary Inflows to Lake Houston, and the Trinity River near Lake Houston," *Water-Resources Investigations Report 99-4129* (August 1983–September 1990), 2; Regional Service Systems Task Force, Water Supply System Task Group, Houston Chamber of Commerce, *Final Review Draft: Water Supply System Plan for the Greater Houston Region* (October 1983), I, 2, 6–7; Planning & Development Department, *Public Utilities Profile for Houston, Texas* (Summer 1994), III–5, III–16, III–20.

74. Ken Kramer, "Water," in *Houston 2001: A Livable City?* (Houston: Institute of Labor and Industrial Relations, University of Houston, 1977), 71–72, 75, 79.

75. Citizens' Environmental Coalition, *2004 Environmental Resource Guide* (Houston: Citizens' Environmental Coalition, 2004), 19. For documentation on some early pollution-control efforts, see City of Houston, Texas, *Public Water Supply System* (January 1948), 13–14; City of Houston, Department of Utilities, *Consolidated Progress Report of the Department of Utilities* (1950), 21; City of Houston, Surface Water Supply Department, *1962 Annual Report*, 4.

76. Bonnie B. Pendergrass, "Water for Houston: The Wallisville Case," (Unpublished paper funded by the Galveston District of the U S. Army Corps of Engineers, 1987), 1–2; Robert J. Dacey, *Record of Decision for Wallisville Lake, Texas* (February 25, 1984), 1.

77. Frank Fuller, prep., *Subsidized Destruction: The Wallisville Lake Project and Galveston Bay* (Austin: Texas Center for Policy Studies, October 1995), i.

78. Pendergrass, "Water for Houston," 1–2.

79. Robert W. McFarlane, "Wallisville Dam—The Persistent Folly," (no date), 1; Gary Cartwright, "Holy Trinity," *Texas Monthly* (October 2003), www.texasmonthly.com; Fuller, *Subsidized Destruction*, i–iv.

80. Pendergrass, "Water for Houston," 1.

81. Ibid., 2–4; Dacey, *Record of Decision for Wallisville Lake, Texas*, 1.

82. Pendergrass, "Water for Houston," 4.

83. Ibid., 5; Colonel John A. Tudela, *Wallisville Lake—Abstract* (Galveston: U.S. Army Corps of Engineers, Galveston District, 1987).

84. Planning and Development Department, *Public Utilities Profile for Houston, Texas*, III–26–III–27; "TRA Makes First Payment on Wallisville Saltwater Barrier Project," *Intra: Newsletter of the Trinity River Authority of Texas* (December 2003/ January 2004): 1, 7; Bill Dawson, "Federal Funds Soon Available for Reservoir, *Houston Chronicle*, November 15, 1989; Harold Scarlett, "Panel's Vote Appears to Be Setback for Wallisville Reservoir," *Houston Post*, February 3, 1989.

85. "TRA Makes First Payment on Wallisville Saltwater Barrier Project," 1; Dr. B. C. Robison, "Wallisville: The Scam Lives On," *Houston Post*, May 23, 1987; Robison, "Wallisville Dam: A Scandal in Disguise," *Houston Post*, October 19, 1986.

86. See Planning and Development Department, *Public Utilities Profile for Houston, Texas* (Summer 1994), V–5–V–6.

87. Rainfall and flood-flow data began as early as 1936 at Buffalo, Brays, and White Oak Bayous. David E. Winslow, "Flood Control in Houston: A Historical Perspective," *LJA Insight* 7 (Summer 2002), online, www.ljaengineering.com; "History: Flooding and Flood Policies"; "Harris County's Flooding History."

88. See Planning & Development Department, *Public Utilities Profile for Houston, Texas* (Summer 1994), V–3; "History: Flooding and Flood Policies."

89. "History: Flood Policies and Sources; Flood Policy 1980 to Present."

90. In this instance more than 65 percent of the areas flooded from Allison were outside the hundred-year floodplain—an area with a one percent chance of being flooded in any given year, which obviously broke all the rules of a more typical flood event. See Tropical Storm Allison Recovery Project, *Off the Charts: Tropical Storm Allison Public Report* (Federal Emergency Management Agency and Harris County Flood Control District, June 2002), 1, 4, 8, 10; "Harris County's Flood History."

91. Tropical Storm Allison Recovery Project, *Off the Charts*, 1, 4, 8, 10; "Harris County's Flood History."

92. Planning and Development Department, *Public Utilities Profile for Houston, Texas* (Summer 1994), V–3, V–8, V–10. On flooding, also see Regional Service Systems Task Force, Drainage and Flood Control Task Group, Houston Chamber of Commerce, *Final Review Draft: Drainage and Flood Control System Plan for the Greater Houston Region* (August 1983), 1, 5.

93. Regional Service Systems Task Force, Drainage and Flood Control Task Group, Houston Chamber of Commerce, *Final Review Draft: Wastewater Treatment System Plan for the Greater Houston Area* (August 1983), 12. See also 1, 3.

94. "The Houston Sewage Program," *American City* 62 (February 1947): 90–91.

95. The reality was that Houston often annexed areas where the treatment system had aged to the point where the city had to invest heavily to replace or

improve the system. See Regional Service Systems Task Force, Drainage and Flood Control Task Group, Houston Chamber of Commerce, *Final Review Draft*, 12.

96. Roger Moehlman, Phillip W. Young, and Meryl L. Olson, *County-Wide Planning for Sewage Treatment* (Reprinted from *Public Works Magazine* for June 1957), 1.

97. Metropolitan Harris County, *A Report of the Harris Home Rule Commission* (1957), 65–66; Moehlman, Young, and Olson, *County-Wide Planning for Sewage Treatment*, 1–3.

98. Moehlman, Young, and Olson, *County-Wide Planning for Sewage Treatment*, 5.

99. U.S. Environmental Protection Agency, *Draft Environmental Impact Statement for District 47 Regional Wastewater Facilities, City of Houston* (Dallas: Office of Grants Coordination, Region VI, Environmental Protection Agency, October 1974), 5–8. See also Houston-Galveston Area Council, *Gulf Coast State Planning Region Waste Treatment Management Study, Appendix II* (May 1975); Harold Scarlett, "Sewage Woes," *Houston Post*, October 29, 1972; Scarlett, "Sewage Solutions Expensive," *Houston Post*, September 23, 1974, City of Houston, Planning Department, *Sewer Plant/Population Study* (November 1975), 20.

100. Regional Service System Task Force, Wastewater Treatment System Task Group, Houston Chamber of Commerce, *Final Review Draft: Waste Water Treatment System Plan for the Greater Houston Area* (August 1983), 18; Niall Q. Washburn, "Houston Sewers and Storm Drains: Looking for Service Equity at Both Ends of the Pipe" (Unpublished paper, May 5, 1991), 19; Thomas Beck, "Preservation of the Buffalo: Modern Wastewater Treatment in Houston" (Unpublished paper, December 10, 1990), 2.

101. Houston-Galveston Area Council, *Gulf Coast State Planning Region, Executive Summary, Areawide Waste Treatment Management Study* (May 1975), 31–32.

102. Turner Collie & Braden, Inc., *A Regional Wastewater Facility Plan for the City of Houston Extraterritorial Jurisdiction, Draft Report* (July 1989), I–1–I–3. See also Texas Department of Water Resources, *Water Planning Information: Southeast Texas and Upper Gulf Coast region with State Summary Data* (Austin: Texas Department of Water Resources, June 1983). In 1983, an enormous sewage treatment plant was completed to relieve overloads at the Northside Plant. The Sixty-Ninth Street Wastewater Treatment Plant, which serves the central business district and major shopping centers and industrial and commercial districts to the north, had a capacity of 200 million gallons of wastewater in the 1990s. A principal element of an extensive capital improvement campaign, the complex was meant to double the city's sewage treatment capabilities. See "69th St. Wastewater Treatment Plant," www.hal-pc.org/~dphan/69.html; Washburn, "Houston Sewers and Storm Drains: Looking for Service Equity at Both Ends of the Pipe," 12, 15.

103. Planning and Development Department, *Public Utilities Profile for Houston, Texas* (Summer 1994), IV–3.

104. Ibid., IV–3, IV–10.

105. City of Houston, Public Works Department, *Draft Final Report* (June 13, 1991).

106. In addition, the growing city had to contend with larger amounts of sedimentation, tank sludge, and excess amounts of activated sludge from two large treatment plants.

107. Houston dried raw activated sludge was sold under the registered name— Hou-Actinite. See J. G. Turney, Samuel A. Greeley, and Paul E. Langdon, "Houston Sludge Disposal Plant Profits from Use of Existing Facilities," *Civil Engineering* 21 (May 1951): 26–29; W.E. White, "From Sewage Sludge Houston Produces Marketable Fertilizer," *Texas Municipalities* 8 (March 1961): 12–14; "Houston Sewerage Program," *American City* 62 (February 1947): 90–91; "City to Receive Federal Grant for Sludge Disposal Facility," *Houston Chronicle*, August 24, 1974.

108. Dr. E. E. Rosaire, "Engineer's Council Raps at City Water Pollution," *Slide Rule* (February 1947): 8.

109. "The Pollution Problem," *Houston Chronicle*, June 28, 1948, Section A, 12; "City Attacks Sewer Stink, But Slowly," *Houston Chronicle*, February 1, 1952, A1.

110. Gordon H. Turrentine, *Clean Air and Water—A Trust; A Review of Houston Chamber of Commerce Efforts in Behalf of Effective Abatement of Pollution, 1941–1972* (Houston: Houston Chamber of Commerce, 1972), 1a.

111. Ibid., 2–3, 6–8, 12–16, 35.

112. Arthur Hill, "Cleanup Proposal for Ship Channel Hits Resistance," *Houston Chronicle*, August 13, 1974, Section 1,1; Tom Kennedy, "Court Orders City to Act 'Without Delay' on Sewage Problem," *Houston Post*, August 21, 1974, A4.

113. Planning and Development Department, *Public Utilities Profile for Houston, Texas* (Summer 1994), IV–10.

114. Jim Morris, "'Benign Neglect' Begets City Filth," *Houston Chronicle*, June 9, 1991, 1C, 3C.

115. Planning and Development Department, *Public Utilities Profile for Houston, Texas* (Summer 1994), IV–10; Bob Burtman, "Below Standards," *Houston Press*, April 2–8, 1998, 7.

116. Rachel Graves, "In Need of Repairs: Public Works Has a Flood of Controversy in Recent Years," *Houston Chronicle*, July 8, 2001, 1A. See also Matt Schwartz, "Public Work Faces Big Woes in Big City," *Houston Chronicle*, July 9, 2001, 1A.

Chapter Eight. Privatization of Water: U.S. and Worldwide Implications

This chapter is adapted from a keynote address, "Privatization of Water: The Worldwide Implications" at the Fifth International Water History Association Conference in Tampere, Finland, Summer 2007; and "Full Circle? Public Responsibility versus Privatization of Water Supplies in the United States," in *Pragmatic Sustainability: Theoretical and Practical Tools,* ed. Steven A. Moore (London: Routledge, 2010), 215–26.

1. John M. Swomley, "When Blue Becomes Gold," *Humanist* 60 (Sept.–Oct. 2000), 6; Maria Alicia Gaura, "Water a Hot Commodity," *San Francisco Chronicle* (December 1, 2002), A3; Peter H. Gleick, "The Big Idea Water, Water-Where?" *Boston Globe* (January 6, 2002), E8.

2. This can be NGOs as well as community organizations but mostly private businesses. See David A. McDonald and Greg Ruiters, *The Age of Commodity: Water Privatization in Southern Africa* (London: Earthscan, 2005), 2.

3. Ibid.

4. Swomley, "When Blue Becomes Gold," 5.

5. Maude Barlow and Tony Clarke, "Who Owns Water?" *Nation* 275 (September 2, 2002), 11.

6. J. R. McNeill, *Something New Under the Sun*, 120–22. See also Joachim Radkau, *Nature and Power: A Global History of the Environment* (Cambridge: Cambridge University Press, 2008), 88.

7. Erik Swyngedouw, *Social Power and the Urbanization of Water* (Oxford: Oxford University Press, 2004), 8.

8. Constance Elizabeth Hunt, *Thirsty Planet: Strategies for Sustainable Water Management* (London: Zed Books, 2004), 48–49.

9. Peter H. Gleick, *The World's Water, 2006–2007: The Biennial Report on Freshwater Resources* (Washington, D.C.: Island Press, 2006), 247–55.

10. Hunt, *Thirsty Planet*, 288.

11. Swyngedouw, *Social Power and the Urbanization of Water*, 60.

12. Meena Palaniappan, Emily Lee, and Andrea Samulon, "Environmental Justice and Water," in *World's Water, 2006–2007*, ed. Gleick, 117.

13. On the relatively recent claim about the commodification of water, see Peter Gleick, et al., *Executive Overview, The New Economy of Water: The Risks and Benefits of Globalization and Privatization of Fresh Water*, www.pacinst.org/reports/new_economy_overview.htm, May 4, 2004. Ken Conca in *Governing Water: Contentious Transnational Politics and Global Institution Building* (Cambridge: MIT Press, 2006), 215, uses the term *water marketization* to refer to "the process of creating the economic and policy infrastructure for treating water as a marketed commodity."

14. United Nations, "International Year of Freshwater 2003," http://www.un.org/events/water/TheRighttoWater.pdf. See also Anthony Lenze, "Liquid Assets," *Pittsburgh Post-Gazette* (September 16, 2003), C–12; Kim Krisberg, "Privatizing Water Systems Draws Mixed Reviews," *Nation's Health* 33 (March 2003): 15.

15. Barlow and Clarke, "Who Owns Water?"13–14; Brad Knickerbocker, "Privatizing Water: A Glass Half Empty?" *Christian Science Monitor* (October 24, 2002), 1; Philip Lee, "The Wellspring of Life, or Just a Commodity," *Ottawa Citizen* (August 16, 2001), A1; Gleick, et al., *Executive Overview: The New Economy of Water*, 5; Swyngedouw, *Social Power and the Urbanization of Water*, 41; Peter H. Gleick, *The World's Water, 2004–2005: The Biennial Report on Freshwater*

Resources (Washington, D.C.: Island Press, 2004), 45; Zachary A. Smith and Grenetta Thomassey, *Freshwater Issues: A Reference Handbook* (Santa Barbara: ABC Clio, 2002), 30.

16. See "Environmental Justice, Political Agenda Setting, and the Myths of History," in *Effluent America,* ed. Melosi, 238–62, 307–13.

17. See Franz Chávez, "Cochabamba's 'Water War', Six Years On," *IPS* (June 22, 2010), http://ipsnews.net/news.asp?idnews=35418.

18. See "Bechtel's Dry Run—Iraqis Suffer Water Crisis," April 17, 2003, http://www.citizen.org/documents/bechteliniraq.pdf.

19. See Tom Lynch, "Toward a Symbiosis of Ecology and Justice," in *The Environmental Justice Reader: Politics, Poetics & Pedagogy,* ed. Joni Adamson, Mei Mei Evans, and Rachel Stein (Tucson: University of Arizona Press, 2002), 247.

20. Nancy J. Jacobs, *Environment, Power, and Injustice: A South African History* (Cambridge, MA: Cambridge University Press, 203), 148.

21. Ibid. For another good example of issues related to water and political power, see Jose Esteban Castro, *Water, Power, and Citizenship: Social Struggle in the Basin of Mexico* (Oxford: Palgrave, 2006).

22. See Sara Grunsky, "Privatization Tidal Wave," *Multinational Monitor* 22 (September 2001): 17–18; Curtis Runyan, "Privatizing Water," *World Watch* 16 (January–February 2003): 36–37; Julie Lanza, "Cities Mull Privatizing Water-works," *Boston Business Journal* 12 (May 11, 1992): 1; Gleick, "The Big Idea Water, Water-Where?" E8; Ursala Hyman, "Wastewater Partnerships," *American City & County* 107 (April 1992): 52.

23. In a few cases the reverse has occurred. For example, city officials in Marysville, Ohio, were preparing to initiate eminent domain proceedings against Ohio Water Service Company in 1990 in an effort to purchase the private company. See Brian R. Ball, "Marysville Seeks Control of Private Water System," *Business First-Columbus* 6 (February 12, 1990), 10.

24. Petri S. Juuti and Tapio S. Katko, eds., *Water, Time, and European Cities* (Tampere, Finland: EU, 2005), 45–46; Ann-Christin Sjolander Holland, *The Water Business: Corporations Versus People* (London: Zed Books, 2005), 8–9.

25. Florencio Lopez-de-Silanes, Andrei Shleifer, and Robert W. Vishny, "Privatization in the United States," *RAND Journal of Economics* 28 (Autumn 1997): 447, 468; Jim Nichols, "Chance to Save Lures Cities to Private Sector," *Cleveland Plain Dealer* (June 22, 1996), 8A; Bret Schundler, "City Chooses Private Manager for Its Water Utility," *American City & County* 112 (March 1997): 45.

26. National Council on Public Works Improvement, *Nation's Public Works: Executive Summaries of Nine Studies,* 37–38.

27. Grigg, *Urban Water Infrastructure,* 7–8; Carol T. Everett, "So Is There an Infrastructure Crisis or What?" *Public Works Management and Policy* 1 (July 1996): 91; Ausubel and Herman, *Cities and Their Vital Systems,* 265.

28. Penn State Public Broadcasting, *Liquid Assets: The Story of Our Water Infrastructure,* 2008.

29. Luken and Pechan, *Water Pollution Control,* 4; Environment and Natural

Resources Policy Division, Congressional Research Service, *Nonpoint Pollution*, 14; McClain Jr., *U.S. Environmental Laws*, 2–1–2–2.

30. American Public Works Association, *Proceedings of the National Water Symposium*, 11, 32; National Council on Public Works Improvement, *Nation's Public Works: Executive Summaries of Nine Studies*, 31.

31. National Council on Public Works Improvement, *Nation's Public Works: Report on Water Supply*, 16; Holtz and Sebastian, *Municipal Water Systems*, 71; Grigg, *Urban Water Infrastructure*, 1, 85.

32. Ross and Levine, *Urban Politics*, 261.

33. Charles Fleming, "Sofia's Choice: Water Business Is Hot as More Cities Decide to Tap Private Sector," *Wall Street Journal* (November 9, 1998), A1.

34. Malcolm Harper, *Public Services Through Private Enterprise: Micro-Privatisation for Improved Delivery* (London: Intermediate Technology Publications, 2000), 17.

35. Charles D. Jacobson and Joel A. Tarr, *Public or Private? Some Notes from the History of Infrastructure: A Report to the World Bank* (Unpublished manuscript, 1996), 2.

36. Fleming, "Sofia's Choice," A1; Schundler, "City Chooses Private Manager for Its Water Utility," 45; Gleick, et al., *Executive Overview: The New Economy of Water*, 5, 7. See also Andrei Shleifer, "State versus Ownership," *Journal of Economic Perspectives* 12 (Autumn 1998): 147; Runyan, "Privatizing Water," 38.

37. Gaura, "Water a Hot Commodity," A3.

38. Estimates do vary. Some observers argue that only about 85 percent of waterworks are publicly owned. See Gaura, "Water a Hot Commodity," A3.

39. In many cases the private water companies are agreeing upon long-term contracts (twenty to twenty-five years) to manage and operate a particular city's waterworks. This has been more typical in recent years than outright purchases.

40. Lenze, "Liquid Assets," 1; Christopher D. Cook, "Drilling for Water in the Mojave," *Progressive* 66 (October 2002): 19–20; Lolis Eric Elie, "Privatization Argument Has Its Leaks," *New Orleans Times-Picayune* (March 31, 2003), 1; Douglas Jehl, "As Cities Move to Privatize Water, Atlanta Steps Back," *New York Times* (February 10, 2003), 14; David Haarmeyer, "Privatize Seattle Water? Study Has Wrong Answer," *Seattle Times* (December 27, 1993), B5.

41. Hunt, *Thirsty Planet*, 285.

42. Matthias Finger and Jeremy Allouche, *Water Privatisation: Trans-National Corporations and the Re-Regulation of the Water Industry* (London: Spon Press, 2002), 62.

43. Peter H. Glieck, "Bottled Water: An Update," in *World's Water, 2006–2007*, ed. Gleick, 169.

44. They also have holdings in other businesses as well.

45. See Grunsky, "Privatization Tidal Wave," 14; Barlow and Clarke, "Who Owns Water?" 12–13; "Veolia Environment," Public Citizen, www.citizen.org/cmep/Water/general/major water/veolia/index.cfm; Veolia Environment, www.vivendienvironment.com/en/activities/water; "Defending the Internal Water

Empire," www.icij.org/water; James K. Glassman, "In Europe, Going for the Water," *Washington Post* (April 7, 1999), E1; Chris Tolhurst, "Drinking at the Front of Opportunity," *Australian Financial Review* (May 18, 1999), 39.

46. Enron was interested in water company acquisitions within the U.S. borders and throughout other parts of the world. For example, they attempted invade the markets in Rio de Janeiro, Berlin, and Panama, and thus posed a threat to the French companies. Fleming, "Sophia's Choice," A1; David Warsh, "What Enron Got Right," *Boston Globe* (December 9, 2001), E2; Andrew Taylor, "Enron Steps into Global Water Market," *Financial Times* (London) (July 25, 1998), 19.

47. "Savoir Faire," *Economist* 368 (July 19, 2003): 7; Lenze, "Liquid Assets," C12.

48. Gleick, et al., *World's Water, 2004–2005,* 47; Smith and Thomassey, *Freshwater Issues,* 29–30.

49. Swomley, "When Blue Becomes Gold," 7; Barlow and Clarke, "Who Owns Water?" 13–14; Fleming, "Sofia's Choice," A1; Runyan, "Privatizing Water," 36; Gleick, "The Big Idea Water, Water-Where?" E8.

50. "Savoir Faire," 7.

51. Barlow and Clarke, "Who Owns Water?" 12–13; Jehl, "As Cities Move to Privatize Water, Atlanta Steps Back," 14; *St. Petersburg* (Florida) *Times* (June 29, 1999), 2E; Samer Iskandar, "Suez Buys Calgon," *Financial Times* (London) (June 16, 1999), 37; Julie B. Hairston, "Treatment Plant Bidding Could Be Fierce," *Atlanta Constitution* (April 9, 1999), 3B; Taylor, "Enron Steps into Global Water Market," 19; Charmagne Helton, "Atlanta's Sewer Problems," *Atlanta Constitution* (March 4, 1997), 5C.

52. Jehl, "As Cities Move to Privatize Water, Atlanta Steps Back," 14.

53. Mary B. Powers and Debra Rubin, "Severed Atlanta Water Contract Was Tied to Unclear Language," *Engineering News-Record* 250 (February 10, 2003): 14–15; Mary Buckner Powers, "Atlanta Ends Privatization Deal and Faces Reservoir Lawsuit," *Engineering News-Record* 250 (February 3, 2003): 14–15; Rick Brooks, "Deals and Deal Makers: A Deal All Wet," *Wall Street Journal* (January 31, 2003), C4; Paul Rosta, "Stockton Mulls Outsourcing After Atlanta Changes Course," *Engineering News-Record* 250 (February 24, 2003): 12; Martha Carr, "Water Board Hopes to Learn from Atlanta: City's Privatization Venture Went South," *New Orleans Times-Picayune* (April 17, 2003), 8. On other debates, see Jim Davis, "Furor over Privatization Stirs Debate Over Its Merits," *Kansas City Business Journal* 17 (June 11, 1999): 4; Jim Hightower, "The Water Profiteers," *Nation* 275 (September 2, 2002): 8; Cook, "Drilling for Water in the Mojave," 20–21; Gordon Russell, "S&WB Adds New Duties for Privatization Bidders," *New Orleans Times-Picayune* (April 4, 2003), 1.

54. Gleick, *World's Water, 2004–2005,* 45–46.

Conclusion

1. R. Coopey and T. Tvedt, eds., *A History of Water,* vol. 2, *The Political Economy of Water* (London: I. B. Tauris, 2006), x.

2. Ibid.

3. Graham and Marvin, *Splintering Urbanism*, 10.

4. Ibid., 33.

5. Martin V. Melosi, *The Sanitary City: Environmental Services in Urban America from Colonial Times to the Present,* abridged ed. (Pittsburgh: University of Pittsburgh Press, 2008), 226.

6. Center for Sustainable Systems, "U.S. Water Supply and Distribution," http://css.snre.umich.edu/css_doc/CSS05-17.pdf.

7. Melosi, *Sanitary City* (abridged edition), 229.

8. Gleick, *World's Water, 2006–2007,* 247–55.

9. Ibid., 1–13.

10. Center for Sustainable Systems, "U.S. Water Supply and Distribution."

11. Intergovernmental Panel on Climate Change, "Climate Change and Water," ed. Bryson Bates, Zbigniew W. Kundzewicz, Shaohong Wu, and Jean Palutikof, *IPCC Technical Paper VI* (Geneva: Intergovernmental Panel on Climate Change, June 2008): vii.

12. Ibid., 3.

13. Ibid., 3–4.

14. See Peter Rogers, "Facing the Freshwater Crisis," *Scientific American* 299 (August 2008): 46–53; Richard Wachman, "Water becomes the new oil as world runs dry," *Observer* (December 9, 2007), http://www.guardian.co.uk/business/2007/dec/09/water.climatechange. For excellent information on world water supplies, see Gleick, *World's Water, 2006–2007.*

Index

Abbott, Carl, 83–84
activated sludge method of wastewater treatment, 130, 142–43, 160, 177, 268n107
Adams, Samuel, 46
aesthetics, threatened by dam building, 79, 95
Africa: water shortage in, 185; water systems in, 192, 194
Age of Miasmas, 40–43, 51, 56; improvements in water systems in, 54–55, 59–60. *See also* filth theory, of disease
agriculture, 22, 83; in competition for water rights, 9, 121; importance of water in, 9, 11, 81; promotion of Western, 23–25, 27; role in economy, 4, 23; runoff from, 20; shipping products of, 11, 22, 131, 133, 141. *See also* irrigation
Alaska, 11; Rampart Dam proposed for, 107–8
Allegheny River, Kinzua Dam on, 81
Allen, Augustus Chapman, 130–32
Allen, John Kirby, 130–32
Allen's Landing, port established at, 132–34
Alviso Water System, San Jose owning, 126
American Bridges and Dams (Zueker), 79–80
American River, as water source, 121
American Water Works Association, 53, 67, 69–70
anticontagionism, 42
aqueducts: Cochituate, 46, 51; Colorado River, 83; Croton, 49–51
Arizona, 25, 221n128; effects of big dams in, 81, 83, 107; water policies in, 11, 107
Army Corps of Engineers. *See* U.S. Army Corps of Engineers
Asia: water industry in, 192, 194; water usage by, 184

Atlanta, Georgia, 41; water system in, 47–48, 194
Atlantic Coast, U.S. Army Corps of Engineers water projects on, 15
Audobon Society, in opposition to big dams, 92, 108
automobiles, influence on Houston's growth, 162
Azurix (water company), 193

bacteria, sewage inoculated with oxidizing, 143
bacteriology, theory of disease transmission, 42, 60; effects of adoption of, 38, 56–57, 75–76; judging water quality and, 44, 62
Baker, M. N., 62–63
Barren River, 17
Battle of Galveston, in Civil War, 141
Battle of San Jacinto, in Texas Revolution, 129, 139–40
Bay Cities Water Company, 117–19, 127
bayous, around Houston: pollution of, 174, 177; stormwater and, 172. *See also* specific bayous
Bayou Ship Channel Company, 136
Baytown, Texas, water for, 155
Bear Wallow Lake Dam, 103
Beaumont, Texas, 135–37
Big Dam Era, 78; desire to control nature in, 84, 237n7; end of, 96–97, 104, 106–7; expected benefits in, 81, 83; goals of, 80, 84; ill-effects of dams built in, 81; safety issues in, 86–89; seeming archaic, 108–9; unequal benefits from, 81–82
Billington, David, 1–2
biofuel production, water used in, 200
Bolivia, privatization of water in, 187, 193
Bonneville Dam, on Columbia River: effects